Regulation and Supervision of the OTC Derivatives Market

The over-the-counter (OTC) derivatives market has captured the attention of regulators after the Global Financial Crisis due to the risk it poses to financial stability. Under the post-crisis regulatory reform the concentration of business, and risks, among a few major players is changed by the concentration of a large portion of transactions in the new market infrastructures, the Central Counterparties (CCPs).

This book, for the first time, analyses the regulatory response of the United Kingdom and the United States, the two largest centres of OTC derivatives transactions, and highlights their shortcomings. The book uses a normative risk-based approach to regulation as a methodological lens to analyse the UK regime of CCPs in the OTC derivatives market. It specifically focuses on prudential supervision and conduct of business rules governing OTC derivatives transactions and the move towards enhancing the use of central clearing. The resulting analysis, from a normative risk-based approach, suggests that the UK regime for CCPs does not fulfil what would be expected if a coherent risk-based approach was taken.

Our comments on the Dodd-Frank Act highlight that the incoherent adoption of a risk-based approach to regulation affects the effectiveness of the US regime for CCPs. Such a regime does not follow the pace of events of 'innovation risk'; in particular, the foreseeable changes FinTech will bring to the OTCDM and central clearing services. The second inadequacy of the US regime concerns the dual regulatory structure of the CFTC and the SEC, and the inadequate adoption of different and not well-coordinated regulatory strategies. We also analyse the cross-border implications of the US regime for non-US CCPs that provide clearing services to US market participants. Finally, we study the negative effects of the absence of a clearly defined resolution regime for CCPs.

Ligia Catherine Arias-Barrera holds a Ph.D. in Law from the University of Warwick, and an LL.M in Commercial and Corporate Law from Queen Mary University of London. She is Associate Professor at the School of Law of the Externado de Colombia University, Private Consultant in Financial Law Services in Colombia and the UK, and Research Associate at the Ibero-American Institute for Law and Finance.

Routledge Research in Finance and Banking Law

Available:

Redefining the Market-State Relationship
Responses to the financial crisis and the future of regulation
Ioannis Glinavos

Financial Stability and Prudential Regulation
A comparative approach to the UK, US, Canada, Australia and Germany
Alison Lui

Law and Finance after the Financial Crisis
The untold stories of the UK financial market
Abdul Karim Aldohni

Microfinance and Financial Inclusion
The challenge of regulating alternative forms of finance
Eugenia Macchiavello

Law and Regulation of Mobile Payment Systems
Issues arising 'post' financial inclusion in Kenya
Joy Malala

Management and Regulation of Pension Scheme
Australia: a cautionary tale
Nicholas Morris

The Regulation and Supervision of Banks
The post crisis regulatory responses of the EU
Chen Chen Hu

Regulation and Supervision of the OTC Derivatives Market
Ligia Catherine Arias-Barrera

For more information about this series, please visit: www.routledge.com/Rout
ledge-Research-in-Finance-and-Banking-Law/book-series/FINANCIALLAW

Regulation and Supervision of the OTC Derivatives Market

Ligia Catherine Arias-Barrera

Routledge
Taylor & Francis Group

LONDON AND NEW YORK

First published 2018
by Routledge

2 Park Square, Milton Park, Abingdon, Oxfordshire OX14 4RN

52 Vanderbilt Avenue, New York, NY 10017

Routledge is an imprint of the Taylor & Francis Group, an informa business

First issued in paperback 2020

British Library Cataloguing-in-Publication Data
A catalogue record for this book is available from the British Library

Library of Congress Cataloging-in-Publication Data
Names: Arias-Barrera, Ligia Catherine, author.
Title: Regulation and supervision of the OTC derivatives market/
  Ligia Catherine Arias-Barrera.
Description: Abingdon, Oxon; New York, NY: Routledge, 2018. |
  Series: Routledge research in finance and banking law | Based on
  author's thesis (doctoral—University of Warwick, 2016) issued
  under title: Fractures of the UK regulation and supervision of
  central counterparties in the OTC derivatives market. | Includes
  bibliographical references and index.
Identifiers: LCCN 2018001657 | ISBN 9781138634787 (hardback)
Subjects: LCSH: Derivative securities—Law and legislation—Great
  Britain. | Over-the-counter markets—Law and legislation—Great
  Britain. | Derivative securities—Law and legislation—United States. |
  Over-the-counter markets—Law and legislation—United States.
Classification: LCC KD1777.D47 A75 2018 | DDC
  346.41/0922—dc23
LC record available at https://lccn.loc.gov/2018001657

ISBN: 978-1-138-63478-7 (hbk)
ISBN: 978-0-367-59092-5 (pbk)

Typeset in Galliard
by Apex CoVantage, LLC

This work is dedicated to my family, thank you for your support and encouragement

Contents

Figures

Cases

Abbreviations

OTCDM	Over-the-Counter Derivatives Market
AIG	American International Group
APER	Statements of Principle and Code of Practice for Approved Persons
APR	Approved Persons Regime
CAs	Clearing Agencies
CASS	Client Assets Sourcebook
CBoT	Chicago Board of Trade
CCPs	Central Counterparties
CDM	ISDA Common Domain Model
CDSs	Credit Default Swaps
CEA	Commodity Exchange Act
CEM	Current Exposure Method
CEs	Clearing Entities
CMA	Competition and Markets Authority
CMGs	Crisis Management Groups
COAGs	Cross-Border Cooperation Agreements
CPMI-IOSCO	Committee on Payments and Market Infrastructures Working with IOSCO
CPSS-IOSCO	Committee on Payment and Settlement Systems Working with IOSCO
CRCs	Credit Risks Committees
CRD IV	Capital Requirements Directive IV
CSI	Council for the Securities Industry
CFTC	Commodity Futures Trading Commission
DCEs	Designated Clearing Entities
DCOs	Designated Clearing Organisations
DFA	Dodd-Frank Wall Street and Consumer Protection Act
DFMUs	Designated Financial Market Utilities
DLT	Distributed Ledger Technology
DMIs	OTC Derivatives Market Intermediaries
EBRM	Exposure Before Risk Mitigates
ECB	European Central Bank

EMIR	European Market Infrastructure Regulation
ESMA	European Securities and Markets Authority
FCA	Financial Conduct Authority
FCAD	Financial Collateral Arrangements Directive
FDIC	Federal Deposit Insurance Corporation
Fed	Federal Reserve
FinTech	Financial Technology
FIT	Fit and Proper Test
fmiCBCM	Cross-Border Crisis Management Group for FMIs
FMIs	Financial Market Institutions
FMUs	Financial Market Utilities
FPC	Financial Policy Committee
FS	Fully Segregated
FSAPs	Financial Sector Assessment Programs
FSB	Financial Stability Board
FSMA 2000	Financial Services and Markets Act
FSOC	Financial Stability Oversight Council
G-SIB	Global Systemically Important Bank
GFC	Global Financial Crisis
IIA Standards	International Standards for the Professional Practice of Internal Auditing
IAIS	International Association of Insurance Supervisors
ICB	Independent Commission on Banking
ICE	Intercontinental Exchange
ICOs	Initial Coin Offerings
IEO	Independent Evaluation Office
IM	Initial Margin
IOSCO	International Organization of Securities Commission
IPPF	Institute of Internal Audit International Professional Practices Framework
ISDA	International Swaps and Derivatives Association
KSPs	Key Supervisory Pillars
MiFID I & II	Market and Financial Instruments Directive I & II
MiFIR	Market and Financial Instruments Regulation
MoU	Memorandum of Understanding
MPBR	More Principles-Based Regulation
MRMAP	Management Responsibility Map
MSPs	Major Swap Participants
MTF	Multilateral Trading Facility
NCA	National Competent Authority
NEDs	Non-Executive Directors
NPRM	New Public Risk Management
ODSG	OTC Derivatives Supervisors Group
OFR	Office of Financial Research
OTF	Organised Trading Facility

PBR	Principles-Based Regulation
PCBS	Parliamentary Commission on Banking Standards
PFE	Potential Future Exposure
PFMIs	Principles for Financial Market Infrastructures
PMP	Public Management Paradigm
PPE	Primary Pooling Event
PRA	Prudential Regulation Authority
PRs	Prescribed Responsibilities
RCH	Recognised Clearing Houses
Regulation SCI	Regulation Systems Compliance and Integrity
ReSG	Resolution Steering Group
RFB	Ring-Fenced Bank
RIEs	Recognised Investment Exchanges
RM	Regulated Market
RMC	Risk Management Committee
RTS	Regulatory Technical Standards
SA-CCR	Standardised Approach for Measuring Derivatives Exposure
SDs	Swap Dealers
SEA	Securities Exchange Act 1934
SEC	Securities and Exchange Commission
SEF	Swap Execution Facility
SIB	Securities and Investments Board
SIFIs	Systemically Important Financial Institutions
SM&CR	New Senior Managers and Certification Regime
SMFs	Senior Management Functions
SoR	Statements of Responsibility
SPR	Senior Persons Regime
SPV	Special Purpose Vehicle
SRB	Systemic Risk Buffer
SRO	Self-Regulatory Organisations
SRR	Special Resolution Regime
SYSC	Senior Management Arrangements, Systems and Controls
TBTF	'Too-Big-to-Fail'
The Bank	The Bank of England
The Board	Board of Governors of the Federal Reserve System
TR	Trade Repository
VMGH	Variation Margin Gains Haircutting

Acknowledgements

Above all, I would wish to thank God and my family.

It gives me great pleasure to thank the many people who have assisted in the completion of this work, in particular, Professor Dalvinder Singh for his supervision of my Ph.D. thesis, and for his guidance and gentle encouragement to publish this book. I am, of course, equally indebted to my Ph.D. examiners, Professor Joanna Gray and Professor Charles Chatterjee, for agreeing to examine my thesis, and for the valuable feedback that they provided. I would also wish to thank Mr. Paul Brione (Bank of England), Ms. Heather Pilley (FCA), and Mr. Tajinder Singh (IOSCO) for their insightful comments about my research. Profound gratitude goes to my dear friend and colleague Dr. Andi Hoxhaj for his continuous and invaluable support. Thank you to faculty members, colleagues, and friends for their guidance and support of my research and teaching at the School of Law of the University of Warwick.

I would like to thank the two funding bodies that sponsored me during my doctoral studies, the Central Bank of Colombia and Externado de Colombia University, for their generous support.

1 Introduction

1.1 The chapters in outline

Following the global financial crisis (GFC), regulators are committed to reduce the likelihood and severity of future crisis. In the area of financial derivatives, regulation is focused on increasing transparency, strengthening market infrastructure, and reducing systemic risk – these post-crisis regulatory reforms frame the research and discussion of this book. Our focus is the major transformation of regulation and supervision of the over-the-counter derivatives market (OTCDM) in the UK and the US, and the consequent move towards the regulation of Central Counterparties (CCPs) as new intermediaries of the market. This is a foundational discussion, revealing that the current UK and US regimes for CCPs are insufficient for a coherent risk-based approach, and highlighting, for the first time, the shortcomings of the UK and the US regimes of CCPs in the OTCDM. Our central hypothesis is that the design and implementation of a coherent risk-based regime would allow regulators to use the approach as the 'route-map' of the regulation and supervision of CCPs. To achieve coherence, a risk-based regime must integrate the perceptions and attitudes of regulators and firms related to the risks manufactured in the OTCDM, and also how they should be managed and controlled. We use a normative risk-based approach to regulation as a methodological lens to analyse the regime, and specifically focus on prudential supervision and the conduct of business rules governing CCPs in the OTCDM.

This work is based, principally, on primary sources of information, and it performs an empirical analysis of the UK and the US regimes of CCPs in the OTCDM. In order to better understand the operation of OTCDM CCPs in the UK regime, the research draws from different empirical sources, including interviews with regulators at the Bank of England (the Bank) and the Financial Conduct Authority (FCA), discussions with officials of international standard-setting bodies such as the International Organization of Securities Commission (IOSCO), interviews with members of CCPs recognised and authorised in the UK, as well as a review of the literature on OTCDM reform and functioning of CCPs. This book is a unique contribution to the field, integrating a legal analysis of the regime of CCPs with sociological perspectives of risk and its role in 'manufactured risk' markets, such as in the OTCDM. We also include broad-policy considerations, like financial stability, to analyse why prudential and conduct of business supervision is necessary. The main contribution of this study is to highlight, from a theoretical perspective, the risk-based shortcomings affecting the regulation and supervision of CCPs in the OTCDM.

The Bank's work, ensuring the safety and soundness of CCPs – and, thereby, the stability of the OTCDM – is currently incomplete. During the first four years of the regime, the Bank set out some key supervisory pillars, anticipating that 'its supervisory effort is based on its assessment of where risks to financial stability are greatest'.[1] This supervision is based on systemic risk management and has been focused on the areas of management of credit, liquidity, and operational risk, continuity of service, and adequate rules in the case of clearing members' default. In this context, this book identifies areas that have been overlooked by regulators.

Our findings exemplify the shortcomings of the UK and the US regimes of CCPs in the OTCDM. In the UK regime, these shortcomings are undermining the success of the regulatory objectives in enhancing market stability. Current inadequacies include the absence of a coherent conduct of business regime of CCPs, the insufficient legal framework underpinning CCPs' operations, the lack of a special resolution regime (SRR) for CCPs, and the failure to rule on 'innovation risk'.

The regulator's objective is to enhance the stability of the OTCDM by ensuring the safety and soundness of CCPs. We identify that the US regime for CCPs in the OTCDM has some shortcomings that hinder the achievement of those objectives. The regime fails to be responsive to the impact that future innovations might have in the derivatives market and central clearing services. Also, the dual regulatory structure affects the efficient supervision of CCPs, undertaken by the CFTC and the Securities and Exchange Commission (SEC). Finally, the cross-border implementation of the US regime exacerbates issues related to CCPs' mutual recognition, and the concerns triggered by the rules governing segregation of assets. In assessing these shortcomings, we will use the risk-based approach as the methodological lens to explain how this regulation strategy can contribute to solving them.

In Chapter 2 we explore the risk-based approach to regulation and provide a framework to analyse the UK regime OTCDM for CCPs. Here we highlight the role that risk has in society and in regulation, emphasising the responsibility financial regulators have to recognise that risks and uncertainties, although at different levels, should inform the regulatory process. Cooperation between regulators and regulated firms is important, not just for information sharing, but the integration between different perspectives of risks in the design and implementation of the regime. Following this line of thought, this chapter provides us with grounds to argue that the OTCDM is a centre of manufactured risks. We analyse how the functioning of the market, the role of CCPs, and the regime are

---

1 Bank of England, 'The Bank of England's Approach to the Supervision of Financial Market Infrastructures' (April 2013), 7.

all continuously manufacturing risks, and then consider the core elements, limits, and shortcomings of risk-based regimes, exploring the UK model of risk-based approach to OTCDM regulation and supervision.

Chapter 3 explores the approach of the UK regime of CCPs in the OTCDM and the first of its shortcomings, using risk-based regulation as a method for our assessment. The two main pillars of prudential supervision and conduct of business are examined, focusing initially on identifying the motivations to implementing CCPs in the OTCDM, and the Bank's regulatory priorities in the first years of implementation of the regime, which are guided by the CPMI-IOSCO Principles for Financial Market Infrastructures. The resulting analysis suggests that the UK regime is affected by two drawbacks of risk-based regimes; namely the absence of an organisational culture in implementing risk-based regulation and how the use of risk-based regulation is creating 'manufactured risks'. Thus, there are some shortcomings that UK regulators should address.

The first weakness is the absence of a conduct of business regime for CCPs; the limited role of the existing rules of conduct of business reveals the need of a coherent regime applicable to CCPs in the OTCDM. This failure goes beyond the lack of design of the regime; it also affects the exercise of enforcement powers. Under the current regime, it is not clear whether the Bank or the FCA could sanction a CCP for the breach of a conduct of business rule.

Adopting a risk-based approach to regulation is useful when regulating systemically important financial institutions (SIFIs), as is the case of CCPs in the OTCDM. However, it is in the nature of a risk-based approach that regulators deliberately overlook certain risks when designing regimes. The attention of the Bank has been focused on managing credit, liquidity, and operational risks faced by CCPs. The result of this prioritisation of risks and their related supervisory actions is that the Bank has abandoned other areas central to the regulation of CCPs. Following this analysis, Chapter 4 explores two more shortcomings; namely the insufficient legal framework underpinning CCPs' operations and the absence of a special resolution regime (SRR) for CCPs. Regarding the insufficient legal framework underpinning CCPs' operations, we expose the issues arising from the contractual relationship between CCPs and their CMs. In particular, we examine how regulators in the UK have conferred a high level of discretion on CCPs related to the performance of their obligations, which in turn diminishes clearing members' and their clients' rights. In order to rebalance the relationship between CCPs and their members, a duty of care predicable of CCPs should be considered.

It might be anticipated that the Bank's focus on ensuring the safety and soundness of CCPs has resulted in a complete regime. However, the Bank's work has been centred exclusively on strengthening loss-allocation and recovery rules for CCPs. Although the remarkable progress concerning the recovery regime is a plausible advance to ensure CCPs' resilience, there is no special regime for the resolution of CCPs. The resolution regime currently applicable to the UK's CCPs is contained in the Banking Act 2009, originally designed for banks, and some aspects of such resolution framework are not suitable for CCPs. Following the benchmark set out in the Financial Stability Board's Key Attributes of Effective Resolution Regimes guide, we explore the reasons for adopting special rules for the resolution of CCPs, as well as emphasise the potential issues that regulators might face when designing and implementing the regime.

In Chapter 5 we highlight how the UK regime of CCPs in the OTCDM is not considering the 'innovation risk'. In a market that exists and evolves by means of innovation, regulators should be aware of the risk it poses to the achievement of their regulatory objectives. Innovation risk can take different forms and might challenge regulators in several ways. In our discussion concerning the role of risk, uncertainties, and manufactured risks, we illustrate the rationale of innovation and how it affects the effectiveness of the regime. We also emphasise the importance of a coordinated approach between regulators and CCPs; in particular, how the innovative or creative compliance of the regime might frustrate the expected outcomes. We refer to the risk that CCPs, in order to remain competitive, might design and offer alternative products to their clients; products that will escape the mandatory clearing requirement. This situation reveals the potential conflict of interests and the position of influence that CMs may have in front of the governance of the CCPs. As the issues posed by financial innovation are different from each other, so are the potential solutions. We explore the suitability of governance rules to solve, at least partially, the issues related to the conflicting interests that converge within the CCP. This chapter also explains how creative compliance is likely to lead to some of the unintended consequences of the CCP regime as well as refers to the potential dangers coming from the innovative financial techniques OTCDM participants will use to meet the high-quality collateral requirements of CCPs and the novel uses of portfolio compression.

Attending to the importance of the US in the OTCDM and in the developments of central clearing, in Chapter 6 we comment on the most concerning shortcomings of the Dodd-Frank Act. In light of the risk-based approach to regulation, we highlight some areas that US regulators have deliberately overlooked in the regulation of CCPs. In this chapter, we argue the existence of several inadequacies of the US regime for clearing houses in the derivatives market, highlighting the limits of the incomplete implementation of risk-based regulation as a regulatory strategy. The central question we seek to solve is whether the implementation of risk-based regimes has contributed to the exacerbation of the flaws revealed in the US derivatives market regulatory structure. Among the shortcomings of the US regime, there is the lack of responsiveness to future innovations: while the current body of regulation seems to tackle past market developments, it deliberately avoids the management of innovation risk. The US regime falls short when approaching issues related to collateral transformation and the expected impact of financial technology (FinTech) – in particular the repercussions that the Distributed Ledger Technology (DLT) might have for CCPs in the OTCDM.

The second regime failure concerns how the US' highly criticised bifurcated regulatory structure hinders efficient supervision of CCPs. We analyse the debate in this section in line with the incoherent adoption of different regulatory strategies by the CFTC and the SEC, as well as how this affects the achievement of regulatory objectives. We then go on to explore the possibility of building a risk-based approach focused on principles as a means to improving the supervision of the OTCDM, and especially the oversight of CCPs. Finally, the chapter studies the shortcomings associated with the extraterritorial application of the US regime, expressly authorised by the Dodd-Frank Act. Both the cross-border implementation of different regimes of CCPs' recognition and the multiple rules governing segregation of assets have been especially problematic. There are both benefits and limitations of current regulatory tools which we identify – for instance the equivalence decision of third-country regimes adopted by the European Commission is a positive and functional approach to solving the issues of extraterritoriality, but there is still room for improvement. Finally, we explore the absence of a determined regime for the resolution of CCPs. Therefore, we discuss the alternatives provided in Title II of the Dodd-Frank Act, the limits of implementing ordinary bankruptcy laws, and the restricted benefits of contractual insolvency provisions.

1.2 Scope and preliminary considerations

The recent financial crisis, and in particular the global financial crisis (GFC) which began in 2007, has had a strong impact on the worldwide economy. What started as a US financial market crash[2] resulted in a truly global economic disaster, affecting both financial and non-financial sectors. One of the markets involved was the derivatives market. As a result, both regulators and regulated firms are aware of the risks and uncertainties manufactured in the derivatives market, and in particular in the OTCDM.

In order to understand the current regulatory reforms of the OTC derivatives, it's helpful to explain the failures affecting the market and the rationale of using regulation to correct them.

1.2.1 *The OTCDM: identified failures*

1.2.1.1 *Lack of transparency in the OTC market*

Transparency 'promotes the orderly and efficient functioning of financial markets by making participants better informed'.[3] The lack of transparency[4] in the market for OTC derivatives allowed companies like American International Group (AIG) to over-extend themselves and sell more credit protection for residential mortgage-backed securities than it could cover.[5] AIG had $1 trillion in assets and

---

2 Financial Crisis Inquiry Commission, *The Financial Crisis Inquiry Report* (Public Affairs New York 2011) (FCIR).
3 Definition used by the IMF <www.imf.org/external/np/exr/ib/2001/042601b.htm.>
4 In the area of the derivatives market, it is debatable whether transparency is achievable and desirable. The ethical aspects of the OTCDM will be studied in future research.
5 Financial Crisis Inquiry Commission, *The Financial Crisis Inquiry Report* (n2).

lost $99.3 billion during 2008.[6] On 16 September 2008 AIG's securities lending business and its credit default swap business – the two main activities that contributed to the AIG crisis – accumulated losses in the order of $50 billion.[7] In the opinion of US Treasury Department Secretary Timothy Geithner,[8] the combination of the lack of transparency in the OTCDM and insufficient regulatory policing powers in those markets left the financial system more vulnerable to fraud and potentially to market manipulation.

The financial crisis in 2008 saw the emergency merger of Bear Stearns[9] with JP Morgan Chase, the failure of Lehman Brothers,[10] and the near-failure of the insurer AIG,[11] all of which were major institutional participants in the derivatives market.[12] Problems within these firms revealed an uncertainty about the amount and interconnectedness of derivatives exposure in the financial system[13] and the weaknesses of the securitisation process, which, in some cases, contributed to the freezing up[14] of markets, or forced the Federal Reserve (Fed) and the federal government to intervene in others.[15]

Derivatives are efficient tools for the hedging and exchange of risk in the financial system. However, the GFC proved that the derivatives market poses a substantial threat to financial stability. The lack of transparent reporting of trades and exposures left both regulators and investors uninformed about where risks are concentrated within the system.

Additionally, the limited transparency of overall counterparty credit risk exposures in the OTCDM precipitated a loss of confidence and market liquidity in times of stress. Financial institutions faced considerable difficulties in monitoring, controlling, and verifying the risks associated with their derivatives dealers.

6 American International Group, 'Form 10-K Annual Report for the Fiscal Year Ended December 31, 2008' (2008) AIG Investor Relations <www.aig.com/Chartis/internet/US/en/2008-10ka_tcm3171-440903.pdf> accessed 18th January 2016.

7 Robert McDonald and Anna Paulson, 'AIG in Hindsight' (Spring 2015) 29 (2) *Journal of Economic Perspectives*, 82.

8 Austin Kilgore, 'Geithner Blames Lack of Transparency for OTC Derivatives Hit on Market' *Housingwire* (July 2009) <www.housingwire.com/news/2009/07/10/geithner-blames-lack-transparency-otc-derivatives-hit-market> accessed 21st June 2013.

9 Corey Hajim, and Adam Lashinsky, 'How Bear Stearns Lost Its Way' *Fortune* (21 August 2007) <http://money.cnn.com/2007/08/20/magazines/fortune/bear_stearns.fortune/index.htm> accessed 24th June 2013.

10 Eric Rosengren, 'Challenges in Resolving Systematically Important Financial Institutions' Federal Reserve Bank of Boston (May 2009) <http://bostonfed.org/news/speeches/rosengren/2009/050509.pdf> accessed 24th June 2013.

11 Adam W. Glass, 'The Regulatory Drive Towards Central Counterparty Clearing of OTC Credit Derivatives and the Necessary Limits on This' (2009) 4 *Capital Markets Law Journal* (suppl 1), S85.

12 Financial Crisis Inquiry Commission, *The Financial Crisis Inquiry Report* (n2).

13 ISDA, 'Transparency and Over-the-Counter Derivatives: The Role of Transaction Transparency' ISDA Research Notes, Number 1 (2009).

14 Paul Mason, *Meltdown: The End of the Age of Greed* (Verso 2010), 105.

15 Kent Cherny and Ben R Craig, 'Reforming the Over-the-Counter Derivatives Market: What's to Be Gained?' Federal Reserve, Bank of Cleveland Economic Commentary (July 2010).

To provide greater transparency, we need access to better information.[16] This is possible when there is an effective and comprehensive clearing system, adequate rules of reporting information, and the constant updating of terms in the documentation.[17]

The lack of transparency as a failure is closely related to information asymmetries affecting the market. The traditional perception of the OTCDM as an ultra-specialised and extraordinarily complex sector is fed by the asymmetries of information, affecting the understanding of these transactions. This issue not only affects third parties, as regulators and consumers, but also dealers and end-users. For instance, it is well known that OTCDM investors transact with little knowledge of the prices that are currently available from other counterparties in the market.[18] The opaqueness of the market keeps investors in the dark about the most attractive contractual terms and who might be offering them.[19] Moreover, information asymmetry in the OTCDM might also be associated with risks and the creditworthiness of those who trade them.[20] Given the complexity of certain transactions – exotic or bespoke products[21] – it is highly probable that end-users enter into such transactions with imperfect information. These asymmetries of information can be divided into two categories, according to the affected market actors.[22]

The first information asymmetry category constitutes the relationship between OTC derivatives dealers and their end-users or clients. This category is usually related to specific expertise and market conditions, as well as pricing information. The second category appears in the context of the relationship between the firms and their security holders. This type of asymmetry is usually related to the impact of OTC derivatives positions on the financial condition of the firm: the level and

16 'G20 Leaders Pittsburgh Summit' (September 2009) <www.g20.utoronto.ca/2009/2009 communique0925.html> accessed 26th May 2013.

17 House of Lords European Union Committee, 'The Future Regulation of Derivatives Markets: is the EU on the Right Track? 10th Report of Session' (2009–2010) 22 <www.parlia ment.the-stationery-office.co.uk/pa/ld200910/ldselect/ldeucom/93/93.pdf> accessed 26th May 2013.

18 Julien Cujean and Rémy Praz, 'Asymmetric Information and Inventory Concerns in Over-the-Counter Markets' (1 April 2014) <www.juliencujean.com/otcInventory.pdf> accessed 18th January 2016.

19 Darrell Duffie, *Dark Markets: Asset Pricing and Information Transmission in Over-the-Counter Markets* (Princeton University Press 2012).

20 Craig Pirrong, 'The Economics of Clearing in Derivatives Markets: Netting, Asymmetric Information, and the Sharing of Default Risks Through a Central Counterparty' (8 January 2009) <http://ssrn.com/abstract=1340660> accessed 18th January 2016.

21 Randy Myers, 'What Every CEO Needs to Know About Weather Risk Management' <www. cmegroup.com/trading/weather/files/WeatherRisk_CEO.pdf> Carter, Ledyard & Milburn LLP, Client Advisory, Forward Freight Agreements <www.clm.com/publication. cfm/ID/85> Cited by Timothy E. Lynch, 'Derivatives: A Twenty-First Century Understanding' (2011) Indiana Legal Studies Research Paper No 187,14 <http://ssrn.com/ abstract=1785634> accessed 22nd November 2017.

22 Dan Awrey, 'The Dynamics of OTC Derivatives Regulation: Bridging the Public-Private Divide' (2010) 11 *European Business Organization Law Review*.

types of risk a firm is taking when trading OTC derivatives change rapidly, making the risk profile and the financial health of the firm difficult to measure. The trace of types of risk in OTC derivatives trading and the difficulty in accessing specific relevant information compound the opacity of the OTCDM.

A tool for improving transparency[23] is the registration of OTC derivative trades in Trade Repositories.[24] A Trade Repository is an entity that maintains a centralised electronic record (database) of transaction data.[25] By centralising the collection, storage, and dissemination of data, 'a well-designed Trade Repository (TR) that operates with effective risk controls can serve an important role in enhancing transparency of information to relevant authorities and the public, promoting financial stability, and supporting the detection and prevention of market abuse'.[26]The study of Trade Repositories rules contained in European Market Infrastructure Regulation (EMIR) goes beyond the scope of this research.

The issues regarding transparency also include the valuation of OTC derivatives. As we have explained, the value of a derivative depends upon the value of the underlying asset. However, this is problematic in the OTCDM, as there is no reference price (as in exchange-traded derivatives), and therefore value determination is less clear. In this sense, the 'OTC derivatives markets may also lead to less efficient underlying markets since information on prices and sizes of the trades is not publicly known'.[27] As a result, regulators and most market participants have an opaque view of the way in which OTC derivatives are valued.

Arguably, the introduction of CCPs to the OTCDM is helping to solve the failure of a lack of transparency. This is a partial solution, in the sense that CCPs represent a step forward; they have an organised structure of the market, or at least a part of it, where the information about contracts, end-users' positions, pricing, and other transaction details will be centrally administered by the CCP and made available to anyone interested, especially regulators. However, some concerns may arise relating to the practical impact that CCPs' access to that information

---

23 Commission Communication to the European Parliament, the Council, the European Economic and Social Committee, the Committee of the Regions and the European Central Bank – Ensuring Efficient, Safe and Sound Derivatives Markets: Future Policy Actions (2009b) COM [2009] 563 final.

24 The regulation applicable to Trade Repositories and Central Counterparties is called EMIR. Regulation (EU) No 648/2012 of the European Parliament and of the Council of 4th July 2012 on OTC derivatives, CCPs, and TRs (EMIR) entered into force on 16th August 2012.

25 EMIR (Titles VI and VII of Regulation EU n648/2012), European Securities and Markets Authority (ESMA) has direct responsibilities regarding the registration, supervision, and recognition of Trade Repositories. In particular, Article 55 of EMIR provides that 'a trade repository shall register with ESMA. The registration of a trade repository shall be effective for the entire territory of the Union' <www.esma.europa.eu/sites/default/files/library/website_tr_registration.pdf> accessed 22nd December 2017.

26 CPSS-IOSCO Consultative Report on Principles for Financial Market Infrastructures 9 (CPMI-IOSCO PFMI) (March 2011). With effect from 1st September 2014, the Committee on Payment and Settlement Systems (CPSS) was renamed the Committee on Payments and Market Infrastructures (CPMI).

27 Schyuler Henderson, *Henderson on Derivatives* (LexisNexis Butterworths 2003), 264.

might have for the benefit of regulation. In other words, the fact that CCPs will have access to all the relevant information does not necessarily mean that those interested, especially regulators, will have a complete knowledge and understanding of the transactions. Access to information in a complete and timely manner is only one part of the correction of the lack of transparency.

1.2.1.2 Inadequate risk management

In order to explain the issue of risk management in the OTCDM, it is first important to clarify that this refers to the management of the risk of contagion of massive defaults – credit risk – and its impact on financial stability. In other words, the credit risk of an individual transaction is not what generates much concern; it is the default multiplied across several OTC derivatives that prompts financial instability and creates systemic risks.

Systemic risk is understood as being 'a trigger event, such as an economic shock or institutional failure with a chain of bad economic consequences'[28] that could impact financial institutions, markets, or both. The OTCDM proved to be one of those markets where systemic risk creeps through the interconnectedness of OTC markets' participants and compounds risk. As opposed to the typical bank systemic risk, where the institutions affected are banks, clearing institutions, and settlement institutions only, the failure of one large OTC derivatives dealer is promptly communicated to other institutions and markets.[29]

The inadequate risk management of the derivatives market was at the heart of the GFC. As explained earlier, many of the risks of credit default swaps (CDSs) and other financial derivatives were concentrated in a few very large banks, investment banks, and others that dominated dealings in the OTCDM. It is reported[30] that among the US Bank holding companies, which were 97 percent of the notional amount of OTC derivatives, millions of contracts were traded by just five large institutions in 2008: JP Morgan Chase, Citi Group, Bank of America, Wachovia, and HSBC. Similarly, other large institutions were teetering on the edge of failure. For instance, through a subsidiary, the nearly collapsed AIG,[31] the largest insurer in the US, had issued large volumes of CDS and faced losses of up to $61.7 billion in 2008.

In the particular case of AIG, its transactions of exotic derivatives had a significant impact on its solvency. AIG needed increasingly large amounts of cash as margin for the CDSs, thus AIG sold to many other investors, as the credit rating agencies downgraded its risk profile.[32] The justification of the massive government assistance to AIG was that if it failed many of the counterparties that had bought the sold swaps would also fail.

---

28 Steven Schwarcz, 'Systemic Risk' (2008) 97 *Georgetown Law Journal*, 193, 198.
29 Ibid 201.
30 Financial Crisis Inquiry Commission, *The Financial Crisis Inquiry Report* (n2), 49.
31 Financial Crisis Inquiry Commission, *The Financial Crisis Inquiry Report* (n2), 50.
32 Charles P. Kindleberger and Robert Aliber, *Manias, Panics, and Crashes: A History of Financial Crises* (4th edn, John Wiley & Sons Inc 2000), ix, 300.

The AIG example leads us to consider that risk-based regulation is 'perhaps a better way to think about systemic risk, not to focus solely on the safety and soundness on critical financial intermediaries',[33] but to aim at financial stability. However, to meet this goal, the risk-based approach needs to move towards an administrative regime to connect macro- and microprudential tools. Such regime would ensure information sharing, joint analysis of risks, and cooperation between authorities.[34] Although macro- and microprudential authorities use prudential policy instruments and tools (e.g. capital and liquidity buffers and balance sheet restrictions) in their pursuit of different objectives, they serve as a backstop of resilience, both to the firm and to the system.[35]

Therefore, regulatory concern lies with the adverse effects that the failure of a large derivatives dealer has for financial stability. In such a case, the consequences extend not only to counterparties, but also damage the liquidity of derivatives markets. This impact is called cross-border transmission of default.[36] Additionally, derivatives markets possess a high risk of cross-market[37] transmission of financial shocks. The proximity between derivatives and the underlying cash markets creates channels among markets for the communication of financial disturbances.

Seen in the light of cross-border failures, the gaps in regulation become evident. In the GFC, while central banks coordinated well in addressing the liquidity crisis, the international financial markets regulators did not know what to do with failing financial institutions.[38] In particular, the massive default showed the weakness of OTCDM regulation when managing the concentration of risk in a few large dealers. In other words, the regulation in place did not allow national regulators, either individually or in cooperation with other regulators, to properly address systemic risk.

In consequence, one of the priorities of the post-crisis regulation should be to address the issues of concentration of risk and excessive interconnectedness of major OTC derivatives dealers with other markets, seeking to avoid the concretion of systemic risk. Most especially, the OTCDM requires effective regulation, otherwise 'the externalities caused by systemic risk would not be prevented or internalized';[39] and since market participants are mainly interested in protecting their own interests,[40] regulators have the responsibility to ensure they have efficient tools to preserve financial stability.

---

33 Steven Schwarcz, 'Systemic Risk' (n28), 203.
34 Jacek Osiński, Katharine Seal, and Lex Hoogduin, 'Macroprudential and Microprudential Policies: Toward Cohabitation' IMF, Monetary and Capital Markets Department (June 2013), 4 <www.imf.org/external/pubs/ft/sdn/2013/sdn1305.pdf> accessed 21st January 2016.
35 Ibid 8.
36 Ibid.
37 BBA, *BBA Credit Derivatives Report 2006 Executive Summary* (2006) 6 <www.bba.org.uk/publication/books-reports-and-subscriptions/bba-credit-derivatives-report-2006/> accessed 10th October 2014.
38 Steven Schwarcz, 'Systemic Risk' (n28), 205.
39 Ibid 206.
40 Ibid.

One of the major changes in OTCDM regulation is the use of CCPs. The traditional instruments used to manage credit risk in OTC derivatives include requiring collateral, entering into netting agreements, and relying on credit ratings to assess risk. But these are only useful in managing the risk of individual transactions; prior to CCPs, there were no regulatory mechanisms designed to manage the concentration of market risk and its consequent implications for financial stability. Hence, the proposition of clearing houses being structured as CCPs has gained acceptance among regulators.

The CCP rationale is that the CCP interposes itself as the legal counterparty to every trade, placing it in 'a unique position in that it has direct interaction and counterparty risk exposure with each trading party'.[41] With the creation of the CCP, all those interested in trading and clearing derivatives must comply with certain membership requirements[42] or become clients of one clearing member. The CCP will support the losses of any cleared transaction and the default will not only affect the large dealer – as without a CCP – but will be mutualised among all the CCP's members. This change in the OTC derivatives post-trade infrastructure 'reduces the risk that failure by single derivatives counterparty can cascade into a system-wide crisis'.[43] Additionally, a CCP has the potential to reduce risks significantly for participants through the multilateral netting[44] of trades and by imposing more effective controls on all participants.

It is important to clarify that CCPs are not new institutions in themselves. What is new is their incorporation in the OTCDM. There are other markets that have used these institutions to clear[45] and settle[46] their transactions, for instance, the securities market[47] and exchange-traded derivatives.[48] The debate lies within the expected benefits of implementing CCPs in the OTCDM (namely improving market resilience by lowering counterparty risk and increasing transparency).

---

41 Douglas D. Evanoff, Daniela Russo, and Robert S. Steigerwald, 'Policymakers, Researchers, and Practitioners Discuss the Role of Central Counterparties' 4Q *Economic Perspectives* – Federal Reserve Bank of Chicago and European Central Bank (2006). <http://econpapers. repec.org/article/fipfedhep/y_3a2006_3ai_3aqiv_3ap_3a2-21_3an_3av.30no.4.htm> accessed 26th May 2013.

42 See Craig Pirrong, 'The Economics of Central Clearing: Theory and Practice' ISDA Discussion Papers No. 1 (May 2011). <www.eachccp.eu/wp-content/uploads/2015/12/ISDA discussion_CCP_Pirrong. Pdf> accessed 22nd November 2017.

43 Adam W. Glass, 'The Regulatory Drive Towards Central Counterparty Clearing of OTC Credit Derivatives and the Necessary Limits on This' (n11).

44 See Philip Wood, *Law and Practice of International Finance* (Sweet & Maxwell 2008), 217.

45 After an exchange is entered into involving a financial instrument, it must be cleared and ultimately settled. These terms have different meanings from market to market; in general, however, 'clearing' involves post-trade operations including trade-matching, confirmation, and risk management; Glass (n11) s 82.

46 'Settlement involves the transfer of money or assets by a party to perform and discharge its obligations under a trade', R. Bliss and Steigerwald, 'Derivatives Clearing and Settlement: A comparison of Central Counterparties and Alternative Structures' (2008) 30 *Economic Perspectives*, 22.

47 Adam Glass, 'The Regulatory Drive Towards Central Counterparty Clearing of OTC Credit Derivatives and the Necessary Limits on This' (n11) s 82.

48 Ibid 3.

However, it is also argued that 'CCPs alone are not sufficient to ensure resilience and efficiency of derivatives markets'.[49]

1.2.1.3 Consequences of these failures: the concretion of systemic risk

The concept of systemic risk[50] surrounds the critiques of the OTCDM and can be identified as the major cause of the failures affecting the market. It is defined as the 'risk of a sudden and anticipated event that would damage the financial system to such an extent that economic activity in the wider economy would suffer'.[51]

After the GFC, regulators aimed to reduce systemic risk in the financial system.[52] In particular, regulators looked at the need to oversee macro- and micro-prudential matters, especially of the markets compromised during the crisis, to avoid gaps in the regulation of the whole financial system which could materialise into possible systemic risks.[53] Regulators are expected to conduct stronger oversight and to provide better regulatory incentives for infrastructure improvements to reduce counterparty credit risk and bolster market liquidity, efficiency, and transparency. Used responsibly with these reforms, OTC derivatives can provide important risk management and liquidity benefits to the financial system.

1.2.2 Regulatory response

1.2.2.1 In the UK

The reaction of regulators in the European Union (EU)[54] was initially focused on increasing transparency and reducing credit risk and operational risk through the use of post-trading market infrastructure.[55] The OTC derivatives regulatory

---

49 Stephen Cecchetti, Jacob Gyntelberg, and Marc Hollanders, 'Central Counterparties for Over-the-Counter Derivatives' (September 2009) *BIS Quarterly Review*, 45.
50 'Systemic risk is probability that the financial system will fail to function as needed to support economic activity in the aggregate', Jack Selody, 'The Nature of Systemic Risk' in John Raymond LaBrosse, Rodrigo Olivares-Caminal, and Dalvinder Sing (eds.), *Managing Risk in the Financial System* (Edward Elgar Publishing Ltd 2011), 20.
51 G30, *Global Institutions, National Supervision and Systemic Risk: A Study Group Report* (Group of Thirty 1997), 3.
52 See IOSCO, 'Global Securities Regulators Adopt New Principles and Increase Focus on Systemic RISK' IOSCO Press Release, (10 June 2010) IOSCO/MR/10.
53 Gillian Garcia, 'The Troubled Asset Relief Program: Has Forbearance as Far as the Eye Can See Saved the US Economy?' in John Raymond LaBrosse, Rodrigo Olivares-Caminal, and Dalvinder Singh (eds.), *Managing Risk in the Financial System* (n51), 409.
54 Gerry G. Kounadis, 'European Market Infrastructure Regulation and Central Clearing: A Conceptual, Legal and Compliance Perspective' (2014) 29 (9) *Journal of International Banking Law & Regulation*, 560.
55 European Commission, 'Impact Assessment – Accompanying Document to the Proposal for a Regulation of the European Parliament and of the Council on OTC Derivatives, Central Counterparties and Trade Repositories' [COM (2010) 484] [SEC (2010) 1059] <http://

reform includes three instruments: EMIR, the Capital Requirements Directive IV (CRD IV), and the Markets and Financial Instruments Directive I and II (MiFID I and II).[56] The EMIR governs CCPs and TRs;[57] the CRD IV includes some rules for OTC centrally cleared derivatives; and the MiFID I and II rule exchange-trade derivatives requirements and standardisation.[58]

The MiFID I and II set out which investment services and activities should be licensed across the EU and the organisational and conduct standards with which those providing such services should comply.[59] In 2011, the European Commission published legislative proposals to amend MiFID by recasting it as a new directive (MiFID II) and a new regulation (MiFIR).[60] After a long political debate, the final texts were published on 12th June 2014 and entered into force 20 days later on 2nd July 2014. Entry into application will follow 30 months after entry into force on 3rd January 2017. However, in February 2016 the European Commission delayed this until 3rd January 2018.

MiFIR complements EMIR,[61] in the sense that it implements the G20 commitment to mandate the trading of standardised derivatives on exchanges and electronic platforms. The regime requires certain derivatives to be traded on a regulated market (RM), a multilateral trading facility (MTF), an organised trading facility (OTF), or in certain trading venues in third countries that have been considered equivalent for that purpose.[62]

The obligation applies to financial and non-financial counterparties that are subject to the clearing obligation in EMIR,[63] as well as third-country entities that would be subject to it if they were established in the EU and either trade

---

ec.europa.eu/internal_market/financial-markets/docs/derivatives/20100915_impact_assessment_en.pdf> accessed 8th May 2013.

56 Directive on Markets in Financial Instruments Repealing Directive [2004/39/EC] of the European Parliament and of the Council, and For the Regulation of Markets in Financial Instruments and Amending Regulation [EMIR] on OTC Derivatives, Central Counterparties, and Trade Repositories <http://ec.europa.eu/internal_market/securities/isd/mifid/index_en.htm> accessed 26th June 2013.

57 On 4th July 2012, the Regulation on OTC Derivatives, Central Counterparties, and Trade Repositories (known as EMIR) was adopted and entered into force on 16th August 2012.

58 Directive of the European Parliament and of the Council of 21st April 2004 on Markets in Financial Instruments [2004/39/EC] Amending Council Directives [85/611/EEC] and [93/6/EEC] and Directive [2000/12/EC] of the European Parliament and of the Council and Repealing Council Directive [93/22/EEC].

59 Alix Prentice, 'Legislative Comment: The Markets in Financial Instruments Directive' (2012) 18 (1) *International Trade Law & Regulation*, 11.

60 Peter Snowdon and Simon Lovegrove, 'MIFID II' COB105 April 1–29 (2013).

61 G. Ferrarini and F. Recine, 'The MiFID and Internalization' in G. Ferrarini and E. Wymeersch (eds.), *Investor Protection in Europe* (Oxford University Press 2006), 235; also see N. Moloney, *EC Securities Regulation* (2nd edn, Oxford University Press 2008), 769–778.

62 Ferrarini, Guido A. and Paolo Saguato, 'Reforming Securities and Derivatives Trading in the EU: From EMIR to MIFIR' (2 January 2014) 13 *Journal of Corporate Law Studies*, 319 <http://ssrn.com/abstract=2386290> accessed 18th January 2016.

63 N. Moloney, 'EU Financial Market Regulation After the Global Financial Crisis: "More Europe" or More Risks?' (2010) 47 *Common Market Law Review*, 1317.

with in-scope EU entities or other third-country entities where their transactions could have a direct, substantial, and foreseeable effect within the EU, or it is appropriate to prevent evasion of MiFIR.

In the UK, the response to the GFC started with the government's commitment to introduce a new approach to financial regulation, 'one which is based on clarity of focus and responsibility, and which places the judgement of expert supervisors at the heart of the regulation'.[64] The changes in financial architecture impose responsibility for financial stability on the Bank and its Financial Policy Committee (FPC),[65] and for prudential regulation on the Prudential Regulation Authority (PRA).[66] Thus, responsibility for business conduct and market regulation is placed upon the new FCA.[67]

These changes mean that supervision actions will be split between the authorities carrying on the conduct of business and those related to prudential supervision. The risk of implementing multiple supervisors is the duplication of sanctions; therefore, attention is focused on the effective coordination among supervisors.[68] The aim is to avoid incompatibilities and to minimise duplication in the exercise of supervision powers; the Bank and the FCA[69] will consult and exchange information 'while recognising that each has distinct objectives and may therefore reach different conclusions'.[70]

In the UK, the rules of cooperation among financial system supervisors are set out in a Memorandum of Understanding (MoU) between the Bank, the PRA, and the FCA. The MoU provides a 'high-level framework that the FCA and the Bank, and where appropriate the PRA, will use to cooperate with one another in relation to the supervision of markets and market infrastructure'.[71]

The regime applicable to CCPs has some special features. In general, the regulation of CCPs was expressly assigned to the Bank.[72] However, the FCA regulates the conduct of participants in relation to the financial instruments and derivatives contracts traded on OTCDM.[73] Consequently, both authorities – the Bank and

---

64   Ibid.
65   Financial Services Act 2012 (FSA 2012) pt 1 A Financial Stability s 9C Objectives of the Financial Policy Committee.
66   FSA 2012 pt1 A The Regulators ch 2.
67   Financial Services and Markets Act 2000 (FSMA 2000) as amended by the FSA 2012 pt 1 A The Regulators ch 1.
68   . See HM Treasury, *Reforming Financial Markets*, para 3.1.
69   FSMA 2000 pt XI.
70   Memorandum of Understanding between the Financial Conduct Authority and the Bank of England, including the Prudential Regulation Authority (MoU FCA-BoE-PRA) 4 <www.bankofengland.co.uk/-/media/boe/files/memoranda-of-understanding/bank-pra-and-fca-supervision-of-markets-and-markets-infrastructure.pdf> accessed 9th May 2013.
71   MoU FCA-BoE-PRA 1.
72   According to the provisions of FSMA 2000, as amended by the FSA 2012, the Uncertificated Securities Regulations 2001 and the Banking Act, the Bank is responsible 'for the oversight of clearing, settlement and payment systems ("post trade systems") in support of its financial stability objective'.
73   Emma Murphy, 'Changes to the Bank of England' (2013) Bank of England, *Quarterly Bulletin*, Q1 20 <www.bankofengland.co.uk/publications/Documents/quarterlybulletin/2013/

FCA – carry out the regulation and supervision of CCPs. In the following chapters, we critically analyse how the Bank has carried out the prudential supervision in the first five years of the regime and assess the limited role of the FCA as the conduct regulator of CCPs.

The regulation of CCPs in the UK is set out in Part XVIII of the Financial Services and Markets Act 2000, and the reforms introduced by the Financial Services Act 2012 and the directly applicable European regulation contained on EMIR. Additionally, the Bank undertakes the supervision following the IOSCO-CPMI Principles of Financial Market Infrastructures.[74]

1.2.2.2 In the US

The derivatives and central clearing reform is embedded in the Dodd-Frank Wall Street Reform and Consumer Protection Act 2010. The Dodd-Frank Act in Title VII established a comprehensive framework for regulating the OTC swaps markets. In particular, the Act provides that the SEC will regulate 'security-based swaps', the Commodity Futures Trading Commission (CFTC) will regulate 'swaps', and the CFTC and the SEC will jointly regulate 'mixed swaps'. Title VII further provides that the SEC and CFTC shall jointly establish such regulations regarding 'mixed swaps' as may be necessary to carry out the purposes of swap and security-based swap regulation under Title VII.[75] Title VIII introduces regulation for central clearing applicable to clearing agencies (Cas) and designated clearing organisations (DCOs).

Regulation and supervision is jointly undertaken by the Fed, the SEC, and the CFTC – these are the financial authorities carrying out derivatives market reform. The policy objectives were announced in November 2008 regarding the OTCDM, with a primary focus on CDSs, which was to [i]mprove market transparency and integrity for CDS, enhance risk management, strengthen OTC derivatives market infrastructure, continue cooperation among regulatory authorities.[76]

The changes introduced by Title VII of the Dodd-Frank Act provide a comprehensive regulatory framework for the OTC swap markets. The Act maintains a division of the regulatory authority between the CFTC and SEC, as follows: the SEC has authority over 'security-based swaps' as financial instruments included within the definition of 'security' provided by the Securities Exchange Act 1934 (SEA) and the Securities Act 1933. Additionally, the SEC has anti-fraud

---

qb130102.pdf> accessed 23rd April 2013. The PRA carries out the 'prudential supervision of many firms that are participants of such systems.

74 CPMI-IOSCO PFMI.

75 Securities Exchange Commission, 'SEC Approves Rules and Interpretations on Key Terms for Regulating Derivatives' (2012) Washington, DC, 9 July 2012 <www.sec.gov/news/press/2012/2012-130.htm> accessed 14th November 2012.

76 US Treasury Department, 'President's Working Group on Financial Market Policy Objectives for the OTC Derivatives Market' (2008) Washington, DC, November 2008 <https://www.treasury.gov/resource-center/fin-mkts/Documents/policyobjectives.pdf> accessed 6th March 2018.

enforcement authority over swaps that do not exactly come within the definition of 'security-based swaps', called 'security-based swap agreements'. The SEC
shares information with the CFTC, clearing institutions, and data repositories.
The CFTC has regulatory authority over all other swaps, mainly energy and agri-
cultural swaps, and shares authority over 'mixed swaps' based on securities but
with commodity components.

The CFTC has proposed and adopted some rules to implement the mandates of
the Dodd-Frank Act. As reported, the Act contains more than 90 provisions that
require SEC rulemaking and others that give the CFTC discretionary rulemaking
authority. Currently, the vast majority of the efforts have been put towards transparency, market access rules, and credit agencies. The process of implementation
is completed by issuing either a 'proposing release' or an 'adopting release'.

1.3 The impact of Brexit for CCPs

The UK's withdrawal from the EU, set for March 2019, is cause for concern for
all derivatives market participants, especially for CCPs based in London. The high
level of uncertainty leading the negotiations between the UK government and
the European Commission (EC) puts CCPs at the centre of the turbulence. Currently, 90 percent of EU clearing takes place in London,[77] but there have been
voices announcing that EU regulators – the European Central Bank (ECB)[78] –
are keen to introduce further regulation on euro-denominated swaps and require
them to be cleared in the EU.

It is worth noting that cooperative arrangements between EU and UK authorities are already in force. In case of a systemic crisis originating in the CCPs' market, the MoU between the ECB and the Bank of England should ensure timely
and sufficient information sharing, as well as enable effective risk management.
However, the high level of interconnectedness between CCPs[79] and other market
participants may be cause for concern. EMIR's regime regarding third-country
CCPs was not designed to cope with major systemic CCPs operating from outside the EU.[80] This appears to be especially problematic because, as we discover
here, the current regime for CCPs relies to a large extent on UK regulation and
supervision.

---

77 'CCPs clear approximately 90% of the euro-denominated interest rate swaps of euro area
   banks, and 40% of their euro-denominated credit default swaps'. ECB calculations based on
   2016Q4. Benoît Cœuré, 'European CCPs After Brexit'. (20 June 2017) Speech, Member
   of the Executive Board of the ECB, at the Global Financial Markets Association, Frankfurt
   am Main <www.ecb.europa.eu/press/key/date/2017/html/ecb.sp170620.en.html#6>
   accessed 28th November 2017.

78 Reuters, 'ECB Wants Extra Shield if it is to Supervise Clearing Houses' <http://mobile.reu
   ters.com/article/amp/idUSKBN1DA1OO> (10 November 2017) accessed 28th November 2017.

79 BIS, 'Analysis of Central Clearing Interdependencies' (5 July 2017) <www.bis.org/cpmi/
   publ/d164.htm> accessed 28th November 2017.

80 Benoît Cœuré, 'European CCPs after Brexit', Ibid.

In June 2017, the EC proposed to reform EMIR, seeking to strengthen the role of EU supervisors and central banks in monitoring and addressing risks to the EU financial system, in particular risks posed by CCPs. The new powers bestowed to the EC, if approved, would allow it to deny recognition of a CCP when it poses excessive risks to the EU financial stability. Additionally, when recommended by the European Securities and Markets Authority (ESMA) and the ECB, the EC would be able to require such a CCP to establish itself in the EU in order to continue providing clearing services in the Union (known as 'CCPs' location policy').[81] The CCP location policy has been highly controversial for EU members[82] that will have to undertake the supervision of systemically important CCPs and market participants[83] that will suffer the consequences of legal uncertainty and market fragmentation.

Under the hypothesis of relocated CCPs, national EU regulators would be compelled to carry out the supervision of certain CCPs. It cannot be denied that, although subject to common principles and rules, not all EU national supervisors have the same level of expertise to deal with systemically important financial institutions. Thus, unless the place of relocation is in certain European countries, the shift of CCPs' location will bring excessive burden on inexperienced EU national supervisors, increasing the risk of ineffective supervision, which might lead to inadequate management and prevention of systemic risk.

The political context of the EC's reform proposal of EMIR is clearly coloured by individual EU Member States' interest to undertake the supervision of CCPs currently based in London and to concentrate their market. However, the implementation of the CCPs' location policy might undermine such purpose and the influence of the political forces behind the reform could backfire, affecting the European market. It is possible that CCPs end up relocated in different EU Member States, putting at risk not only the financial stability of the EU, but also

---

81 The idea is not new. Initially, on July 2011, the ECB issued the 'Eurosystem Oversight Policy Framework'. It would require clearing houses with daily exposures of more than 5 billion Euros in one of the main euro-denominated categories of derivative to be located in the Eurozone. However, the rule was overturned in March 2015 when the General Court of the EU considered that 'the ECB location policy was of a binding nature and that the ECB had no autonomous regulatory competence in respect of all clearing systems under the Treaty on the Functioning of the EU'. Therefore, the ECB had to continue the cooperation with the Bank of England 'to seek a coordinated and shared approach for achieving the common objective of financial stability and the smooth functioning of financial market infrastructures'. ECB, 'ECB Takes Note of General Court Judgment on Location Policy For CCPs' (4 March 2015) Press Release <www.ecb.europa.eu/press/pr/date/2015/html/pr150304.en.html> accessed 28th November 2017.

82 Costas Mourselas and Jean Comte, 'EU Member States Clash on CCP Location Policy' (7 September 2017) <www.globalcapital.com/article/b14n76v9rrp6j0/eu-member-states-clash-on-ccp-location-policy> accessed 28th November 2017.

83 Blackrock, 'European Market Infrastructure Regulation 2.0 (CCP Location Policy) Key Issues for End-Investors' <www.blackrock.com/corporate/en-at/literature/publication/proposal-on-more-robust-supervision-of-central-counterparties-ec-170717.pdf> accessed 28th November 2017.

triggering market fragmentation. The movement of CCPs from London to several European countries would 'artificially split the Euro market into small pools of liquidity'.[84] Along with the repercussions of a fragmented market associated with liquidity and increased costs for end-users, there is a possible backlash from market actors, affecting EU market competitiveness. It might be anticipated that the relocation policy of the EC will make split on-shore markets in the Eurozone less liquid than offshore markets outside the Eurozone. The impact might also be reflected on prices differences between EU and non-EU CCPs on the same products.

The International Swaps and Derivatives Association (ISDA) conducted a survey among its members to determine the effects of the CCPs' location policy, which confirmed the potential negative consequences of the policy on market participants. It estimates that to require Euro-denominated interest rate derivatives to be cleared post-Brexit in a EU-based CCP would result in an overall IM increase in the range of 15 to 20 percent.[85] The adoption of the CCPs' location policy is likely to trigger concentration of risk in some smaller EU CCPs. This might impede EU investment and cause some risks to go un-hedged, as end-users struggle to get connected to a new CCP.[86]

Thus, the issues triggered by such fragmentation do not only concern the EU and the UK, but international markets and regulators. Indeed, the EC proposal seems to take a step away from the G20 principles, in particular, overlooking the commitment to avoid fragmentation, protectionism, and regulatory arbitrage. Moreover, the implementation of post-GFC regulatory reform emphasises the importance of the principle of deference and international comity in international forums.[87] The G20 Pittsburgh Summit coined the concept of regulatory deference to ensure an efficient cross-border implementation of the OTC derivative clearing obligation. This notion embeds the commitment of 'regulators to defer to each other when it is justified by the quality of their respective regulatory and enforcement regimes, based on similar outcomes, in a non-discriminatory way, paying due respect to home country regulation regimes'.[88]

Against this background, the recommendation of industry-led associations such as the ISDA and the Investment Association[89] is that EU and UK regulators

84 Ibid.
85 ISDA letter to the EC Communication, 'Responding to the Challenges for Critical Financial Market Infrastructures and Further Developing the Capital Markets Union' (8 June 2017) <www.isda.org/a/YIDDE/isda-final-response-to-ec-communication-8-june-2017.pdf> accessed 28th November 2017.
86 Ibid.
87 See World Federation of Exchanges, 'Financial Markets and International Regulatory Dissonance: A WFE Position Paper' (November 2017) <www.world-exchanges.org/home/index.php/files/51/Recent-Publications-2017/487/WFE-Financial-Markets-and-International-Regulatory-Dissonance:-Position-Paper-%E2%80%93-22-November-2017.pdf> accessed 1st December 2017.
88 G20 Leaders' Statement The Pittsburgh Summit September 24–25 2009.
89 IA Response to European Commission CCP Proposal <https://ec.europa.eu/info/law/better-regulation/feedback/6851/attachment/090166e5b4f2a52a_de> accessed 1st December 2017.

work towards a close cooperation to ensure that non-EU CCPs are sufficiently supervised and therefore do not pose excessive risk to the financial stability of the Union. In line with this trend, Mark Carney, governor of the Bank of England, stated the need for 'robust cross-border arrangements for the supervision of CCPs'.[90]

On 20th December 2017, the Bank issued a guidance of its approach to the authorisation and supervision of international CCPs.[91] The Bank advises non-UK CCPs that have been authorised and recognised under EMIR to prepare themselves for the upcoming regulatory changes. After the UK's withdrawal from the EU is completed, non-UK CCPs will be subject to a new process of recognition carried out by the Bank. There are three conditions that determine if a CCP would need to apply for UK recognition. These are: the CCP seeks to provide clearing services to CMs established in the UK, the CCP will be used by market participants required to clear their transactions according to UK domestic law, and the CCP is regarded as a Qualifying CCP under UK domestic law for capital requirement purposes.

It is expected that UK-EU negotiations[92] will grant an implementation period[93] in which current regulation will be applicable. Also, the UK government has emphasised its intention to convert current EU law into UK domestic law. Therefore, Article 25 of EMIR on the recognition of third-country CCPs – currently under reform – will not only rule during the implementation period, but it is also likely to guide the new UK domestic law requirements for recognition of non-UK CCPs.[94] The objective is to minimise the impact of Brexit in the continuous provision of central clearing services and to give certainty to non-UK CCPs and their users, i.e. CMs and their clients. The Bank is keen to facilitate the transition process and intends to cooperate with CCPs and their domestic supervisory authorities in different jurisdictions. In this regard, it might be anticipated that

---

90 Mark Carney, 'Speech at the Mansion House' (20 June 2017) <www.bankofengland.co.uk/speech/2017/a-fine-balance> accessed 20th December 2017.
91 Bank of England, 'Letter to International Central Counterparties' (20 December 2017) <www.bankofengland.co.uk/-/media/boe/files/letter/2017/letter-to-ccps.pdf?la=en&hash=544DA5A3C8759C5D16D66FC5C269452912B8EF3F> accessed 20th December 2017.
92 The European Council authorised the opening of the second phase of the negotiations in January 2018. According to Article 50 TEU, this phase will seek to define a framework for the UK's future relationship with the EU. European Council, '(Art. 50) meeting' (Guidelines, 15 December 2017) <www.consilium.europa.eu/media/32236/15-euco-art50-guidelines-en.pdf> accessed 20th December 2017. See also EC, 'Brexit: European Commission Recommends Draft Negotiating Directives for Next Phase of the Article 50 Negotiations' (Press Release, 20 December 2017) <http://europa.eu/rapid/press-release_IP-17-5342_en.htm> accessed 20th December 2017.
93 Philip Hammond, 'Financial Services Update: Written statement – HCWS382' (20 December 2017) <www.parliament.uk/business/publications/written-questions-answers-statements/written-statement/Commons/2017-12-20/HCWS382/> accessed 20th December 2017.
94 Bank of England, 'Letter to International Central Counterparties' (20 December 2017) (n91).

those jurisdictions that have been assessed as equivalent to the EU will also be deemed as equivalent to the new UK domestic law.

The UK's withdrawal from the EU is also problematic, especially if the UK loses access to the EU single market and is not granted passporting rights.[95] In such an event, UK CCPs would be subject to 'third-country' authorisation and recognition process. The EC would have to issue an equivalence decision with the UK regime and then UK CCPS would need to submit an application to ESMA for recognition. In contrast, if Brexit negotiations allow the UK to retain access to the EU single market that would grant passporting rights for UK-based firms, UK CCPs would be allowed to continue providing clearing services to EU clients.

Besides the future of regulation and supervision of CCPs after Brexit, the ISDA has suggested to UK and EU authorities to agree on a set of transitional rules based on English contract law to be applicable to derivatives contracts after March 2019.[96]

Notwithstanding the terms of the Brexit deal and the effects of a change of regime applicable to UK CCPs, UK regulators would benefit from the coherent adoption of a risk-based approach. The challenges of the after-Brexit period will require collaborative work between regulators and market participants to maintain the stability of the financial system and to safeguard the place of London as the largest market for OTCDM. We are not suggesting that regulators should lighten the regime – indeed Mark Carney has been clear in anticipating that London will not lower its requirements to retain investors after Brexit. Instead, we suggest UK regulators take advantage of the approach to regulation proposed in this book as a means to facilitate the process of design and implementation of post-Brexit rules. In the particular case of OTCDM and the rules applicable to CCPs, the cooperation should be not only with European Supervisors, but also with market participants to ensure no disruption is caused to the provision of central clearing services. A regime of incentives seems to be better suited to keep the OTCDM and CCPs as successful as they have been since 2013, when the current regime entered into force.

1.4 Remarks

Financial derivatives are contracts whose value is based or derived from the value of another underlying asset. The range of derivatives contracts include vanilla

95 'In the field of banking and other financial services, the passport gives banks in the EU the right to provide financial services throughout the EU, under the license granted by their home country and under the home country supervision. The passport relies on two elements: i) a set of prudential requirements harmonised under EU law; and ii) mutual recognition of licenses'. (12 July 2017) Briefing European Parliament, Economic Governance Support Unit <www.europarl.europa.eu/RegData/etudes/BRIE/2016/587369/IPOL_BRI(2016)587369_EN.pdf> accessed 1st December 2017.

96 ISDA, 'Brexit – CCP Location and Legal Uncertainty' (August 2017) Whitepaper <www.isda.org/a/U8iDE/brexit-paper-1-final1.pdf> accessed 28th November 2017.

products, i.e. options, futures or forwards, swaps and credit derivatives, as well as exotic or bespoke derivatives. They are traded in exchange and in OTC markets, and they perform several functions. The most important function is to hedge risks generated in any other type of contract. They are also used to control business risks associated with the volatility of prices, to obtain funding at a preferential rate, and to take speculative advantage. Although the risk management function predicable of derivatives seeks to reduce and reallocate, rather than to create risks, this benign tool might not always operate in the way anticipated, transforming them into 'risk-bearing' instruments. Hence, derivatives themselves can represent various types of risks (e.g. credit, liquidity, legal and operational risks). Thus, as a fundamental concept in financial derivatives, risk is not only managed but can also be manufactured in the market.

The role that the OTCDM played in the GFC and its market failures motivated the move towards more formal regulation and supervision. The post-GFC regulatory reforms have modified the structure and functioning of the OTCDM. After the introduction of CCPs to the OTCDM, the traditional bilateral structure of derivatives transactions changed. As the CCP places itself in the middle of the transaction and becomes the counterparty of the two initial counterparties, there is a shift in the allocation of risks that is now transferred to the CCP. As a result, the risk of each individual transaction is mutualised across all CCPs' members.

The OTCDM post-crisis regulatory reform follows the international commitment of reducing systemic risk in the financial system. The emphasis is on the need to oversee macro- and microprudential matters in markets that, as the OTCDM, were compromised during the crisis. In particular, the case of the OTCDM in the international regulatory agenda has been focused on strengthening market infrastructure by introducing TRs and CCPs, as well as on regulating non-centrally cleared derivatives. This is in line with the aim of the G20 Pittsburgh Summit 2009 to improve transparency, mitigate systemic risk, and protect against market abuse.

The critical analysis of the UK, and comments on US regimes of CCPs in the OTCDM and its shortcomings now follow, in subsequent chapters.

2 The risk-based approach to regulation

2.1 Introduction

In this chapter, we will principally consider whether risk-based regulation is an efficient approach to the CCP regime in the OTCDM. We will first attempt to throw some light on the role of risk in society and in regulation, as well as on the way risk-based regulation operates. This discussion highlights the benefits, limits, and complexities tied to the adoption of risk-based approaches to regulation. Then, at the core of the chapter, we will go on to analyse the parameters that risk-based regulation offers within the current CCP regime in the OTCDM in the UK and the US.

This chapter is the framework of the regulatory analysis of this book. The research explores the UK and the US risk-based models of regulation and supervision governing CCPs in the OTCDM, as well as highlights the importance of the increasing tendency towards using CCPs.[1] We especially focus on the study of prudential supervision and conduct of business rules. Using the core features of the risk-based[2] model we will then identify and assess the risks posed by CCPs to the regulator's objectives[3] and address those risks using various regulatory tools.[4]

Different models of regulation could be considered to analyse the new UK and US approaches. However, this study uses risk-based regulation – adopted in both jurisdictions – as a method of analysing the CCP regime in the OTCDM. Risk-based regulation exposes the reality that there might be a limit on the resources

1 Daniel Heller, and Nicholas Vause, 'Expansion of Central Clearing' (June 2011) (67) *BIS Quarterly Review*, 68.
2 Robert Baldwin, and Julia Black, 'Really Responsive Regulation' (2008) 71 *Modern Law Review*, 59.
3 Robert Baldwin, Martin Cave, and Martin Lodge, *Understanding Regulation* (Oxford University Press 2012), 283; Stuart Bazley, and Andrew Haynes, *Financial Services Authority Regulation and Risk-Based Compliance* (2nd edn, Tottel 2007).
4 See Julia Black, 'The Development of Risk Based Regulation in Financial Services: Canada, the UK and Australia a Research Report' ESRC Centre for the Analysis of Risk and Regulation London School of Economics and Political Science (September 2004) <www.lse.ac.uk/collections/law/staff%20publications%20full%20text/black/risk%20based%20regulation%20in%20financial%20services.pdf> accessed 21st January 2016.

that can be spent on controlling certain types of risk.[5] In addition, this method allows us to analyse how the regimes are satisfying expectations regarding transparency and accountability.[6]

The risk-based approach is a particularly interesting way to analyse the regulation of CCPs. Indeed, a general concern after the GFC[7] was that risk-based regulation tends to be operated in a manner that places too much emphasis on 'individual sites'[8] and that, as a result, this approach is slow to come to terms with systemic and cumulative risks.[9] We must question the emphasis that has been placed on the regulation of CCPs in the UK and the US. Is the use of a risk-based approach *restricting* the UK and US regimes – rather than ensuring their focus on the safety and soundness of CCPs, both as individual sites, and by simultaneously promoting the stability of the OTCDM? In other words, is risk-based regulation the appropriate approach for ensuring the effective management of systemic risk[10] in the OTCDM? Does it need to be complemented with other strategies of regulation? If so, what are those strategies likely to be?

2.2 Risk in context

The 'Risk Society' theory provides us with an interesting perspective to understand the phenomenon of risk in the OTCDM. The main argument put forward here is that the OTCDM is a market of 'manufactured risks'.[11] We consider how Risk Society theory provides a basis on which to frame the role of innovation in the OTCDM. The origin and growth of the OTCDM is led by innovation[12] and, in that way, it creates multiple and evolving types of risks; as it occurs in other areas, the pace and impact of innovation does not necessarily increase certainty but, perhaps, the very opposite.[13]

Here we explain how risk-based regulation helps regulators to control the risk manufactured in the OTCDM and thereby cope with the impact of innovation.

---

5 Robert Baldwin, Martin Cave, and Martin Lodge, *Understanding Regulation* (Oxford University Press 2012) (n3), 293.
6 Ibid.
7 US Government Accountability Office, *Financial Crisis: Recent Crisis Reaffirms the Need to Overhaul the US Regulatory System* GAO-09–1049T Washington, DC (2009) in Ibid 283.
8 Julia Black, 'The Role of Risk in Regulatory Processes' in Robert Baldwin, Martin Cave, and Martin Lodge (eds.), *The Oxford Handbook of Regulation* (Oxford University Press 2010); also see Julia Black and Robert Baldwin, 'Really Responsive Risk-Based Regulation' (2010) 32 *Law and Policy*, 184.
9 Julia Black, 'The Emergence of Risk-Based Regulation and the New Public Risk Management in the United Kingdom' (2005) 512 *Public Law*, 535.
10 Steven Schwarcz, 'Systemic Risk' (2008) 97 *Georgetown Law Journal*, 193, 198.
11 Joanna Gray, and Jenny Hamilton, *Implementing Financial Regulation: Theory and Practice* (John Wiley & Sons Ltd 2006), 7.
12 Darrell Duffie, Ada Li, and Theo Lubke, 'Policy Perspectives on OTC Derivatives Markets Infrastructure' (2010) Federal Reserve Bank of New York) 10 <www.newyorkfed.org/media library/media/research/staff_reports/sr424.pdf> accessed 15th January 2016.
13 Anthony Giddens, 'Risk and Responsibility' (1999) 62 (1) *Modern Law Review*, 1.

Risk-based regulators should acknowledge the difference between risk and uncertainties. Regulators have a limited capacity to anticipate uncertain and unknowable events (e.g. large-scale losses)[14] – however, they should acknowledge that there are other types of uncertainties: the knowable uncertainties that might inform and contribute to the process of regulation. In this context, risks continue to be the 'drivers' of regulatory actions whereas uncertainties perform a secondary role. To accept that uncertainties might inform a risk-based regime is not at all perpetuating the unrealistic idea that risk-based regimes are broad or powerful enough to 'capture' all sources of risks, nor that they promise 'zero-failure'.[15] Instead, it is to emphasise that risk-based regimes are not informed exclusively by quantifiable and objective risks, but are fed by unknown but knowable uncertainties. Thus, we argue that regulators in risk-based regimes should acknowledge that not all uncertainties are equal.[16] Although all uncertainties are unknown, they can be knowable or unknowable[17] and the knowable uncertainties are the ones that might assist the design and implementation of risk-based regimes. Those are the uncertainties that can be reasonably anticipated when regulators design and implement a regime. Effective cooperation between regulators and regulated firms, throughout the process of regulation, facilitates the exchange of their multiple perceptions about the future and the identification of knowable uncertainties.

Uncertainties in risk-based regimes allow regulators to face contingent phenomena and, in particular, innovation. The occurrence of innovation is uncertain and unknown, but the form or content of innovation might be knowable. Under this rationale, regulators – by means of effective cooperation – are expected to be diligent in the task of foreseeing the *form* of innovation.

One possible shortcoming of this proposition is that in introducing one indeterminable element (i.e. 'knowable uncertainties'), we undermine the clarity of what regulators should do or are expected to do. To overcome this, regulators can define the parameters of responsibility and shape public and political expectations accordingly. This is to openly reaffirm the distinction between risks and knowable uncertainties, as well as the role and limits regulators have in each case. Therefore, while regulators will continue to use risk as a driver for regulatory decisions, and by so doing have a mechanism of risk identification and assessment, in the area of knowable uncertainties the role of regulators is more of a commitment to use strategies (e.g. cooperation, information sharing with firms) that allow the timely identification of such uncertainties.

To develop this argument, we also consider approaches to the problem of risk in sociological studies, explaining the most relevant concepts of the theory of

---

14 Joanna Gray, 'Is It Time to Highlight the Limits of Risk-Based Regulation? (2009) 4 (1) *Capital Markets Law Journal*, 51.

15 Ibid 53.

16 Ibid 60. (Emphasis added).

17 Barbara Adam, Ulrich Beck, and Joost van Loon (eds.), *The Risk Society and Beyond: Critical Issues for Social Theory* (Sage Publications 2000), 8.

Figure 2.1 Risks and uncertainties

Risk Society and how risk has become central to financial regulation. We then address the question of how the notion of 'manufactured risk' is applicable to the OTCDM.

2.2.1 Risk Society

The study of risk has occupied scholarship in a wide variety of special research areas,[18] among them legal[19] and sociological studies.[20] Hence, different approaches have been used to provide an explanation of what risk means; how it is identified and selected; and how society, governments, and institutions respond to the risk they face. Although the studies regarding the role of risk are approached differently according to the discipline, in the social sciences there is a constant

---

18 See Frank Knight, *Risk, Uncertainty and Profit* (Houghton Mifflin 1921); in management, for decision theory, see James G. March, and Zur Shapira, 'Managerial Perspectives on Risk and Risk Taking' (1987) 33 *Management Science*, 1404, 1413; Mary Douglas, and Aaron Wildavsky, *Risk and Culture: An Essay on Selection of Technological and Environmental Dangers* (Berkeley 1982); and Branden B. Johnson and Vincent T. Covello (eds.), *The Social and Cultural Construction of Risk: Essays on Risk Selection and Perception* (Dordrecht 1987).
19 See Nicklas Luhmann, *Risk: A Sociological Theory* (Aldine De Gruyter 1993), 1; Nicklas Luhman, Elizabeth King-Utz, and Martin Albrow (trs.), *A Sociological Theory of Law* (2nd ed, Routledge 2014), 193.
20 Nicklas Luhmann, *Risk: A Sociological Theory* (n19) Ibid 1.

interaction, and sometimes contradiction,[21] between areas. Luhmann and Beck are the most prominent sociologists in the debate over regulation and the role of risk.[22]

Ulrich Beck has built the concept of the so-called Risk Society in order to analyse the phenomenon of risk and its role in society. According to Beck, risk means anticipation of a positive or negative situation in the future; risk exists in a state of virtuality and only when it is anticipated does it become topical.[23] The rationale of the Risk Society is the distribution of 'bads' and 'dangers'.[24] In a Risk Society, there is a constant development of innovative technology that is not fully understood. In such a society, there is no end in production of possible futures.[25] These theoretical considerations are particularly helpful to study the dynamics of markets in constant evolution and led by innovation, such as the OTCDM.

The origin of the Risk Society was the result of evolution and recognition of social changes present in the industrial society. It was a time to understand that society lives beyond nature and tradition, and people no longer live their lives as if determined by fate.[26] Beck's work attributes reflexive modernity as the process that allowed the surge of the Risk Society.[27] Reflexive modernity is characterised as a period of prominent individualism, where the manual worker society was displaced by the educated and informational society. This transformation of society caused Risk Society theorists to question the role of risk.

This transition could be compared to the well-known commercial practice of brokers offering life insurance. All human beings are aware of their mortality, but after a talk with a life insurance broker, their perception of the risk of death increases. Similarly, what occurs with the emergence of a Risk Society is that society becomes consciously aware and worried about two notions: future and safety. As a result of that collectively shared perception,[28] the idea of risk surges.[29] It is not that Risk Society represents an increase in dangers; the change is in the perception and reaction of society towards those same risks. Moreover, as the traditional institutions – conceived during industrial society – are no longer sufficient to monitor and protect people from risk, those institutions and agencies contribute to produce and legitimate risks themselves. This scenario feeds open-ended discussions regarding the challenges of a global society and the risks it faces.

---

21 Baruch Fischhoff, Stephan R. Watson, and Chris Hope, 'Defining Risk' (1984) 17 *Policy Sciences*, 123–139.
22 Joanna Gray, and Jenny Hamilton, *Implementing Financial Regulation: Theory and Practice* (n11).
23 Ulrich Beck, 'World Risk Society and Manufactured Uncertainties' (2009) 1 *IRIS* 292 <www.fupress.net/index.php/iris/article/view/3304/2906> accessed 18th January 2016.
24 Ulrich Beck, *Risk Society: Towards a New Modernity* (Sage Publications 1992), 3.
25 Anthony Giddens, 'Risk and Responsibility' (n13), 3.
26 Ibid.
27 Ulrich Beck (n24) 3.
28 'B. Latour, and K. Knorr-Cetina would mention the "networks" through which they become established', Ulrich Beck, 'World Risk Society and Manufactured Uncertainties' (n23), 297.
29 Anthony Giddens, 'Risk and Responsibility' (n13) 3.

A discussion concerning the theories of risk built in sociology scholarship goes beyond the scope of this book; it is sufficient to say that, for sociologists, the theory of risk is one part of the formation of modern society.[30] In this sense, we understand that in advanced modernity the generation of wealth is inextricably linked to the social production of risks.[31] Then, in late modernity, the change is the move towards distribution of risks.[32] The modernisation process triggers progress in several areas (e.g. technology, science) that results in a multiplication of known risks, while at the same time it questions our ability to prevent or minimise the impact of such risks. Also, the appearance of unknown risks challenges the modernisation of society. It requires the identification of the potential unintended effects or unknown risks, and to delimit what is actually tolerable. These considerations concerning the creation of known and unknown risks, as well as unintended effects, will inform our later analysis of the OTCDM as a centre of production of risks and uncertainties.

In order to understand the transformations that feature in the Risk Society, it is also important to see that the risks can have positive and negative aspects. In a Risk Society, risks are not only hazards, but also an expansion of choices.[33] Therefore, when society is linked to technological progress and innovation, the number of choices available increases for those in the position to take and afford the choice. Giddens and Pierson[34] exemplified this with the situation of a woman – we would say a couple – with fertility problems. The scientific progress has made available a variety of treatments for infertility, but only couples with a high income can afford them. The positive and negative effects of risks are also a key concept in the OTCDM, since both sides impact the management of risk and profitability in derivatives transactions.

Under this rationale, the modern society, in its latest stage, represents an explosion of identified and unidentified risks. A basic element of risk, distinguishing it from uncertainty, means that its consequences are not necessarily destructive: the future component of risk makes it measurable, or quantifiable. This means that society holds enough knowledge to foresee, control, mitigate, and even sometimes eliminate risk. Moreover, the possibility to measure risk determines the potential to calculate its probability of occurrence. This attribute allows Risk Society theorists to differentiate risk from uncertainty. Unlike risk, uncertainty cannot be measured and thereby cannot be controlled, because its outcomes cannot be predicted. In the words of Joanna Gray, the outcomes of uncertainty are 'unknown and unknowable'.[35] In this regard, the regulation of OTCDM faces

---

30 Nicklas Luhmann, *Risk: A Sociological Theory* (n19), 6.
31 Ulrich Beck, *Risk Society: Towards a New Modernity* (n24).
32 Ibid 20.
33 Anthony Giddens, and Christopher Pierson, *Conversations with Anthony Giddens: Making Sense of Modernity* (Stanford University Press, 1998), 212.
34 Ibid.
35 Joanna Gray, and Jenny Hamilton, *Implementing Financial Regulation* (n11).

considerable challenges. As we will go on to explain, risk and uncertainty may well receive similar treatment in the areas of investment and finance.

The debate in the discourse of risk embeds the idea of differentiating risk from uncertainty.[36][37] The traditional dichotomy[38] in the study of risk and risk regulation attends to two lines of thought. One the one hand, the 'scientific-rationalist', 'absolutist', or 'modernist' model[39] understands risk as an objective concept, which can be quantified and measured, and is linked to the probability[40] and severity[41] of occurrence. Under this model, the regulation of risk should be the result of a technocratic process where experts lead the decision-making. The technocrats hold knowledge and expertise, and are in the position to analyse and decide the risk that individuals and society should tolerate. This model considers that uncertainty is unknown and possibly unknowable, mainly because it is derived from perception and lacks verifiable data.[42] Uncertainties are merely speculative, and the result of qualitative judgements or predictions. The scientific-rationalist method is also criticised for being utilitarian[43] because it privileges the total benefit, even if it exceeds the total costs or risks. Hence, it is irrelevant whether those assuming the costs or risks are in a good position to manage them.[44] The OTCDM evidences the shortcomings of using this model, because a purely mathematical study of risk is insufficient to control the market for manufactured risks.

On the other hand, there is the 'social-constructivist' 'socio-political' 'post-modernist' model.[45] According to this model, risk is constantly merging with uncertainty and, as such, it cannot always be quantified and measured.

36 Hazel Kemshall, *Risk, Social Policy and Welfare* (Open University Press 2002), 11; C. Hood, and D.K.C. Jones (eds.), *Accident and Design: Contemporary Debates in Risk Management* (UCL Press 1996).

37 Ian Bartle, 'Risk-Based Regulation and Better Regulation in the UK: Towards What Model of Risk Regulation?' (2008) 2nd Biennial Conference of the ECPR Standing Group on Regulatory Governance, Utrecht University, the Netherlands' Regulation in the Wake of Neoliberalism. Consequences of Three Decades of Privatization and Market Liberalization' <http://regulation.upf.edu/utrecht-08-papers/ibartle.pdf> accessed 15th January 2016.

38 Robert Baldwin, and Martin Cave, *Understanding Regulation: Theory, Strategy and Practice* (Oxford University Press, 1999), 145,148.

39 Deborah Lupton, *Risk* (Routledge 1999), 6.

40 Frank H. Knight, *Risk, Uncertainty and Profit* (n18) in Lupton Ibid 9.

41 D. Smith, and B. Toft, 'Risk and Crisis Management in the Public Sector' (1998) *Issues in Public Sector Risk Management*, 18 (4) *Public Money and Management*, 10.

42 Sven O. Hansson, 'Risk', *The Stanford Encyclopedia of Philosophy* (2007) <http://plato.stan ford.edu/entries/risk/> accessed 15th January 2016.

43 The first systematic account of utilitarianism was developed by Jeremy Bentham, 'Introduction to the Principles of Morals and Legislation' (1781) <www.utilitarianism.com/jeremy-bentham/index.html> accessed 15th January 2016.

44 Hélène Hermansson, 'Consistent Risk Management: Three Models Outlined' (2005) 8 (7–8) *Journal of Risk Research*, 562.

45 Barbara Adam, and Joost van Loon, 'Introduction: Repositioning Risk: The Challenge for Social Theory' in Barbara Adam, Ulrich Beck, and Joost van Loon (eds.), *The Risk Society and Beyond, Critical Issues for Social Theory* (n17), 8.

Moreover, risk and uncertainty can easily overlap each other. Contrary to the technocratic approach, this model asserts that the circumstances from which probabilities are derived are always different and, as a result, the outcomes of analytical models are flawed and based on uncertain knowledge.[46] This model argues that purely statistical and mathematical identification of risks done by experts lacks democratic legitimacy. Under this model, regulation of risk should involve all the interested actors, not just the technocrats, and the risk-based regime of the CCPs in the OTCDM should integrate the multiple perceptions of risks and uncertainties that regulators and firms have. Although regulators are challenged to achieve a balance between potential conflicting interests (i.e. interests of the public and interests of firms), cooperation with regulated firms would contribute to the design and facilitate the effective implementation of the regime.

The importance of this second model lies with the development of the idea of 'subjective risks'. Such risks are derived from other types of knowledge – not just mathematical – and their perception is usually influenced by cultural, social, and political factors.[47] Surprisingly, therefore, subjective risks might not merge with objective risks. Here, subjective perceptions of risk affect behaviour and thereby can change actual objective outcomes.[48]

2.2.1.1 *Manufactured risk*

Studying Beck's Risk Society, Giddens identifies a category of risks called 'external risks'. These were recognised in the midst of the Welfare State in the post-war period after 1945,[49] when the role of the State was to protect society against risks (e.g. provide insurance for sickness, unemployment, disabilities). Society started to leave the external risks attached to the notions of nature and tradition, whilst transitioning to a society marked by 'manufactured risks'. Certainly, the appearance of 'manufactured risks' challenged the Welfare State as conceived in the post-war period. They triggered a crisis in the management of risks, as now new types of risks were beginning to lead society.[50]

Beck and Giddens have led the study of 'manufactured risks'. Giddens defines manufactured risks as 'risks created by the very progression of human development, especially by the progression of science and technology'.[51] The particular characteristic of this type of risk is that, as it comes with progress and innovation,

---

46 Pat O'Malley, *Risk, Uncertainty and Government* (Routledge-Cavendish 2004), 18. Studying the idea of external factor and subjectivity in the data used to create sustainability standards.
47 Robert Baldwin, and Martin Cave, *Understanding Regulation* (n38), 141.
48 John Adams, *Risk* (London, UCL Press, 1995), 23.
49 Anthony Giddens, 'Risk and Responsibility' (n13), 3.
50 Anthony Giddens, and Christopher Pierson, *Conversations with Anthony Giddens: Making Sense of Modernity* (n33), 216.
51 Anthony Giddens, 'Risk and Responsibility' (n13), 3.

it can be hardly measured or quantified. The data available from history cannot fully inform the probabilities of occurrence.[52]

As we might anticipate, the idea of manufactured risks challenges the assertion that all risks can be measured or are calculable based on data which, as was explained earlier, is the traditional way to distinguish risk from uncertainty. Indeed, Giddens seems not to be concerned with the distinction, as he uses the terms 'manufactured risk' and 'manufactured uncertainty'[53] interchangeably, while Beck prefers the use of the term 'manufactured uncertainties'. Hence, Beck considers that risks are different from manufactured uncertainties, because they are dependent on human-to-human decisions, created by the society itself, collectively imposed and individually unavoidable.[54] There is an inherent impossibility to calculate manufactured uncertainties, because they break with known risks and the ways institutions have dealt with them. Notwithstanding the distinction between risk and uncertainty, when it comes to manufactured risks there is limitless creativity triggered by incalculable uncertainty.[55]

Another characteristic of manufactured risk is that it presumes new politics,[56] a reorientation of values and the relevant strategies attached. This means that society – in the era of 'reflexive modernity' – is aware of its limits and contradictions, and those of the modern order. The limits that take the form of manufactured risks[57] require an update of the politics and the strategies to manage them. Such a review of politics and strategies might bring positive outcomes: for instance, enhancing engagement with certain areas and types of risks. New politics require that any of the actors involved call attention when he/she has identified a serious risk.[58]

Although the reshape and update of politics might contribute to better manage manufactured risks, the *ethos* of this type of risk limits the reaction of society. Beck draws our attention to the fact that the issues of de-location,[59] incalculableness, and non-compensability of manufactured uncertainties prevent integral protection against them.[60] Moreover, the speed with which politics evolves is heavily influenced by cultural perceptions in each country. In the words of Beck, 'the pace of development outstrips the cultural imagination of society'.[61] In this scenario, manufactured risks provoke extensive debates regarding the limits they

---

52 Anthony Giddens, and Christopher Pierson, *Conversations with Anthony Giddens: Making Sense of Modernity* (n33), 210.
53 Anthony Giddens, 'Risk and Responsibility' (n13), 4.
54 Ulrich Beck, 'World Risk Society and Manufactured Uncertainties' (n23), 298.
55 Ibid 291.
56 Anthony Giddens, and Christopher Pierson, *Conversations with Anthony Giddens: Making Sense of Modernity* (n33), 212.
57 Ibid.
58 Anthony Giddens, 'Risk and Responsibility' (n13), 5.
59 The term 'de-location' indicates that manufactured risks are not always constrained to a specific geographical area.
60 Ulrich Beck, 'World Risk Society and Manufactured Uncertainties' (n23), 293.
61 Ibid 297.

pose and how they should be managed. The discussion results in new forms of institutionalisation (e.g. regulation) and decision-making processes that respond to conditions of manufactured uncertainty.[62] Hence, the traditional institutional mechanisms to manage risks are not enough to cope with manufactured risks.

2.2.2 Risk-government

The theory of Risk Society is not, however, a unique explanation for the role of risk in society and in regulation. Initially, the need to control risks through regulation was perceived as a response from governments after they had experienced crises which were not well managed. For strategic and political reasons, governments seek to restore public confidence by introducing new regulation, tackling the risks that caused previous crises.[63] Indeed, the initial efforts to impose legal controls to risk date from the mid-1960s, when specialised agencies were created in the US to directly regulate particular risks.[64] The work of Foucault[65] and the theory of governmentality provide one answer to the question of how to be governed, and particularly how to be governed by the State, or as Foucault called it, 'the political form of government'.[66] According to the theory of governmentality and its analysis of *The Prince* of Nicholas Machiavelli, the exercise of power is 'to reinforce, strengthen and protect the principality'.[67] Hence, the government is organised according to the needs of modern societies. However, the extent of such needs varies and is usually determined by liberalist and neo-liberalist discourses.[68] At this stage, technical experts are in a privileged position to define and select risks according their own conceptions.[69]

From the Risk Society theory perspective, risk governance is associated with the absence of control.[70] The awareness of risk in government is, in fact, recognition of the limits of our ability to control uncertainties.[71] However, the role of risk in the 'governmentality theory' is as a tool to control and shape behaviours.[72] Indeed, risks are means to guide what governments and individual should do,

---

62 Ibid.
63 Joanna Gray, and Jenny Hamilton, *Implementing Financial Regulation* (n11).
64 George L. Priest, 'The New Legal Structure of Risk Control' ch 7 in Pat O'Malley (ed.), *Governing Risks* (The International Library of Essays in Law and Society 2005), 205.
65 Graham Burchell, Colin Gordon, and Peter Miller, *The Foucault Effect: Studies in Governmentality* (Chicago University Press 1991) <https://laelectrodomestica.files.wordpress.com/2014/07/the-foucault-effect-studies-in-governmentality.pdf> accessed 13th January 2016.
66 Ibid.
67 Ibid.
68 D. Hodgson, '"Know Your Consumer": Marketing, Governmentality and the New Consumer of Financial Services' (2002) 40 (4) *Management Decision*, 318–328 in Joanna Gray, and Jenny Hamilton, *Implementing Financial Regulation* (n11), 9.
69 Ulrich Beck, *Risk Society: Towards a New Modernity* (n24).
70 Anthony Giddens, *Runaway World: How Globalization is Reshaping our Lives* (Profile Books 1999) in Joanna Gray, and Jenny Hamilton, *Implementing Financial Regulation* (n11), 8.
71 Ibid.
72 Pat O'Malley, 'Risk, Power and Crime Prevention' (1992) Economy and Society, 252 Ibid 9.

according to political views. The way in which risk is used in risk governance is influenced by the particularities of the environment in which it operates.[73] Similarly, the governmental authorities start to develop methodologies and strategies according to their own definition of risks. As Joanna Gray explains, the adoption of risk-based regulation by the Financial Services Authority is one example of an authority designing its own 'powerful rhetorical framework'.[74]

2.2.3 Risk and regulation

The dynamic of risk as a driver of regulatory decisions reveals the complexity of implementing risk-based regimes. In his highly controversial[75] work, *Breaking the Vicious Circle: Towards Effective Risk Regulation*, Stephen Breyer[76] demonstrates how, in a world of 'newfound risks',[77] it is impossible to reconcile the gap between scientific methods of measuring risk and political pressures. Breyer criticises risk-based regulation, arguing that its implementation is a vicious circle that tends to fail due to three shortcomings: over-regulation, random selection of priorities, and inconsistent implementation across government agencies and areas. Hence, the design of a coherent risk programme and a set of rational priorities covering risk regulatory programmes[78] is key to breaking the vicious circle.

Furthermore, there are some issues triggered in the implementation of risk-based regulation. Such process cannot be limited to the simple integration of multiple perceptions of risks. When government authorities face some conflict between different risk-based regimes, the use of risk allows regulators to shift responsibility for certain risks to the regulated firms.[79] As a result, it is arguable whether the element of risk effectively depoliticises the regulatory process.[80]

Despite the critiques of risk-based regimes, the adoption of risk-based regulation in a world of 'newfound risks' does not necessarily undermine the role of uncertainty[81] and its democratic character. It seems clear that uncertainty and

73 Pat O'Malley, *Risk, Uncertainty and Government* (n46).
74 Joanna Gray, and Jenny Hamilton, *Implementing Financial Regulation* (n11), 12.
75 Joan Biskupic, 'Senators Question Breyer's Economics; Biden Calls Cost-Effective Approach to Environmental Protection "Elitist"' *Washington Post*, 15 July 1994 A6 in Todd C. Zubler, 'Book Note: 'Breaking the Vicious Circle: Toward Effective Risk Regulation' (Fall 1994) 8 (1) *Harvard Journal of Law & Technology*, 1 <http://jolt.law.harvard.edu/articles/pdf/v08/08HarvJLTech241.pdf> accessed 15th January 2016.
76 Stephen Breyer, *Breaking the Vicious Circle: Towards Effective Risk Regulation* (Harvard University Press 1993).
77 Todd C. Zubler, 'Book Note: 'Breaking the Vicious Circle: Toward Effective Risk Regulation'(n75).
78 Robert Baldwin, and Martin Cave, *Understanding Regulation* (n38) in Ian Bartle, 'Risk-Based Regulation and Better Regulation in the UK: Towards What Model of Risk Regulation? (n37).
79 Joanna Gray, and Jenny Hamilton, *Implementing Financial Regulation* (n11).
80 Ibid.
81 Sanjay G. Reddy, 'Claims to Expert Knowledge and the Subversion of Democracy: The Triumph of Risk Over Certainty' (1996) 25 *Economy and Society*, 222, 254.

risk might now align and form a hybrid system.[82] Regulators adopting a socio-logical model to study risk – the decision-making process concerning what risk exists, the level of tolerance, and how to control it – are not restricted to only mathematical methods. Instead, this model is shaped through the integration of different sources of knowledge and with the participation of all interested actors. This argument, translated into the dynamics of risk-based regulation, can be identified by means of a regulatory process that welcomes cooperation between firms and regulatory authorities.

In order to understand the cooperation between firms and regulators, it is important to highlight that, as the Risk Society theory asserts, the perception of risk varies and is influenced by cultural, political, and social factors. Hence, it is perfectly possible that regulators perceive some types of risk as most promi-nent, while financial firms recognise the existence of different risk. Similarly, there might be different perceptions of risks within the firm.[83] Therefore, when risk-based regulation is designed and implemented, different risks should be con-sidered in order to create a coherent approach. In the ideal scenario, risk-based regulation would imply the appropriate and timely cohesion of multiple percep-tions of risks to integrate the perception of government, regulators, and firms. The adequate integration of these perceptions would allow regulators to balance the multiple interests in play and to use risk as a driver of regulatory decisions.

These considerations are relevant to financial services regulation, where the concept of risk has been adopted as a benchmark. Hence, as explained by Joanna Gray, 'regulation has to be proportionate to the risks'.[84] Then, the extent to which risk influences the content of financial regulation delimits the decision-making process; more importantly it contributes to define what regulators do and what they are expected to do.

In financial services regulation, the role of risk is not only considered from the regulators' perspective, but also the role of individuals within the firm. Although the detailed discussion of risk-based regimes is in the next part of this chapter, it is important to explain that the adoption of a risk-based approach to regulation involves the desire to shape firms' internal cultures and processes. This is not only to integrate firms' perception and attitude towards risk. It also embeds rules of senior management and staff, and hence accountability.[85] Thus, the phenomenon of risk within the firm considers the internal structure of control, as well as the role of boards and risk committees. The rationale is, as Joanna Gray explains, that financial regulation has extended its reach 'downwards' into the level of the regu-lated firm to impose specific responsibilities on individuals within those firms, particularly on senior managers.[86] The senior managers' regime imposes specific

---

82 Pat O'Malley, 'Imagining Insurance: Risk, Thrift and Industrial Life Insurance' (1999) 5 (2) *Connecticut Insurance Law*, 675, 705.
83 See Joanna Gray, and Jenny Hamilton, *Implementing Financial Regulation* (n11), 44.
84 Ibid.
85 Ibid 46.
86 Ibid 55.

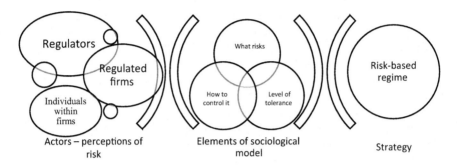

Figure 2.2 Regulators adopting a sociological model to study risk

duties to members of the board and individuals performing managerial roles. Moreover, the firm's internal control system is expected to contribute to the achievement of regulators' objectives. Therefore, the effective implementation of risk-based regimes relies on the effective cooperation and a coherent dialogue between regulators and firms. Such a model of cooperation integrates regulators' and regulated firms' perceptions of risks and uncertainties, as well as how they should be managed and controlled.

Bearing all of our previous insights in mind, we will now briefly consider how Risk Society and Beck's theory frame the evolution of OTC derivatives as an example of a 'manufactured-risk-market'.

2.2.4 The OTCDM is a 'manufactured-risk-market'

The Risk Society theory gives us the context to argue that the OTCDM is a 'manufactured-risk-market' and a formation of the modern society in financial markets. The OTCDM creates risks and accumulates uncertainties. The uncertainties might be known-unknowns or unknown-unknowns that the OTCDM brings to regulators and firms. These uncertainties in turn show the limits of the expertise and regulation of the market. As part of a Risk Society, regulators and firms are aware of the risks and uncertainties manufactured in the OTCDM.

The awareness of such limits might assist regulators and market participants, allowing regulators and firms to manage risks and, if possible, uncertainties. There might be, however, some challenges. Firstly, regulators and firms have to identify uncertainties.[87] Due to the incalculable nature of uncertainties, their anticipation, although useful, might be difficult in practice. Secondly, in an ideal scenario, regulators and firms are expected to coordinate the management of

---

87 'Uncertainty represents a distinctive way of governing through the future' Pat O'Malley, 'Uncertain Subjects: Risks, Liberalism and Contract' ch13 in Pat O'Malley (ed.), *Governing Risks* (n64), 349.

risks. The coordination requires a constant sharing of information and expertise, so regulators and firms have timely access to the same information about the market and participants' practices. However, such a level of coordination is usually challenged by the interaction between potential conflicting interests.

Notwithstanding the challenges, risks and uncertainties manufactured in the OTCDM have the potential to inform the design process and implementation of regulation, especially in risk-based regimes. As Joanna Gray asserts, in the areas of finance and investment, 'the difference between risk and uncertainty is (perhaps deliberately so) not commonly maintained'.[88] It follows that uncertainties receive a veil of certainty and objectivity, regardless of the impossibility in measuring or quantifying them. Recognising this predicament, we would emphasise that, in risk-based regimes, the role of risk and uncertainties is different. To use a metaphor, while the known risks are the drivers of regulatory actions, the uncertainties are the co-drivers, or co-pilots; they have a secondary function, but in a risk-based approach, they still contribute towards the expected outcomes.

The OTCDM is a manufactured-risk-market because risks exist as an integral part of the activities performed in the market. In order to develop this argument, we must first bring into this section the functions derivatives perform and the reasons they were created. The defenders of the derivatives market argue that derivatives improve economic efficiency by dividing risks and allocating them to the most willing risk-bearers.[89] OTC derivatives[90] are useful in completing asset markets and enhancing price discovery; although this is debatable, we argue that they contribute to absorbing systemic risk.[91]

Financial derivatives were created to manage and control the risk triggered by the volatility of financial markets.[92] These instruments are useful to hedge[93] risk – basically any type of risk. The purpose of hedging is to provide protection when an entity is exposed to potential risk by reducing or reallocating risk instead of creating it. However, this tool of risk management does not always bring the expected benefits. In practice, the hedging of risk might be affected when the derivative does not cover the targeted risk or when the counterparty of the derivative transaction – this is the provider of protection – defaults. Thus, derivatives

88 Joanna Gray, and Jenny Hamilton, *Implementing Financial Regulation* (n11).
89 David Mullins, 'Remarks on the Global Derivatives Study Sponsored by the Group of Thirty' (1993) ISDA Summer Conference 1 <https://fraser.stlouisfed.org/scribd/?item_id=35397&filepath=/docs/historical/federal%20reserve%20history/bog_members_statements/mullins_19930728.pdf#scribd-open> accessed 18th September 2015.
90 Dan Awrey, 'The Dynamics of OTC Derivatives Regulation: Bridging the Public-Private Divide' (2010) *European Business Organization Law Review*, 11.
91 Roger Lowenstein, 'When Genius Failed: The Rise and Fall of Long-Term Capital Management' (2000) and Thomas F. Siems, '10 Myths About Financial Derivatives' (1997) Cato Inst, *Cato Policy Analysis*, 283, 8–9.
92 Henry TC Hu, 'Misunderstood Derivatives: The Causes of Informational Failure and the Promise of Regulatory Incrementalism' (1993) 102 *Yale Law Journal*, 1457, 1464–65.
93 Carolyn H. Jackson, 'Have You Hedged Today? The Inevitable Advent of Consumer Derivatives' (1999) 67 *Fordham Law Review*, 3206.

are not always performing their risk management function. When financial derivatives do not contain risks, they become multipliers of risks.

Similarly, financial derivatives are instruments that allow speculation. Speculation occurs when the parties enter into a derivative transaction with the sole purpose of taking advantage of the future movements of prices and obtaining the respective profit.[94] Also, financial derivatives might be used to obtain funding at a preferential rate.[95] Another common practice in the use of financial derivatives is arbitrage: using market imperfections as mismatches in market movements, artificially restricting opportunities, and so on to generate profits. Arbitrage might consist in staking positions before markets react to certain events.[96]

As might be anticipated, risk is the common element to all the functions performed by financial derivatives. Indeed, risk is the driver of derivatives transactions. Hence, what derivatives markets do is to isolate and transfer both negative and positive outcomes of risk. While the negative effect of risk is managed to avoid losses, the positive effect represents the possibility to gain profit.[97]

If financial derivatives are instruments of risk management, we can argue that they fit into the category of manufactured risks. Their manufactured risk character is composed of two essential factors: firstly, the primary purpose of the markets in which derivatives are traded, exchange and OTC, is to provide tools to manage risk. Both financial and non-financial firms use derivatives to that end.[98] Hence, financial derivatives are a creation; they are the result of the progression of finance and financial technology (FinTech), and thereby manufactured. Secondly, this manufactured market itself represents various types of risks,[99] including credit, market, liquidity, legal, and operational risks. We will later discuss the particularities of each one of the risks brought by the derivatives market.

Additionally, the inclusion of the CCPs in the OTCDM is adding complexity to the structure of the market. Although we will discuss the role of CCPs in the OTCDM more later on, this is an opportune moment to explain that CCPs are the new intermediaries of the OTCDM. A CCP interposes itself in the middle of the transaction and becomes the counterparty of the two initial counterparties. As a result, there is a change in the allocation of credit risk, now transferred to the

94 Norman Menachem Feder, 'Deconstructing Over-the-Counter Derivatives' (2002) 677 *Columbia Business Law Review*, 719; Don M Chance, 'Losing Money with Derivatives' (1998) *Essays in Derivatives*, 289, 300.
95 Peter A. Abken, 'Over-the-Counter Financial Derivatives: Risky Business?' (9 March–April 1994) *Federal Reserve Bank of Atlanta Economic Review*, 5.
96 Norman Menachem Feder, 'Deconstructing Over-the-Counter Derivatives' (n94), 720.
97 Desmond Eppel, 'Risky Business: Responding to OTC Derivatives Crises', (2002) 40 *Columbia Journal of Transnational Law*, 677, 687.
98 Anatoli Kuprianov, 'The Role of Interest Rate Swaps in Corporate Finance' (Summer 1994) Federal Reserve Bank *Bank Richmond Economic Quarterly*, 53, 58.
99 Brandor Becker, and Francois-Ihor Mazur, 'Risk Management of Financial Derivatives Products: "Who's Responsible for What?"' (Fall 1995) 21 *The Journal of Corporation Law* 177, 183.

CCP.[100] CCPs are crucial nodes in the financial system, hence their systemic importance in terms of managing, reducing, and allocating the inherent risks arising from transactions between market participants.[101] Notwithstanding the benefits of the use of CCPs, their systematically important position creates and deepens some risks in the OTCDM. As CCPs are highly interconnected, their failure might prompt negative externalities.[102] Moreover, the establishment of a CCP creates the risk of contagion[103] of shocks and losses. Also, CCPs in the OTCDM are too difficult to substitute,[104] which is problematic when one of just a few operating CCPs ceases to provide services. Thus, the introduction of the CCPs in the OTCDM might be a manufactured risk source when they fail to solve and, instead, deepen issues such as concentration of risks and excessive interconnectedness, and when the operation or failure of the CCPs creates new risks.

2.2.4.1 *The role of innovation*

The manufactured nature of the OTCDM shows that purely mathematical studies of risks are not enough to control manufactured risks. Entrepreneurialism is at the heart of the OTCDM and 'uncertainty is the timeless reality of entrepreneurial activity'.[105] The OTCDM relies on the liberty to create new products and the use of probabilistic calculations of future harms that, by nature, neglects the 'liberty to create the future'.[106] The OTCDM is a hotbed of entrepreneurial behaviour.[107] Indeed, success and profitability are mostly derived from innovation (how different the new products and practices are from those of the past, that have been already controlled by regime). Hence, if OTCDM regulators seek to inform regulatory reforms solely based on previous experiences or crises that put in the forefront the 'known risks' of the market, they are likely to fail in dealing with innovative sources of risks, or 'innovation risk'.

---

100 Douglas D. Evanoff, Daniela Russo, and Robert S. Steigerwald, 'Policymakers, Researchers, and Practitioners Discuss the Role of Central Counterparties' (2006) 4 *Economic Perspectives Federal Reserve Bank of Chicago and European Central Bank*. <http://econpapers. repec.org/article/fipfedhep/y_3a2006_3ai_3aqiv_3ap_3a2-21_3an_3av.30no.4.htm> accessed 26th May 2013.
101 Nikil Chande, Nicholas Labelle, and Eric Tuer, 'Central Counterparties and Systemic Risk' *Bank of Canada Financial System Review* (December 2010).
102 IMF, 'Central Counterparties: Addressing Their Too Important to Fail Nature' Working Paper (January 2015).
103 CCPs actions may have 'pro-cyclical' effects by exacerbating other stresses in the financial system.
104 IMF, 'Central Counterparties: Addressing their Too Important to Fail Nature' (n102).
105 Frank H. Knight, *Risk, Uncertainty and Profit* (n18).
106 Pat O'Malley, 'Consuming Risks: Harm Minimization and the Government of "Drug Users"' in Russell Smandych (ed.), *Governable Places: Readings in Governmentality and Crime Control* (Advances in Criminology Series 1999).
107 David Osborne, and Tedd Gaebler, *Reinventing Government: How the Entrepreneurial Spirit is Transforming the Public Sector* (Plume Books 1993).

The OTCDM itself is a product of innovation rather than evolution – proof of that is the fact the products currently traded are substantially different from those designed in the 1970s.[108] Innovation usually increases the complexity[109] of the market by means of introducing certain types of products and market practices that are not fully understood by regulators and market participants. Indeed, intermediaries are usually the precursors of such innovation. Their interest is to take advantage of the new products and information that only they hold. Thus, innovation challenges regulators and their ability to keep pace and anticipate, if possible, the direction of such innovation. Moreover, innovation has an important effect, explained further in following chapters, which is the possibility to increase complexity through the generation of what Awrey calls 'unanticipated and undetected interconnections'.[110] The unintended interconnections between different markets and participants are channels of communication of risk. The UK regime of CCPs in the OTCDM is an example of how innovation in compliance might result in the transfer of risks from the OTCDM to the repo market. In other words, how the current regime's 'creative compliance' might frustrate the objective of enhancing the risk management in the OTCDM.

In particular, OTCDM innovation is not restricted to applying to technological inventions[111] seeking to facilitate trade. Instead, innovation occurs when hedging, speculation, and market-making converge. Although this tripartite categorisation of activities has been used to explain innovation in the exchange-traded market,[112] it also guides innovation in the OTCDM. Similar to the exchange market, the OTCDM allows the performance of these activities. Also, the features that traditionally distinguished the OTC and exchange markets are being progressively blurred as a result of the post-GFC regulatory reforms, and now both markets share some common characteristics. The context in which innovation takes place in the OTCDM is a source of manufactured risks that are not always foreseen by regulators. Therefore, the argument here is not restricted to the evolution of the OTCDM and how the 'pace of innovation has left financial regulators and regulation behind the curve'.[113] Instead, we emphasise that the OTCDM is itself a manufactured-risk-market and, as such, the use of the risk-based approach to regulation should respond to the classical financial system risks – credit, liquidity,

---

108 Donald McKenzie, 'The Material Production of Virtuality: Innovation, Cultural Geography and Facticity in Derivatives Market' (August 2007) 36 (3) *Economy and Society*, 359 <www.tandfonline.com/doi/pdf/10.1080/03085140701428332> accessed 14th January 2016.

109 Dan Awrey, 'Complexity, Innovation, and the Regulation of Modern Financial Markets' (2012) 2 *Harvard Law Review*, 267.

110 Ibid.

111 Barry Barnes, and David Edge (eds.), *Science in Context: Readings in the Sociology of Science* (MIT Press 1982).

112 Donald McKenzie, 'The Material Production of Virtuality: Innovation, Cultural Geography and Facticity in Derivatives Market' (n108).

113 Dan Awrey, 'Complexity, Innovation, and the Regulation of Modern Financial Markets' (n109), 239.

and operational risks – as well as those created by the particular dynamics of the market and the regulation in place.

2.2.4.2 Creative compliance

The behaviour of firms participating in the market, and particularly complying with regulation, is sometimes heavily influenced by creativity. Here we will explore this creativity in terms of a form of innovation that characterises the OTCDM and creates manufactured risks. There are mainly two forms of enforcement methods to ensure the observance of rules: compliance (cooperation) and deterrence[114] (punishment). Under the rationale of Risk Society, both models are forms of controls against[115] risks, but compliance might be more effective, as it ensures observance through the use of few resources.[116] To persuade is less expensive than to punish.[117] However, when firms incur gross non-compliance, regulators are almost compelled to use punishment[118] (e.g. when non-compliance is causing substantial damages). According to the compliance method of enforcement, the idea behind regulation is securing compliance.[119] This means that the first approach of regulators is to expect that firms will voluntarily observe rules and principles. However, when firms do not act accordingly, regulators have enforcement powers and a sanctions system that are the deterrence[120] mechanisms.

Along with the incentives provided by regulators,[121] in the area of compliance, industry and firms model their perceptions and attitude towards risks[122] and regulation. The key notion to consider here is the existence of 'subcultures of resistance to regulation'[123] that represent the interests of the firm, but more importantly the industry forces. For instance, in the derivatives market, firms tend to follow the advice of the International Swaps and Derivatives Association

---

114 Ian Ayres, and John Braithwaite, *Responsive Regulation: Transcending the Deregulation Debate* (Oxford University Press 1992), 39.

115 Roger Cotterell, *The Sociology of Law: An Introduction* (Butterworths 1992), 245.

116 John T. Scholz, 'Voluntary Compliance and Regulatory Enforcement' (October 1984) 6 *Law and Policy*, 385, 404.

117 Ian Ayres, and John Braithwaite, *Responsive Regulation: Transcending the Deregulation Debate* (Oxford University Press 1992) (n114), 26.

118 Keith Hawkins, 'Law as Last Resort' in Robert Baldwin (ed.), *Reader on Regulation* (Oxford University Press 1998), 298.

119 Ian Ayres, and John Braithwaite, *Responsive Regulation: Transcending the Deregulation Debate* (n114) 39.

120 See Thomas Schelling, *Arms and Influence* (Yale University Press 1966); Laura Langbein, and Cornelius Kervin, 'Implementation, Negotiation and Compliance in Environmental Safety Regulation' (1985) 47 *Journal of Politics*, 854, 880.

121 Peter N. Grabosky, 'Regulation by Reward: On the Use of Incentives as Regulatory Instruments' (1995) 17 (3) *Law & Policy*, 257.

122 See Mary Douglas, Cultural Bias (Occasional Paper 35, London, Royal Anthropological Institute) in Joanna Gray, and Jenny Hamilton, *Implementing Financial Regulation* (n11) 41.

123 Ian Ayres, and John Braithwaite, *Responsive Regulation: Transcending the Deregulation Debate* (n114), 39.

(ISDA) to cooperate with the regulatory process. The attitude of individual firms and industry towards risks can become sources of manufactured risks. The perception of the risks created in the OTCDM, and how they should be managed, is influenced not only by the dynamics of the individual firm but also by the 'industry subculture' and by shared interpretational frameworks that the industry creates.[124] Whilst such industry subculture sometimes might be aligned to regulators' objectives (e.g. when communication and education persuade firms to comply),[125] when the costs of compliance are less than the benefits firms accrue, they will tend to avoid total and uncontested compliance. In such a situation, there are basically two options: to negotiate compliance with the regulator[126] or to find creative forms of compliance that leave the regulator lagging behind the avoidance activities.[127] We will focus on the creative compliance option and examine how it leads to innovation.

Creative compliance is defined as 'using the law to escape legal control without actually violating legal rules'.[128] It is a reaction from regulated firms to the content of certain regulation. In this sense, the attitude towards rules is not to observe them, but to find the way to work with them[129] and actively manipulate the law.[130] This means that regulated firms are creating new ways to escape the intended consequences of the regime and thereby comply with the letter of the law 'while undermining the policy behind it'.[131] The importance of compliance performed with high standards of honesty and integrity has been recognised as a central element to preserve the reputation of financial firms and its members.[132] In times of multiple regulatory reforms, financial markets are living in the 'age of the compliance officer'.[133] The role of compliance officers within the structure

---

124 Joanna Gray, and Jenny Hamilton, *Implementing Financial Regulation* (n11), 42.
125 K.O. Hawkins and J.M. Thomas, 'The Enforcement Process in Regulatory Bureaucracies' in K.O Hawkins and J.M Thomas (eds.), *Enforcing Regulation* (Kluwer Nijhoff 1984), 82.
126 Ian Ayres, and John Braithwaite, *Responsive Regulation: Transcending the Deregulation Debate* (n114), 26.
127 Doreen McBarnet, 'Law, Policy and Legal Avoidance: Can Law Effectively Implement Egalitarian Policies?' (Spring 1988) *Journal of Law and Society*, 113.
128 Doreen McBarnet, 'Law and Capital: The Role of Legal Form and Legal Actors' (1984) 12 *International Journal Sociology of Law*, 233; Doreen McBarnet, 'Law, Policy and Legal Avoidance' (1988) 1 *Journal of Law & Society*, 13; Doreen McBarnet, 'It's Not What You Do But The Way That You Do It: Tax Evasion, Tax Avoidance and the Boundaries of Deviance' in D. Downes (ed.), *Unraveling Criminal Justice* (Macmillan 1991); Doreen McBarnet, and Christopher Whelan, 'The Elusive Spirit of the Law: Formalism and the Struggle for Legal Control' (1991) 54 (6) *Marvard Law Review*, 848.
129 Doreen McBarnet, 'Law and Capital: The Role of Legal Form and Legal Actors' (n128) 3.
130 Doreen McBarnet, and Christopher Whelan, 'The Elusive Spirit of the Law' (n128).
131 Doreen McBarnet, 'When Compliance is not the Solution but the Problem: From Changes in Law to Changes in Attitude' (The Australian National University, Australian Taxation Office, Centre for Tax System Integrity Working Paper N 18 August 2001), 8.
132 BIS, 'Compliance and the Compliance Function in Banks' (April 2005) <www.bis.org/publ/bcbs113.pdf> accessed 19th January 2016.
133 Sam Fleming, 'The Age of the Compliance Officer' (2014) FT Report, April 24, 12:19 am <www.ft.com/cms/s/0/cadd54a6-c3bd-11e3-a8e0-00144feabdc0.html#axzz3xiWFXGRl> accessed 19th January 2016.

of financial firms is pivotal to keeping up with new and changing regulatory requirements.

Compliance officers are those employees required to have compliance knowledge and expertise in the firm, as well as be up to date with regulatory changes; they usually are a multidisciplinary group of experts in law, finance, and accountancy.[134] It is precisely within pockets of such a high level of knowledge and scrutiny of the law that creative compliance might take place. The window of creativity is into the gaps, exemptions, and exclusions of the law, as well as the literal interpretation of restrictive rules. Thus, creative compliance exposes the limits of formalism as a mechanism of law and control,[135] especially because it uses specific rules and legal forms to deceive the purpose of regulation. Creative compliance might be triggered when the regulator tries to cover all the possible areas – and correlated risks – with over-prescriptive rules, but also when the rules are too general and leave gaps and fractures in the regulation.

To reduce the events of creative compliance, McBarnet and Whelan[136] propose the adoption of an anti-formalist approach to the law. Even though the adoption of the approach might be criticised,[137] its main attribute is that anti-formalism is policy oriented[138] and entails an emphasis on substance[139] to avoid tight definitions, benefit the use of broad criteria still preserving coherence,[140] and interpret reality according to the spirit of the law. This involves a constant review of the regulated firms' practices in line with the policy guiding the regime. This argument supports our emphasis on the importance of designing and implementing a coherent risk-based approach as the 'route-map' of the regulation of CCPs in the OTCDM. Coherence is reached when a risk-based regime integrates the perceptions of regulators and firms related to the manufactured risks of the OTCDM and how they should be managed. Also, regulators should be bestowed with sufficient enforcement powers to ensure compliance.

The findings of this work exemplify the shortcomings of the UK and the US regime of CCPs in the OTCDM. Such shortcomings are affecting the achievement of the regulatory objective of enhancing the stability of the market. In the UK, the absence of a coherent conduct of business regime of CCPs, the insufficient legal framework underpinning CCPs' operations, the lack of a special resolution regime for CCPs, and the failure to rule on innovation risk are flaws

---

134 Athul Shah, 'Creative Compliance in Financial Reporting' (1 January 1996) 21 *Accounting, Organizations and Society*, 23.

135 Mark Kelman, *A Guide to Critical Legal Studies* (Harvard University Press 1987).

136 Doreen McBarnet, and Christopher Whelan, 'The Elusive Spirit of the Law' (n128), 851.

137 See Doreen McBarnet, and Christopher Whelan, 'The Elusive Spirit of the Law' (n128), 856.

138 Jason Scott Johnston, 'Uncertainty, Chaos and the Torts Process: An Economic Analysis of Legal Form' (1991) 76 (341) *Cornell Law Review*, 97.

139 The concept of substance over form is highlighted in *Ramsay (WT) Ltd v IRC* [1982] AC 300; *Furniss v Dawson* [1984] AC 474; *Helby v Mathews* [1895] AC 471,475; *Re Curtain Dream* [1990] BCLC 925, 935. See Duncan Kennedy, 'Form and Substance in Private Law Adjudication' (1976) 89 *Harvard Law Review*, 1685, 1775.

140 Ernest Weinrib, 'Legal Formalism: On the Immanent Rationality of Law' (1988) 97 *Yale Law Journal*, 949.

that hinder the attainment of regulatory objectives. The regulator's objective is to enhance the stability of the OTCDM by ensuring the safety and soundness of CCPs. Similarly, in the US regime, the incomplete implementation of risk-based regulation triggers some shortcomings related to a flawed regulatory structure that renders inefficient supervision of CCPs and a precarious adoption of multiple regulatory strategies. Also, the US regime fails to rule on the impact that future innovations – e.g. FinTech developments and market practices such as collateral transformation – might have in the functioning of the derivatives market and central clearing services. We would emphasise that the current management of innovation risk is incipient. Moreover, the extraterritorial implementation of the US regime of CCPs poses serious concerns related to CCPs' mutual recognition and rules of segregation of assets.

If we understand that the OTCDM is indeed a manufactured-risk-market, there are several risks produced in the market and by the current regulation. The purpose of this book is to call attention to how some manufactured risks have not yet been adequately addressed in the UK and US CCP regimes in the OTCDM.

2.3 Addressing the argument in favour of principles-based regulation

In financial regulation, the debate regarding which strategy to implement is somehow a cyclical discussion. Sometimes the result is, like the quote from a very famous song,[141] that: 'You can't always get what you want, but if you try sometimes, you might find you get what you need'. The reader of the regulation strategies continually realises that the practical distinction between one strategy and another is sometimes very subtle, and that the integration between them might offer better results than their individual implementation.[142] The defenders of one or another strategy of regulation tend to promise that it will contribute to overcome all the potential issues regulators face in practice. Indeed, there is a well-intentioned objective of continuously trying to improve the content and features in order to suggest the 'best strategy'. However, our experience during times of crises always seems to see new waves of debate and criticism of the just-abandoned latest 'best' strategy.

That was the fate of principles-based regulation (PBR). PBR was heavily criticised, particularly in the UK, after the GFC. Nonetheless, there were some defenders of the strategy – immediately after the GFC, Awrey proposed that the PBR would be one of the most appropriate strategies to rule innovation and complexity in financial markets, particularly in the OTCDM.[143] In short, he argued

---

141 Rolling Stones, 'You Can't Always Get What You Want'.
142 Joanna Gray, 'Is It Time to Highlight the Limits of Risk-Based Financial Regulation? (n14) 50, 62.
143 Dan Awrey, 'Regulating Financial Innovation: A More Principles-Based Alternative?' (2011) 5 (2) *Brooklyn Journal of Corporate, Financial & Commercial Law*, 273 <http://ssrn.com/abstract=1702457> accessed 17th January 2016.

that a 'more principles-based regulation' (MPBR) has the potential to respond to the challenges steaming from the complexity and innovativeness of financial markets[144] and he studied the case of the OTCDM. He asserts that MPBR can ameliorate asymmetries of information and expertise between regulators and regulated firms, 'constrain agency costs, promote harmonisation and generate more responsive and durable regulation'.[145]

MPBR shows us that similar benefits can be attributed to the use of risk-based regimes. Risk-based regulation, despite its drawbacks, is also a mostly efficient approach to regulate CCPs in the OTCDM and the related innovation risk. In the next section, we will explain in detail the benefits and shortcomings of a risk-based approach and how it can be complemented with other strategies.

2.4 Taxonomy of a risk-based approach

'Risk-based regulation' is a general set of principles that seeks to find common and homogenous elements to rationalise the regulatory process.[146] In particular, having assessed the risk that the parties will present to the regulatory body achieving its objectives,[147] it prioritises regulatory actions accordingly. This approach to regulation comprehends two stems: conduct of business and prudential regulation. It requires regulators to clearly define its objectives from the outset; therefore, regulatory agencies conduct a process of decision-making to determine how to address and when to prioritise risks. It is highly likely that such a process is biased and affected by some errors in judgement. Consider the following theory,[148] developed in societal risk regulation.[149] This theory describes two types of errors: type I, erring on the side of caution (judging something as risky when it is not), and type II, erring on the side of risk (judging something as safe when it is not). When applied to the process of selection of risks, the theory illustrates how the judgement of regulators is greatly subjective and, thus, it might be affected by inner perceptions and external factors.

Risk-based regulation requires a strategy of regulation[150] in which the quality of a firm's internal controls is the paramount focus of attention. The rationale

---

144 Ibid.
145 Ibid.
146 Julia Black, 'The Development of Risk-Based Regulation in Financial Services: 'Just 'Modelling Through'?' 156 in Julia Black, Martin Lodge and Marck Thatcher, *Regulatory Innovation a Comparative Analysis* (Edward Elgar Publishing 2005).
147 Julia Black, 'The Emergence of Risk-Based Regulation and the New Public Risk Management in the United Kingdom' 512–535 (n9).
148 Julia Black, 'The Development of RBR Just 'Modelling Through'?' (n146); Julia Black, 'Risk and Regulatory Policy: Improving the Governance of Risk. Risk-based Regulation: Choices, Practices and Lessons Being Learnt' (2010) *OECD*, 185 <www.keepeek.com/Digital-Asset-Management/oecd/governance/risk-and-regulatory-policy/risk-based-regulation_9789264082939-11-en#page6> accessed 9th October 2015.
149 Kriston Schrader-Frechette, *Risk and Rationality* (University of California Press 1991).
150 Julia Black, and Robert Baldwin, 'When Risk-Based Regulation Aims Low: A Strategic Framework' (2012) 6 (2) *Regulation and Governance*, 131.

is 'to ensure that a firm's own system of regulation is enhanced to enable the regulator to spend fewer resources monitoring in the future'.[151] This is possible when there is a cooperation scheme between regulators and regulated firms. Such a scheme relies on the idea that, primarily, the responsibility rests with firms' self-regulation and that these self-directed rules are in line with regulators' objectives. However, such cooperation is only likely to be effective when regulators control and guide the self-directed rules and enforce their powers to implement their own rules.[152] Such reliance on the firm's internal control is no different to the firm simply transplanting risk-based supervision at a firm-level. Although regulators might require firms to adopt certain rules in order to minimise the regulator's exposure to risk, the implementation of such rules is also benefiting the firm. This is because when the firm is operating under risk-based rules, it is reducing the risk of failure, as well as lowering the risk of litigation.[153] However, the process of designing and enforcing such rules sometimes, as in the case of large conglomerates, requires a negotiation between regulators and those firms. The negotiation usually consists of firms proposing risk management techniques and regulators reviewing whether those techniques and procedures are sufficient.[154]

Risk regulation in general is about far more than the dry and technical implementation of risk assessment and risk management techniques.[155] The adoption of risk-based regulation[156] and the 'concomitant development of its risk-based operating framework for supervision'[157] is of central importance within financial services[158] and has been developed in financial services through a two-stemmed approach: prudential regulation and conduct of business.[159]

The first stem is prudential regulation. Prudence is a standard to judge behaviour; to act prudently means 'acting with or showing care and thought for the future'.[160] In tort, prudence refers to acting with reasonable care.[161] In company law, the concept has been developed in the area of Directors' Duties[162] and 'prudence' is related to the 'reasonable care' of directors in the exercise of their duties. In the area of regulation, prudential regulation and supervision is part of the command and control strategy developed in the risk-based approach. It

151 See Robert Baldwin, Martin Cave, and Martin Lodge, *Understanding Regulation* (n38), 105.
152 Julia Black, and Robert Baldwin, 'When Risk-Based Regulation Aims Low: Approaches and Challenges' (2012) 6 *Regulation and Governance*, 1, 2.
153 Stuart Bazley, Andrew Haynes, and Tony Bluden, *Risk-Based Compliance* (Butterworths Compliance Series 2001), 2.
154 Ibid.
155 Joanna Gray, and Jenny Hamilton, *Implementing Financial Regulation* (n11), 15.
156 Clive Briault, 'The Rationale for a Single National Financial Services Regulator' (1999) FSA Occasional Paper No 2; See HM Treasury, *Reforming Financial Markets* (2009).
157 Michael Foot, 'Delivering Cost-Effective Regulation Through Risk-Based Supervision' (1999) 89 *Journal of International Financial Management*, 2.
158 Jón Daníelsson, 'On the Feasibility of Risk Based Regulation' (2003) 49 Institute for Economic Research, *CESifo Economic Studies*, 2, 1.
159 Julia Black, 'The Emergence of Risk-Based Regulation and the New PRM in the UK' (n9) 20.
160 (Concise Oxford English Dictionary 2011).
161 *Blyth v The Company of Proprietors of the Birmingham Waterworks* (1856) 11 Ex 781, 782.
162 *Leeds Estate, Building and Investment Company v Shepherd* (1887) 36 ChD 787, 804.

involves monitoring the compliance of both individual firms and financial firms with safety and soundness[163] standards, but also evaluating whether these standards are sufficient. The safety and soundness of a firm means it is adequately capitalised, and as a result it is protected from insolvency and liquidity problems. The aim of prudential supervision is to reduce the sources of risk – originated within the firm and the market – that can affect the safety and soundness of regulated firms. To that end, regulators set prudential measures (e.g. capital requirements, risk management methods) that in the UK are included in the FSMA 2000 and subsequent reforms.

The second stem of risk-based regimes is conduct of business, concerned with consumer[164] protection. Rather than focusing on the protection of clients from the insolvency of individual financial institutions, this measure emphasises safeguarding clients from unfair practices.

The adoption of risk-based regulation is motivated by multiple factors.[165] It usually involves a concern of regulators to enhance its legitimacy and accountability; hence, it is expected to have a clear demarcation of supervisors' roles, what they are expected to achieve, and thus what they should be responsible for. Also, when adopting the risk-based model, supervisors expect to have sufficient intervention tools, such as an enforcement regime. When supervisors are bestowed with enforcement powers, they can ensure compliance. As discussed earlier the initial approach is to expect that regulated firms will voluntarily observe rules (compliance), but if this is insufficient, regulators are entitled to use deterrence mechanisms (sanction systems).[166]

2.4.1 The path towards the current model of risk-based regulation

Risk-based regulation is an enthusiastic response to the call for a more efficient approach to regulation. It emerged after a period of strong rhetoric towards deregulation, aiming to overcome the issues of inflexibility, legalism, and in general over-regulation that affected the costs of regulation itself.[167] Such an environment embraced the approaches to regulation that incorporated costs-benefits analysis[168] and appeared to be more objective and transparent. It was the perfect

163 Bert Ely, 'Financial Regulation', *The Concise Encyclopedia of Economics* (2008) Library of Economics and Liberty <www.econlib.org/library/Enc/FinancialRegulation.html> accessed 18th January 2015.

164 HM Treasury-FCA (2011b), *A New Approach to Financial Regulation: The Blueprint for Reform*, CM8083 (June 2011) FCA.

165 Ibid.

166 Ian Ayres, and John Braithwaite, *Responsive Regulation: Transcending the Deregulation Debate* (n114), 39.

167 Bridget M. Hutter, 'The Attractions of Risk-Based Regulation: Accounting for the Emergence of Risk Ideas in Regulation' (2005) Discussion Paper N 33 ESCR Centre for Analysis of Risk and Regulation, 1 <www.lse.ac.uk/accounting/CARR/pdf/DPs/Disspaper33.pdf> accessed 20th October 2015.

168 Christopher Hood, Henry Rothstein, and Robert Baldwin, *The Government of Risk: Understanding Risk Regulation Regimes* (Oxford University Press 2004).

scenario for risk-based regulation as an approach that provided efficient instruments for policymaking and illustrated effective decision-making.

Risk-based regulation was conceived for the first time in the 1980s, emerging in the midst of the rise of the 'Regulatory State'.[169] The rationale of the Regulatory State[170] is driven by the move from public and centralised control to privatised institutions through new forms of state regulation.[171] This revolutionary fragmentation of the regulatory environment created new dynamics of cooperation between the existing regulatory agencies and the new self-regulatory bodies.[172] Although the integration of private institutions to the state regulatory function is attractive, it also has shortcomings. The concern is regarding the capacity of governmental agencies to conduct an effective oversight of private institutions and the consequences in terms of regulators' accountability.[173]

Breaking the traditional paradigm of the centralisation of regulatory functions to welcome the fragmentation of the regulatory environment has rendered some of the further developments in the management of the Regulatory State.[174] Several structural changes were associated with new Public Management Paradigm (PMP).[175] Strategies of privatisation, liberalisation and de-regulation, fiscal retrenchment, and economic and monetary integration contributed to limiting the role of the interventionist state[176] while enhancing the power of rulemaking and the rise of the Regulatory State.[177] Meta-regulatory strategies, risk-based regulation, and the enhancement of regulators' enforcement powers are all part of the establishment of the Regulatory State. Even though the term 'de-regulation' might misleadingly suggest the return of the *laissez-fair laissez-passer* situation, in the context of the Regulatory State this means a combination of de-regulation and re-regulation.[178] This change highlights the reality of regulation in practice, in particular, that regulation is de-centralised and involves a broader spectrum of state and non-state actors, operating at a transnational, supranational, national, and sub-national level. This interaction among multiple actors blurs the traditional boundaries between the regulators and regulated firms.[179]

In the context of the Regulatory State, the most notorious feature of risk-based regulation is that it tackles the institutional risk – that the regulator might not

169 Julia Black, 'Tensions in the Regulatory State' (2007) *Public Law*, 1.
170 See Giandomenico Majone, 'From the Positive to the Regulatory State: Causes and Consequences of Changes in the Mode of Governance' (1997) 17 *Journal of Public Policy*, 2.
171 Giandomenico Majone, 'The Rise of the Regulatory State in Europe' (1994) 17 (3) *West European Politics*, 78.
172 John Braithwaite, 'Accountability and Governance under the New Regulatory State' (1999) 58 (1) *Australian Journal of Public Administration*, 90.
173 Julia Black, 'Tensions in the Regulatory State' (n169), 2.
174 Ibid.
175 Giandomenico Majone, 'From the Positive to the Regulatory State' (n171), 140.
176 Ibid.
177 Ibid 140.
178 Ibid 143; Giandomenico Majone (1994) 'The Rise of the Regulatory State in Europe' (n171) 97.
179 Julia Black, 'Critical Reflections on Regulation' (2002) 27 *Australian Journal of Legal Philosophy*, 1.

achieve its objectives. Hence, the risk-based approach is a strategy that not only targets the risks that pose the greatest threat to the regulators, but also promotes the rational allocation of regulatory resources.

Those appealing features of risk-based regimes have attracted regulators around the globe. Several international organisations and committees have adopted the risk-based[180] approach to regulation and supervision.[181] The Basel Committee requires supervisors to adopt risk-based supervision in the 2012 revised Core Principles for Effective Banking Supervision.[182] Similarly, IOSCO[183] and the International Association of Insurance Supervisors (IAIS) have produced sets of principles or best practice standards, on regulation and supervision in the areas of securities regulation and insurance respectively, that are illustrated by a risk-based approach to regulation. The Financial Stability Board (FSB) Recommendations for the Supervision of Global Systemically Important Financial Institutions[184] emphasise the adoption of a risk-based approach. In 2010, the IMF decided that the financial sector assessment programs (FSAPs) would follow a risk-based approach[185] based on two main criteria of the financial sector of a country: size and interconnectedness with financial services in other countries.[186] At the national level, Australia, Canada,[187] the UK, and the US[188] lead the development of the risk-based approach to regulation. In other jurisdictions, in

180 Kern Alexander, Rahul Dhumale, and John Eatwell, *Global Governance of Financial Systems: The International Regulation of Systemic Risk* (Oxford University Press 2006), 4.
181 Cynthia C. Lichtenstein, 'The Fed's New Model of Supervision for "Large Complex Banking Organizations": Coordinated Risk-Based Supervision of Financial Multinationals for International Financial Stability' (2006) *American Journal of Law & Medicine* 8, 283 <http://lawdigitalcommons.bc.edu/cgi/viewcontent.cgi?article=1130&context=lsfp> accessed 21st January 2016.
182 BIS, 'Core Principles for Effective Banking Supervision' (BCBS, September 2012) <www.bis.org/publ/bcbs230.pdf> accessed 21st January 2016.
183 IOSCO Guidelines to Emerging Market Regulators Regarding Requirements for Minimum Entry and Continuous Risk-Based Supervision of Market Intermediaries (December 2009) <www.iosco.org/library/pubdocs/pdf/IOSCOPD314.pdf> accessed 21st January 2016.
184 FSB, 'Increasing the Intensity and Effectiveness of SIFI Supervision. Progress Report to the G20 Ministers and Governors' (1 November 2012) <www.fsb.org/wp-content/uploads/r_121031ab.pdf?page_moved=1> accessed 21st January 2016.
185 IMF, 'Integrating Stability Assessments under the Financial Sector Assessment Program into Article IV Surveillance: Background Material' (27 August 2010) <www.imf.org/external/np/pp/eng/2010/082710.pdf> accessed 21st January 2016. See Carlo Gola, Francesco Spadafora, 'Financial Sector Surveillance and the IMF' IMF, Working Paper, 1 November 2009.
186 Inge Govaere, Reinhard Quick, and Marco Bronckers, *Trade and Competition Law in the EU and Beyond'* (Edward Elgar Publishing 1 October 2011), 46.
187 Julia Black, 'The Development of RBR in Financial Services' (2004) (n4).
188 Arthur Wilmarth, 'The Transformation of the US Financial Services Industry, 1975–2000: Competition, Consolidation, and Increased Risks' (2002) *University of Illinois Law Review*, 215; Patricia A. McCoy, Andrey D. Pavlov, and Susan M. Wachter, 'Systemic Risk Through Securitization: The Result of Deregulation and Regulatory Failure' (2009). 41 *Connecticut Law Review*, 493 <http://ssrn.com/abstract=1367973> accessed 21st January 2016; Arthur Wilmarth Jr, 'Reforming Financial Regulation to Address the Too-Big-to-Fail Problem' (2010) 35 *Brooklyn Journal of International Law*, 707.

particular other financial regulation systems, the adoption of risk-based regulation has been partial.

Julia Black suggests that the introduction of risk-based regulation might be regarded as a 'regulatory innovation' in both subjective and objective terms.[189] To paraphrase Black: accordingly, each regulator subjectively decides to adopt the risk-based approach through new organisational and decision-making processes, while at the same time implementing integrated frameworks that objectively assess the risk across regulated firms. Whatever the reasons to adopt risk-based regulation, whether fully or partially introduced into domestic regimes, regulators expect that the risk-based approach will help them overcome their limited capacity to administer the traditional command and control regimes.[190]

However, in spite of this chorus of approval, the question of how novel or innovative risk-based regimes are persists.[191] It is not prescriptive of these risk regimes to see how regulatory agencies are continuously prioritising resources and activities; neither is it novel that the assessment of areas of policy attention and decision-making respond to the most urgent of risks. So then, if the problem is old, the question is what is novel in adopting a risk-based approach to regulation. One possible answer is that risk-based regulation, unlike other approaches, involves not only the analysis of economic costs and benefits, but also considers the concept of uncertainties.[192] This is the differential feature of the risk-based approach: it allows regulators to design and implement regimes that consider unknown but foreseeable events, which in turn might represent a threat to the achievement of regulatory objectives. Moreover, risk-based regimes offer a new element, especially relevant in financial regulation, which is an integrated decision-making framework applicable to all levels of risk and firms.[193]

The study of risk-based regulation literature leads us to argue that this approach is part of a trend surrounding risk management practices in the private and public sectors.[194] It is a strategy that offers alternative tools to regulatory agencies for better design and conduct regulation in the midst of the institutional risk; it also enhances the efficient allocation of resources. However, despite the expected benefits, if regulators want to benefit from the adoption of risk-based regulation, they should ensure that the regime coherently includes the basic elements of the approach. Otherwise, we suggest that regimes end up following a 'language of risk',[195] where the observer can identify some diverse elements of the risk-based

189 Julia Black, 'The Development of RBR Just 'Modelling Through'?' (n146).
190 Ibid 17.
191 Julia Black, 'The Emergence of Risk-Based Regulation and the New PRM in the UK' (n9).
192 Ibid.
193 Julia Black, 'The Development of RBR Just 'Modelling Through'?' (n146), 156.
194 Julia Black locates risk-based approach as part of the movement called 'New Public Risk Management' (NPRM). The NPRM has two strands: the internal risk management practices and risk-based regulation. Black, 'The Emergence of Risk-Based Regulation and the New PRM in the UK' (n9).
195 Joanna Gray, and Jenny Hamilton, *Implementing Financial Regulation* (n11).

approach in the regime, but not a consistent adoption of it. One example of a risk-based element in the regime, which we will look at in detail later, is the Bank's regulatory priority, stated in 2013, to design a recovery and resolution regime that would enhance the safety and soundness of CCPs. The element of risk-based regulation to highlight here is the identification and prioritisation of risk – in this case, the risk of CCPs' financial distress or insolvency. In practice, however, the Bank has focused its prudential regulation on the development of loss-allocation and recovery rules, leaving aside the design of a special resolution regime. The absence of clarity prevents the efficient implementation of the approach. It triggers confusion because neither regulators nor regulated firms understand what risk-based regulation looks like in practice: the benefits and the limits, to what extent risk-based regulation is the complete 'route-map' to conduct regulation and supervision, or whether it needs to be merged with other complementary strategies, as well as its impact on accountability.

In order to illustrate what risk-based regulation comprehends, we will explain the basic elements of the approach in the next section.

2.4.2 Elements of risk-based regulation

Although the content of risk-based regulation varies according to the area and the jurisdiction where it is implemented, there are some common elements. These elements will be the parameters to assess the CCP regime in the OTCDM in the UK and the US.

2.4.2.1 Risk tolerance

The first element of a risk-based approach to regulation is 'risk tolerance':[196] the discretion that regulators have when choosing what type of risk they are prepared to tolerate and at what level. Not surprisingly, for regulators, this is a highly appealing feature of risk-based regulation regimes. Regulators are equipped with a high level of discretion to choose the risks that the regime will prioritise, and those they will not.[197] However, such power does not come without restraints; the discretionary selection of risks is a double-edged sword. Regulators are deciding the risks that merit priority and special attention while at the same time excluding others; as a result, the scope of the regime is limited from the outset. An example of the level of risk tolerance in the UK financial services regulation is the approach of the Bank and the PRA to operate a 'non-zero-failure' regime.[198] This means that the PRA is willing to tolerate the risk of failure of regulated firms,

---

196 Julia Black, 'Risk and Regulatory Policy: Improving the Governance of Risk' (n148), 186.
197 Julia Black, 'The Development of RBR Just 'Modelling Through'?' (n147), 158.
198 The Bank of England, Prudential Regulation Authority, 'The PRA's approach to Banking Supervision' (October 2012) <www.bankofengland.co.uk/publications/Documents/praapproach/bankingappr1210.pdf> accessed 22nd January 2016.

but with minimum disruption of services and without spillovers to the wider financial sector.[199]

It is true that the initial selection of risks is not a straitjacket for regulators, but it is the 'route-map' that illustrates the primary areas of focus. Power[200] argues that risk-based regulation requires a new 'politics of uncertainty'. The politics of uncertainty will allow regulators to review the assessment of risk and to include future types of risks. Accommodating this new politics of uncertainty in risk-based regulation requires us to consider two factors. The first is that although regulators are vested with the power to review, adjust, and complement the strategy of regulation, the issue is that such reforms are not effective unless they are in place in a timely manner. In other words, unless the review of the risks is continuous and as dynamic as market changes, regulators might react only when 'non-regulated' risks have crystallised. However, this could be avoided, or at least minimised, with a move towards an administrative regime to connect macro- and microprudential regimes. It is a regime that ensures information sharing, joint analysis of risks, and cooperation between authorities.[201] Although macro- and microprudential authorities use prudential policy instruments and tools (e.g. capital and liquidity buffers and balance sheet restrictions) with different objectives, they serve as a backstop of resilience both to the firm and to the system.[202]

The second factor of the 'new politics of uncertainty' is that, as Joanna Gray explains,[203] regulators need to be clear about the differences between risk and uncertainty,[204] as well as how they are limited by this reality, when implementing risk-based regimes. Regulators need to draw the line to differentiate between future events that can be predicted and measured (risks) and those that cannot be reasonably foreseen (uncertainties). The difficulty is to restrict risk-based regimes to actually avoidable risks. The reliance on efficient and up-to-date models of risk identification and assessment assist regulators in delimiting the risks that can be controlled. Also, this avoids creating overly ambitious expectations of the regime.[205] To complicate things further, regulators are not completely free from external influence. Particularly, the political context usually determines the extent of regulators' tolerance of failure. One illustrative example is the post-GFC

199 Paul Fisher, 'The Financial Regulation Reform Agenda: What Has Been Achieved and How Much Is Left to Do?' Speech at Richmond, the American International University, London (30 September 2015) <www.bis.org/review/r151009b.pdf> accessed 22nd January 2016.
200 Michael Power, *The Risk Management of Everything: Rethinking the Politics of Uncertainty* (Demos 2004).
201 Jacek Osiński, Katharine Seal, and Lex Hoogduin, 'Macroprudential and Microprudential Policies: Toward Cohabitation' (IMF, Monetary and Capital Markets Department June 2013), 4 <www.imf.org/external/pubs/ft/sdn/2013/sdn1305.pdf> accessed 21st January 2016.
202 Ibid.
203 Joanna Gray, 'Is It Time to Highlight the Limits of Risk-Based Financial Regulation?' (n14).
204 Frank H. Knight, *Risk, Uncertainty and Profit* (n18); M. Power, *Organised Uncertainty* (Oxford University Press 2007) in Joanna Gray, 'Is it Time to Highlight the Limits of Risk-Based Financial Regulation?' (n14).
205 Ibid.

regulatory reforms. In the immediate aftermath of the GFC, financial regulators were compelled by the G20 leaders to regulate any market that had the potential to become a source of systemic risk;[206] as a result, regulatory reforms moved towards enhancing macroprudential regulation and supervision[207] in different markets that might trigger financial instability.

Within the post-GFC regulatory reforms, financial regulators reinstated the limits of their accountability by adopting a 'non-zero-failure' policy,[208] which means they should not be expected to prevent all future failure. Instead, they are responsible for using all the regulatory tools available to better manage the risks and the consequent negative effects in case of its crystallisation in order to preserve the financial stability. This example illustrates how public expectations and political influence[209] impact the regulators' areas of attention, as well as similarly affect the stage of risk identification.

2.4.2.2 Risk identification

The second element of risk-based regimes is risk identification.[210] At this stage, regulators identify the risks that might impact the achievement of their objectives. To this end, regulators collect relevant information about the market, participants, transactions, and so on. This means that regulators only identify risks that they know and are confident they can manage. Perhaps the key to overcome the difficulties in identifying risks, which arise from flawed information, is to ensure the access to correct and complete data.

Nonetheless, access to information does not complete the equation here; there are further indicators that contribute to having a clear view of the risks. Regulators determine some risk indicators that are 'activities or events that are likely to result in the risk crystallising'.[211] Objective and subjective factors concur in the selection of risk indicators. Regulators tend to analyse previous failures and the tacit knowledge about warning signs of risk crystallisation. For instance, in financial regulation, there are specialised studies conducted by academics[212] and

206 Contemporary financial regulation attempts to ensure that no systemic risks can harm the financial system. The most prominent examples are the Basel III framework, the Dodd-Frank Act, the Alternative Investment Fund Manager Directive (AIFMD), and EMIR.
207 See Martin Day, 'Macro-Prudential Regulation' Financial Regulation International (1 October 2010) <www.financialregulationintl.com/regulation/regulatory-reforms/macro-prudential-regulation--1.htm?origin=internalSearch> accessed 5th December 2017. Also see FSA, Turner Review: A Regulatory Review to the Global Banking Crisis (August 2009); Bank of England, 'The Role of Macroprudential Policy' (Discussion Paper November 2009).
208 Financial Services Authority, 'Reasonable Expectations' (2003) FSA<www.fsa.gov.uk/pubs/other/regulation_non-zero.pdf> accessed 15th January 2016.
209 Bridget M. Hutter, 'The Attractions of Risk-Based Regulation' (n167).
210 Julia Black, 'Risk and Regulatory Policy: Improving the Governance of Risk' (n148), 186.
211 Ibid 195.
212 Charles P. Kindleberger, and Robert Z. Alibe, *Manias, Panics and Crashes: A History of Financial Crises* (6th edn, Palgrave Macmillan 2011); Christopher Kobrak, and Mira Wilkin (eds.), *History and Financial Crisis: Lessons from the 20th Century* (Routledge 2013).

international regulators[213] about previous crises and what markets are likely to be the epicentre of the next financial distress. The study of the causes of previous crisis is only one helpful tool to consider proposals for mitigation and prevention of future crises. For instance, the GFC revealed, amongst other issues, the fundamental flaws in the rating agencies' business model[214] – and regulators decided to enhance the regulation of credit rating agencies.

Moreover, financial regulators also consider indicators as the assessment of management, governance, and culture of control functions, and risk arising from dealing with customers.[215] Financial regulators assess these risk indicators with qualitative methods rather than quantitatively, because they are risks to the firm from the external market environment.[216] In the process of risk identification, regulators consider all the factors and indicators to constitute risk categories. These include the risk factors, which regulators identify from previous crises, failures, and tacit knowledge, as well as the risk indicators identified in the regulated firms. At the firm-level, risk indicators are influenced by the internal organisation and dynamics of the firm, and particularly by the market environment. Therefore, the aim of regulators is to find the balance among all risk indicators, enhancing the synergy and reducing the tensions between macroprudential and microprudential policies.

The OTCDM post-GFC reform is an illustrative example of how previous crises inform regulators' identification of risks and the course of their supervisory actions. The move towards the implementation of CCPs was motivated and informed by the largely documented success of LCH Clearnet, the CCP that cleared large part of the Lehman Brothers' OTC derivatives in the heat of the GFC. The experience of LCH Clearnet is an example of how a CCP can effectively manage a clearing member's default and decrease systemic risk.[217] The default of Lehman Brothers was of $9 trillion.[218] Upon default, LCH Clearnet had three options; namely, to liquidate the portfolio directly in the market, unwind the book through a dealer who would act as an agent for the CCP, or auction off the

213 Claudio Borio, and Piti Disyatat, 'Global Imbalances and the Financial Crisis: Link or no Link?' BIS Working Papers No 346, Monetary and Economic Department May 2011; Már Gudmundsson, 'How Might the Current Financial Crisis Shape Financial Sector Regulation and Structure?' (BIS, Deputy Head of the Monetary and Economic Department, at the Financial Technology Congress 2008, Boston, 23 September) <www.bis.org/speeches/sp081119.htm> accessed 15th January 2016.
214 Willem H. Buiter, 'Lessons from the 2007 Financial Crisis' (2007) CEPR Discussion Paper No DP6596, December <http://ssrn.com/abstract=1140525> accessed 22nd January 2016.
215 Julia Black, 'Risk and Regulatory Policy: Improving the Governance of Risk' (n149), 196.
216 Ibid.
217 Julia Lees Allen, 'Derivatives Clearinghouses and Systemic Risk: A Bankruptcy and Dodd-Frank Analysis' (2012) 64 *Stanford Law Review*, 1079.
218 Paul Cusenza, and Randi Abernethy, 'Dodd-Frank and the Move to Clearing' (INSIGHT, September 2010), 22, 23; LCH Clearnet, '$9 Trillion Lehman OTC Interest Rate Swap Default Successfully Resolved' Press Release (8 October 2008) <www.lchclearnet.com/Images/2008-10-08%20SwapClear%20default_tcm6-46506.pdf> accessed 16th January 2016.

positions as a package.[219] LCH Clearnet chose the auction. However, before the auction took place, LCH confidentially hedged and neutralised the 'macro-level risk of Lehman'.[220] As the default could be managed within the margin LCH held for Lehman, there was no need to use any of the default fund.[221] It is reported that approximately 35 percent of Lehman's initial margin was used to hedge risk and auction the total house portfolio.[222] This means that LCH Clearnet not only demonstrated efficient clearing members' default management, it also protected all other market participants from counterparty and systemic risk. Accordingly, the G20 leaders decided that, attending to the complexities tied to the default management process, the best mechanism to manage counterparty credit risk in the OTCDM was the use of central clearing, through CCPs.

In the stage of risk assessment, financial regulators refer to impact and probability,[223] as well as to weighting of risks. Weighting is to give more importance to certain risks than others – it reveals the risk appetite of the regulator and in turn the amount of resources that is willing to devote to manage the relevant risks. The weighting shows the level of risk the regulator is prepared to accept; weighting is also used to incentivise an individual firm's compliance. This is to consider the inherent risk of firms' activities and to acknowledge the measures taken by them to manage those risks effectively.[224]

Nevertheless, the initial weighting of risks is not static and it is likely to change once the regime is being implemented. New phases and concerns prompt changes in regulators' perspective of risk. The OTCDM reform illustrates the dynamics regulators face when weighting risks – the assessment of where risks to financial stability are greatest and the according prioritisation of regulatory actions. Initially, the OTCDM regulatory reform was focused on promoting the use of central clearing for all OTC derivatives transactions to better manage counterparty credit risk. Therefore, the regulatory priority was the management of credit risk, whilst other risks, such as liquidity risk, were underestimated. This is a reflection of the flip side of risk-based regimes, as regulators have to identify which risks they are not prepared to devote their resources to preventing.[225] However, after some years of implementation, regulators, CCPs, clearing members, and clients have realised that the imposition of mandatory clearing to a large portion of the OTC derivatives transactions would affect the liquidity of the CCP. This is because the suitability for mandatory central clearing depends, among

---

219 Julia Lees Allen, 'Derivatives Clearinghouses and Systemic Risk: A Bankruptcy and Dodd-Frank Analysis' (n 217).
220 Press Release, LCH Clearnet, '$9 Trillion Lehman OTC Interest Rate Swap Default Successfully Resolved' (n 218).
221 Ibid.
222 Natasha de Terán, 'How the World's Largest Default Was Unravelled' (FIN NEWS 13 October 2008) <www.efinancialnews.com/story/2008-10-13/how-the-largest-default-was-unravelled> accessed 16th January 2016.
223 Julia Black, 'Risk and Regulatory Policy: Improving the Governance of Risk' (n149), 196.
224 This use of weighting has been recognised in environmental regulation.
225 Julia Black, 'Risk and Regulatory Policy: Improving the Governance of Risk' (n149), 186.

other factors, on product and process standardisation, and on market liquidity.[226] Therefore, the initially underestimated management of the liquidity risk of CCPs has now become a regulatory priority. Liquidity is a recognised constraint that may require CCPs to review and modify risk management models.[227]

As we said earlier, regulators are expected to establish the risks that can potentially affect the achievement of their objectives during the stage of identifying and evaluating risks.[228] In order to control those risks, regulators usually match their statutory objectives with them.[229] Therefore, the clarity of the statutory objectives is a key part of an effective design and implementation of the risk-based approach.

Both explicit and implicit objectives are significant to the relationship between risks and statutory objectives. Explicit objectives are clearly stated by the regulator from the outset: for instance, the grounds of the supervision of CCPs are closely linked to the Bank's aim to preserve financial stability. Since the goal is a sound and safe financial system by ensuring institutional stability, the Bank's aim is to ensure that CCPs' rules and policies are designed and applied to monitor, manage, and mitigate risks, especially systemic risk. Similarly, the Bank 'seeks to ensure that sufficient priority is given to continuity of key services, without systemic disruption and without recourse to public funds'.[230] These objectives show that the priority is on counterparty credit risk management for CCPs. The supervision relies on systemic risk management[231] through principles of governance, management of operational risk, continuity of service, and adequate rules in case of participants' default. The purpose of the Bank is to manage the risks concentrating in the CCP. The rationale is that risks posed by individual firms might fly under the radar when the regulator identifies and assess risks. However, as those individual firms converge into a new intermediary – the CCP – by means of regulating CCPs, the Bank seeks to indirectly manage and control the risks posed by collective group of firms. These risks are linked to implicit objectives of the Bank.

To clarify this point further, OTCDM participants in bilateral trading both pose and face credit risk. Due to the high level of interconnectedness and concentration of risk amongst few market participants, the default of one of them affects not only the direct counterparty. The consequences of default will multiply,

226 Che Sidanius, and Anne Wetherilt, 'Thoughts on Determining Central Clearing Eligibility of OTC Derivatives' (BoE, Financial Stability Paper No 14 – March 2012) <www.bankofengland.co.uk/financialstability/Documents/fpc/fspapers/fs_paper14.pdf> accessed 16th January 2016.

227 See John Dizard, 'Clearing House Push Created Unforeseen Systemic Risks' *Financial Times* (29 January 2016) <www.ft.com/cms/s/0/455c589a-c663-11e5-808f-8231cd71622e.html#axzz3ymqKotn9?ftcamp=engage%2Femail%2Fnewsletters%2Fsmart_brief%2Fsmartbriefnewsletterscontrafcf%2Fauddev&segid=0800933> accessed 1st February 2016.

228 One example of this 'risk-to-objectives' approach was the FSA in the UK.

229 Robert Baldwin, Martin Cave, and Martin Lodge, *Understanding Regulation* (n3), 283.

230 Bank of England, 'The Bank of England's Approach to the Supervision of Financial Market Infrastructures' (April 2013), 4.

231 Ibid.

affecting not only the OTCDM but also other markets. This is how credit risk can grow into systemic proportions. In this scenario, the role of regulators would be to identify the risks that each high-risk individual firm poses to the market and to the financial stability. However, this role changed with the introduction of mandatory clearing in the OTCDM.

Mandatory central clearing, through CCPs, for a large part of the OTCDM implies not only a change in the structure of OTC derivatives transactions, but also a change in regulation of the market and its participants. The CCP interposes itself in every trade and becomes the new counterparty of the two initial parties. The change in terms of regulation and supervision of the risks is that CCPs are nodes of risks that contribute to enhance credit risk management in the OTCDM. Therefore, regulating CCPs allow regulators to identify, assess, and control the risks collectively. Instead of supervising individual firms that raise high risks, the regulator oversees CCPs, which are intermediaries that gather those high-risk firms. The attention is on the risks that the sum of high-risk firms may pose to financial stability.

Thus, the regulatory priority of the Bank on counterparty credit risk management for CCPs and the supervision of systemic risk management is indirectly serving some implicit objectives of the Bank, as regulator. Implicit objectives concern the regulation of the market, individual firms, and the subsequent enhancement of OTCDM stability. This is to identify and capture the risks of the OTCDM by bringing together both strategic and firm-specific risks.[232] This facilitates conducting supervision by integrating macro- and microprudential tools. The safety and soundness of CCPs is a means to pursue the stability of the OTCDM. Hence, the regime does not only cover risks affecting CCPs, but also their members, high-risk firms.

The clarity of statutory objectives and their link to key risks should be predicable to the stages of design and implementation of the regime. For instance, if statutory mandates assign the functions of prudential supervision and conduct of business to two authorities, it's expected that in practice both authorities will be actively involved in the respective stems of supervision. Each mandate – prudential supervision and conduct of business – should be matched with specific risks. However, this is not always the case. To briefly anticipate the discussion of the following chapters, the CCP regime in the UK OTCDM clearly states that the Bank is the prudential supervisor of CCPs, while the FCA oversees the conduct of business of CCPs. However, after three years of the CCP regime, it is not clear what authority is responsible for the conduct of business supervision. Despite the fact that UK authorities adopt a risk-based approach to regulation, in the specific regime of CCPs in the OTCDM, the conduct of business supervision is abandoned.

Finally, the evaluation of risk demands regulators to identify those managerial attitudes and practices which will adversely affect the level of risk presented by the

---

232 Julia Black, 'Risk and Regulatory Policy: Improving the Governance of Risk' (n149), 192.

firm. This is to assess, on a case-by-case basis, the internal management and risk control, as well as to establish whether the firm's internal control system might exacerbate or mitigate the risks. Indeed, this stems from the risk-based approach's commonly substantial delegation of control functions down to the risk management systems of the firms being regulated and the inevitable 'meta-regulation'.[233]

2.4.2.3 Categorisation according to the level of risk

The third element of risk-based regulation is that, after the assessment, regulators categorise firms and activities according to the level of risks.[234] This categorisation determines how the sources available will be distributed within the different levels of risk. Efficient resource allocation is, therefore, one of the most advocated benefits of risk-based regulation systems and the drive of 'better regulation'.[235] The rationale is to conduct the risk assessment and to shift the resources within the categorised firms accordingly – something that is challenging for regulators in practice.[236] The risk rating of a firm structures the supervisory response.[237] Therefore, the allocation of those sources is translated into the number of inspections, the imposition of sanctions when there have been breaches, the monitoring of compliance, and so on.

As might be anticipated, one shortcoming of risk-based regulation is that it tends to place too much emphasis on individual sites. Therefore, it is not always the most effective strategy to manage systemic risks, which are at the core of financial regulation.[238] Arguably, if regulators centre their attention on those firms posing the greatest risks,[239] this means that some firms can fly under the radar to a greater or lesser degree.[240] Thus, for a risk-based regime to be efficient, it is desirable that it regulates all the firms according to their particular level of risk, instead of simply prioritising the supervision of the riskiest firms.

The issue regarding low-level risk firms affects any regulator implementing the risk-based approach. The question is what level of resources should be applied to them. Regulators tend[241] to use alternative regulatory tools such as information

---

233 Julia Black, 'Emergence of Risk-based Regulation', 544 in Robert Baldwin, and Martin Cave, and Martin Lodge, *Understanding Regulation* (n3), 289.
234 Julia Black, 'Risk and Regulatory Policy: Improving the Governance of Risk' (n149), 190.
235 In the UK, the 'Better Regulation' policy is explained in the Better Regulation Framework Manual: Practical Guidance for UK Government Officials (July 2013) <www.gov.uk/government/publications/better-regulation-framework-manual>; in the EU several policy documents explain the Better Regulation Package, <http://ec.europa.eu/smart-regulation/index_en.htm>. accessed 18th January 2018.
236 Julia Black, 'Risk and Regulatory Policy: Improving the Governance of Risk' (n149), 211.
237 Julia Black, 'The Development of RBR Just "Modelling Through"?' (n147).
238 Niamh Moloney, 'Financial Services and Markets' in Robert Baldwin, Martin Cave, and Martin Lodge (eds.), *The Oxford Handbook of Regulation* (n8) 1; George J Stigler, 'The Theory of Economic Regulation' (1971) 6 (2) *Bell Journal of Economics*, 114.
239 Julia Black, and Robert Baldwin, 'When Risk-Based Regulation Aims Low: Approaches and Challenges' (n152) 2.
240 Robert Baldwin, Martin Cave, and Martin Lodge, *Understanding Regulation* (n3), 284.
241 Julia Black, 'Risk and Regulatory Policy: Improving the Governance of Risk' (n149), 201.

campaigns, random inspections, and/or theme inspections. The use of these less costly techniques ensures the rationalised distribution of resources, while at the same time enhancing the effectiveness of the risk-based regulation strategy.

The combination of the dynamic nature of the regulated firms and their level of risk is challenging for regulators adopting the risk-based approach. Regulators should have in place different mechanisms to manage those risks that are not easy to graduate. For instance, the former FSA issued a revised framework, 'Arrow 2', requiring supervisors to enter a judgement to avoid leaving 'dark holes'[242] in the classification of risks. However, although this requirement was helpful, the Northern Rock case showed that it was not sufficient to cover all types risks firms may pose.

2.4.2.4 Link organisation enforcement resources to risk scores

The fourth element of risk-based regulation is closely linked to the third. Risk-based regimes provide the framework to link the organisation enforcement resources to the risk scores assigned to individual firms or activities.[243] This means that the resources available to regulate are allocated among supervised firms according to the level of risk assigned. Thus, the higher the level of risk a firm poses, the higher the amount of resources regulators will dispose to supervise that firm. The drawback to this element is that this assumes there are always enough resources available and that regulators are capable of overseeing firms at all levels of risk. However, reality shows that regulatory resources are mostly scarce, which implies that regulators tend to allocate the available resources solely on the supervision of the riskiest firms.[244]

2.4.3 Risk-based regulation and accountability

The prioritisation of resources under a risk-based approach to regulation triggers special challenges of justification and legitimation, particularly in explaining who should be making decisions about the risks that are important and those that are not.[245] Legitimation and justification in the process of risk selection also raise important concerns in terms of the accountability of the regulators[246] adopting risk-based regimes.

The implementation of risk-based regulation in terms of accountability is mixed,[247] as it involves managerial accountability and political accountability. Managerial accountability coming from the internal organisation and structure of the regulator; political accountability coming from the public. In both scenarios, the content and extent of the accountability is determined, at an early stage, by the regulator itself. The regulator identifies the most significant risks and then

---

242 Ibid 214.
243 Ibid.
244 Ibid 285.
245 Ibid 294. See Power, *The Risk Management of Everything* (n200); Julia Black, 'The Emergence of Risk-Based Regulation and the New PRM in the UK' (n9).
246 Julia Black, 'Tensions in the Regulatory State' (n169), 7.
247 Ibid.

distributes the resources accordingly. This means that the exercise of such discretion limits the extent of regulators' accountability.[248]

This line of thought in the literature[249] explains why a risk-based regulation approach represents a limit to regulators' accountability, but it does not analyse the effects of risk-based regimes on the accountability of regulated firms and activities. It might be argued that the accountability of the regulated firms is also limited in risk-based regimes – if regulators choose certain risks, it is not clear whether regulated firms will be accountable when their conduct triggers other types of risks, i.e. risk objectives which are not covered, or are less significant to regulators.

Furthermore, when defining parameters of responsibility, it is necessary to shape public and political expectations accordingly. For instance, the former FSA designed the risk-based approach partly to clarify 'what regulators should be expected to achieve, and thus what they should be accountable for'.[250] The benefit of implementing a system in these terms is that both parties' – regulators and firms – know the 'rules of the game' from the beginning. The potential drawback here appears when there is an error in judgement, when regulators decide to assume that certain firms pose no risk when they do, and vice versa.

2.4.4 The adoption of risk-based regulation

There are several reasons to adopt risk-based regulation. Regulators incorporate a risk-based approach to regulation seeking to improve their performance. In particular, the effective source distribution is a helpful tool when such resources are scarce. Similarly, when there have been changes in the regulatory architecture (i.e. mergers, divisions, or the creation[251] of regulatory bodies), the use of a risk-based regime contributes to address several organisational concerns.[252] Moreover, changes in the markets regulated and periods of 'regulatory failures' are attractive contexts where risk-based regulation germinates and develops. Most notably, risk-based regulation is adopted as a functionally efficient tool for improving 'better' regulation.[253] Better regulation[254] is a movement that aims to improve the quality of the regulatory environment[255] by devoting attention to regulatory policies, tools, and institutions.[256]

---

248 Julia Black, 'The Emergence of Risk-Based Regulation and the New PRM in the UK' (n9).
249 Julia Black, 'Tensions in the Regulatory State' (n169), 8; Julia Black, 'The Emergence of Risk-Based Regulation and the New PRM in the UK' (n9); Power, *The Risk Management of Everything* (n200).
250 Julia Black, 'The Emergence of Risk-Based Regulation and the New PRM in the UK' (n9).
251 Bridget M. Hutter, 'The Attractions of Risk-Based Regulation' (n167).
252 Julia Black, 'Risk and Regulatory Policy: Improving the Governance of Risk' (n149), 189.
253 In the UK, regulators are now subject to new statutory duties of 'better regulation' set out in the Compliance Code. These include the requirement to adopt a risk-based approach to inspection. (DBERR 2007).
254 Neil Gunningham, Peter N. Grabosky, and Darren Sinclair, *Smart Regulation* (Clarendon Press 1998).
255 OECD, 'Regulating Policies in OECD Countries' (OECD 2002).
256 Robert Baldwin, 'Is Better Regulation Smarter Regulation?' (2005) Public Law (Autumn) 489.

Beyond the broader motivations to use risk-based regulation regimes, regulators use these frameworks to serve more immediate purposes. For instance, gathering information on the regulated population more efficiently, and in that way improving compliance.[257] One example is the supervision of CCPs in the OTCDM. The rationale of the risk-based regime is that CCPs will gather information on a large portion of transactions and participants, as well as contribute to the supervision by making that information available to regulators.

2.4.5 Drawbacks of risk-based regulation

Despite the claimed benefits of risk-based regulation, there are some important drawbacks. The first challenge of the risk-based approach is the need for the regulator to clearly identify its objectives and the risks that regulated firms may present in achieving those objectives.[258] As we explained earlier, several factors influence the identification of risks and how risk is matched to regulators' objectives. Similarly, the assessment of risks[259] might be difficult. Regulators need to evaluate the distinction between the intrinsic dangerousness of the activity and the propensity of a firm's internal control to mitigate or exacerbate those risks. Moreover, the initial identification and evaluation of risks needs to include not only present but future risks.[260] To be effective, such assessment of risk needs to go beyond the individual firm[261] and to integrate firms' risks with industry wide risk assessments. The difficulty is, however, to reconcile the individual evaluation of the firm and its portfolio with the assessment of industry risk and portfolio.

Some other drawbacks of risk-based regulation are related to the capacity of regulators to implement the approach. Implementation is successful when regulators have sufficient access to information and specialised knowledge[262] of the regulated market. The effective analysis and use of the data collected allow a better understanding of the particularities of firms and markets, as well as the risks they face on a daily basis.

Similarly, the implementation of the risk-based approach requires being clear about how the risk evaluations will be used as drivers for regulatory actions. Other requirements include identifying intervention tools that are likely to have the most potential and provide a rational and defensible basis for decisions,[263] as well as attending to the broader institutional and political context that regulators face, akin to ensuring that the various strategies do not undercut each other or the rationale of risk-based regulation itself.[264]

257 Julia Black, 'Risk and Regulatory Policy: Improving the Governance of Risk' (n149) 212.
258 Robert Baldwin, Martin Cave, and Martin Lodge, *Understanding Regulation* (n3), 281.
259 Ibid.
260 Julia Black, 'Risk and Regulatory Policy: Improving the Governance of Risk' (n149), 193.
261 Ibid.
262 Ibid.
263 Julia Black, and Robert Baldwin, 'When Risk-Based Regulation Aims Low: A Strategic Framework' (n150), 131.
264 Robert Baldwin, Martin Cave, and Martin Lodge, *Understanding Regulation* (n3), 287.

Each regulator has the discretion to integrate risk assessment with supervisory response. However, the initial identification and assessment of risk inform the allocation of resources and the method of enforcement. The interaction between regulators' risk assessments and a particular enforcement approach depends upon the design of the enforcement strategy.[265] The coherent integration of risk assessment and effective enforcement might be achieved by several means: for instance, by creating integrated inspection and enforcement teams, or by designing intervention strategies directly linked to the level of risk. One example of specialised supervision teams is the new Directorate for FMIs created within the Bank. Recognising the systematic importance of FMIs, the new Directorate[266] will conduct a more intense supervision of all of them, including CCPs.

The effective implementation of risk-based regulation determines whether the approach accomplishes the aim of changing regulated firms' behaviour.[267] In this area there is an interesting debate: on the one hand, Gray and Hamilton assert that:

> [R]isk-based systems have the potential to reshape relationships between those who govern and those who are governed, to embedded norms of behaviour, to attribute blame and to define and delimit both responsibility and accountability.[268]

On the other hand, Black and Baldwin argue that risk-based regulation is limited to one part of the task, because there is a gap between the risk-based assessment and the enforcement process. They argue that such a gap exists, because while the intervention in risk-based regime is driven by risk, the enforcement approach considers that the regulatory response depends on the attitude of the regulated firms and their capacity to comply.[269] This means that in order to determine the right enforcement action – whether compliance or deterrence – it is necessary to identify whether regulatees form a cohesive group or a sum of disparate groups. Hence, the regulator should choose a range of enforcement methods in the pursuit of compliance.

Similarly, risk-based regulation has an impact on regulators' culture and behaviour.[270] As we discussed earlier, risk-based regulation is a strategy that represents the 'route-map' of regulation. Hence, the implementation of risk-based regulation implies that regulators have a complete understanding of the approach. However, this is a progressive process and it should involve all levels of the regulatory agency, i.e. senior management and staff. On this point, it is advisable

265 Julia Black, 'Risk and Regulatory Policy: Improving the Governance of Risk' (n149), 215.
266 The Bank of England's *Supervision of Financial Market Infrastructures Annual Report* (March 2015).
267 Cento Veljanovski, 'Strategic Use of Regulation' in Robert Baldwin, Martin Cave, and Martin Lodge (eds.), *The Oxford Handbook of Regulation* (n8), 1.
268 Joanna Gray, and Jenny Hamilton, *Implementing Financial Regulation* (n11), 1.
269 Julia Black, and Robert Baldwin, 'When Risk-Based Regulation Aims Low: A Strategic Framework' (n150), 132.
270 Julia Black, 'Risk and Regulatory Policy: Improving the Governance of Risk' (n149), 190.

to develop internal systems[271] to ensure that supervisors are implementing the framework as it was designed and bearing in mind the projected outcomes. Regulators should apprehend the risk-based approach at the design stage, and even more importantly during implementation, in order to put in place an organisational culture guided by the approach.

Organisational culture[272] is a key element of an efficient risk-based approach. Such organisational culture guided by the risk-based approach should be consistent in the design and the implementation stages. Otherwise, the regime will be frustrated in the implementation phase and, in turn, it will not deliver the expected outcomes, but only partially accomplish the regulatory objectives. Organisational culture implies that regulators should be sufficiently trained not just in the mechanics of risk assessment, but also in the whole rationale of risk-based regulation.[273] Moreover, it includes understanding the behaviour of regulators in performing risk assessments. This is whether regulators understand the firms and markets they supervise, and how regulated firms respond to the implementation of the regime. It also considers, particularly in financial regulation, the assessment of the firm's internal control and management of risk. The challenge in this area is to clearly identify whether in practice the system of a firm's internal control is contributing to *managing* risks or *creating* risks – i.e. control itself creates risks.[274]

We can see how the inconsistency between design and implementation affects the achievement of the regime objectives. UK regulators do not fully understand the rationale of risk-based regulation. As a result, their regulatory actions are limited to identifying and assessing the most prominent risks present in the OTCDM, and in particular those posed and faced by CCPs. But there is no awareness regarding the distinction between ensuring mechanical compliance of the regime and the implementation of the risk-based approach to regulation. We see this manifested in two ways: on the one hand, in the interviews conducted during this research, officials from the FCA and the Bank seemed to be unfamiliar with the philosophy behind risk-based approach to regulation and with the way it interacts with other strategies of regulation, such as judgement-based and meta-regulation. On the other hand, in the UK regime of CCPs in the OTCDM, there is a huge fracture between the design of the approach – in particular the mandates of the Bank and the FCA – and the implementation of the regime's two pillars, of prudential supervision and the conduct of business. Whilst prudential supervision carried out by the Bank is, in general, well designed and its implementation is presumably making OTCDM more resilient, the conduct of business is completely absent, and so is the role of the FCA as conduct regulator of CCPs.

To sum up, we have considered the dynamics of the risk-based regulation by highlighting the benefits, limits, and complexities tied to the adoption of this

271 Ibid.
272 Julia Black, 'The Development of RBR in Financial Services' (n4).
273 Julia Black, 'Risk and Regulatory Policy: Improving the Governance of Risk' (n149), 207.
274 Ibid 208.

approach to regulation. Risk-based regulation is a comprehensive control strategy[275] that assists regulators in the efficient supervision, and the two pillars (conduct of business and prudential supervision) provide an organised structure to regulation. Nonetheless, as with any strategy, it is limited in some other aspects. To overcome its drawbacks, risk-based regulation needs to be designed and implemented to deal adequately with the challenges and critiques we have discussed; one alternative is to combine a risk-based approach with other strategies of regulation.

For instance, in 2013 the UK financial regulators decided to integrate risk-based regulation with the judgement-based approach. This integration of multiple strategies is expected to improve, complement, and reinforce the conduct of supervision. Following this line of thought, we will now go on to look at the content of the judgement-based approach and address the question of how it complements the risk-based approach in UK financial regulation.

2.5 Complementing the traditional risk-based approach to regulation

Along with the reforms of the regulatory architecture in the UK, and the adoption of a twin peaks system, there has also been an emphasis on integrating other regulation strategies into the inherited risk-based approach. To that end, UK regulators decided to adopt judgement-based regulation.

2.5.1 Judgement-based regulation

With the adoption of the Financial Services Act 2012, judgement-based regulation was launched as a new approach to regulation and supervision. Not surprisingly, regulators have high expectations and confidence in their capacity to implement the approach.[276] The approach presupposes that regulators will have greater discretion[277] to exercise their powers, and as a result supervision will be more intrusive. Among other aspects, the mechanical compliance assessment and the 'tick-box' exercise are replaced by the use of pre-emptive tools in the detection of future risks.[278]

Regulation always involves judgement.[279] The difference is to do with the degree to which judgement is based on *observable facts*, as opposed to the degree to which judgement is based on speculation over what might happen in the future.[280] Thereby, when adopting judgement-led regulation, it is crucial to

275 Robert Baldwin, Martin Cave, and Martin Lodge, *Understanding Regulation* (n3), 105.
276 Draft Financial Services Bill, Draft Financial Services Bill Joint Committee, Contents (19 December 2011) para 188.
277 Andromachi Georgosouli, 'Judgement-Led Regulation: Reflections on Data and Discretion'(3–4 July 2013) 14 *Journal of Banking Regulation*.
278 FSA, 'The FCA Approach to Regulation' (FSA, June 2011) ch 5 (para 5.6 to 5.9).
279 Sants, H Draft Financial Services Bill, (2012) para 190.
280 Andromachi Georgosouli, 'Judgement-Led Regulation' (n278).

clearly set out the degree of discretion regulators will have. This is translated into powers of intervention, and the expectation that regulators will be more intrusive in order to pre-empt the materialisation of future risks.[281] These are key features in the forward-looking nature of judgement-led regulation.

Risk-based regulation, which will be continuously guiding the regulation approach in the UK, is complemented by the judgement-based approach.[282] The latter requires a regulatory approach that takes into account risks that may pose a threat to the financial stability.[283] Hence, the early intervention powers, conferred to regulators in the judgement-based approach, overcome the drawbacks of the gap between risk assessment and implementation identified in the risk-based regime. Similarly, the forward-looking nature of a judgement-based approach complements the risk-based approach, as it educates firms by setting examples of conduct that must be avoided in the future.[284] As risk-based regulation relies heavily on a strategy focused on the quality of a firm's internal controls, the judgement-led approach might contribute to enhancing the standards of conduct of regulated firms, making them consistent with regulators' objectives.

The implementation of a judgement-led approach is proactive in its nature. Along with the leading role of regulators, it calls for the active involvement of regulated firms. The rationale is to allow discretion within the framework and control of regulators. Hence, firms will 'be granted freedom' to manage their affairs according to the expected outcomes set by regulators.[285] From this it follows that the firms' internal control systems are expected to guarantee full disclosure to the regulator.[286] Therefore, there must be a greater willingness to comply with supervisors' instructions and directions. A judgement-led approach also requires firms to cooperate with regulators by making available all its resources and expertise.[287] Although successful implementation of the judgement-based approach includes an undeniable component of self-regulation,[288] it is also true that it is very much in line with 'the change in the character of financial regulation away from facilitating market discipline and towards providing the public good of consumer protection and financial stability'.[289]

Those opposing integrating risk-based and judgement-based approaches argue that adoption of risk-based regulation undermines the judgement-led approach. They argue that risk-based regulation 'makes assumptions about risk and about

---

281 Ibid.
282 Julia Black, 'The Rise, Fall and Fate of Principles Based Regulation' (2010) LSE Law, Society and Economy Working Papers 17.
283 Andromachi Georgosouli, 'Judgement-led Regulation' (n277).
284 Ibid.
285 Rosa Lastra, 'Defining Forward Looking, Judgement-Based Supervision' (3/4 July–November 2013) 14 *Journal of Banking Regulation*.
286 Andromachi Georgosouli, 'Judgement-led Regulation' (n277).
287 Rosa Lastra, 'Defining Forward Looking, Judgement-Based Supervision' (n285).
288 Andromachi Georgosouli, 'Judgement-led Regulation' (n277).
289 Mads Andenas, and Iris H-Y Chiu, *The Foundations and Future of Financial Regulation: Governance for Responsibility* (Routledge 2014).

the likely impact of risk materialisation'[290] and that those assumptions may be mistaken from the outset. However, this critique fails to consider the bigger picture. The real debate is not solely about the *assumptions* about risks, but about the decisions when taking pre-emptive actions and how to measure the quality of such judgements; in particular, whether regulators should be accountable for the outcome of the pre-emptive actions they took. Implementing strong and updated methods of risk assessment, as well as reasoned and accountable decision-making processes, can counter the arguments of those against integration.

Despite the benefits of judgement-led regulation, regulators still face some challenges when implementing the approach. Firstly, the access to data provided by regulated firms is in the thick of the discussion. Firms are expected to submit all the relevant information that will allow the regulators' intervention, the communication of system-wide risk, and the prescription of certain modes of action. Access to information is the first step to anticipate, when possible, the risk and its occurrence. However, it is equally important that all the collected data is efficiently analysed in order to avoid spending valuable time on analysis rather than on taking action.

Additionally, the supervisory data requires a determination of how intrusive should a supervisor be 'in order to operationalize a more forward-looking and judgement-led approach to supervision'.[291] In this sense, the UK authorities have introduced reforms to strengthen the supervisors' powers to collect data.[292] However, the crux of the debate is about effective analysis and use of the collected data, and how it guides supervisors' judgement when taking supervisory actions.

The second challenge in implementing judgement-led supervision is to set a clear goal and have adequate supervisory tools and resources. Rosa Lastra asserts that to be able to supervise 'regulators must have knowledge and exercise judgement'.[293] Thus, regulators' knowledge should be built upon access to adequate and complete information, as well as regulators' familiarity with market dynamics and evolution.

There is also a debate on whether the adoption of rule-based regime can fill the gaps related to the insufficient society protection when regulators exercise judgement. In other words: whether judgement is limited and the rules sufficiently can complement it. This is particularly important in the case of complex structures or products used by financers with the purpose of avoiding regulation and control. Thus, it is desirable to reach a coherent dialogue between rules and discretionary judgement. This is to understand that the balance between rules and discretion is different in each of the supervisory stages.[294]

---

290 Ibid.
291 Joanna Gray, and Peter Christian Metzing, 'Defining and Delivering Judgement-Based Supervision: The Interface with the Legal System' (3–4 July 2013) 14 *Journal of Banking Regulation*.
292 P. Tucker, 'The Debate on Financial System Resilience: Macroprudential Instruments', Speech to Barclays Annual Lecture, London, 22 October 2009.
293 Rosa Lastra, 'Defining Forward Looking, Judgement-Based Supervision' (n285).
294 Rosa Lastra identifies three stages of the supervisory process: the entry into the business, the supervision stricto sensu, and the sanctioning. Ibid.

In summary, then, judgement-based regulation helps to overcome some of the drawbacks of the risk-based approach. However, the road to designing the best version of a risk-based regime must go further, considering the role that regulated firms have in the implementation stage. Though there might be room for debate, there is a general acceptance that meta-regulation assists risk-based regimes. We will now go on to consider the content of meta-regulation and how it contributes to boost the risk-based approach to regulation.

2.5.2 Meta-regulation of the OTC derivatives market

Meta-regulation as a regulatory strategy is one example of the decentred regulatory space.[295] Regulated firms are expected to produce internal governance and controls that contribute to the public justice of accountability.[296] Along with risk-based regimes, meta-regulation has been heralded as one of the hallmarks of the 'new regulatory state'.[297] Hence, the strategy permeates two of the functions carried out by supervisors in risk-based regimes, namely microprudential regulation and risk management.[298] The rationale is that regulated firms become centres of self-control that facilitate the achievement of public regulatory needs in pursuing safe and sound financial institutions.[299] However, one disadvantage of this is when the firm's internal control system is oriented to different ends to those of the regulator.[300]

Meta-regulation involves cooperation between regulators and regulated firms. The cooperation is guided and controlled by regulators, and regulated firms have broad frameworks[301] that illustrate the shape of internal control systems and governance, risk management systems, internal audits, and so on. The task is to develop firm-based systems and procedures accordingly. Such firm-based systems will complement regulatory actions since regulators cannot excessively prescribe the firm organisational structures. The expected outcome is that regulated firms will design an internal organisation which achieves a proportionate and appropriate form of compliance to meet regulatory objectives.[302] Nevertheless, one foreseeable challenge is how regulators effectively assess the risk management systems

---

295 Mads Andenas, and Iris H-Y Chiu, *The Foundations and Future of Financial Regulation: Governance for Responsibility* (n289).
296 Christine Parker, *The Open Corporation* (Cambridge University Press 2000), 246.
297 Peter Grabovsky, 'Using Non-Governmental Resources to Foster Regulatory Compliance', (1995) 8 (4) *Governance*, 529.
298 Mads Andenas, and Iris H-Y Chiu, *The Foundations and Future of Financial Regulation: Governance for Responsibility* (n289).
299 Ibid.
300 Peter Grabovsky, 'Using Non-Governmental Resources to Foster Regulatory Compliance' (n297), 529.
301 In the EU, the markets in Financial Instruments Directive 2004 (MiFID) provides for broad principles of organisational soundness.
302 Mads Andenas, and Iris H-Y Chiu, *The Foundations and Future of Financial Regulation: Governance for Responsibility* (n289).

that will reflect the conflict of interest between firms' and regulators' inner interests.[303] In other words, while firms design and conduct risk management systems bearing their own interests, regulators are not able to critically evaluate those systems in light of regulatory objectives.

Baldwin and Black[304] propose the adoption of really responsive regulation to solve this issue. The really responsive regulation model implies that regulatory strategies are not designed to be solely adapted to the behaviour of regulatees, but should seek to establish a synergy between punishment and persuasion.[305] To this end, the responsive regulation reaches compliance when regulators operate an 'explicit enforcement pyramid'.[306] According to the enforcement pyramid, governments should seek to offer self-regulatory solutions, but if the regulatory objectives are not met, the State should escalate to enforce such self-regulation to command regulation with discretionary or non-discretionary punishment.[307]

Furthermore, responsive regulation is attentive to five key factors; namely: 'the behaviour, attitudes, and cultures of regulatory actors, the institutional setting of regulatory regime, the interactions between the different logics of regulatory tools and strategies, the regime's own performance over time, and the changes in each of these elements'.[308] These factors are considered to be at the core of the regulators' role and are central challenges to achieve regulatory objectives over time.[309] In addition to these factors, the really responsive regulation ought to consider the way that regulatory challenges vary across the core regulators' tasks with respect to individual firms and in developing strategies.[310] A novel element of the really responsive regulation model is the early identification of undesirable and non-compliant behaviour. This allows regulators to develop tools and strategies, assess the outcomes, and then reform the regulatory actions accordingly. This is closely linked to the enforcement strategy that combines elements of compliance and deterrence; it is accomplished through a system of incentives and different levels of civil, administrative, and, as a last resort, criminal sanctions.

Attending to the participation of market actors in the regulatory process, this research supports the argument that meta-regulation is applicable to the OTCDM. In particular, it considers how certain features of the meta-regulation can be articulated with the regime adopted by the Bank, as well as the issues it brings to the supervision. The Bank designed the supervision regime to cover both 'design of Financial Market Institutions – including CCPs – rules and the

---

303 Ibid.
304 Julia Black, and Robert Baldwin, 'Really Responsive Risk-Based Regulation' (n8).
305 Ian Ayres, and John Braithwaite, *Responsive Regulation: Transcending the Deregulation Debate* (n114) 25.
306 Julia Black and Robert Baldwin, 'Really Responsive Risk-Based Regulation' (n8), 259.
307 Ibid.
308 Ibid.
309 Neil Gunningliam, 'Enforcement and Compliance Strategies', in Robert Baldwin, Martin Cave, and Martin Lodge (eds.), *The Oxford Handbook of Regulation* (n8).
310 Ibid.

use of management discretion in the application of these rules'.[311] This means that CCPs, as market participants, will have a certain level of discretion to implement the new regulation. Thus, this work questions the limits of such CCPs' discretion and how this could adversely affect the implementation of the new rules.

2.6 Risk-based regulation of CCPs in the OTC derivatives market

2.6.1 The UK

Although risk-based regulation started with the FSA, the two new UK supervision authorities PRA[312] and FCA are also implementing such an approach to regulation. However, each of them is developing separate risk assessment frameworks. The PRA will design and implement a risk assessment for prudential issues and the FCA for conduct of business. This book argues that CCPs in the UK OTCDM should be regulated and supervised by the FCA in the matters of conduct of business and by the Bank for prudential matters.

The FCA is responsible for regulating conduct in retail and wholesale markets (including both exchange-operated markets and OTC dealing), supervising the trading infrastructure that supports those markets, and ensuring prudential regulation of firms not prudentially regulated by the PRA.

The regulation and supervision of clearing and settlement systems (trading infrastructure), including CCPs, was expressly assigned to the Bank. However, it has been stated that in its supervision the Bank will work closely with the FCA, reflecting the FCA's responsibilities for the trading infrastructure and market product.[313]

The risk-based approach entitles the FCA to detect and act on risks that are identified in the marketplace, ensuring that potential problems are identified early to meet FCA objectives.[314] The FCA has explained its approach to risk-based regulation through the steps it will use, namely: to identify and assess risks both emerging and current to consumers and firms; to identify the risks that market failures exist that impede effective competition in relevant markets; to develop a general understanding of the risks and issues in financial markets to support authorisation, supervision, and enforcement functions; to prioritise, manage, and mitigate risks consistently and use a risk-based approach for making decisions; to establish common standards and principles for measuring and assessing risk across the organisation; and to put in place the infrastructure, systems, and tools to catalogue, analyse, and assess risk.[315]

---

311 Bank of England, 'The Bank of England's Approach to the Supervision of Financial Market Infrastructures' (n230).
312 Proposed reforms will replace the PRA with the Prudential Regulation Committee of the Bank of England, Bank of England and Financial Services Bill 2015–2016.
313 First and second MoUs between the FCA and the Bank.
314 The FCA's approach to advancing its objectives (July 2013).
315 Ibid.

The Bank is responsible for regulating and supervising post-trading market infrastructures, within them OTCDM's CCPs. To this end, the Bank has set out some key supervisory pillars (KSPs), anticipating that 'its supervisory effort is based on its assessment of where risks to financial stability are greatest'.[316] In general, the supervision relies on systemic risk management[317] through the principles of: governance, management of operational risk, continuity of service, and adequate rules in case of participants' default. Certainly, some of the elements announced on the Bank policy documents could be indicative of the adoption of a risk-based approach; however, there is not an explicit mention of the adoption of such an approach. This raises some concerns regarding the coherent approach to regulation and supervision of CCPs. Our findings indicate that the FCA and the Bank are not following a consistent risk-based approach to CCPs' regulation and supervision.

The development of the risk-based regulation approach is focused on the management of systemic risk.[318] Hence, the post-GFC regulatory reforms highlighted the need to oversee macro- and microprudential matters, to reduce systemic risks.[319] The aim is to avoid gaps in regulation, which could materialise into possible systemic risks – therefore, one of the remedies for mitigating potential systemic fragilities is to monitor and constrain the behaviour of key financial institutions[320] and intermediaries. In the case of the OTCDM, the regulatory response to the system failure of a fragile market infrastructure is the adoption of the CCPs, mutualising trading risk and enhancing system stability.[321]

2.6.2 The US

The debate surrounding the complete adoption of risk-based regulation in the US securities market is not new.[322] It has been argued that a transition from a rule-based regime – as the one embedded in the Securities Exchange Act 1934 – to a risk-based approach – found in the Commodities Futures Modernization Act 2000 – is the key to implementing more effective, comprehensive compliance, rather than an enforcement focus of US securities regulation.

---

316 Bank of England, 'The Bank of England's Approach to the Supervision of Financial Market Infrastructures' (n230), 7.
317 Ibid.
318 Jack Selody, 'The Nature of Systemic Risk' in John Raymond LaBrosse, Rodrigo Olivares-Caminal, and Dalvinder Singh (eds.), *Managing Risk in the Financial System* (Edward Elgar Publishing Ltd 2011), 26.
319 Dalvinder Singh, 'The US Architecture of Bank Regulation and Supervision' in Raymond LaBrosse, Rodrigo Olivares-Caminal, and Dalvinder Singh (eds.), *Managing Risk in the Financial System* Ibid 409.
320 Jack Selody, 'The Nature of Systemic Risk' (n318), 26.
321 Ibid.
322 International Securities Exchange. Proposal for Regulatory Reform for the US Financial Markets, (March 2009), 4.

In July 2011, the CFTC, the SEC, and the Federal Reserve's Board issued a report to Congress identifying the common elements of risk-based supervision for clearing entities (CEs). The three common elements are: objectives, standards, and processes and tools for the assessment of CEs or financial market utilities (FMUs). Moreover, during the constant review of such elements, it might happen that supervisors find deficiencies and – more importantly for this analysis – unaddressed risks. Hence, supervisors will seek to address such shortcomings by putting in place a wide range of enforcement actions.

The task to develop a set of standards as a background of risk management assessment embeds the relevant provisions of the Exchange Act,[323] the core principled established in section 5b of the Commodity Exchange Act (CEA) and the CFTC regulations, as well as the CPSS-IOSCO basis for management of risks in systemically important systems. The enforcement of this body of regulation starts with the initial registration or application process, ongoing monitoring[324] and examinations,[325] cooperation with other national and international authorities, and agreements on corrective actions[326] when material weaknesses in risk management or violations of statutory provisions have been identified.

As in any other regime, the strategy of regulation to be implemented is central to the achievement of the regulatory objectives. Thus, the adoption of risk-based regulation as an approach that strengthens the supervision of systemically important financial institutions, instead of implementing a compliance rules and principles-based strategy, avoids the issues associated with the 'tick-box exercise' of sets of rules.

Reflecting the typical elements of risk-based approaches to regulation, the US regime assesses the importance of conducting a supervision that entails the evaluation of how a DCO identifies, measures, controls, and monitors diverse types of risks (among them, country and economic risk, as well as credit, market, liquidity, legal risks, and so forth). Once the identification of risk has been completed, regulatory agencies – the CFTC and the SEC – are expected to focus their resources on those entities that pose higher risks.

The CFTC tends to hire professionals from diverse areas to carry out risk identification and assessment, and to implement risk measurement models. Examiners should conduct a detailed study of the board of directors and senior management within DCOs so they can determine their risk philosophy, culture,

---

323 Sections 17, 17A, and 19.
324 Conducting periodic (such as daily or monthly) testing, including back testing and stress testing, to verify the CE's or FMU's measurements of credit, market, and liquidity risks; reviewing internal audit reports.
325 Examinations consist of a review and evaluation of internal CE and FMU reports and analysis related to risk management and verification by examiners of the information contained in the CE's and FMU's reports and analysis.
326 This authority includes enforcement, such as the institution of a civil or administrative action against a CE or FMU leading to the imposition of sanctions such as a civil monetary penalty, a cease and desist order, or suspension or revocation of the CE's or FMU's registration, authorisation, or charter.

policies, and procedures. Along with this process, examiners should consider what financial safeguards are in place, as well as the effectiveness of the account segregation at DCOs.

Furthermore, the role of credit risks committees (CRCs) within DCOs is also central to the implementation of a risk-based approach to regulation. CRCs assess levels of risk by conducting processes of due diligence on potential clearing members and their credit quality. Moreover, general market situations as credit spreads and stock prices should also be considered, especially when the intersections between Basel III, DFA, and EMIR are putting excessive pressure on having highly liquid and unencumbered collateral. The focus should be on ensuring that DCOs are accurately accepting only the highest-quality collateral and increasing transparency on how they calculate haircuts. Also, the information collected during the oversight process should be sufficiently accurate to assess the type of data for low-probability, high-adverse impact events, and to measure whether DCOs are capitalised enough to manage unexpected losses.

In contrast to the UK regime, the US regime (or at least the applicable rules as issued to DCOs)[327] includes a balanced combination of prudential and conduct of business rules. According to the CEA,[328] DCOs must comply with certain core principles associated with adequate financial, operational, and managerial resources; appropriate standards for participant and product eligibility; adequate risk management capabilities; efficient and fair default rules and procedures; governance arrangements and fitness standards; rules to minimise conflicts of interest in the DCO's decision-making process; a process for resolving any conflicts; and avoidance of actions that are unreasonable restraints of trade or that impose anti-competitive burdens, among others.

2.7 Conclusion

Risk is central to financial regulation. The rationale of the risk-based approach to regulation is based on the understanding that regulators ought to recognise the difference between risks and uncertainties, and thereby the limits and opportunities that such a distinction brings to the process of regulation. Whilst risks are measurable and quantifiable, uncertainties stem from qualitative judgements or predictions. However, the traditional dichotomy is not always clear, as risks and uncertainties easily overlap. Hence, risks and uncertainties might align and form a hybrid system, where the role of each category in the regulatory process is established from the outset. Regulators acknowledge that risks are the drivers of regulatory actions and uncertainties, especially knowable uncertainties, are co-drivers that, with a secondary function, contribute to conduct risk-based approaches to the expected outcomes.

---

327 Criteria, procedures, and requirements for registration as a DCO are set forth in s 5b of the CEA, 7 USC s 7a-1, and Part 39 of the CFTC's regulations.
328 S 5b, 7 USC s 7a-1, of the Commodity Exchange Act (CEA).

Accepting the interaction between risks and uncertainties will assist regulators in their task of managing and controlling new types of risk resulting from the progression of human development, science, and technology. These are manufactured risks, challenging the idea that all risks can be measured. Moreover, the identification and assessment of different types of risks and uncertainties require regulators to interact and cooperate with regulated firms. The cooperation between regulators and regulatees will facilitate the integration of different sources of knowledge that, in turn, will inform the decision-making process concerning what risks exist, the level of tolerance, and how to control them.

As different elements informing regulation, the recognition of risk and uncertainties reshapes and reorients the strategies attached to risk-based regimes. Such recognition also determines the limits that financial regulators face and the complexity tied to the implementation of risk-based regimes. Regulators and regulated firms are aware of the difficulties in coping with manufactured risks and knowable uncertainties. This reality is revealed in markets as the OTCDM that are a limitless source of new risks, triggered by innovation and entrepreneurial activity.

The integration of regulators' and regulated firms' perceptions and attitudes towards risk informs the stages of risk identification and assessment, as well as the resulting prioritisation of resources. On the one hand, regulators conduct a process of decision-making to determine how to address and when to prioritise risks. Following this rationale, risk-based regulators are expected to develop the two stems of the approach: prudential regulation and conduct of business. At the same time, in order to cooperate with regulators, regulated firms will adjust their internal system of control and regulation to enable the regulator to spend fewer resources supervising.

There are several benefits of adopting risk-based regimes. They allow the design and implementation of regimes that consider unknown but foreseeable events. Risk-based approaches offer an integrated decision-making framework applicable to all levels of firms and risks. Risk-based regimes enhance the efficient allocation of resources according to the risks regulators decide to prioritise, and the exercise of such discretion limits the extent of regulators' accountability.

However, despite the benefits we have discussed, risk-based regulation has some drawbacks. Particularly challenging is the need for the regulator to clearly identify its objectives and the risk that regulated firms may pose to the achievement of those objectives. Also, the limited capability of regulators to implement the approach, as well as the related issues concerning access to information and specialised knowledge, pose significant difficulties. Regulators are expected to make clear how risk evaluations will be used as drivers of regulatory actions and will inform the method of enforcement. Moreover, risk-based regimes are expected to accomplish changes in regulated firms' behaviour and have an impact on regulators' culture and behaviour. To overcome these drawbacks, risk-based regimes need to be designed and implemented coherently, and with cooperation between regulators and regulated firms. They also need to be combined with other strategies of regulation, such as judgement based and meta-regulation.

Considering everything we have examined so far, risk-based regulation would seem to be a partially efficient approach to regulate CCPs in the OTCDM, in that it allows an efficient allocation of sources, one of the most concerning challenges of regulators. Moreover, risk-based regulation is broad enough to design and implement a regime for CCP in the OTCDM that contributes effectively to achieve regulators' objectives. In this case, the safety and soundness of CCPs are in line with financial stability.

Four points support our conclusion that the risk-based approach is efficient but still could be improved. Firstly, the Bank's decision to create a special division to carry out the policy analysis and supervision of CCPs is evidence of one of the key benefits of risk-based regulation, wherein it provides a means of linking the organisation enforcement resources to individual firms and activities.

Secondly, the decision of both the Bank and US regulators to intervene in the OTCDM by regulating CCPs is an example of the implementation of two elements of risk-based regulation: risk-tolerance and risk-identification techniques. UK and US regulators identified and assessed the risks the CCPs posed to its regulatory objectives and designed the regime accordingly. In this sense, they linked the risks posed by CCPs to the objective of financial stability and the safety and soundness of the CCPs. Bear in mind, however, that risk-based regimes involve a selection of risks that entails the correlative exclusion of other types of risk. This shortcoming is a notable feature of the UK and US risk-based regimes of CCPs. Regulators are prioritising their regulatory actions and resources to manage credit, liquidity, and operational risk, whilst other types of risk, such as the innovation risk have been implicitly excluded.

In the US, both the CFTC and the SEC are committed to the objective of financial stability and prevention of systemic risks. Like the UK, the US regime has given priority to rule the recovery of CCPs. Such prioritisation is an effect of the international regulatory agenda. As we will go on to consider in later chapters, international regulators have been working on the design of recovery rules for financial market institutions (FMIs), whilst the resolution is regarded as less urgent. The rationale is that having a strong and efficient regime of CCPs' recovery will ensure resolution is avoided. Therefore, the design and particularities of resolution rules are not an immediate cause of concern. This is another example of the imperfect implementation of the risk-based approach to regulation. The prioritisation of certain risks (in particular the risk consistent with a CCP's crisis, that has the potential to be solved only with recovery rules) implies that regulators have overlooked the design of CCPs' resolution.

In Chapter 6 we will discuss this aspect in greater depth, but in brief, the Dodd-Frank Act does not sufficiently clarify whether Title II is applicable to the resolution of all types of CCPs. If the Financial Stability Oversight Council (FSOC) designates a CCP as a systemically important financial institution,[329] the

---

329 Dodd-Frank Act, s 804.

DFA provides such a CCP with access to emergency funding[330] and the CCP might be subject to more stringent regulation. However, it is not clear if the regime is applicable if the CCP fails. One interpretation might lead commentators to assert that even if Title II is not applicable, the ordinary bankruptcy laws are. However, the implementation of Chapter 11 (US insolvency law for private companies) is not unburdened either.

Thirdly, one of the features of risk-based regulation is that it facilitates the gathering of information about the regulated population. This feature sheds light on the Bank's approach to the regulation of CCPs in the OTCDM. The Bank prioritises the regulation of CCPs because they gather information of a large part of the OTCDM; CCPs are channels of communication and information, and, in that sense, facilitate the regulators' access to information of the market.

Finally, and more broadly, risk-based regulation assists the study, design, and implementation of the regime by providing a comprehensive structure in the two traditional stems of financial regulation; namely prudential regulation and conduct of business.

Furthermore, a risk-based approach can be a useful tool to assist the regulator in the management of systemic risk, specifically in the regime of CCPs in the OTCDM. Although the risk-based approach to regulation was criticised after the GFC for being slow in managing cumulative risks, it has the potential to assist the regulation of markets that might be sources of systemic risk.

The key to achieving the efficient management of systemic risk is in the implementation. Risk-based regulation needs to be conducted in a manner that does not place attention exclusively on the riskiest firms, but instead ensures the efficient supervision of firms at all levels of risk. The UK regime is designed and implemented to ensure that CCPs, as new intermediaries in the OTCDM, are sufficiently resilient. The priority of the Bank is to enhance the robustness of these entities, to avoid any disturbance of their services, and to ensure they have efficient loss-allocation, recovery, and resolvability rules. Risk-based regimes allow regulators to take advantage of the risk identification, risk assessment, and respective allocation of sources to reduce, though not eliminate, the events that could trigger systemic risk. Thus, risk-based regulation is an efficient approach to deal with systemic risk when it has been designed and implemented amidst the financial stability objective.

Nonetheless, the risk-based approach to regulation needs to be complemented by other regulatory strategies, particularly in the UK where regulators have combined approaches to regulation. The integration of multiple regulatory strategies helps the approach to overcome its shortcomings. Complementary strategies, such as judgement based and meta-regulation, are the most relevant for the study of the regime of CCPs in the OTCDM. Indeed, the Bank's regime includes two elements that reflect those complementary strategies: the importance of the

---

330 Dodd-Frank Act, s 806 provides access to the Federal Reserve's discount window.

cooperation of CCPs in the design and implementation of the regime, and the range of early intervention tools to supervise CCPs.

In contrast, in the US, the most suitable alternative is the adoption of a risk-based approach to regulation guided by principles. This is similar to the strategy adopted by the CFTC, in order to avoid the negative effects that a purely rules-based approach brings to the regime and, especially, the consequences that a system of strict rules enforcement might have for the competitiveness of the US market against international markets.

3 Shortcomings of the UK regime of CCPs in the OTC derivatives market

3.1 Introduction

This chapter is devoted to exploring the approach of the UK regime of CCPs in the OTCDM, and the first of its shortcomings. Using a risk-based regulation approach to assess the regime, we will examine the two main pillars of the regime: prudential supervision and conduct of business. Taking into account our parameters, outlined in the first chapter of this book, here we identify the two drawbacks of risk-based regimes affecting the UK regime of CCPs in the OTCDM. These are the absence of an organisational culture in implementing risk-based regulation and that the use of risk-based regulation is, itself, creating manufactured risks. In adopting risk-based regulation, the UK regime of CCPs is prioritising prudential matters and at the same time ignoring almost completely the conduct of business regulation. Such prioritisation is reflected in the wrongful interpretation of the supervisory mandates of the Bank and the FCA. This lack of clarity regarding the role of UK authorities affects the organisational implementation of the risk-based approach.

The chapter starts with a brief explanation of the rationale behind the adoption of the CCPs in the OTCDM. We then present an overview of the UK regime of CCPs in the OTCDM and the Bank's approach to the supervision of CCPs. The purpose of these first two sections is to address the questions regarding the motivations to implementing CCPs in the OTCDM and to identify the Bank's regulatory priorities in the first years of regime implementation. Thirdly, we explain a key failure of the UK CCPs regime in the OTCDM – the absence of a conduct of business regime. We question the limited role that the current conduct of business rules have in the UK regime of CCPs and how it needs to be further developed. In explaining this inadequacy, we address several questions: firstly, the concern regarding the role that the FCA *should* have as the conduct regulator of CCPs. We then argue the importance of having a conduct of business regime for CCPs in the OTCDM and, finally, highlight the elements that such a regime should have.

3.2 Rationale of the CCPs in the OTCDM

The OTCDM has traditionally been a self-regulated market of bilateral and non-standardised contracts and transactions, privately negotiated between the parties involved. However, after the GFC, regulators decided to intervene in the market through more comprehensive regulation, along with a more intrusive approach to supervision. The regulatory focus was to provide a better counterparty risk management through the adoption of new FMIs: CCPs and TRs.

Central Counterparties are the not-so-novel[1] solution that financial regulators adopted post-GFC to solve some of the market's failures.[2] The reasons that such a reaction came about, as argued by the G20 in 2009 and as continuously restated in subsequent summits, were to increase transparency in the market, promote the standardisation of OTC derivatives products, and promote tools for better risk management.[3]

TRs will collect all the relevant information regarding trades, dealers, and investors with the aim to provide better access to relevant information.[4] Access to information is an efficient tool to enhance transparency[5] in the OTCDM. However, the TRs' regime and concerns about the efficiency of such systems are beyond the scope of this book.

Financial market infrastructures lie at the heart of the financial system[6] and improve market resilience in times of stress.[7] In particular, CCPs locate themselves as crucial nodes in the financial system, hence their systemic importance in terms of managing, reducing, and allocating the inherent risks arising from transactions between market participants.[8] In carrying out their typical functions, CCPs run a 'matched book'. This means that 'any position taken on with one counterparty is always offset by an opposite position taken with a second counterparty'.[9] Although the CCPs do not take on market risk in their normal

1 Christian Chamorro-Courtland, 'The Trillion Dollar Question: Can a Central Bank Bail-Out a Central Counterparty (CCP) Clearing House Which Is 'Too Big To Fail'?' (Spring 2012) *Brooklyn Journal of Corporate, Financial & Commercial Law*, March.

2 Paul Tucker, 'Central Counterparties in Evolving Capital Markets: Safety, Recovery and Resolution' Banque du France, Financial Stability Review N17 (April 2013).

3 Robert Steigerwald, 'Chapter 7: Central Counterparty Clearing and Systemic Risk Regulation' (2014) Federal Reserve Bank of Chicago, Revised draft: 05/16/2014.

4 Darrell Duffie, Ada Li, and Theodore Lubke, 'Policy Perspectives on OTC Derivatives Market Infrastructure' (March 2010) FRB of New York Staff Report No 424 <http://ssrn.com/abstract=1534729> accessed 3rd October 2015.

5 Colleen Baker, 'Regulating the Invisible: The Case of Over-the-Counter Derivatives' (2009–2010) 5 *Notre Dame Law Review*, 1287.

6 Amandeep Rehlon, and Dan Nixon, 'Central Counterparties: What Are They, Why Do They Matter and How Does the Bank Supervise Them?' (Bank of England, Quarterly Bulletin, Q2 2013).

7 Jacques Aigrain, and M. Gex, 'CCPs as Instruments of Stability and Risk Mitigation' in 'OTC Derivatives: New Rules, New Actors, New Risks' Banque du France – Financial Stability Review (n3).

8 Nikil Chande, Nicholas Labelle, and Eric Tuer, 'Central Counterparties and Systemic Risk', *Bank of Canada Financial System Review* (December 2010).

9 Amandeep Rehlon, and Dan Nixon, 'Central Counterparties: What Are They, Why Do They Matter and How Does the Bank Supervise Them?' (n6).

course of business, they are exposed to the risk that a counterparty may default. In such a case, the CCP would be subject to market risk.[10]

As noted, the main reason for introducing CCPs to the OTCDM is to provide a better management of counterparty credit risk, particularly in markets such the OTC derivatives, where the losses are severe enough to become a channel of contagion and be the potential source of systemic risk.[11] CCPs are used to reduce and mutualise the counterparty credit risk in the markets in which they operate.[12] CCPs reduce counterparty credit risk through multilateral netting – that is, 'offsetting an amount due from a member on one transaction against an amount owed to that member on another, to reach a single, smaller net exposure'.[13]

Equally important to the functioning of CCPs is the orderly management of a member's default and of any other source of losses. To that end, CCPs count with loss-allocation rules and mechanisms to act in the event of a member's default. Some of these mechanisms include an auction of the defaulter's positions and more commonly the use of CCPs' default waterfall. Although there is no standard 'default waterfall',[14] the mechanism usually involves: defaulting member's initial margin and default fund contribution, part of the CCP's equity, a surviving member's default fund contributions, rights of assessment, and the CCP's margin equity.[15] The aim of having these mechanisms in place is to avoid the failure of the CCP and its systemic implications. However, CCPs should also have a special resolution regime to be enforced when the recovery measures have been exhausted. In such an event, the priority of supervisors will be ensuring the continuity of the clearing services.

There are notable advantages and limits posed by the use of CCPs.[16] A detailed consideration of the benefits and limits of the use of CCPs in the OTCDM is beyond the scope of this study – however, it is important for us to briefly look at the advantages and limits CCPs have. The most prominent benefits that CCPs bring to the OTCDM include the discipline of an independent valuation of market positions, rigorous full collateralisation, and clear default rules and procedures.[17] CCPs are said to increase market safety and integrity by mitigating and managing

---

10 BIS, 'Recovery of Financial Market Infrastructures' CPMI-IOSCO (October 2014).
11 Ibid.
12 Jon Gregory, *Central Counterparties: Mandatory Clearing and Bilateral Margin Requirements for OTC Derivatives* (Wiley Finance Series 2014), 4.
13 Amandeep Rehlon, and Dan Nixon, 'Central Counterparties: What Are They, Why Do They Matter and How Does the Bank Supervise Them?' (n6).
14 ISDA, 'CCP Default Management, Recovery and Continuity: A Proposed Recovery Framework' (January 2015).
15 Craig Pirrong, 'The Economics of Central Clearing: Theory and Practice' (ISDA Discussion Papers Series, May 2011).
16 Ben S. Bernanke, 'Clearing and Settlement During the Crash' (1990) Princeton University, 3 (1) *The Review of Financial Studies*, 133.
17 Jacques Aigrain, and M. Gex, 'CCPs as Instruments of Stability and Risk Mitigation' in 'OTC Derivatives: New Rules, New Actors, New Risks' (n7).

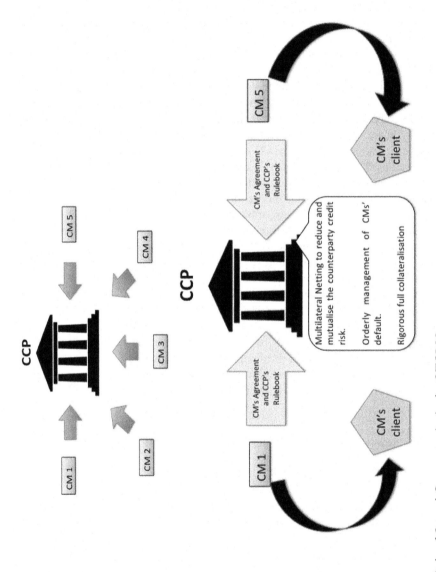

Figure 3.1 Role of Central Counterparties in the OTCDM

counterparty credit risk, mitigating liquidity and operational risks, addressing information asymmetries, reducing complexity, and increasing efficiency.[18] Such benefits are achieved when CCPs feature strong regulatory regimes, high standards of governance, and risk management.[19] However, the shape of the regulation varies in each jurisdiction, and the effectiveness of the regulation in achieving these outcomes depends heavily on the availability of market infrastructure and the use that market participants make of that infrastructure.[20]

Nonetheless, the adoption of CCPs in the OTC derivatives is not perfect. Pirrong, one of the strongest critics of CCPs, argues that in the aftermath of the GFC central clearing was wrongfully considered a panacea that would prevent future panics and ensure financial stability.[21] He argues that there is considerable room for scepticism about the excessive hope placed upon the CCPs' role. On the one hand, CCPs are highly interconnected[22] intermediaries and the consequences of their failure might prompt negative externalities.[23] The establishment of a CCP creates the risk of contagion[24] of shocks[25] and losses that may occur as a result of two events – the CCP's actions to survive, following the default of a clearing member or a CCP's eventual default. Moreover, CCPs in the OTCDM are characterised by a lack of substitutability;[26] as the market is highly concentrated, they are too difficult to substitute in case one of them ceases to provide services.

These concerns explain the content of the post-GFC regulatory reforms that moved towards enhancing central clearing for OTC derivatives, but more importantly, are designed to ensure the safety and soundness of CCPs. As has been discussed in this research, the UK regime – in line with the international regulatory reform – is heavily seated in the prudential supervision of CCPs. The priority is to ensure the safety and soundness of CCPs, with the expectation that this will result in stability for the OTCDM.

18 Marcus Zickwolff, 'The Role of Central Counterparties in Financial Crisis Recovery' (World Federation of Exchanges, 2010) <www.world-exchanges.org/insight/views/role-central-counterparties-financial-crisis-recovery> accessed 5th October 2015.

19 HM Treasury, 'Financial Reform: A Framework for Financial Stability (Group of Thirty) and a New Approach to Financial Regulation: An Analysis' (November 2010).

20 FSB, 'OTC Derivatives Market Reforms Eighth Progress Report on Implementation' (7 November 2014).

21 Craig Pirrong, 'The Inefficiency of Clearing Mandates' Policy Analysis, CATO Institute (July 2010).

22 David Murphy, Michalis Vasios, and Nick Vause, 'An Investigation into the Procyclicality of Risk-Based Initial Margin Models' (Bank of England Financial Stability Paper No. 29, May 2014).

23 IMF, 'Central Counterparties: Addressing their Too Important to Fail Nature' (IMF, Working Paper, January 2015).

24 CCPs actions may have 'pro-cyclical' effects by exacerbating other stresses in the financial system.

25 Li Lin, and Jay Surti, 'Capital Requirements for Over-The-Counter Derivatives Central Counterparties' (IMF, WP/13/3 January 2013).

26 IMF, 'Central Counterparties: Addressing Their Too Important to Fail Nature' (n23).

The introduction of mandatory clearing also brings some benefits in terms of supervision of the OTCDM. From the regulators' perspective, one of the benefits of CCPs is that they contribute to enhancing standardisation. When the G20 leaders agreed on the need to improve standardisation of OTC derivatives transactions, the working group of the FSB was engaged with the task to translate the G20 commitments into standards and implementing regulation. The aim of standardisation was to achieve consistency in implementation across jurisdictions, to promote greater use of OTC derivatives products in standardised form, and to minimise potential regulatory arbitrage. Hence, the October 2010 report from the FSB[27] set out recommendations for authorities to work with market participants to increase standardisation, including the introduction of incentives and, where appropriate, regulation.

These recommendations and the work of the OTC Derivatives Supervisors Group (ODSG) help to explain how standardisation contributes to regulators' work. On 31st March 2011, the ODSG[28] took the commitment to achieve the benefits of standardisation[29] by providing supervisors with ongoing qualitative and quantitative indicators to inform supervisory and regulatory priorities. One of the objectives of standardisation is to develop the foundation for implementing market reforms, allowing more automated processing, expanded central clearing, and enhanced transparency.

The aim of standardisation is materialised in three initiatives: firstly, to develop an ongoing analysis for the purposes of benchmarking the level of standardisation in each asset class related to derivatives (credit, interest rates, equities, commodities).[30] Secondly, the product standardisation, including the development publication and take-up of standardised product documentation.[31] This second initiative requires explaining the role of ISDA issuing standard documentation used on OTC derivatives transaction. Thirdly, process standardisation:[32] continuing the work with CCPs, TRs, and other infrastructure providers to standardise processes in each asset class.

Besides the advantages of standardisation, CCPs also play an active role in increasing transparency of the OTCDM. The problem before the GFC was that the bilateral structure of OTC derivatives transactions impeded the adequate monitoring of exposures and the assessment of potential risks for financial stability.[33]

---

27 FSB, 'Implementing OTC Derivatives Market Reforms' (25 October 2010).
28 'This is the roadmap of the G14 members to initiatives and commitments regarding central counterparties, infrastructure providers and global supervisors to continue to make structural improvements to the global OTC derivatives markets' <www.newyorkfed.org/medialibrary/media/newsevents/news/markets/2011/SCL0331.pdf> accessed 4th December 2017.
29 FSB, 'Implementing OTC Derivatives Market Reforms' (n27).
30 Ibid.
31 Legal standardisation is the use of common legal documentation, including master netting agreements, definitions, confirmations, etc. Ibid.
32 Operational standardisation seeks to manage all product trade cycles in common terms, and it is beneficial to central clearing systems. Ibid.
33 Daniela Russo, 'OTC Derivatives: Financial Stability Challenges and Responses from Authorities' (Banque du France, Financial Stability Review N 14 Derivatives Financial Innovation and Stability July 2010).

Hence, the regulatory response was to introduce several mechanisms to increase the transparency of the market – one route being the use of CCPs. The justification is that CCPs maintain transaction records, including notional amounts and counterparty identities.[34] A CCP contributes to transparency because it provides the centralised administration of long and short positions of clearing members.[35] However, the role of CCPs needs to be complemented with other mechanisms.[36]

As the CCPs are assuming a position of special importance, in each transaction and in the market more generally, they fall into the category of systemically important financial institutions (SIFIs).[37] The systemic importance of CCPs and the undesirable consequences of their failure have inspired the content of the regulatory reform. Regulators have been particularly devoted to ensure, to the best of their capacity, that the CCPs will provide the clearing services[38] with no interruption or disturbance, even if the CCPs are facing financial distress. Hence, the regulatory reform includes loss-allocation and recovery rules to be adopted by the CCPs, and it is expected to develop a special resolution regime in the near future.

3.3 UK regime of CCPs in the OTCDM

We will now address the questions concerning the role of the UK regulators of CCPs in the OTCDM and the role that the Bank and the FCA should take when conducting their prudential supervision and conduct of business supervision. Since our overarching purpose is to critically assess the UK regime of CCPs, rather than to describe in detail its content, this chapter only explores the most relevant provisions regarding UK regulation and the relevant provisions of EMIR. Finally, this section also highlights the areas of supervision that the UK regime prioritises in order to help us understand the findings of this study, the shortcomings of the UK regime of CCPs in the OTCDM.

3.3.1 Regulatory architecture

The reform of the financial regulation and supervision regime in the UK began by proposing the introduction of a new approach to financial regulation – one which is based on clarity of focus and responsibility, and which places the judgement of expert supervisors at the centre of regulation. Hence, the responsibility for financial stability rests with the Bank[39] and its FPC; the PRA oversees the

---

34 IMF, 'Making OTC Derivatives Safer: The Role of Central Counterparties (FMI, Global Financial Stability Report, April 2010).
35 IMF, 'Central Counterparties: Addressing Their Too Important to Fail Nature' (n23).
36 ISDA Report <www2.isda.org/functional-areas/technology-infrastructure/data-and-reporting/reporting/> accessed 15th October 2014.
37 George Walker, 'Systematically Important Institutions Too Big To Fail' (2012) (Financial Regulation International October 26, 2012).
38 FSB, 'OTC Derivatives Market Reforms Eighth Progress Report on Implementation' (n20).
39 See Graham Nicholson, and Michael Salib, 'The Regulatory Powers and Purview of the Bank of England: Pre- and Post-Crisis' (2013) 10 *Journal of International Banking and Financial Law*, 636.

prudential matters. Moreover, responsibility for conduct of business will still sit with the new FCA. As part of this approach, regulators are empowered to look beyond compliance and to supervise proactively. To introduce these reforms, the government amended the Financial Services Market Act 2000. The most recent reform is proposed in the Bank of England and Financial Services Bill 2015–2016; it attributes the functions of the PRA to the Bank. Such functions are to be exercised by the Bank acting through its Prudential Regulation Committee.[40] Regarding the CCPs, we would argue that the competent authorities are the Bank and the FCA.[41]

3.3.2 UK statutory regime and European regulation (EMIR)

The Financial Services and Markets Act 2000 (FSMA 2000) Part XVIII regulates CCPs, entities subject to the recognition requirements as recognised clearing houses (RCHs). However, the legal obligations to be satisfied are defined in large part by European law. For the purpose of this study, our focus is on the regulation of CCPs contained in the European Regulation on OTC derivatives, Central Counterparties, and Trade Repositories, commonly known as EMIR.[42] A systematic interpretation of both bodies of regulation aims to ensure that the Part XVIII regime can be more efficient and responsive to the more complex and challenging environment, which both CCPs and regulators now face.[43]

The main obligations under EMIR include the central clearing obligation[44] through a CCP for certain classes of OTC derivatives; application of risk mitigation techniques for non-centrally cleared OTC derivatives;[45] reporting on all OTC derivatives to Trade Repositories;[46] application of organisational, conduct of business, and prudential requirements for CCPs; and application of requirements for TRs, including the duty to make certain data available to the public and relevant authorities. This study is focused on analysing the provisions in EMIR related to CCPs, the prudential regulation, conduct of business, and organisational requirements.

---

40 'The Bank of England and Financial Services Bill 2015–2016' <www.publications.parlia ment.uk/pa/bills/lbill/2015-2016/0065/lbill_2015-20160065_en_3.htm#pt1-pb3-l1g12> accessed 21st October 2015.

41 FSB, 'Resolution of Systematically Important Financial Institutions: Progress Report' (November 2012).

42 On 4th July 2012, the Regulation on OTC Derivatives, Central Counterparties, and Trade Repositories (known as EMIR) was adopted and it entered into force on 16th August 2012.

43 HM Treasury-FCA (2011b), *A New Approach to Financial Regulation: The Blueprint for Reform*, CM8083 (June 2011) 20 (hereinafter HM Treasury-FCA (2011b), *A New Approach to Financial Regulation: The Blueprint for Reform*).

44 Art 4 EMIR.

45 Art 11 EMIR.

46 Art 9 EMIR.

CCPs must be recognised[47] and authorised[48] by the national competent authority[49] – the Bank of England[50] in the UK – within the EMIR transitional period. These provisions are under reform.[51] The period to decide if the application is complete is 30 working days,[52] and 'once complete, a further four months to make a recommendation for authorisation to a supervisory college'.[53] Additionally, CCPs must comply with the UK requirements on monitoring and mitigating financial crime and market abuse.[54]

Section 286 of FSMA also makes clear[55] that any applicant for recognition must comply with all the requirements established by the MiFID,[56] as prescribed by Section 290 (1A).[57] The relevant provisions of MiFID I impose the pre-trade transparency requirements; Article 29 establishes the general obligation to make current bid or other prices and the depth of trading interest at these prices public, which are then advertised through their systems in respect of shares admitted to trading on a regulated market. This obligation is further developed in Article 44 of MiFID I, where the competent authorities in each Member State are allowed to waive the obligation to make the information public attending to market size

47 For the clearing houses, the recognition requirements are set out on FSMA 2000 Part III and IV of the Schedule. Section 286 establishes the process of Qualification for Recognition; Section 288 Application by a clearing house.

48 EMIR Title III AUTHORISATION AND SUPERVISION OF CCPs (hereinafter EMIR Title III. A & S of CCPs) Chapter 1 Conditions and procedures for the authorisation of a CCP.

49 EMIR Article 2 Definitions defines (13) 'competent authority'.

50 Bank of England, 'The Bank of England's Approach to The Supervision of Financial Market Infrastructures' (April 2013), 5 (hereinafter the Bank's Approach to FMIs' Supervision, 2013).

51 The EC explains that reform is needed because under current supervisory arrangements for EU CCPs national authorities in the Member States where the CCP is established take the main decisions, and this is inadequate given the volume of cross-border activity by CCPs. Also, a significant volume of financial instruments denominated in the currencies of Member States are cleared by recognised CCPs in non-EU countries, and EMIR's current rules on equivalence and recognition have notorious shortcomings as regards ongoing supervision in third countries. See EC, 'Further Amendment to the European Market Infrastructure Regulation (EMIR) <https://ec.europa.eu/info/law/better-regulation/initiatives/com-2017-331_en> accessed 22nd November 2017.

52 EMIR Title III A & S of CCPs, Chapter 1, Article 17 Procedure for Granting and Refusing Authorisation.

53 EMIR Title III A & S of CCPs, Chapter 1, Article 18, College 2.

54 The Financial Services and Markets Act FSMA 2000 (Over the Counter Derivatives, Central Counterparties, and Trade Repositories) Regulations 2013. PART 4 Amendments to the Financial Services and Markets Act 2000 (Recognition Requirements for Investment Exchanges and Clearing Houses) Regulations 2001 (6).

55 FSMA 2000 Part XVIII Recognised Investment Exchanges and Clearing Houses (hereinafter FSMA Part XVIII) Section 286 (6).

56 The Commission adopts proposals for a Directive on markets in financial instruments repealing Directive 2004/39/EC of the European Parliament and of the Council, and for a Regulation on markets in financial instruments and amending Regulation [EMIR] on OTC derivatives, CCPs and TRs.

57 FSMA Part XVIII Section 290 Recognition orders (. . .) (1A). See HM Treasury-FCA (2011b), *A New Approach to Financial Regulation: The Blueprint for Reform* (n43).

reasons, as well as the adopted market model. Similarly, Article 30 considers the deferred publication of the transactions based on their type and size.

Additionally, it is first important to clarify that the FCA has, as part of its handbook, a sourcebook for recognised investment exchanges (RIEs).[58] These rules and guidance apply to recognised bodies and to applicants for recognition as RIEs under Part XVIII of FSMA 2000, under the section on 'Recognised Investment Exchanges and Clearing Houses'.[59] The handbook develops the recognition requirements set out on Part XVIII FSMA 2000. At first sight, it may be expected that these rules, initially designed for clearing houses providing services in the exchange market, would be at least partially applicable to the clearing houses operating in the OTCDM. However, this is not the case in practice; the rules that are enforced by the FCA are not applicable to CCPs in the OTCDM.

3.3.3 Prudential supervision of CCPs

Using a top-down approach, we will now examine the role of prudential supervision in the context of the stability of the entire market; later we will consider prudential regulation and the stability of individual financial firms, and, finally, conduct of business matters. Prudential supervision involves 'not only monitoring the compliance of systemically important institutions with safety and soundness standards,[60] but also evaluating whether these standards are sufficient to protect the rest of the economy adequately from financial distress in a systemically important firm'.[61] This is the macroprudential supervision seeking to limit financial system distress, in this case focused on regulating CCPs as systemically important institutions of the OTCDM.

Macroprudential supervision can be broadly defined as the 'oversight of the financial system as a whole'.[62] More specifically, it involves the 'analysis of trends and imbalances in the financial system and the detection of systemic risks'.[63] This function is generally carried out by the central bank, which in the UK is the Bank of England, and the specific delegation of this function to the FPC. The

---

58 Financial Conduct Authority (FCA) Handbook, Recognised Investment Exchanges (REC) <www.fshandbook.info/FS/html/FCA/REC> accessed 6th October 2015.
59 Financial Conduct Authority FCA Handbook, Recognised Investment Exchanges (REC) (n58) Chapter 1 1.1 Application, Ibid 2.
60 Bert Ely, 'Financial Regulation' *The Concise Encyclopedia of Economics* (2008) Library of Economics and Liberty (27 June 2013) <www.econlib.org/library/Enc/FinancialRegulation.html> accessed 15th October 2015.
61 Frederick S Mishkin, 'Prudential Supervision: Why Is It Important and What Are the Issues?' (University of Chicago 2000) <www.neber.org/chapters/c10756> accessed 31st May 2013.
62 Martin Wolf, 'Seven Ways to Fix the System's Flaws' (FT, London, 23 January 2012) <www.ft.com/cms/s/0/c80b0d2c-4377-11e1-8489-00144feab49a.html#axzz41Y0Y7ydi> accessed 15th October 2015.
63 Rosa Lastra, 'Defining Forward Looking, Judgement-Based Supervision' (July–November 2013) 14 (3/4) *Journal of Banking Regulation*.

aim is to have the overall picture of the systemic risks[64] and the interconnectedness between financial institutions.[65][66] The supervisory approach greatly relies on the information it acquires in monitoring and assessing systemic risk in financial markets. Therefore, it is important to enforce the rules on information reporting, and exercise extensive information surveillance.[67] Particularly in complex and structured markets, there is a call for sufficient disclosure of relevant matters; hence supervisors do not operate under the assumption that market discipline is enough to rule those markets.[68] Indeed, supervisors are expected to carry out a more proactive role when conducting supervision.

In coordination with the macroprudential supervision in April 2013, the Bank received the mandate to carry out the 'microprudential' supervision of FMIs,[69] among them CCPs. Microprudential supervision refers to day-to-day supervision of individual financial institutions.[70] The focus of microprudential supervision is to ensure the safety and soundness of individual institutions, which in turn contributes to achieving financial stability.

The grounds of the supervision of FMIs are closely linked to the Bank's aim to preserve financial stability. Since the goal is a sound and safe financial system by ensuring institutional stability, 'the Bank's role as supervisor is to ensure that the infrastructures are managed in a manner consistent with public interest'.[71] To this end, the Bank's aim is to ensure that FMIs' rules and policies are designed and applied to monitor, manage, and mitigate risks, especially systemic risk. Similarly, the Bank 'seeks to ensure that sufficient priority is given to continuity of key services, without systemic disruption and without recourse to public funds'.[72] The supervision regime closely follows the general objective set by the G20 to avoid creating a new class of too-important-to-fail institutions.[73]

Conducting the supervision of CCPs, the Bank has set out some KSPs, anticipating that 'its supervisory effort is based on its assessment of where risks to financial stability are greatest'.[74] Although the emphasis is on counterparty credit risk management for CCPs, in general the supervision lies on systemic risk

---

64 G30 Working Group on Macroprudential Policy Enhancing Financial Stability and Resilience: Macroprudential Policy, Tools and Systems for the Future (2010).

65 Mad Andenas, and Iris H-Y Chiu, *The Foundations and Future of Financial Regulation: Governance for Responsibility* (Routledge 2014).

66 FSA, 'The Turner Review: A Regulatory Response to the Global Banking Crisis' (March 2009).

67 Iris H-Y Chiu, 'Transparency Regulation in Financial Markets: Moving into the Surveillance Age?' (2001) 3 *European Journal of Risk and Regulation*, 303.

68 See Richard E. Mendales, 'Collateralised Explosive Devices: Why Securities Regulation Failed to Prevent the CDO Meltdown' (2009) *University of Illinois Law Review*, 1359.

69 .Bank's Approach to FMIs' Supervision, 2013 (n50), 3.

70 Rosa Lastra, 'Defining Forward Looking, Judgement-Based Supervision' (n63).

71 Ibid.

72 Bank's Approach to FMIs' Supervision, 2013 (n50), 4.

73 Jon Cunliffe, 'Speech: Is the World Financial System Safer Now?' Bank of England (17 March 2014).

74 Bank's Approach to FMIs' Supervision, 2013 (n50), 7.

management[75] through principles of: governance, management of operational risk, continuity of service, and adequate rules in case of participants' default.

The governance principle seeks that FMIs feature governance rules and decision-making processes that reflect the purpose of the institution and are consistent with the interests of the financial system as a whole. To this end, the Bank proposes a risk assessment model[76] which considers internal and external risks, the potential systemic impact, and the context. Moreover, the model includes mitigating factors divided into operational and financial mitigants, structural mitigation, and recovery and resolvability.

As a second principle, the Bank incorporates the promotion and maintenance of standards.[77] The rationale is to seek that FMIs impose standards and disciplines on individual participants, achieving the strengthening of FMIs' operations. Therefore, FMIs are expected to lead industry thinking and enhance the standards used in the market. In the view of the Bank, this process includes product standardisation[78] that occurs alongside the improvement of ISDA documentation, as a contribution tool to the management of operational risks of the CCPs.

In the process of promoting and maintaining standards during the last year, the Bank has considered the introduction of tiering arrangements across FMIs.[79] Tiering embeds the agreements whereby direct participants provide operational access to indirect participants. In the case of central clearing, tiering would allow the expansion of 'indirect clearing'. The foreseeable effect of tiering is a considerable increase in exposures between direct and indirect participants that might result in further operational dependencies.[80] Thus, the Bank has been working with CCPs to identify the potential sources of risks and related action plans to better monitor and control them.

Furthermore, the financial risk mitigants principle plays a central role in the Bank's supervision, especially the loss-absorbency rules. There are several ways to implement such rules. Therefore, the Bank takes a close interest in how supervised FMIs assess the adequacy of their loss-absorbing resources. The methodology of assessing risks must meet at least the minimum standards set out in the CPSS (now CPMI)[81]-IOSCO Principles, as well as EMIR.[82]

Additionally, the Bank supervisory approach carefully considers recovery and resolvability rules to manage the default of a participant and the potential disruption it might cause. Along with the guidance of CPMI-IOSCO and the regulation of EMIR, the Bank proposes some principles. Such principles indicate that loss-allocation rules should include comprehensive, clear, transparent, and

---

75 Ibid.
76 Ibid.
77 Ibid 8.
78 IMF, 'Making OTC Derivatives Safer: The Role of Central Counterparties' (n34).
79 *Bank's Supervision of FMIs 3rd Annual Report 2016–2017.*
80 Ibid.
81 The CPSS changed its name to the Committee on Payments and Market Infrastructures (CPMI) on 1st September 2014.
82 Bank's Approach to FMIs' Supervision, 2013 (n50), 9.

expeditious methods to allocate losses. Also, contractual procedures for the tear-up of contracts should be only used as a last-resort mechanism. Where a tear-up is used, it should be isolated to the affected clearing services, so that the CCPs' other services can in principle be maintained. Finally, the design of loss-allocation rules should be sensitive to the incentives that they provide to participants.

Moreover, the Bank establishes that, if recovery plans are not comprehensive and sufficient, 'the authorities are able to step in to resolve the FMI in a way that prevents or limits systemic disruption without calling on public funds'.[83] The Bank has the attribution to resolve a troubled CCP according to the amendments to the Banking Act 2009 done by the Financial Services Act 2012. The resolution procedure will follow the FSB's Key Attributes of Effective Resolution Regimes.

Thus, the accomplishment of the aforementioned principles in practice urges the Bank to take a comprehensive approach. With this compromise, the Bank has made clear that its supervision goes beyond assessing compliance with rules and requirements. It also includes continuous supervisory assessment and intervention, aside from active cooperation with national and overseas authorities.[84]

The principles reflect the supervisory priorities of the Bank in the first years of the regime. The Bank has issued three Annual Reports on the supervision of FMIs to assess the progress against such principles. The reports inform how the Bank has met its financial stability objective through the supervision of recognised CCPs.[85] In its first-year report, the Bank stressed that the UK CCPs have improved their risk management by introducing new and enhanced margin models.[86] Similarly, the CCPs have been working on new arrangements to allocate clearing member default losses that exceed the pre-funded resources,[87] consistent with the new UK recognition requirements that came into force in 2014.

The First Annual Report explains the progress against 2013 supervisory priorities. Accordingly, the judgement of the Bank is setting these priorities to highlight the areas in which a major effort is required from the FMIs in order to reduce risks in the system. As described in the report, this judgement and assessment is based on a risk review conducted by supervisory staff and reviewed by senior bank officials. Thus, elements of risk-based regulation, combined with judgement-based regulation, can be clearly identified in the Bank's approach to CCPs' supervision.

Moreover, to integrate the FMIs to the process of supervision and in line with international regulatory requirements,[88] the Bank includes a process of 'self-assessment' that each FMI must conduct. The process requires the evaluation of

---

83 Ibid.
84 Ibid.
85 *The Bank of England's Supervision of Financial Market Infrastructures, Annual Report* March 2014 (hereinafter *Bank's supervision of FMIs 1st Annual Report 2014*).
86 Ibid.
87 Ibid.
88 The self-assessment followed the disclosure framework and applied the assessment methodology recommended by CPMI-IOSCO.

compliance against the Principles for Financial Market Infrastructures (PFMIs). The self-assessment is a mechanism that facilitates the cooperation between FMIs and the Bank, as well as contributes to delivering more efficient supervision. The first assessments have already been published.[89]

Recognising the systemic importance of FMIs, the Bank created a new Directorate[90] that will conduct a more intense supervision. According to the Second Annual Report of March 2014, the Bank's new division is exclusively dedicated to conducting the risk-based supervision of FMIs and guiding the policy development. Additionally, the Bank stresses that a large part of the second year of supervision was focused on enhancing loss-allocation and recovery rules. The Bank's aim in developing this aspect was to put in place a regime that ensures the continuous provision of critical services, in the event that an FMI is in financial distress.

The Bank's annual reports present the progress regarding 2013 and 2014 supervisory priorities, highlighting developments related to credit and liquidity risk, recovery and resolution, operational risk management, governance, disclosure, and use of the Bank's powers. Moreover, in 2016, the IMF[91] and the Bank's own Independent Evaluation Office (IEO)[92] reviewed the supervision of FMIs, CCPs among them. Overall the Bank's oversight of CCPs was praised as a leading example for international regulators.[93]

In 2016 and 2017, the Bank proposed the implementation of two complementary sets of activities to enhance its supervisory approach: a forward-looking assessment of the risks FMIs face and a core assurance programme.[94] The adoption of these sets of activities is a remarkable advance towards a risk-based approach that continuously updates the identification and assessment of emerging risks to the firm. Besides the traditional focus on margin and default requirements, the Bank's assessment seeks to centre attention on areas of FMI operations likely to result in risks to financial stability.[95] Moreover, the core assurance programme introduces more in-depth on-site inspections and seeks to ensure FMIs' compliance with the PFMIs on a regular basis. It brings a structural review of all the critical areas affecting FMI operations. It is notable how these reforms to the Bank's supervisory approach might result in highly efficient early identification and mitigation of upcoming key risks and uncertainties.

---

89 LCH Clearnet Ltd published in June 2014, CME Clearing Europe Ltd in March 2015, LME Clear Ltd in June 2015, EuroClear UK & Ireland Ltd in May 2015.
90 *The Bank of England's Supervision of Financial Market Infrastructures, Annual Report* March 2015 (hereinafter *Bank's Supervision of FMIs 2nd Annual Report 2015*).
91 FMI, FSAP: *Supervision and Systemic Risk Management of Financial Market Infrastructures – Technical Note* IMF Country Report No 16/156 June 2016.
92 Bank of England, 'Evaluation of the BoE's Approach to FMI Supervision' Independent Evaluation Office (February 2017).
93 *The Bank of England's Supervision of FMI – Annual Report from 5th March 2016 to 22nd February 2017* (hereinafter *Bank's Supervision of FMIs 3rd Annual Report 2016–2017*).
94 *Bank's Supervision of FMIs 3rd Annual Report 2016–2017*.
95 Ibid.

3.3.3.1 *Progress in credit and liquidity risk management*

Regarding the development of credit and liquidity risk management, the Bank restates the importance of the CCPs' main function: to take and manage counterparty credit risk.[96] To this end, the CCP collects margins from its clearing members, and that margin should correspond to the amount of credit risk the CCP is managing. The attention of the supervisor in the first year of the regime was focused on the margin models and stress tests. In particular, the Bank examined the key elements of the CCP's margin and default fund calculation to ensure the CCP is sufficiently protected against potential member failure.[97]

During 2014, the Bank's concern was the assessment of initial margin (IM) models. In accordance with EMIR requirements, the Bank evaluated how the models used by CCPs to calculate IM strike an adequate balance between risk-sensitivity and pro-cyclicality.[98] This balance ensures that if market conditions change, the CCP will have enough resources to manage losses without the need to alter IM requirements, which in turn might affect the liquidity of clearing members. Moreover, the Bank conducted the supervision to assess whether the UK CCPs have sized their default funds to ensure it is enough to absorb the losses arising from the default of its two largest members in 'extreme-but-plausible' market conditions. The default fund is comprised by IM, a default fund, and a contribution of the CCPs' own capital.

As noted, the Bank implements the parameter of 'extreme-but-plausible' market conditions. This parameter is developed through stress tests that are based upon hypothetical scenarios. CCPs design their own stress tests and the Bank only analyses the suitability of the scenarios that CCPs include in their tests.[99] In contrast to the stress tests of Banks, the CCP stress tests are not uniform. The Bank view is that CCPs conduct their business in many different markets and with different types of transactions – therefore, standardised stress test for CCPs would be a futile exercise.[100] Nonetheless, at the international level, CPMI-IOSCO is developing additional regulatory guidance on the design of standardised CCPs stress test, as a means of enabling regulators to compare the resilience of CCPs. In early 2016, ESMA published its first multi-jurisdiction supervisory tests of CCPs, concluding that EU CCPs – including the four based in London – would be sufficiently resilient to extreme-but-plausible market conditions.[101] The

---

96 *Bank's Supervision of FMIs 1st Annual Report 2014.*
97 'The two largest UK CCPs have made a number of significant enhancements to their margin methodologies since the PSOR was published in 2013'. Ibid.
98 *Bank's Supervision of FMIs 2nd Annual Report 2015.*
99 Ibid.
100 Interview with Mr Paul Brione Head of Central Counterparty Supervision, Bank of England, London, 25th September 2015.
101 ESMA, 'EU-wide CCP Stress test 2015' (Report 2016/658) (29 April 2016) <www.esma.europa.eu/sites/default/files/library/2016-658_ccp_stress_test_report_2015.pdf> accessed 7th December 2017.

2017 stress test results, which engaged multiple regulators (among them the Bank),[102] and include a different methodology,[103] have not yet been published.

The CFTC also conducted a stress test exercise[104] on five CCPs registered with them, among them two supervised by the Bank (i.e. LCH and ICE Clear Europe). The results found that both met and even exceeded required resiliency levels.

Finally, the Bank reports that, in seeking to enhance the mechanisms CCPs use to manage liquidity and credit risk, it will allow them to participate in its Sterling Monetary Framework (SMF).[105] The participating CCPs will have sterling reserve accounts at the Bank, access to operational sterling facilities, and access to sterling liquidity insurance.

After completing the 2016 assessment, the Bank's review confirmed that CCPs have adequate liquidity frameworks, albeit with potential for improvement. The area of concern is finding alternatives to further mitigate risks associated with investment margin.[106]

3.3.3.2 Progress in recovery and resolution rules

Regarding the recovery and resolution of CCPs, the Bank required all supervised FMIs to work on developing recovery plans. The importance of this regime lies on the systemic consequences of a CCP's failure – implementing effective loss-allocation rules to protect the CCPs is a key part of ending the concerns regarding the 'too-big-to-fail' character of these institutions. Moreover, this regime seeks to ensure the continuity of CCPs' services even in times of financial distress. Although the majority of the losses suffered by a CCP come from members' default, it is equally important to develop loss-allocation arrangements for non-default losses.

Here, the Bank reported some advances following the reform of FSMA introduced in July 2013. In particular, the reform imposed the obligation on UK CCPs to maintain recovery plans from 1st February 2014 in order to meet the new recognition requirements. Moreover, CCPs are required to have in place rules to allocate the losses in the event of a clearing member's default. Similarly, the Bank took this opportunity to go beyond the EMIR regime by requiring

---

102 *Bank's Supervision of FMIs 3rd Annual Report 2016–2017.*

103 ESMA, '2017 EU-wide CCP Stress Test Exercise' (Methodological ESMA70–708036 281–51) (1 February 2017) <www.esma.europa.eu/sites/default/files/library/esma70-708036281-51_public_framework_2017_ccp_stress_test_exercise.pdf> accessed 7th December 2017.

104 CFTC, 'Supervisory Stress Test of Clearinghouses' November 2016 <www.cftc.gov/idc/groups/public/@newsroom/documents/file/cftcstresstest111516.pdf> accessed 7th December 2017.

105 Bank of England Press Release, 'European Central Bank (ECB) location policy for Central Counterparties (CCPs)' (4 March 2015) <www.bankofengland.co.uk/publications/Pages/news/2015/036.aspx> accessed 16th October 2015.

106 *Bank's Supervision of FMIs 3rd Annual Report 2016–2017.*

that by May 2014 CCPs must put arrangements in place to allocate non-default losses. These are the losses that might threaten the solvency of the CCP and are not caused by clearing members' default.

Furthermore, some legislative changes took place in 2014. The resolution regime contained in the Banking Act 2009 was extended to include CCPs. In July 2014, the HM Treasury issued secondary legislation that gave powers to the Bank to resolve a failing CCP. Although it was expected that the European Commission would issue legislation or guidance on CCP resolution, there has not been any progress.

During 2016, the Bank conducted a review of CCPs recovery plans. Breaking with its initial approach, the Bank accepts that a CCP resolution event cannot be ruled out. It highlighted the importance of the role of crisis management groups (CMGs) in providing a framework for authorities to plan CCPs' orderly resolution. Accordingly, acting in its capacity as resolution authority, the Bank established two CMGs for ICEU in 2016 and for LCH in 2015.

Regarding the national and international development of regulation for CCPs' recovery and resolution, the Bank continues to play a central role. The Bank has actively participated in the discussion led by the FSB[107] on the issues affecting the development of resolution plans for CCPs. The latest FSB guidance[108] is focused on five features: the point of entry to resolution, the tools available to a resolution authority, allocating losses to equity holders in resolution, CMGs, and the adequacy of financial resources.

3.3.3.3 Progress in operational risk management

Regarding the operational risk management, the Bank's work has been focused on ensuring operational resilience.[109] This is the management of 'cyber risk' by controlling any attempt to penetrate, shut down, or manipulate FMIs' computer systems. To that end, the Bank has been implementing a programme to act against cyber-attacks.[110] The programme includes enhancing understanding of the threat to the financial sector, strengthening work to assess the sector's current resilience to cyber-attacks, developing plans to test the resilience of the sector, and improving the sharing of information.[111]

Ensuring operational resilience of CCPs is a key area of focus for 2017.[112] The Bank seeks to enhance the system of assessment of CCPs' IT infrastructure,

---

107 FSB, 'Essential Aspects of CCP Resolution Planning Discussion Note' 16 August 2016 <www.fsb.org/wp-content/uploads/Essential-Aspects-of-CCP-Resolution-Planning.pdf> accessed 7th December 2017.

108 FSB, 'Guidance on Central Counterparty Resolution and Resolution Planning' 5 July 2017 <www.fsb.org/wp-content/uploads/P050717-1.pdf> accessed 7th December 2017.

109 *Bank's Supervision of FMIs 2nd Annual Report 2015.*

110 *Bank's Supervision of FMIs 1st Annual Report 2014.*

111 Ibid.

112 *Bank's Supervision of FMIs 3rd Annual Report 2016–2017.*

aiming at ensuring such infrastructure is resilient to the changes and operational outages.

The FCA – in collaboration with the Bank – leads the supervisory work on the most recent developments in FinTech and Distributed Ledger Technology (DLT). The progress is reflected in the collaboration among regulators, financial services firms, and technology firms. All of them have analysed the multiple uses of DLT, smart contracts, and blockchain as innovations changing capital markets. Although the efficiency of the current regime will only be tested in the coming years, the most recent FCA report suggests that current rules are flexible enough to regulate applications of various technologies in the financial system.[113]

3.3.3.4 Lack of progress in governance

The annual reports of 2014 and 2015 reveal the limited progress made in the supervision of CCP governance. The only advancement was the conformation of board risk committees composed of representatives of clearing members and clients. The primary task of these risk committees is to advise the CCP's board on any measures that might have an impact in the risk management of the CCP.

Although the Bank recognises that CCP governance is a supervisory priority, the regime does not include any rules regarding the quality of that governance.[114] Such a regime needs to consider the potential conflicts between the CCPs' commercial objectives and their role in systemic risk management. Some of the shortcomings of the UK regime of CCPs in the OTCDM allude to the need to enhance the governance of CCPs.

In 2016, some small progress took place, as the Bank's review focused on the structure and composition of CCPs' boards.[115] The resulting recommendation was to increase the number of independent directors.

3.3.3.5 Progress in disclosure

The advance in terms of disclosure is an important step towards enhancing the transparency of the OTCDM. Experience over the past three years shows that CCPs are working to meet the requirements of the CPMI-IOSCO Disclosure Framework. The aim is to improve the quality and quantity of the information available to stakeholders. In particular, supervisors are interested in assessing the information about the functioning of FMIs and the level of compliance with the

---

113 FCA, 'Distributed Ledger Technology Feedback Statement on Discussion Paper (17/03 December 2017) <www.fca.org.uk/publication/feedback/fs17-04.pdf?utm_source=Trig germail&utm_medium=email&utm_campaign=Post%20Blast%20%28bii-fintech%29:%20 Allianz%20invests%20%2496%20million%20in%20an%20insurtech%20–%20Regulators%20 speak%20out%20on%20DLT%20rules%20-%20JPMorgan%20Chase%20to%20launch%20a %20robo-advisor&utm_term=BII%20List%20Fintech%20ALL> accessed 28th December 2017.
114 *BoE's Supervision of FMIs 2nd Annual Report 2015.*
115 *Bank's Supervision of FMIs 3rd Annual Report 2016–2017.*

PFMIs. The first self-assessments were published during 2014 and 2015. Similarly, CCPs have published Accounts Disclosure Documents according to Article 39 of EMIR.

3.3.3.6 *Enforcement powers of the Bank of England*

Finally, the Bank restates that, according to the regulation contained in the FSMA 2000 and the Banking Act 2009, the Bank has the power to require FMIs to provide information, commission independent reports, make on-site inspections, require changes to FMIs' rules, and give directions.

In exercising these powers, the Bank is required by the FSMA 2000 to publish certain statements of procedure relating to the decisions resulting in statutory notices and publishing details of these statutory notices. Accordingly, in September 2013, the Bank issued a consultation paper on the proposed statutory statements of procedure in respect of the Bank's supervision of financial market infrastructures.[116] In this document, the Bank proposed the decision-making framework for giving warning notices and decision notices in the course of the Bank's supervision of recognised clearing houses.[117]

By establishing a multi-tier structure, the proposed decision-making process aims to ensure that a supervisory team of experts have the guidance and advice of senior bank officials. Decisions will be taken at different levels, depending on the impact, and will involve representatives from different areas of the Bank. There will be two decision-making committees responsible for issuing statutory notices: the Financial Market Infrastructure Board and the Financial Market Infrastructure Review Committee. The FMI board members are part of the Bank's executive management structure and are chaired by the deputy governor for financial stability. The FMI Review Committee consists of representatives from various areas of the Bank and is chaired by the executive director for financial stability.

The decision-making committees will seek to reach a consensus on the decisions. However, when a consensus is not possible, they will vote. In order to support effective decision-making, the Bank has categorised the FMIs to be under its supervision. Category One includes those FMIs which pose the greatest risks to financial stability in the event of disruption or failure, whilst Category Two captures the remainder. This classification is other indicia to demonstrate that the Bank is implementing the risk-based approach to regulation in the sense of prioritising regulatory actions according to the level of risk of regulated firms.

The Bank develops the procedure of decision-making by considering two types of notices: the warning notice and the decision notice. Before explaining how

---

116 Bank of England, 'Proposed Statutory Statements of Procedure in Respect of the Bank's Supervision of Financial Market Infrastructures' BoE, Consultation Paper (September 2013).

117 FSMA s 395 requires the Bank to establish a decision-making procedure for statutory notice decisions that is designed to ensure, amongst other things, that at least one of the decision-makers has not been directly involved in establishing the evidence on which the decision is based.

each of them works, it is important to recognise the warning notice as a demonstration of the judgement-based regulation and the early stage intervention powers of regulators. As we will see, the warning notice procedure is how the Bank issues pre-empting communication when suspicious actions have been identified in supervising the firm.

The warning notices regime provides that, if Bank staff believe that action requiring a warning notice is appropriate, they will recommend to the relevant decision-making committee to give the notice. In taking the decision, the committee will consider whether the recommendation is appropriately supported, as well as the responses received from the FCA in light of the MoU between the Bank and the FCA, and decide whether to give notice according to the requirements of Section 387 FSMA 2000.

Once the warning notice has been released, there will be a specific time, of no less than 14 calendar days, to make representations. The period may be extended by request. The recipient of the warning notice and third parties are entitled to make representations and respond to points made by the decision-making committee.

Similarly, the decision notices regime prescribes that the committee will review the material before them, consider the representations and comments made by Bank staff, and issue the decision notice, meeting the requirements of Section 388 FSMA 2000. In the decision notice, the Bank will include a brief summary of how it has dealt with the key representations made and make any other decision related to the statutory notice.

Additionally, the proposal includes the 'further decision notice' – before the Bank takes action, it may give notice relating to a different action concerning the same matter, conditioned to the recipient's consent.

According to Section 395 of FSMA 2000, the Bank must publish information about statutory notice decisions in the course of the Bank's supervision. This would assist the achievement of the Bank's supervisory goals – for example, 'by informing the financial services industry of behaviour on the part of the relevant body which the Bank considers unacceptable'.[118] This attribution could be considered as an early intervention mechanism in front of the risks posed by specific firms, which is an element of the risk-based approach to regulation. Indeed, the factors the Bank will consider when deciding whether to publish or not include the potential advancement of its supervisory goals, enhancement of financial stability, providing a signal to relevant bodies as to the types of behaviour it considers being unacceptable, and preventing more widespread breaches of its requirements.

Another development of the Bank's CCP supervision is the policy statement giving directions to qualified parent undertakings of UK recognised clearing houses. The analysis of this policy is beyond the scope of this study.

Finally, closely related to the Bank's role as CCPs' supervisor are the challenges posed by the UK's withdrawal from the EU.[119] In particular, the requirement

---

118 FSMA s 395.
119 *Bank's Supervision of FMIs 3rd Annual Report 2016–2017.*

to have in place the necessary arrangements for providing cross-border clearing services. The Bank is committed to fostering cooperation with EU supervisors to ensure that CCPs are able to continue to provide services to EU counterparties, as well as to identify and mitigate the risks triggered by Brexit.

3.3.3.7 *The role of the Principles for Financial Market Infrastructures (PFMIs)*

The Bank's approach to FMI supervision is guided by the international CPMI-IOSCO PFMIs.[120] These principles refer to the management of risks faced by FMIs including credit, liquidity, operational and legal risks, as well as governance, default management, and transparency. The PFMIs were designed to ensure that the infrastructure supporting global financial markets is 'more robust and thus well placed to withstand financial shocks'.[121] In light of that premise, the Bank is focusing intervention on the areas that represent a clear threat to stability and will accordingly exercise its enforcement powers.[122]

Although the Bank repeatedly insists that the PFMIs are at the core of supervision of CCPs, in fact, they are only parameters that illustrate how supervision is conducted to foster financial stability. The principles published in April 2012 seek to harmonise and strengthen the existing international standards for FMIs and, within them, CCPs. The PFMIs incorporate specific minimum requirements to ensure a common base level of risk management across FMIs and countries,[123] but each jurisdiction is expected to further develop the rules that materialise the principles.

Moreover, the PFMIs establish a series of responsibilities of central banks, market regulators, and other relevant authorities for financial market infrastructures. The primary responsibility is to incorporate these principles and their responsibilities in their own regulatory framework. Once they have been incorporated, central banks and regulators are expected to follow up the implementation, use, and assessment of observance of such principles by the FMI. That stage of assessment is further assisted by the CPMI-IOSCO Assessment Methodology that provides guidance for assessing and monitoring compliance. The Assessment Methodology is a useful tool for FMI when self-evaluating its performance in front of the principles; it also helps regulators to evaluate the way they discharge their own responsibilities as regulators and supervisors.

3.3.3.8 *Summary of the Bank of England supervision*

To sum up, the Bank's supervisory regime is constructed upon the objective of CCP robustness. In so doing, the Bank has built a system of rules focused

---

120 'CPMI-IOSCO Principles of Financial Market Infrastructures' <www.bis.org/publ/cpss101a.pdf> accessed 22nd May 2013 (hereinafter CPMI-IOSCO PFMI).
121 Ibid.
122 Emma Murphy, 'Changes to the Bank of England' (Bank of England, Quarterly Bulletin Q1, 2013), 26.
123 CPMI-IOSCO PFMI, 12.

on the management of credit, liquidity, and operational risks. From the Bank's perspective, the safety and soundness of CCPs is achieved by means of prudential supervision. Therefore, the strengthening of loss-allocation and recovery rules has occupied the Bank's attention in the first years of the regime.

It is also notable that the Bank, in implementing the risk-based approach to regulation, is prioritising its intervention in certain areas – those which the Bank considers to represent a threat to the achievement of its objectives. As a result, other areas of supervision have not been sufficiently developed, such as governance, disclosure, and resolvability of CCPs. In light of these shortcomings, we will now explore in the next section and Chapters 4 and 5 the weaknesses of the UK CCP regime in the OTCDM.

3.4 Shortcomings of the UK regime of CCPs in the OTCDM

In the introduction to this chapter, we promised to organise the analysis of the CCPs regime following the two stems of risk-based regulation: prudential supervision and conduct of business. However, this poses a problem, as after exploring the prudential supervision conducted by the Bank, it has become clear that, in fact, there is no conduct of business regulation in place. This is the first and key weakness of the UK's CCP regime in the OTCDM.

3.4.1 The absence of a coherent conduct of business regime for CCPs

The FCA is responsible for regulating conduct in retail and wholesale markets (including both exchange-operated markets and OTC dealing), as well as for supervising the trading infrastructure that supports those markets. However, the FCA has not designed a regime of conduct of business for CCPs, which are part of the post-trading market infrastructure of the OTCDM. We would argue that this is because the FCA's mandate has been misinterpreted and that the Bank, the FCA, and the CCPs themselves have all inaccurately believed that the Bank is the only CCP regulator. In the interviews conducted during the course of this research with all of these parties, it became clear that none of them were aware of the conduct of business regulation and supervision, and who should be in charge of it. The problem concerning the lack of a conduct of business regime for CCPs goes beyond the lack of design; it also affects the exercise of enforcement powers. Under the current regime, it is not clear whether the Bank could sanction a CCP for the breach of a conduct of business rule.

In order to explain this shortcoming, in this section we will address several questions concerning the limited role that the existing rules of conduct of business have in the UK's CCP regime and how a coherent regime should be further developed: firstly, we argue that the FCA should be the conduct regulator of CCPs in the OTCDM. Secondly, we must consider the importance of having a conduct of business regime and the issues it would solve. Finally, we recommend the necessary elements that such a regime would have, including consumer protection and competition.

3.4.1.1 The FCA must play a role

The FCA is responsible for regulating conduct in retail and wholesale markets (including both exchange-operated markets and OTC dealing), supervising the trading infrastructure that supports those markets, and for prudential regulation of firms not prudentially regulated by the PRA.

Even though the regulation and supervision of clearing and settlement systems (trading infrastructure), including CCPs, was expressly assigned to the Bank, it has been stated that in its supervision the Bank will work closely with the FCA, reflecting the FCA's responsibilities for the trading infrastructure and market product.[124] Accordingly, in the MoU between the Bank, the FCA, and the PRA:

> FCA is responsible for regulation of organised financial markets including RIEs and other trading platforms, and the conduct of participants in relation to the financial instruments and derivatives contracts trades both on those markets and in the OTC financial markets.

A comprehensive interpretation of this mandate leads us to conclude that the FCA carries out the conduct of business of the OTC derivatives participants, including CCPs. It then follows that the FCA will design the conduct of business regime for CCPs, and then supervise (in coordination with the Bank), the compliance of such rules through a toolkit of enforcement powers. However, in practice this is not the case.

An alternative interpretation prevalent amongst UK authorities is that the only regulator and supervisor of the CCPs in the OTCDM is the Bank of England, and that the FCA supervision of OTCDM participants does not include CCPs – in other words, that CCPs are not 'OTCDM participants', and therefore are not supervised by the FCA in any matter. Following this interpretation, the Bank would be the prudential *and* conduct of business supervisor. However, the first stumble of this interpretation is that the Bank is not a conduct supervisor – this is not part of the Bank's mandate.

Even accepting the second interpretation of the mandates – that the FCA has no supervisory functions over the CCPs in the OTCDM – the critique regarding the absence of a conduct of business regime remains. Irrespective of the authority responsible to implement conduct rules, the UK regime of CCPs in the OTCDM is fractured.

Our findings are supported by the interviews conducted at a CCP operating in London, CME Clearing Europe Ltd,[125] and officials of the FCA[126] and the Bank, all of whom were questioned about the role of the FCA as conduct of business supervisor of CCPs. The responses were different in each of the three cases.

---

124 Two MoUs between the FCA and the Bank of England, including the PRA.
125 Interview Grant Elliot (Senior Analyst Clearing and Business Development), Matthew Gravelle (Government Relations Team) and Huong Auduc (Legal Department) CME Clearing Europe Ltd, London (12 June 2014).
126 Heather Pilley, 'Technical Specialist, Derivatives Reform Team, FCA', Phone Interview (19 August 2015).

Our path to discovering the issues concerning the conduct of business rules for CCPs began with the first interview, conducted at CME Clearing Europe Ltd. The staff members interviewed clearly stated that the only UK authority overseeing the CCPs' operation in the national OTCDM was the Bank. Moreover, when questioned about the parameters of conduct they follow in providing their services, they made reference to internal Codes of Conduct and Corporate Governance. Even so, this study recognises the important role that self-regulation instruments have in the CCPs regime: state regulation and concomitant supervision are fundamental to ensure compliance. As the interview was conducted in the first year of regime implementation, the preliminary conclusion was to understand that the FCA would issue a conduct of business regime during the next year.

Later on, we undertook a second interview at the FCA, after the second year of regime implementation. This time, when we asked about the role of the FCA in front of CCPs in the OTCDM, the interviewee explained that the Bank definitely has the leading role in supervising CCPs; however, the FCA is very much involved with CCPs' work through two mechanisms. Firstly, the FCA participates in the EMIR College of Supervisors; this follows the EMIR mandate that, for each EU-based CCP, a college of supervisors will be established that is made up of relevant national regulators and ESMA; these colleges are responsible for authorising and supervising EU CCPs. Although this part of the answer seems to be confusing and suggests that the FCA is indeed acting as a supervisor of CCPs, Article 18 of EMIR[127] helps to clarify why the FCA participates in these colleges. The FCA is responsible for the supervision of clearing members; hence, besides the CCPs' competent authority (which in the UK is the Bank), the FCA sits in the college of supervisors, but in its capacity as clearing members' supervisor. This is one of the first aspects that delimits this research, which is exclusively devoted to the study of the regulation and supervision of CCPs; clearing members' supervision is beyond the scope of this book.

Secondly, the FCA actively conducts the supervision of what is called 'client clearing',[128] which is the method that allows non-clearing members to have the benefits of clearing. According to the FCA, this is a conduct matter, to do with how clearing members deal with their clients. Therefore, according to the FCA, its role in the OTCDM is supervising the conduct of clearing members and their clients. However, the issue remains, because the client clearing regime is part of the supervision of clearing members, and not the supervision of the CCPs.

The scenario of uncleared derivatives is different altogether; this is the category of transactions that are not subject to the clearing obligation. The FCA has an important role for the uncleared derivatives, along with the PRA. Therefore, once the definitive uncleared derivatives regime is in place, the implementation

---

127 EMIR Title III Authorisation and Supervision of CCPs. Chapter 1 Conditions and procedures for the authorisation of a CCP. Article 18. College.
128 FCA Seminar (July 2015) <www.fca.org.uk/static/documents/emir-obligation-clear-mar gin-otc-derivative-trades.pdf> accessed 6th October 2015.

will fall mostly on the PRA for their regulated firms, and in the FCA for the solely regulated firms, whilst the Bank would be looking at this part of the market for systemic risk matters. In this part of the OTC market, it is perfectly clear that the three authorities will be involved, albeit in slightly different ways.

Our third interview was conducted at the Bank.[129] This confirmed the confusion surrounding the implementation of the conduct of business supervision of CCPs in the OTCDM. In particular, we drew two conclusions: firstly, the Bank is completely focused on the prudential supervision of CCPs. From the Bank's perspective, CCPs' standards of conduct are not areas that pose a significant threat to the Bank's regulatory objectives and, therefore, the conduct of business supervision is not a priority. This finding has profound implications concerning risk-based regimes. It means that the process of risk identification and allocation of sources is leading regulators to prioritise prudential supervision over conduct of business in the case of the CCPs regime in the OTCDM. The inevitable conclusion is that the use of a risk-based approach in the CCPs regime in the OTCDM is fracturing the UK regulation and supervision. The shortcoming consists of breaking the balance between the two stems of the risk-based approach: prudential supervision and conduct of business. Our concern is that the Bank is privileging the prudential regulation of CCPs, while overlooking the importance of conduct rules, and as a result the UK does not have a conduct of business regime for CCPs in the OTCDM.

Our second conclusion is that the Bank reaffirms its position as the only supervisor of CCPs and in practice the FCA has no direct role in terms of conduct of business supervision. In the hypothetical event that a CCP breaches a typical conduct rule – for instance, client asset management – the Bank would be the authority expected to impose sanctions. However, we would argue that this is not clear whatsoever, in light of a mandate wherein the Bank is the CCP regulator. Moreover, regarding conduct of business, the only existing rules are the provisions of the European Regulation EMIR. This situation demonstrates the notorious poor, secondary role that conduct of business has in the current UK's CCP regime. The Bank monitors whether CCPs observe the conduct rules of EMIR, but it has not developed any further regulation. Although it is true that EMIR is directly applicable in the UK, at least until March 2019, it is also true that EMIR is a guide, and that national competent authorities are entitled to further develop rules and carry out their domestic implementation. Neither the Bank, nor much less the FCA, have focused their regulatory attention on developing the conduct of business standards for CCPs in the OTCDM.

To sum up, the lack of clarity concerning the conduct of business regime for CCPs in the OTCDM in the UK has longstanding implications. It reveals that the regime is affected by two drawbacks of the risk-based approach to regulation: the absence of organisational culture UK regime of CCPs in implementing

---

129 Interview with Mr Paul Brione Head of Central Counterparty Supervision, Bank of England, London (25 September 2015).

risk-based regimes; and the use of risk-based regulation is creating manufactured risks, because it has allowed prioritisation of prudential matters over conduct of business. The inconsistency of the regime shows that the risk-based approach to regulation is not effectively assisting the supervision of CCPs in the OTCDM. The rationale of adopting an approach to regulation is to have a 'route-map' that will guide the way regulation and supervision are conducted. However, the findings of this research show that no such route-map exists in the case of the UK's CCP regime in the OTCDM, because one of the pillars of the risk-based approach – the conduct of business – is missing. Lewis Carroll illustrates this predicament for us perfectly: 'If you don't know where you're going, any road will get you there'.[130] UK regulators know and hope that CCPs will make OTCDM safer, and therefore regulation must ensure the robustness, safety, and soundness of the CCPs. To that end, regulators chose to follow an approach to regulation that integrates prudential and conduct areas, but when designing and implementing the regime, they decided to take a step back from the original route-map, confident that they would achieve the same outcome. If the UK regime is guided by risk-based regulation, but in practice is being partially implemented, the approach is not serving its purpose; the partial route-map will not lead us to the required destination. As a result, the Bank as regulator is judiciously supervising the most urgent needs of the market, seeking to ensure the safety and soundness of CCPs in the OTCDM, while deliberately overlooking that the robustness of CCPs should be built upon conduct of business rules, as well as prudential ones. It seems that regulators are aware that conduct of business should be part of the regime but decided to prioritise the prudential regulation.

Additionally, the lack of clarity about the conduct of business regime for CCPs in the OTCDM causes us to question the effectiveness of regulators' enforcement powers. The Bank's enforcement powers, as explained before, allow it to require CCPs to provide information, commission independent reports, make on-site inspections, require changes to CCP's rules, and give directions. However, the absence of a conduct of business regime prompts confusion about the role that the Bank or the FCA[131] would play in the event of a breach of the EMIR conduct standards. This fundamentally creates doubt about how the system of enforcement would work.

In other words, we cannot with certainty assume that the Bank, as the only regulator of CCPs in the OTCDM, could use its enforcement powers in an event of non-compliance of conduct of business standards, especially because the Bank does not have the mandate of a conduct regulator.[132] Neither is it certain to that the FCA is the competent authority to enforce conduct standards, because the FCA is not supervising CCPs in the OTCDM.

---

130 Lewis Carroll *Alice's Adventures in Wonderland* (Macmillan 1865).
131 Lista M. Cannon, and Paul Adams, 'Twin Peaks Regulation' (2012) 162 *National Law Journal*, 440. (Emphasis added).
132 HM Treasury, *A New Approach to Financial Regulation: The Blueprint for Reform* (n43), 5.

3.4.1.2 Why do CCPs need a conduct of business regime?

The second part of this section addresses the importance of a conduct of business regime for CCPs in the OTCDM. If the most notorious concerns surrounding the CCPs functioning in the OTCDM are resilience, safety, and soundness, and if these objectives can be achieved to a great extent by means of prudential rules, then the question is: why is the conduct of business regime of CCPs in the OTCDM needed, and why should it be developed by UK regulators?

The first part of the answer is in the role that CCPs have in the OTCDM. This is different from the role they play in exchange markets: in the OTCDM, CCPs are particularly focused on credit risk management.[133] As explained before, CCPs replace the traditional bilateral structure of OTC derivatives transactions. A CCP imposes itself as the new counterparty for the two initial counterparties. This change in structure means that there are contractual arrangements between the CCP and the clearing members; these arrangements are ruled by contracts and mainly by CCPs' rulebooks. This study argues that there are certain elements of that relationship between the CCPs and clearing members that could be overseen by means of conduct of business rules; in particular, the extent that the term 'consumer' in the broadest sense could include clearing members, and so, as a result, they would be subject to a consumer protection regime.

There must be a consumer protection regime that includes clearing members, because the content of the CCPs' rulebooks heavily benefits the contractual position of CCPs. For instance, the limitation of CCPs' liability reflects how some clauses of CCPs' rulebooks greatly undermine the contractual rights of clearing members. Regulators privilege the CCPs' capacity to rule their own contracts in these 'unfair' terms, on the basis that allowing it contributes to the robustness of the CCP. Therefore, a consumer protection regime would help to correct the imbalance[134] in the relationship between CCPs and clearing members.

Similarly, the UK regime of CCPs in the OTCDM would benefit from protecting consumers. After the GFC[135] there has been an increasing recognition of the relevance that consumer protection has in capital markets regulation. It has been argued that 'capital markets require transparency, fairness, equal access, competition and investment soundness'.[136] In this sense, the reforms to the UK regime

---

133 Gregory, *Central Counterparties: Mandatory Clearing and Bilateral Margin Requirements for OTC Derivatives* (n12), 37.

134 See Justin O'Brien, and George Gilligan, 'Culture and the Future of Financial Regulation: How to Embed Restraint in the Interests of Systemic Stability' (2014) 8 (2) *Law and Financial Markets Review*, 115–127 See S. Miller, *The Moral Foundations of Social Institutions: A Philosophical Study* (Cambridge University Press, 2010).

135 Alexander Stöhr, 'Approaches to Financial Regulation in View of the Crisis: Report About the 34th Meeting of the German Comparative Law Society' (2015) 23 (1) *Journal of Financial Regulation and Compliance*, 73–83.

136 Rosa Lastra, and Andrea Miglionico, 'The House of Lords Report on the Post-Crisis EU Regulatory Framework: Where Does the UK Stand?' (2015) 5 *Journal of International Banking and Financial Law*, 303B 2.

should grant authorities with greater powers to intervene in the market. The exercise of powers should not be restricted to prudential supervision, but also to further develop the conduct of business rules through consumer protection.[137]

A second reason highlighting the relevance of conduct of business regime is the potential issue regarding competition originating among CCPs. There are competition issues that might adversely affect the growth of OTCDM; for instance, the concentration of the market.[138] As we will go on to explain, there are certain market practices of CCPs that will need to be regulated in the UK.

However, the challenge is to justify the need for a special regime of conduct of business for CCPs in the OTCDM, while general consumer protection and competition law can help to solve the respective issues triggered in the market. This rationale goes back to the issues affecting the conduct of business regulation in general. MacNeil[139] categorises such issues, saying that the scope of conduct of business is limited, because it is trying to do what can be done with general law. Furthermore, it is unclear what relationship conduct of business rules might have with ethics. Such a high level of complexity prevents conduct of business regulation to be effectively applied. Thus, it could be argued that these issues are transmitted to the CCPs' conduct of business regimes, and that laws of consumer protection and competition provide enough regulation to solve these matters. However, the primary reason to argue for a further development of conduct of business rules lies in the recognition of the potential problems that can affect the functioning of the CCPs and their relationship with clearing members and their clients. Certainly, a special regime would not exclude or replace the use of general rules; instead it will reinforce it. Such a regime will promote the design and implementation of a body of regulation that attends to the needs arising from CCPs' legal status as market infrastructures, and in turn it will contribute to ensure the robustness of these institutions, which is in the interest of UK regulators. Contrary to the opinion that fragmentation does little to promote the clear and consistent development of standard market practices,[140] we would argue that a special regime of conduct of business for CCPs in the OTCDM will *enhance* the functioning of the market.

Moreover, we recognise that a special conduct of business regime for CCP would not necessarily extend the enforcement powers of the FCA as conduct regulator. This is to accept that other authorities (for instance, the Competition and Markets Authority (CMA)) and courts will continue to solve matters related to conduct of business violations, issues concerning consumer protection, unfair

---

137 See Howard Davies, 'Why Regulate?' *FSA*, Speech (4 November 1998) <www.fsa.gov.uk/Pages/Library/Communication/Speeches/1998/sp19.shtml> accessed 25th January 2016.

138 FCA, 'Wholesale Sector Competition Review 2014–15' *FCA* (February 2015) 94 <www.fca.org.uk/static/documents/feedback-statements/fs15-02.pdf> accessed 12th October 2015.

139 Iain MacNeil, 'Rethinking Conduct Regulation' (2015) 7 *Journal of International Banking and Financial Law*, 413.

140 Ibid 418.

contract terms, competition, and so on. Instead, the FCA will design and implement standards of conduct relevant to the role CCPs play in the OTCDM, and will have efficient enforcement tools. This argument reinstates the importance of the mandate that the FCA has as conduct regulator of financial markets. The FCA has sufficient knowledge of the particularities and dynamics of conduct in each of the regulated firms and markets, and that places the FCA in a special position to enforce conduct of business standards in financial markets, regardless of the other instances and authorities where some of the conduct issues can be solved.

3.4.1.3 *Morphology of a conduct of business regime for CCPs*

We will now address the question concerning what a conduct of business regime for CCPs in the OTCDM would look like. The aim is to consider some of the elements that are particularly relevant to the regulation of conduct of CCPs in the OTCDM. To build up the proposal, we have considered the UK conduct of business rules, and the creation of the FCA, to understand what conduct of business entails, and the conduct of business rules of the EMIR that are directly applicable to CCPs recognised and authorised in the UK.

3.4.1.3.1 CONSUMER PROTECTION

Financial regulators are working on the development of regimes that require regulated firms to follow certain standards of conduct when carrying out their business. This means that the pillar of conduct of business is developed along with prudential regulation. As we have seen, conduct of business is also a fundamental part of risk-based regimes. However, there is no single definition of what conduct of business means; in each jurisdiction, regulators design standards of conduct that mostly include consumer protection, market conduct rules, and some minimal ethical codes of conduct.[141]

The history of the conduct of business in the UK[142] combines statutory and self-regulation elements. Although a detailed description of the regulatory evolution is not the purpose of this section, it is important to highlight the dynamics of the conduct of business regime in the history of the UK financial system.[143] The interest in regulating conduct of market participants can be traced back to

---

141 In an attempt to understand what 'conduct of business' includes, the firm Norton Rose published a document that, although it is centred on the insurance market, is illustrative about the identifiable elements of this part of the regulatory approach <www.nortonrose fulbright.com/knowledge/publications/115387/beyond-law-understanding-the-scope-of-conduct-regulation> accessed 6th October 2015.

142 George Gilligan, 'The Origins of UK Financial Services Regulation' (1997) 18 (6) *The Company Lawyer*, 167–176, 1997 <http://ssrn.com/abstract=2213218> accessed 24th October 2015.

143 For a historic study about the patterns of the UK financial regulation and how they have emerged repeatedly, see Ibid.

1967.[144] However, the first call for a formal[145] conduct of business regime[146] appeared when it was recognised that the application of fiduciary law was simply too unclear to provide firms with the certainty as to their duties and obligations which they needed in order to function efficiently.[147] As common law could not provide this certainty, it is reported that the Council for the Securities Industry (CSI) and the Stock Exchange introduced their codes for conflicts of interest in 1984; however, there were concerns regarding the legitimacy and the use of self-regulatory instruments to rule conflicts of interest. After a long process of regulatory and institutional reforms, the FSMA of 1986 conferred wide regulatory powers to the Securities and Investments Board (SIB). The SIB issued some conduct of business rules[148] applicable to, among other firms, recognised clearing houses. However, the Companies Act 1989 altered such an attribution of powers, and in relation to the conduct of business, it granted the SIB with the power to issue statements of principle 'as to conduct and financial standing of firms to all authorised persons';[149] this included the members of self-regulatory organisations (SROs). The role of SROs was, therefore, to enforce such principles and codes of practice in relation to their members.[150]

It is relevant for this study to highlight the elements that, from the beginning, have been part of the conduct of business regimes. The focus of the conduct of business in the reform introduced by the Companies Act 1989 was to ensure that the principles issued by the Securities and Investment Board (SIB) and related SRO rules provided an adequate level of investor protection[151] according to the different types of customer. The reform also emphasised the promotion of high standards of integrity and fair dealing; the duty of authorised persons to act with due skill, care, and diligence; the obligations concerning relationships with customers including the timely provision of information to inform investment decisions; the duty to keep inspection of records; and so on.

---

144 Ibid.
145 There were previous statutory regimes related to certain elements of the conduct of business, but these instruments were dispersed: Prevention of Fraud (Investments) Act 1958 and then the 1986 Act Licensed Dealer (Conduct of Business) Rules 1960. Afterwards the process of reform started with several reports: The 'Wilson Report', *Report of the Committee to Review the Functioning of Financial Institutions*, Cmnd.7937 (HMSO, 1980); and the 'Gower Report', *Review of Investor Protection, Report, Part I* (Cmnd 9128) (London 1984); LCB Gower, *Review of Investor Protection, Report, Part II* (London 1985) and Gower, *Review of Investor Protection, Discussion Document* (HMSO, London 1982) Julia Black, *Rules and Regulators* (Oxford University Press 1997), 47.
146 Ibid 54.
147 Law Commission, 'Fiduciary Duties and Regulatory Rules: A Consultative Paper', CP No. 124 (London 1992) and Fiduciary Duties and Regulatory Rules, LC No 236 (London 1995) in Ibid.
148 S 48 Financial Services Act 1986.
149 S 47A, inserted by s192 Companies Act 1989 (hereinafter CA 1989).
150 S 206 CA 1989.
151 S114 (9) CA 1989.

Afterwards, with the creation of the FSA, there was a strong emphasis on recognising that prudential supervision and conduct business are closely related, even though it is not easy to draw a clear dividing line between the two.[152] Clive Bruilt, who was the first FSA director of central policy, accepted that there is a considerable overlap – both conceptually and in practice – between prudential and conduct of business regulation, especially in risk-based approaches to regulation.[153] This difficulty accompanied the FSA supervision from the beginning. Nevertheless, the FSA diligently designed a large part of the current conduct of business rules[154] and codes,[155] including conduct rules for the OTCDM[156] – but the problem was the implementation[157] of the regime. The FSA was blamed for not balancing prudential and conduct of business supervision. This is inextricably similar to what is happening to the Bank in the supervision of CCPs in the OTCDM.

In this context, the creation of the FCA provided an opportunity to develop a new approach to conduct regulation.[158] The FCA's mandate might be illustrative as to what a conduct of business regulator is responsible for. The FCA was created to fulfil three operational objectives: protect consumers; enhance the integrity of the UK financial system; and help to maintain competitive markets and promote effective competition in the interests of consumers.[159] In order to conduct the supervision of these areas, the FCA will make rules, prepare and issue codes, provide general guidance, and determine the general policy and principles.[160] Moreover, under the new regime, the government intended to vest the FCA with new and more intrusive powers of intervention. For instance, they were now granted the power to direct firms to withdraw or amend misleading financial promotions

---

152 Clive Briault, 'The Rationale for a Single National Financial Services Regulator' (1999) FSA Occasional Paper No 2, 14.

153 Ibid 20.

154 Interpreting the content of COBS *Re Lehman Brothers International (Europe) (in administration)* [2010] EWCA Civ 917 Lord Neuberger MR, Arden LJ and Sir Mark Waller 2 August 2010.

155 The FSA attempted to harmonise the relevant provisions in the Conduct of Business Code (COB). The main provisions apply with regard to the relationship between regulated firms and their customers are set out in the COB module of the Handbook.

156 Blair, Allison, Morton, Richards-Carpenter, Walker and Walmsley, *Banking and Financial Services Regulation* (3rd ed, Butterworths LexisNexis 2002), 507.

157 Nicola Brittain, 'PRA: FSA Botched "Conduct" and "Prudential" Regulation Mix' Professional Adviser (2 May 2013) <www.professionaladviser.com/ifaonline/news/2265707/pra-fsa-botched-conduct-and-prudential-regulation-mix> accessed 7th October 2015.

158 HM Treasury, 'A New Approach to Financial Regulation: Building a Stronger System' CM8012 (February 2011), 59 (hereinafter HM Treasury, A New Approach to Financial Regulation: Building a Stronger System' (2011).

159 FSMA 2000 as amended by the FSA 2012 pt1A The Regulators, ch1 The Financial Conduct Authority; pt1B The FCA's general duties.

160 The Financial Services and Markets Act 2000 as amended by the Financial Services Act 2012 pt1A The Regulators ch1 The Financial Conduct Authority, The FCA's general duties pt1B The FCA's General Duties.

with immediate effect and to publish warning notices in relation to disciplinary matters.[161]

Hence, the FCA approach includes preventive actions in relation to the operation of markets for financial products and services, where there is evidence that these are not operating in the interests of the wider economy.[162] Similarly, the regime allows the FCA to intervene early in relation to products where risks are likely to outweigh the benefits the product will bring, or when the product does not meet regulatory standards and consumer detriment is occurring.

Crucially important for us in this analysis is the FCA's proposition to adopt a differentiated approach. The FCA is expected to tailor its approach and the use of its regulatory tools to the particular risks in the sectors, firms, and products. This emphasis, which includes major firms and market infrastructure providers, 'will be more thematic work, targeting product services and practices which have the potential to cause consumer or market detriment, than on firm specific risk'.[163] The forthcoming conclusion is, therefore, that the conduct of business regime for CCPs would take into account the particularities of their role in the OTCDM.

In addition, the FCA's work is conducted to intervene proactively to make markets more efficient and resilient, as well as to enhance integrity and choice.[164] The aim is to ensure that the conduct of market participants, as in OTCDM, is compatible with a fair and safe market, deterring market abuse and pursuing transparency.[165] The implementation of the new approach is part of the FCA Handbook and the Business Standards, which includes the Conduct of Business Sourcebook and the Code of Market Conduct, relevant for the OTCDM.

Following this line of thought, the first element that can be extrapolated from the UK experience is that the conduct of business regime is concerned with consumer[166] protection. But rather than focusing on the protection of clients from the insolvency of individual financial institutions, it emphasises safeguarding clients from unfair practices.[167] Moreover, the UK conduct regulation also extends to corporate governance and incentives, organisational systems, competition and antitrust, 'fit and proper' requirements and professionalism, and more recently 'product governance'.[168]

The EMIR developed some minimum conduct of business standards for CCPs. The standards are especially illustrative, because they attend to the systemic importance of CCPs. According to the regulation, 'CCPs shall act fairly and professionally in accordance with the best interests of such clearing members and

---

161 HM Treasury, A new approach to financial regulation: building a stronger system' (2011).
162 FSA, 'The FCA approach to regulation' (FSA, June 2011) 23.
163 Ibid 23.
164 Ibid 24.
165 Ibid.
166 Ibid.
167 Ibid.
168 Alix Prentice, and Caroline Bystrom, 'MiFID II: Regulating Investment Firms from the Inside Out' (2015) 6 *Journal of International Banking and Financial Law*, 364B.

clients and sound risk management'.[169] This makes clear how multiple interests converge in the CCP, and how regulators seek to make CCPs conduct themselves in a manner that contributes to the stability of the market. To develop the conduct of business rules, EMIR establishes the participation requirements – the criteria that CCPs will apply when admitting clearing members, which are not only limited to avoid discrimination, but also 'to ensure that clearing members have sufficient financial resources and operational capacity to meet the obligation arising from the participation in a CCP'.[170] The requirements illustrated in EMIR are the minimum parameters to be applied by the CCPs; however, national regulators and CCPs are able to strengthen those requirements. The monitoring of compliance of these financial resources and operational capability is controlled by the subsequent and periodic assessment conducted by the CCP, at least once a year.

Similarly, in order to avoid the excessive concentration of risks, those clearing members that clear transactions on behalf of their clients shall gather all the relevant information to identify, monitor, and manage the potential concentration of risk. Although the rules of access to information and the monitoring task are among the CCPs' obligations, the clearing members remain responsible for ensuring that clients comply with their respective obligations.

In the event that the initial criteria are not being met by clearing members, the CCP shall have in place 'objective and transparent procedures for the suspension and orderly exit'[171] of those clearing members. The orderly exit of a clearing member is vital for the CCPs to ensure the continuity of services and should be as minimally disruptive as possible.

Finally, the CCP is allowed to impose some additional obligations on its clearing members; for instance, to participate in auctions of a defaulting clearing member's position. The only limitation to such additional obligations is not to restrict participation to certain categories of clearing members.

The conduct of business rules of EMIR also make reference to the transparency[172] that CCPs and their clearing members shall observe. Article 38 sets out that there must be public disclosure regarding the prices and fees associated with the services provided, the risks associated with those services, the volumes of the cleared transactions for each class, the operational and technical requirements relating to the communication protocols with third parties, and any breaches by clearing members of the criteria and requirements to participate in the CCP. All this information is available to national competent authorities and ESMA. The access to better information is one of the fundamental objectives of the OTC derivatives market reform; timely access to accurate, relevant data allow

---

169 Art 36 EMIR.
170 Art 37 EMIR.
171 Ibid.
172 Schuyler K. Henderson, 'The New Regime for OTC Derivatives: Central Counterparties Part 1' (2011) 4 *Journal of International Banking and Financial Law*, 207.

authorities to effectively supervise the operation of the CCPs, as well as to ensure compliance to rules, and to use of early intervention mechanisms.

In Article 39, EMIR approaches the concepts of segregation and portability.[173] This provision imposes an obligation to CCPs to

> [K]eep separate records and accounts that shall enable [the CCP] to distinguish in accounts with the CCP the assets and positions held for the account of one clearing member from the assets and positions held for the account of any other clearing member and from its own assets.[174]

The rationale of segregation[175] is to have transparent and up-to-date information regarding the financial capability of the CCP and each of its clearing members to perform its obligations. With that information, the control on the volume of transactions and the subsequent risks involved is more effective, resulting in a constant control to avoid any concentration of risks. As ruled in Article 39 of EMIR, the requirement to distinguish assets and positions with the CCP taken into account is satisfied where:

> a) the assets and positions are recorded in separate accounts, b) the netting of positions recorded on different accounts is prevented, c) the assets covering the positions recorded in an account are not exposed to losses connected to positions recorded in another account.[176]

Moreover, the concept of assets refers to the collateral held to cover positions and, importantly, it covers 'the right to the transfer of assets equivalent to that collateral or the proceeds of the realization of any collateral'.[177] This rule allows clearing members to freely move their assets in the normal course of business; what is required is that the value of such collateral remains enough to guarantee the positions and exposures of the clearing member.[178] Further regulation about collateral requirements is developed in Article 46 of EMIR.

The concept of segregation is vital for the CCPs' functioning as the intermediary expected to provide better risk management in the OTC derivatives market. On the one hand, the segregation obligation applied to CCPs will allow them to clearly comply and remain compliant with the financial requirements to provide clearing services. This is a core tool to ensure the continuity of services and the

---

173 Tariq Zafar Rasheed, 'We Live in Regulatory Times: The Regulatory Capital Implications for Cleared Derivatives' (2014) 6 *Journal of International Banking and Financial Law*, 385.

174 Art 39 EMIR.

175 Tariq Zafar Rasheed, and Bas Zebregs, 'Can a House Divided Between Itself Stand? Segregation in Derivatives Clearing' (2012) 5 *Journal of International Banking and Financial Law*, 293.

176 Art 39 (9) EMIR.

177 Art 39 (10) EMIR.

178 Tariq Zafar Rasheed ' "Rings to Bind Them All": Central Counterparties and Collateralisation Issues' (2011) 6 *Journal of International Banking and Financial Law*, 331.

safety and soundness of the CCP. On the other hand, the segregation empowers the CCP, and in turn supervisors, to monitor and control the level of compliance of the clearing members, as well as to assess rigorously the level of exposure, positions, and assets each member is allowed to have.

EMIR distinguishes between two types of segregation. The 'omnibus client segregation' operates when the CCP 'keeps separate records and accounts enabling each clearing members to distinguish in accounts with the CCP the assets and positions of that clearing member from those held for the accounts of its clients'.[179] The 'individual client segregation' works when the CCP 'offers separate records and accounts enabling each clearing member to distinguish in accounts with the CCP the assets and positions held for the account of other clients'.[180] After the client has received all the relevant information and advice by the clearing member, it can choose between the two types of segregation offered by the CCP.

A third element of the consumer protection concerns the management of information and assets. CCPs are obliged to publicly disclose the prices and fees associated with the clearing services, the risks associated with those services, the volumes of the cleared transactions, the operational and technical requirements relating to the communication protocols with third parties, and of any clearing members' breaches of the criteria and requirements to participate in the CCP. Timely access to complete information ensures that clearing members are sufficiently informed when deciding the CCP in which they will clear their OTC contracts, as well as trace any changes in the functioning of the CCP to which they belong.

Furthermore, according to the segregation requirement, CCPs are compelled to keep separate records and accounts for each clearing member. A clear and supervised system of segregation benefits the clearing member, in the sense that the CCP is able to distinguish in accounts with the CCP the assets and positions held for the account of one clearing member from the assets and positions held for the account of any other clearing member and from its own assets. Such a separation of assets offers a layer of protection for clearing members' assets when the CCP is in financial distress, in particular in a resolution event. Segregation rules help to control the functioning of the CCP as provider of better risk management, and contribute to ensuring the continuity of clearing services, which is in the interest of clearing members.

To sum up, EMIR contributes to the conduct of business regime by developing the content of consumer protection in terms of the obligation of CCPs to act fairly and professionally, in accordance with the 'best interest of clearing members'. The conduct regulator in the UK would have the first task to explain what is the best interest of clearing members and clients, and how it is articulated with the systemic role CCPs have in the OTCDM. In so doing, the conduct regulator is expected to identify foreseeable conflicts of interests and how they could be

---

179 Art 39 EMIR.
180 Art 39 EMIR.

solved. Moreover, and in line with the transparency that should rule the functioning of CCPs, the conduct regulator should ensure the existence and compliance of objective procedures for the suspension and orderly exit of clearing members.

3.4.1.3.2 COMPETITION REGIME

Besides the broad category of consumer protection, competition is also a highly relevant topic to consider in the regime of conduct of business. Indeed, the FCA has the mandate to promote effective competition when addressing the consumer protection objective.[181] In line with this mandate, the conduct of business regime for CCPs in the OTCDM has the potential to help solve issues regarding 'unfair contract terms' and anti-competitive practices.

In pursuing this objective, the FCA conducted the wholesale sector competition review.[182] Although it is not a regulatory priority, the FCA recognises some of the competition issues that might affect the functioning of the OTCDM. In particular, the review mentions that the vertical integration model of CCPs and trading venues may create barriers to entry/expansion for standalone providers trying to compete, and the reduction in the number of clearing providers and the impact they have in terms of fair, reasonable, and transparent access to clearing services. Moreover, the review emphasises one of the most notorious features of CCPs market – the high level of concentration. The small number of CCPs and, in turn, the concentration of certain instruments that can be cleared, facilitates the emergence of monopolistic practices, such as price controls and restrictions to market entry.

Similarly, the FCA accepts that increased competition between CCPs could lead to competition in risk management techniques, which in turn could affect financial stability. For instance, as users select CCPs based on the instrument traded, the membership requirements, and the available liquidity,[183] CCPs might seek to present themselves as more attractive by reducing the margin requirements. The FCA believes that EMIR provides the solution to some competition issues when it sets out that access between CCPs and trading venues should be provided on a non-discriminatory basis for OTC derivatives. Nonetheless, whilst this provision of EMIR might solve the vertical integration[184] problem affecting the links between trading venues and CCPs, it does not solve the competition

---

181 The Bank of England and Financial Services Act 2016 takes further steps to promote diversity and competition in the banking sector, by ensuring that regulators take into account different business models as part of their competition objectives.

182 See FCA, 'Wholesale sector Competition Review 2014–15' (n138).

183 A survey conducted by COO Connect Peer Group Network and Derivative Consulting. The criteria fund managers should use to choose the CCP that clears their derivatives shows that the most important factors are the Products and Services (e.g. Portfolio Compression), Asset Safety (e.g. collateral segregation), and counterparty risk management. COO Connect Breakfast Briefing, (20 October 2015).

184 Vertical integration happens when two firms in different stages of a supply chain merge. An example of this would be the merger of a CCP with a trading venue.

issues involving the practices CCPs might adopt to gain more clearing members. Therefore, there are some areas that could be further regulated by national conduct authorities.

Furthermore, there is some concern regarding the access to clearing services by clearing members and their clients. Some respondents of the review emphasised that there are few options for OTC clearing in the UK; the limitation in number of entities that can offer clearing services in the OTCDM is attributable to the regulation in place. The regulatory requirements for the recognition and authorisation of CCPs in EMIR and domestic legislation, but also the capital requirements imposed in Basel III, mean that only large financial institutions will be able to become clearing members. Similarly, there are potential issues arising from indirect clearing. Indirect clearing – also known as 'client clearing' – is a method allowing OTCDM participants to benefit from the clearing services, without becoming clearing members themselves. In particular, there are legal and operational risk management challenges in the clearing chain and the number of clearing members and CCPs that will be able to provide clearing services to clients. This uncertainty is increased by the upcoming European regulation[185] and the impact it will have.

Therefore, it is important for UK authorities to ensure that there are enough arrangements to guarantee access to clearing.[186] This can be achieved by expanding direct access to CCPs, which in turn reduces concentration of risk and enhances competition, and through safe and efficient indirect clearing rules.

One additional consideration regarding the increase of access to clearing is to acknowledge the impact it might have for CCPs. CCPs are entities subject to a progressive pressure to increase the number of products they clear. Indeed, one of the regulatory reforms coming from Market and Financial Instruments Directive II (MiFID II), in force since 3rd January 2018, is precisely the implementation of a policy of open access to CCPs in the OTCDM; that is, to broaden the spectrum of products that will be centrally cleared and to facilitate 'client clearing'. Under MiFID II, CCPs will have to open up to any participant that meets the minimum criteria. The rules are intended to introduce a level playing field for securities trading and clearing in Europe. However, the concern is whether, in an 'open-access environment', CCPs are sufficiently robust to handle a potential crisis.

Some have compared this expansion of CCPs clearing in the OTCDM with the phenomenon faced by rating agencies before the GFC. Pre-crisis, rating agencies

---

185 On 2nd October 2015, ESMA informed the delay in the issue of the regulatory technical standards (RTS) on indirect clearing for OTC derivatives. ESMA Press Release <www.esma. europa.eu/system/files/2015-1498_-_letter_to_european_commission_-_technical_ standards_on_indirect_clearing_under_emir_and_under_mifir.pdf> accessed 13th October 2015.

186 BIS, 'The Macro Financial Implications of Alternative Configurations for Access to Central Counterparties in OTC Derivatives Market' (Paper Committee on the Global Financial System CGFS Papers No 46, November 2011).

faced pressure to increase their product coverage[187] because of the privileges of official ratings. In the case of CCPs, despite the fact that the open-access policy of MiFID II is said to introduce a real competition to the clearing services, it should not be ignored that it also puts high pressure on CCPs. The expansion of clearing services requires paying careful attention to the risks a CCP is in a position to manage.

Although the FCA recognises these aforementioned competition issues, it adopted a passive approach towards them. In the review, the FCA explains that many of these competition issues are dependent on the implementation of EMIR and complementary legislation. Thus, the real effects of EMIR cannot be identified in the current status of the market. The market study conducted by the FCA contributes to support the argument in favour of designing a conduct of business regime that includes competition rules. There are competition issues arising in the CCPs market that can affect the functioning of the market, and therefore need to be considered by UK regulators. As already explained, some of the foreseeable effects that EMIR will have in terms of competition of CCPs in the OTCDM can greatly affect the functioning of the market in terms of access to clearing and efficiency of risk management techniques. Therefore, UK regulators are in time to design the regime and to provide some clarity regarding the authority that would carry out the regulation and supervision of this matter.

Our research emphasises the importance of clarifying the authority that will oversee competition of CCPs in the OTCDM. According to the review, several competition concerns are not regulated by the FCA, and would be regulated by the Bank.[188] However, this straightforward conclusion has some shortcomings in practice. Despite the fact that the Bank is the leading CCP supervisor, it is not clear how the Bank would act as a competition regulator. So, if CCPs engage in any anti-competitive practice, the regulation applicable would be the general competition regime,[189] enforced by the CMA[190] and not the Bank.

In this sense, the FCA is in the best position to become the authority responsible for the oversight of competition of CCPs in the OTCDM. Firstly, the FCA, as conduct regulator, is related to the market, and concerned with OTCDM competition issues due to its supervisory role of clearing members and their clients.

---

187 In 2006 Moody's reported that structured products (largely CDOs) accounted for 44 percent of their income; for Fitch the proportion was 51 percent. See Richard Tomlinson and David Evans, 'The Ratings Charade' (Bloomberg Markets, July 2007) 51 <www.jour nalism.columbia.edu/system/documents/524/original/2008_Evans_The_Ratings_Cha rade_MAG_July_2007.pdf> accessed 29th February 2016.

188 FCA, 'Wholesale Sector Competition Review 2014–15' (n138), 50.

189 Competition Act 1998 (CA 1998); the Financial Services and Markets Act 2000 (FSMA); the Enterprise Act 2002 (EA 2002); the Enterprise and Regulatory Reform Act 2013 (ERRA 2013); the Financial Services (Banking Reform) Act 2013; The Competition Act 1998 (Concurrency) Regulations 2014; and the CMA's Guidance on Concurrent Application of Competition Law to Regulated Industries.

190 The predecessor of the CMA is the Office of Fair Trading (OFT), which had an MoU with the FSA to coordinate the supervision of competition in financial markets.

The study contained in the Wholesale Markets Competition Review demonstrates that some of the competition concerns tend to involve CCPs, clearing members, and clients all at once. Thus, to assign the function of supervision of competition of CCPs to the FCA would prevent unnecessary overlaps between the FCA and the CCPs' competition supervisor in the event of anti-competitive practices. Secondly, the FCA has the operational objective of promoting effective competition, and in doing so counts with new statutory enforcement powers and a MoU with the CMA. Under the Financial Services (Banking Reform) Act 2013, the FCA is to become a concurrent competition authority from 1st April 2015. The concurrency[191] means that the FCA will have the power to enforce the competition prohibitions against anti-competitive agreements and abuse of a dominant position contained in the Competition Act 1998. Moreover, the Enterprise Act 2002 allows the FCA to carry out market studies and refer markets to an independent panel within the CMA for detailed investigation. Alongside these powers, the MoU between the FCA and the CMA seeks to maximise the effectiveness of both authorities in making financial services markets work well for consumers.[192] Thus, the new enforcement powers and framework of cooperation put the FCA in a privileged position to oversee competition issues of CCPs.

Finally, the FCA already has a conduct of business regime applicable to recognised clearing houses that operate in the exchange-traded market. Although the central clearing (CCPs service) in the OTCDM is focused on credit risk management whilst in the exchange market, CCPs' primary role is to standardise and simplify operational processes; the experience the FCA has in supervising in the exchange market can be useful in the OTCDM.

Additionally, the benefits of regulating the competition of CCPs in the OTCDM are not limited to conduct of business matters or exclusively linked to consumer protection. Beyond these direct effects of a competition regime, well-designed and enforced regulation can contribute to control, though not solve, the too-big-to-fail[193] character that CCPs have. The role of the competition regime is necessarily secondary but useful when integrated with public policy in pre- and post-crisis periods.[194] It contributes to maintain as much as possible the fair conditions of access and participation of the market where too-big-to-fail

---

191 See Deb Jones, 'The FCA's New Competition Powers: What Do They Mean for The Financial Services Industry?' Speech, Scottish Financial Enterprise Lunch, Edinburgh (21 November 2014) <www.fca.org.uk/news/new-competition-powers-what-do-they-mean-for-the-financial-services-industry> accessed 13th October 2015.

192 'Memorandum of Understanding between the Competition and Markets Authority and the Financial Conduct Authority' (12 June 2014) <www.gov.uk/government/uploads/system/uploads/attachment_data/file/325666/MoU_FCA-CMA_Final.pdf> accessed 13th October 2015.

193 Jesse W.W. Markham Jr, 'Lessons for Competition Law from the Economic Crisis: The Prospect for Antitrust Responses to the "Too-Big-To-Fail" Phenomenon' (2011) 16 *Fordham Journal of Corporate & Financial Law*, 2.

194 'Antitrust enforcement is not a luxury reserved for more prosperous times', Maurice E. Stucke, 'New Antitrust Realism' (January 2009) *Global Competition Policy Magazine*, 20.

institutions are implicitly allowed to interfere in the functioning of the market. In the case of CCPs, the interference is the result of the systemic relevance they have in the OTCDM. Such a privileged position indirectly allows CCPs to impose limits to market access, to limit their liability regime, to impose 'unfair' contract terms, and so on. Therefore, the role of competition law can complement the regulation in place by enabling[195] a fair conduct of business, which protects CCPs but still enhances the robustness and resilience of the CCPs in the OTCDM.

3.5 Conclusion

The introduction of CCPs to the OTCDM aims to provide better management of counterparty credit risk. This is central in markets, such as the OTCDM, where losses are severe enough to become a channel of contagion and be the potential source of systemic risks. CCPs reduce and mutualise the credit risk. CCPs are said to increase market safety and integrity by mitigating and managing credit, liquidity, and operational risks. The functioning of CCPs relies heavily on the orderly management of a member's default and of other sources of losses. Moreover, it is argued that the intermediation of CCPs contributes to address information asymmetries and increases efficiency of the market. Similarly, the introduction of mandatory central clearing through CCPs brings some benefits in terms of supervision of the OTCDM. This is because CCPs contribute to enhance standardisation of OTC derivatives transactions and have an active role in increasing transparency of the OTCDM.

The downside, however, is that CCPs are assuming a position of special relevance in each transaction and in the market, and are considered SIFIs. CCPs are highly interconnected, and thereby their failure might prompt negative externalities. Moreover, CCPs in the OTCDM are characterised by lack of substitutability when one of them ceases to provide services. These concerns surrounding the functioning, safety, and soundness of CCPs explain the content of the post-GFC regulatory reform; in particular, the special focus on strengthening the prudential regulation of CCPs.

The UK regime – in line with international regulatory agenda – is heavily seated in the prudential supervision of CCPs. The reform in the UK started with the introduction of a new approach to financial regulation that empowered regulators to look beyond compliance and to supervise proactively. Such an approach combines some elements of risk-based regimes and places the judgement of expert supervisors at the centre of regulation. Regarding the supervision of CCPs, this research argues that the competent authorities are the Bank and the FCA.

The Bank, in coordination with its macroprudential supervision, carries out the microprudential supervision of CCPs. The Bank's aim is to ensure that CCPs'

---

195 Joseph William Singer, *No Freedom without Regulation: The Hidden Lesson of the Subprime Crisis* (Yale Press September 2015).

rules and policies are designed and applied to monitor, manage, and mitigate risks, especially systemic risks. Moreover, in line with the CPMI-IOSCO PFMIs, the Bank has set out supervisory priorities, anticipating that its supervisory effort is based on its assessment of where risks to financial stability are greatest. This judgement and assessment is based on a risk review conducted by supervisory staff and reviewed by senior bank officials. Thus, some elements of risk-based and judgement-based regulation can be identified in the Bank's approach to CCP supervision.

The influence of the risk-based approach to regulation is also revealed in the Bank's enforcement powers. In particular, the decision-making committees within the Bank rely on a categorisation of the FMIs according to the level of risk they pose to financial stability in the event of disruption or failure. The classification indicates that the Bank is implementing a risk-based approach to regulation in the sense of prioritising the regulatory actions according to the level of risk of regulated firms. However, the adoption of a risk-based approach is incomplete. Our findings suggest that the UK regime for CCPs does not fulfil what would be expected if a coherent risk-based approach were taken.

Along with the rules contained on EMIR, the FSMA 2000 Part XVIII regulates CCPs, entities subject to the recognition requirements as recognised clearing houses. In this chapter we explored the provisions in EMIR related to CCPs, prudential regulation, conduct of business, and organisational requirements. Moreover, we highlighted the Bank's system of rules and progress regarding the management of credit, liquidity, and operational risks.

The Bank's supervisory regime seeks to achieve the robustness, safety, and soundness of CCPs by means of prudential supervision. However, other areas, such as the conduct of business regime, have not been considered. The implementation of a risk-based approach in the CCPs regime affects the effectiveness of the UK regulation and supervision. This shortcoming consists of breaking the balance between the two stems of risk-based regimes: prudential regulation and conduct of business. As a result, the UK does not have a coherent conduct of business regime for CCPs in the OTCDM and the only rules are those included in EMIR.

The lack of a conduct of business regime for CCPs might have a negative impact in terms of enforcement. Unfortunately, the Bank considers that setting standards of conduct is not a priority, as it does not endanger the achievement of its regulatory objectives. Moreover, the FCA's mandate has been wrongfully interpreted and, as such, the Bank is considered the only regulator of CCPs. Thus, it is unclear whether the Bank or the FCA would be entitled to sanction a breach of a conduct of business rule.

Going beyond the critique, in this chapter we presented some considerations about the role that the FCA should have, the importance of the design and implementation of a conduct of business regime for CCPs, and the elements that such a regime should include. A conduct of business regime for CCPs would help to solve some of the issues rising from the contractual arrangements between CCPs and clearing members; arrangements that until now have been exclusively ruled by CCPs' rulebooks and contracts. There are certain elements of that relationship that could be overseen by means of conduct of business rules. In particular, the chapter emphasised the need to design a consumer protection regime that includes clearing members. The consumer protection regime would help to correct the imbalances in the relationship between CCPs and clearing members; would safeguard clearing members from unfair practices, as well as strengthen the rules of management of information and assets; and would be the opportunity to further develop the conduct rules contained in EMIR, including segregation and portability rules. In doing so, the conduct regulator would explain how CCPs have to act fairly and professionally, in accordance with the best interest of clearing members and their clients, and how it is articulated with the systemic role of CCPs in the OTCDM.

Similarly, a conduct of business regime would be central to solving issues regarding competition among CCPs. The regime would help to solve issues concerning unfair contract terms and anti-competitive practices. There are several competition issues that need to be regulated. For instance, how increased competition among CCPs could lead to competition in risk management techniques, which in turn could adversely affect financial stability. Also, the extent to which the current regime limits the access to clearing services by clearing members and their clients. Here, the role of UK regulators could be to ensure that there are enough arrangements to ensure broader access to central clearing without sacrificing the robustness of CCPs and their ability to manage financial distress scenarios. Thus, the rationale is that the design and implementation of competition rules and clarity about the competent authority would enable a fair conduct of business, which benefits CCPs and enhances the robustness of CCPs in the OTCDM.

4 Shortcomings – the insufficient legal framework underpinning CCPs' operations and the absence of a special resolution regime for CCPs

4.1 Introduction

The shortcomings affecting the regulation and supervision of the UK regime of CCPs in the OTCDM go beyond the lack of conduct of business explained in Chapter 3. In this chapter, we explore two more weaknesses: the insufficient legal framework underpinning CCPs' operations and the absence of a special resolution regime for CCPs. Both shortcomings exemplify the central argument of this book: due to the adoption of a risk-based approach to regulation, UK regulators have focused their attention and regulatory actions on the most urgent needs of the market – ensuring the safety and soundness of CCPs in the OTCDM – whilst overlooking other areas of concern that could affect the functioning and robustness of CCPs and thereby the market. Risk-based regulation is, therefore, creating manufactured risks.

The first part of this chapter explores the insufficient legal framework underpinning CCPs' operations. Prioritising risks and regulatory actions has led regulators to abandon the design and implementation of rules to govern the contractual relationship between CCPs and clearing members. In order to explain the difficulties this poses, we address several questions concerning the contractual provisions governing the CCP-clearing member relationship. We explain how CCPs' rulebooks limit the liability of CCPs, and question how several contractual provisions limit the possibility of clearing members (and indirectly, clearing members' clients) to enforce their rights. Moreover, we consider segregation and portability, as has been disclosed by the CCPs operating in the UK. This chapter presents the debate about the shortcomings of the 'legal segregation' included in EMIR, and how these weaknesses could be overcome with complementary UK regulation. Finally, we argue for the recognition of the existence of a duty of care applicable to CCPs, exploring the content of the duty and the issues it would help to solve. We also identify the drawbacks of the proposal, highlighting the need to reform Section 291 of the FSMA 2000 and anticipating the potential difficulties faced by such a duty of care in being recognised in English courts.

The second part of this chapter is devoted to explaining another shortcoming of the UK regime, the absence of a special resolution regime for CCPs. Although the prudential supervision of the Bank of England is focused on ensuring the safety and soundness of CCPs, priority has been given almost exclusively to the development of loss-allocation and recovery rules. During the first years of the regime, the Bank has been reluctant to recognise that CCPs might fail and therefore has not designed a regime to rule on CCP resolution. This approach overlooks the fact that a core feature of a stable financial system depends on recognising that all financial institutions are resolvable, including those that are systemically important. The discussions in this section attempt to throw some light on key aspects in considering the resolution of CCPs. We argue the importance of designing a different regime to the one of the Banking Act 2009, which is currently applicable to CCPs. To this end, we call regulators to recognise that CCP failure is a possibility, addressing the question of what a special resolution regime for CCPs might look like, and highlighting possible regime shortcomings concerning the exercise of rights for clearing members and their clients, as well as financial stability.

4.2 Insufficient legal framework underpinning CCPs' operations

When examining the legal framework governing the relationship between CCPs and their clearing members, we must understand that this discussion is part of a larger concern regarding certain provisions of CCPs' rulebooks that almost exclusively govern the relationship between CCPs and clearing members. The content of such rulebooks is, except for the risk management part, left to the autonomy of CCPs. Regulators do not control a large part of the contractual content, nor how obligations should be performed under such terms. Even some clauses that might not be considered fair to clearing members and their clients are seen as acceptable by the regulator, because the priority is to ensure the 'robustness' of the CCP.[1] As a result, CCPs have a high level of discretion when performing their obligations, which in turn diminishes clearing members' and their clients' rights and opens sources of potential litigation. Although in this study we accept that any contractual relationship might be contentious, we argue that regulators can mitigate the sources of dispute by regulating certain contractual provisions that clearly unbalance the relationship between CCPs and clearing members. The regulation of contractual matters could complement the protection of clearing members and their clients as consumers of CCPs' services. Therefore, this shortcoming is not limited to merely contravening the 'abusive or unfair' contractual clauses, but we would also seek to emphasise the importance of considering the existence of a duty of care predicable of CCPs in the performance of their contractual obligations.

Furthermore, this issue relates to the compliance with one of the PFMIs, the principle of legal basis. According to this principle, '[a]n FMI should have a

---

1 Interview with Mr Paul Brione Head of Central Counterparty Supervision, Bank of England, London, 25th September 2015.

well-founded, clear, transparent, and enforceable legal basis for each material aspect of its activities in all relevant jurisdictions'.[2] The management of legal risk and the consequences in terms of certainty and predictability are at the core of the CCPs' soundness.[3] Hence the Bank, whose supervision is guided by the PFMIs, is bestowed to issue legal guidance to illustrate the content of the duty of care expected from CCPs, as well as to control the content of potentially 'abusive' contractual terms.

4.2.1 Regulation of CCPs' contractual relationships

The role of CCPs in the OTCDM is to provide better credit risk management. In performing their functions, they act according to a legal framework that controls their functioning. The UK regime, in line with international regulation, is focused on ensuring the robustness of CCPs. This is to ensure their resilience and, most importantly, to preserve the continuity of services even in the event of CCPs' financial distress. Although this area of focus of the regulation and supervision of CCPs is predominant in the post-GFC regulatory reforms, we argue that the robustness of CCPs is not limited to prudential matters. According to the PFMIs, a CCP is robust not only when its stability contributes to the stability of the system, but also when its functioning agrees with the robustness of its clearing members and their clients. In this sense, this work argues against the notion that making CCPs safe and sound justifies the imposition of excessive restrictions on the clearing members' rights and, indirectly, their clients' rights.

The PFMIs are the guide for the regulation and supervision of CCPs in the OTCDM. The first principle requires regulators to have in place a well-founded, clear, transparent, and enforceable legal basis for each material aspect of FMIs' activities.[4] The principle of legal basis seeks to provide the foundation to clearly define from the outset the set of rights and obligations of the CCPs, clearing members, and clearing members' clients.[5] The aim is for national laws to govern all the CCPs' rules, procedures, and contracts, so that they provide a high degree of legal certainty.

The UK regime of CCPs in the OTCDM sufficiently regulates areas such as netting arrangements, enforceability of members' default, and recovery; as such, we will not analyse these here. Instead, this section explains some of the contractual issues that are absent from the current regime, according to the legal basis principle that should guide the regulation of CCPs, in line with the PFMIs. The areas that pose particular concern are: the limitation of CCPs' liability related to management of clearing members' positions, assets and value related to collateral, and the content of the duty of care that would be expected from CCPs

---

2 CPMI-IOSCO Principles of Financial Market Infrastructures (hereinafter CPMI-IOSCO PFMI).
3 Ibid 27.
4 Ibid.
5 Ibid.

when performing contractual obligations. The discussions presented here are an example of the absence of rules protecting clearing members' and their clients' rights from the imposition of unfair contract terms, or from the inadequate performance of CCPs' obligations.

In order to explain this weakness, we will address questions about how the relationship between CCPs and clearing members is regulated and, in particular, the analysis of the clauses that show most prominently the dominant position of CCPs. We then characterise CCPs' obligations related to the management of assets and positions of clearing members, the requirements of segregation and portability created by EMIR, and the potential issues they raise. We also discuss whether there is, or should be, a duty of care applicable to the CCPs performing their contractual obligations, as the recognition of the duty of care would balance the contractual relationship between CCPs and clearing members, promote consumer protection, and strengthen the obligation of CCPs to act 'fairly and professionally in accordance with the best interests of such clearing members and clients and sound risk management'.[6]

4.2.1.1 *The contractual relationship between CCPs and clearing members*

Amongst other areas, the UK regime of CCPs in the OTCDM, including EMIR,[7] regulates the clearing obligation, the type of contracts subject to clearing, reporting of transactions, the CCP authorisation and recognition, the minimum requirements clearing members should meet to be part of CCPs, and so on. Similarly, the regime imposes some obligations on CCPs and clearing members related to segregation and portability of positions and margins. However, the core of the rights and obligations of the contractual relationship between CCPs and clearing members is not part of the regime. The task to define contractual arrangements is left completely within the autonomy of the parties involved. Hence, CCPs have drafted rulebooks to rule their contractual relationships. The obligations and rights of CCPs and clearing members are contained in the rulebook, together with the Clearing Membership Agreement and any other documentation given contractual force pursuant to the rulebook.[8] Therefore, general laws rule the enforceability of the contractual arrangements[9] and courts will decide any related dispute.

---

6 Art 36 EMIR.
7 Including regulatory technical standards (RTS) and implementation technical standards of EMIR.
8 CME Clearing Europe Ltd, 'Rulebook Clearing Rules ch 2 General Provisions' Last updated: (19 December 2015), 35 <www.cmegroup.com/europe/clearing-europe/membership/files/CMECE-Rulebook.pdf> accessed 29th February 2016.
9 Contract law and tort law.

As might be anticipated, the content of CCPs' rulebooks is not uniform – each CCP drafts it differently.[10] There are, however, some clauses common to all of them. For instance, the rules regarding the amendments to the content include the consultation proceeding and the subsequent publication. Such provisions allow clearing members, or part of them,[11] to know the amendment in advance and to submit the relevant comments.[12] The CCP has the unilateral right to amend the clearing arrangement. Accordingly, the CCP might decide to cease the clearing of a certain contract, or to introduce amendments to contract specification; that is the part of the contract module setting out the terms of a particular type of transaction.[13]

Moreover, CCPs' rulebooks include provisions delimiting the liability of clearing members. Those provisions say that clearing members are liable for any losses, liabilities, damages and claims, costs suffered by the CCP arising out any breach of the obligations included in the rulebook and clearing membership agreement, or costs arising out of any contract entered into by the clearing member.[14] Such a liability regime applies, excepting the events of bad faith, fraud, wilful default, or gross negligence on the part of the CCP. The obligation to indemnify will consider the steps taken by the clearing member to mitigate the losses. Accordingly, the attribution of liability will follow the general rules of contract law and tort. There is no exemption or limitation to clearing members' liability, which is the opposite to the clauses of CCPs' liability. The imbalance of the liability regime shows how the clauses of rulebooks privilege CCPs' position to the detriment of clearing members' rights.

Regarding the liability of CCPs, the rulebook broadly sets out the events in which such a liability arises. It starts by delimiting the beginning of the liability to the moment when the contract exists. This means that there is no possibility to consider any potential liability arising from the period of contractual negotiations. Although English law does not recognise a liability in the pre-contractual period,[15] there are some areas that remain debatable.[16] The liability of pre-contractual arrangements might change when a contract is agreed or when the negotiations end with no agreement.[17] In the event where negotiations end with

---

10 CCPs' rulebooks are published on CCP websites. This book uses the rulebooks of the CCPs authorised in the UK.
11 CME Clearing Europe Ltd Rulebook 2.2.3.
12 CME Clearing Europe Ltd Rulebook 2.2 Amendments.
13 CME Clearing Europe Ltd Rulebook Rule 2.2.8 and ss.
14 CME Clearing Europe Ltd Rulebook Rule 2.3.
15 See H.G. Beale (ed.), *Chitty on Contracts* (28th edn, Sweet & Maxwell 1999) 2–103ff; GH Treitel, *The Law of Contract* (14th edn, Sweet & Maxwell 2015), 20.
16 Paula Giliker, 'A Role for Tort in Pre-Contractual Negotiations? An Examination of English, French and Canadian Law' (2003) 52 *International & Comparative Law Quarterly*, 969.
17 'In *Regalian Properties plc v London Dockland Development Corporation* [1995] 1 WLR 212, Rattee J held that there could be no recovery of pre-contractual expenses when a contract did not result between the parties. When parties use the expression "subject to contract" in

the agreement of a contract, under English law, the liability for pre-contractual negotiations is limited to the counterparty's will. Hence, in *Investors Compensation Scheme Ltd v West Bromwich Building Society*[18] (No1), it was held that 'the law excludes from the admissible background the previous negotiations of the parties and their declarations of subjective intent'. However, in *In ProForce Recruit Ltd v Rugby Group Ltd*,[19] the Court said that the effect of such negotiation arrangements might be considered in the construction of the contractual terms only when parties do not exclude them. In this area, the drafting of CCPs' rulebooks does not present major concerns.

However, there are other sources of potential liability in the negotiation period for a contract that is void or voidable. For instance, if the content of the negotiation arrangements that might result in liability incited in the contract, under certain conditions these arrangements can give the counterparty the right to rescind the contract, or part of it, according to the Misrepresentation Act 1967. There is statutory liability under the Misrepresentation Act 1967 in the event of intentional, negligent, and innocent misstatements. In those events, the affected counterparty can demand for a rescission[20] of the contract and claim damages. Also, there is the possibility of liability in tort for negligence in common law.[21] The negligence is configured when there was a reasonable reliance of the parties on each other and of any evidence of an assumption of responsibility for statements made during negotiations.[22] Thus, when a contract is voided, the benefits of the period of negotiations might be recovered under the principles of the law of restitution.[23]

Therefore, if any of the hypotheses considered before affect the relationship between the CCP and its members, it could be anticipated that the clause of

---

their negotiations, the parties had accepted that any pre-contract costs were incurred at that party's own expense'. In contrast, in *Countrywide Communications Ltd v ICL Pathway Ltd* [2000] CLC 324, Nicholas Strauss QC accepted that, in 'exceptional cases' in which the contract failed to materialised, a claimant would be able to recover on quantum merit for expenditure incurred in anticipation of such contract, Jill Pole, *Casebook in Contract Law* (Oxford University Press 2014), 79.

18 *Investors Compensation Scheme Limited v West Bromwich Building Society* [1998] 1 WLR 896.
19 *ProForce Recruit Ltd v Rugby Group Ltd* [2006] EWCA Civ 69 (CA).
20 *Halpern v Halpern* [2007] EWCA Civ 291, [2007] 3 WLR 849, Jill Pole, *Casebook in Contract Law* (n17).
21 *Caparo Industries plc v Dickman* [1990] 2 AC 605, [1990] UKHL 2, [1990] 1 All ER 568.
22 Stahis Banakas, 'Liability for Contractual Negotiations in English Law: Looking for the Litmus Test' (2009) *Revista para el Analisis del Derecho*, Barcelona.
23 *Lipkin Gorman v Karpnale Ltd* [1991] 2 AC 548, (affirmed in subsequent decisions: see, e.g. *Woolwich Equitable Building Society v IRC* [1992] 3 All ER 737; *Westdeutsche Landesbank Girozentrale v Islington London Borough Council* [1996] AC 669; *Kleinwort Benson Ltd v Glasgow City Council* [1998] 1 AC 153), where the House of Lords acknowledged for the first time the existence of an autonomous cause of action in unjust enrichment, Robert Pearce, and Warren Barr, *Pearce & Stevens' Trusts and Equitable Obligations* (Oxford University Press 2014), 270.

the rulebook limiting the liability to the existence of the contract would be unenforceable.

According to CCPs' rulebooks, the liability of CCPs is restricted to the events of bad faith, fraud, wilful default, or gross negligence.[24] These provisions exclude any responsibility for any suspension of services or closure of the CCP; any errors and inaccuracies in any information used by the CCP; any warranties, representations, and undertakings which might be implied; any exercise or failure to exercise the discretion or right conferred by the rulebook; any dispute relating to the validity, existence, or terms of any contract, loss,[25] or diminution of value of collateral and any contribution; and loss of anticipated profit or revenue regardless of whether the CCP has been advised of the possibility of such loss or it could be foreseen. Moreover, any liability of the CCP will be recoverable by the clearing members limited to the portion of collateral held by the CCP pro rata to the relevant clearing member and the related guarantee fund.

The clauses limiting the liability of CCPs are allowed by Section 291 of the FSMA 2000. CCPs are recognised bodies that can delimit their liability only to acts of bad faith and similar occurrences. As we will go on to explain, this regime prevents clearing members from exercising their contractual rights when the CCPs are acting negligently. Under the current regime, the performance of CCPs' obligations is not regulated by the general regime of contract law and tort. In order to illustrate how problematic this is in practice, in the next section we will explore some of the obligations of CCPs in holding and managing clearing members' positions, assets, and collateral. This study argues for the design and implementation of regulatory guidance related to the standard of diligence and duty of care that CCPs should observe when performing their contractual obligations.

4.2.1.2 CCPs' management of assets

4.2.1.2.1 CCPS' HOLDING ASSETS

According to the terms of the contract between the CCP and clearing members, clearing members are required to provide collateral by transferring the full ownership of eligible cash, title of eligible securities, or eligible precious metals.[26] The transfer of those assets is done directly to the CCP or to the order of the CCP. Hence, when the collateral is in cash, the CCP will deposit it in a bank account; such collateral could remain deposited or be invested through an investment

---

24 S 291 of the FSMA 2000 clearly states the liability in relation to a recognised body's regulatory functions. The statutory provision limits the liability recognised bodies, among them CCPs. Hence, CCPs 'are not to be liable in damages for anything done or omitted in the discharge of the recognized body's regulatory functions unless it is shown that the act or omission was in bad faith'.
25 Including major investment loss.
26 CME Clearing Europe Ltd, Rulebook ch 6 Collateral, Rule 6.3 Holding Collateral, 96.

agent. When the collateral is the title of securities, the CCP will deposit it with a custodian,[27] or in the case of a fully segregated account, to a fully segregated custodian. Precious metals will be deposited with a settlement agent for precious metals. In any event, the collateral is held in the name of the CCP, unless otherwise stated. Moreover, the risk management procedure of the CCP rules the deposit of all the assets.

Similarly, clearing members are required to keep separate accounts for their clients' assets and positions, when they are clearing on behalf of their clients.[28] In these events, the CCP will open accounts (records and books) for administrative purposes only. The intermediation of the CCP does not affect the liability of the clearing members for their clients' accounts. Hence, clearing members are obliged to verify the quality and the availability of the collateral, and report it to the CCP. Also, the clearing members that are firms regulated by the FCA are obliged to manage their clients' assets according to the CASS Client Assets.[29] However, as the FCA does not regulate CCPs in the OTCDM, CASS Client Assets are not applicable to CCPs management of clearing members' assets, though it would be helpful to use these or similar rules to guide CCPs' management of assets.

In order to clarify the nature of the contractual positions of CCPs and clearing members, we must first recognise that clearing members hold different types of accounts in CCPs. Firstly, when the clearing members is clearing on its own behalf, the account is called a house account – the CCP records the positions entered between the CCP and the clearing member. Secondly, when the clearing member is clearing on behalf of its clients, the clearing member has several client accounts, which might be an omnibus client account,[30] an individual client account,[31] or a fully segregated client account. Under the clients' accounts, the obligation of CCPs is to record on their books the positions entered between the CCP and the clearing member acting on behalf of their clients, as well as the collateral received by CCPs in relation to such positions. From this structure of accounts, it follows that CCPs face the clearing member only in relation to registered cleared contracts and receive collateral from the clearing member only in respect of their positions, even when those positions are held on behalf of clearing members' clients.[32]

27 Charles Hewetson, and Nicholas Elliots Q.C. (eds.), *Banking Litigation* (3rd edn, Sweet & Maxwell 2011), 185.
28 CME Clearing Europe Ltd Rulebook ch 4 Accounts, 81.
29 The FCA updated the Client Assets Rules on August 2015, CASS Client Assets <www.hand book.fca.org.uk/handbook/CASS/1/2.html> accessed 20th October 2015.
30 CME Clearing Europe Ltd, 'Account Disclosure' (28 July 2014) <www.cmegroup.com/ europe/clearing-europe/membership/files/CMECE-Account-Disclosure-Document.pdf> accessed 19th October 2015.
31 This account records positions entered into by a clearing member in respect of a single client of the clearing member and the collateral, which relate to such positions separately from those of both the clearing member and any other client of the clearing member. The clearing member can have as many individual client accounts as it chooses. Ibid.
32 LCH Clearnet Ltd Disclosure for Purposes of Article 39(7) of EMIR <www.lchclearnet. com/documents/731485/762693/Legal+Implications+Article+39.7> accessed 20th October 2015.

Furthermore, any distribution or interest in respect to assets will belong to the CCP, which in turn will transfer an equivalent distribution or interest to the clearing member.[33] The exception to this rule is in the event of a clearing member's default, in which case any distribution or interest will be withheld by the CCP and, once the declaration of default is issued, they will form part of the portable net sum, single net sum, or CCP's default single net sum.

The holding of clearing members' assets is ruled by imposing on CCPs the obligation related to segregation and portability.[34] EMIR imposes the obligation on CCPs and clearing members to segregate the assets and positions. The 'legal segregation' included in EMIR requires that assets and positions with the CCP are recorded in separate accounts, positions recorded on different accounts cannot be netted, and the assets covering the positions recorded in one account are not exposed to losses connected to positions recorded in other accounts. As a result, in the insolvency of any counterparty, it should be possible to distinguish the positions and assets attributable to the insolvent and the others.

Nonetheless, there are some issues that are not considered in EMIR and that the UK regulators have not clarified. The first source of concern is that the 'legal segregation' of EMIR works in an ideal scenario where the records of the CCP and the clearing member coincide – but if they are different, there is a potential source of litigation. Similarly, 'legal segregation' does not necessarily mean that collateral is also operationally segregated;[35] operational segregation means that collateral is held in different segregated accounts. Thus, the formality of the segregation obligation is a step towards clearing members' and clients' asset protection, but it does not ensure the actual separation of assets.

The concerns surrounding the legal segregation contained in EMIR have not been further considered in the UK's regime for CCPs in the OTCDM. Indeed, information concerning how segregation and portability are working in practice is found in the Accounts Disclosure Documents published by CCPs,[36] and not in a body of regulation issued by UK authorities. We would argue the need for UK regulators to consider the design of a regime of segregation that goes beyond mere legal segregation and tackles deeper issues. Firstly, the new UK rules should ensure the actual segregation of collateral, rather than just complying with the segregation obligation and only requiring separate records of positions, types of assets, and value related to collateral to be kept. The aim is to achieve the asset protection for clearing members, clients, and the CCP itself, especially but not exclusively in the event of the insolvency of the CCP. Secondly, it would also be

---

33 CME Clearing Europe Ltd Rulebook ch 6 Collateral, Rule 6.3, Holding Collateral, 96.
34 Art 39 (2) EMIR.
35 Tariq Zafar Rasheed, and Bas Zebregs, 'Can a House Divided Between Itself Stand? Segregation in Derivatives Clearing' (2012) 5 *Journal of International Banking and Financial Law*, 293.
36 'CME Clearing Europe Ltd Accounts Disclosure Document' <www.cmegroup.com/europe/clearing-europe/membership/files/CMECE-Account-Disclosure-Document.pdf> accessed 20th October 2015; LCH Clearnet Ltd, Disclosure for Purposes of Article 39(7) of EMIR (n32).

advisable for UK segregation rules to impose a duty on CCPs to confirm the information that has been given by clearing members concerning their clients' positions, types of assets, and value related to collateral. The current regime puts the CCP in a purely administrative function, maintaining the register of positions, assets, and value related to collateral. In carrying out this function, the CCP relies completely on the information given by clearing members relating to their clients' types of assets and value related to collateral. As a result, if a dispute arises regarding those positions, assets, and value, such a dispute will involve the clearing member and the client on one side, and the CCP on the other. The latter will argue that it holds information considered complete and reliable. This foreseeable scenario leads us to question whether it is useful for CCPs to carry out segregated information. If the CCP will not be accountable, because any misleading information is not its responsibility but the clearing members', there is not much sense in imposing the obligation to carry out segregated clients' information.

However, if legal segregation is complemented with a duty to verify the information given by clearing members, CCPs will be compelled to be more vigilant regarding the information they receive. Moreover, the CCPs' commitment to the veracity of recorded information would reinforce their enthusiasm in achieving the segregation objective; the CCP will benefit by being able to verify the information clearing members deliver about their clients. For instance, in the omnibus client account, clearing members do not always provide information about the identity of their clients. As a result, any delay in receiving information or inaccuracy in such information could jeopardise the CCP's ability to port positions and collateral.[37] In that scenario, if the CCP were allowed to verify the accuracy of information, it would not face any such issues.

4.2.1.2.2 CCPS' OBLIGATIONS RELATED TO CLEARING MEMBERS' POSITIONS

The rules regarding the management of clearing members and their clients' positions are almost exclusively left to the CCPs' rulebooks, and the CCP role varies according to the type of account. The role of the CCPs includes: recording of positions and margin, management of collateral including the excess of it, liquidation of collateral and portability, management of mutualisation risk and other shortfalls, and in some types of accounts, the management of clearing members' clients' default.

4.2.1.2.3 OMNIBUS CLIENT ACCOUNT

The omnibus account will record positions entered into by a clearing member in respect of more than one client. The account records the types of assets and value of collateral. This type of account is also called an omnibus segregated account.[38]

---

37 Ibid 5.
38 LCH Clearnet Limited (the 'Clearing House') Disclosure for Purposes of Article 39 (7) of ('EMIR') (n32) 2.

The omnibus account can take several forms.[39] Net omnibus client account: the CCP records all positions, types of assets and value of related collateral relating to the omnibus client as whole. Thus, the CCP cannot identify the records of positions and collateral by each client, nor net positions against each other, unless the clearing member authorises it to do so. The second is the gross omnibus account, in which the CCP records positions by client according to the information provided by the clearing member. The types of assets and value-related collateral are recorded for the entire account, and not by the client. These two types of omnibus accounts comply with the minimal requirements of Article 39(2) EMIR.

The treatment of collateral follows some general rules. Each clearing member is required to deposit or deliver to the CCP with respect to each account in which it holds assets. The collateral is formed by initial and variation margins. Hence, the CCP determines the amount of margin for each account following the risk management procedure that the CCP has in place.[40] The sole discretion of the CCP is the parameter to modify or adjust initial and variation margins, as well as the reference prices it uses. Here the expectation is that the decision of the CCP is motivated by the best interest of the clearing members and the CCP itself.[41]

When there is an excess of collateral[42] in the omnibus client accounts, there is no provision in EMIR on whether such excesses should be transferred to the CCP. Therefore, these assets will receive the same treatment as collateral; the CCP will record the type of assets and the value related to the excess collateral for the entire omnibus account. However, in the event of the clearing members' default, the treatment of the excess collateral changes. In such an event, the CCP may take and liquidate all the collateral in the form of cash or securities in the omnibus client account, for the purpose of offsetting any amounts owing by the defaulting clearing member.

The client's default in the omnibus client account, should not, in principle, have a direct effect on the clearing arrangements of other clients of the clearing members, unless the default is significant and might cause the default of the clearing member.[43] In that case, the collateral of other clients in the same omnibus client account could be subject to mutualisation risk. According to the

---

39 Each CCP adopts forms and names of omnibus accounts that, although similar in nature, receive different names. For instance, LCH Clearnet Ltd offers: the non-identified client omnibus net segregated account (the NOSA), the identified client omnibus segregated account (the IOSA), and the affiliated client omnibus segregated account (the AOSA). LME Clear Ltd called them omnibus segregated client accounts.

40 CME Clearing Europe Ltd Rulebook Procedures, 93 ss.

41 The CCP will notify any changes to the clearing members, CME Clearing Europe Ltd Rulebook 92.

42 Excess collateral in relation to an omnibus client account is any collateral that the CCP receives in respect of that account which is greater than the collateral it has called from the clearing member.

43 European Union Emissions Trading Scheme, 'Client Segregation and Portability under EMIR' <www.emissions-euets.com/collateral-segregation-and-portability> accessed 29th February 2016.

mutualisation risk, the client in the omnibus client account takes a degree of risk against other clients of the clearing member in the same omnibus account only upon the default of the clearing member.[44]

On the default of a client, the clearing members may decide to transfer any positions relating to a defaulting client to the house account so that they become house positions; alternatively, the clearing member may choose to close those positions out. Also, the collateral relating to the defaulting client, according to the identification made by the clearing member, could be transferred to the house account and become house collateral, if requested by the clearing member in accordance with the CCP rules. Until the defaulting client positions have expired, the clearing member is responsible for meeting the relevant margin requirements. Alternatively, the clearing member may close out those positions.

Regarding the portability obligation, in order to mitigate triggered upon the default of the clearing member, CCPs are allowed to port positions and related collateral within a certain period of time. The value of both the positions and the collateral may fluctuate, and the CCP will not be receiving a variation margin from the defaulting clearing member to reflect such fluctuations. Nonetheless, it is also possible that the CCP cannot port.[45] In such an event, CCPs will close out the positions in the relevant omnibus client account, as well as calculate and return a sum. When the CCP is able to identify the client, the relevant sum will be returned to that client; otherwise the sum will be returned to the clearing member.

There are other risks that are shared under the structure of the omnibus client account – the risks relating to fluctuation in the value of collateral. During business as usual, CCPs allocate collateral to each omnibus client account by value and types of assets, which are recorded by an issue identifier and nominal amount. Given that the collateral is not allocated by the client and is held in a pool for all clients within the same omnibus client account, clients' share increases and decreases in the value of collateral. In the case of a clearing member's default, CCPs are allowed to liquidate any non-cash collateral at such a time and at such a rate as it, in its reasonable discretion, determines. All the clients in the omnibus client account share the risk arising from the fluctuation of prices and rates, and the CCPs are not obliged to explain the reasons they had to act in a certain way.

The explanation of the omnibus client accounts and the risk they pose to clients and clearing members shows the privileged position of CCPs. Although the proceedings are explained in CCPs' rulebooks and the Accounts Disclosure Documents, CCPs have a high level of discretion when deciding to opt for one option or another, and the exercise of that discretion might become a source of litigation. Thus, if the UK regulator issues additional guidance by means of principles or duties expected from CCPs, it would contribute to increased transparency and control over the CCPs decision-making process.

---

44 CME Clearing Europe Ltd Accounts Disclosure Document (n36) 4.
45 LCH Clearnet Ltd calls this 'porting windows' to include all the portability proceedings. LCH Clearnet Ltd (the 'Clearing House') Disclosure for Purposes of Article 39 (7) of ('EMIR') 6.

An additional source of litigation is concerning the event of insolvency of the custodians chosen by the CCP to hold the cash, securities, or precious metals that make up the collateral. In the event of insolvency of the custodian, or in case of a negligent, fraudulent, or wilful default act that causes the loss of the money or assets, the liability of the CCP is limited. According to the CCP rulebooks, the clearing members' claim against the CCP will be limited to the current value of the assets that the custodian makes available to the CCP, whilst all the clients of the omnibus account would share the losses. The responsibility of the CCP is restricted to having used appropriate skill, care, and diligence when choosing the custodian. CCPs have no obligation to exercise vigilance over how custodians perform their obligations.

4.2.1.2.4 INDIVIDUAL CLIENT ACCOUNT

Individual client accounts record positions entered into by a clearing member, in respect of a single client of the clearing member and the collateral relating to such positions separately, from those of both the clearing member and any other client of the clearing member. This type of account is also called an individual segregated account.[46] The benefits EMIR expects from this form of segregation are the complete separation of one client's positions and collateral from the clearing member and its other clients. Upon a clearing member default, CCPs will liquidate the collateral of the defaulting clearing member and facilitate the porting in the individual client account with the value of the related collateral to an adopting clearing member, in accordance with the CCP rulebook. The positions and collateral associated with each individual client account can be ported to a different adopting clearing member, but if porting is not possible, the CCP might decide to close out the clients' positions. Therefore, the CCP will exercise its discretion in deciding the procedure to follow in each case.

The principal advantage of using an individual client account is that the client's collateral, including the excess collateral, is legally segregated and cannot be used to cover any losses relating to the positions of other clients or other accounts.

4.2.1.2.5 FULLY SEGREGATED (FS) ACCOUNT

In contrast to the accounts created by CCPs and clearing members is the fully segregated (FS) account. FS accounts are the only ones that protect clearing members and their clients from CCP insolvency. The FS individual client account is an account created in the CCP and the FS account is an account with the FS Custodian. The CCP, the clearing member and the client will enter into an FS

---

46 LCH Clearnet Limited (the 'Clearing House') Disclosure for Purposes of Article 39 (7) of ('EMIR') p2. LME Clear Ltd calls them individual segregated client accounts, and offers three types of direct individual segregated accounts, indirect individual segregated client accounts, and indirect omnibus segregated client accounts. LME Clear Disclosure, Disclosure under EMIR Art 39 (7) p 3.

Settlement Deed in relation to each FS individual client account. Accordingly, the collateral related to an FS individual client account is delivered directly to the FS account, and vice versa. Such collateral satisfies the client's margin obligations to the clearing member, and the clearing member's margin requirement in relation to the FS individual client account. Thus, the CCP creates a security interest over each FS account in favour of an FS Security Trustee. The FS Security Trustee will hold the security on trust for the benefit of the clearing member and the relevant client in the terms of the Security Interest Document, which will be enforceable when the CCP enters into an insolvency proceeding.

The procedure upon the default of the CCP shows the unprotected position of the clearing members and clients. In the FS account, the default of the CCP triggers the right of each clearing member to calculate a CCP Default Sum for each of its FS individual client accounts, by netting positions and the value of the collateral recorded; the CCP shall verify every calculation, but if there is dispute, the final decision is the CCP's calculation. Similarly, the collateral related to the FS account and the FS individual client account is available to meet the losses incurred by the CCP, and the only remaining collateral – if any – is the one secured by the relevant FS Security Interest Document in favour of the FS Security Trustee. The Trustee will enforce the Security Interest Document against the collateral and can instruct the FS Custodian to liquidate or transfer the securities or cash. The powers that the Trustee can exercise depend upon the contractual terms, which should be known by clearing members and clients.

In the current status of the clearing regime, it is possible for CCPs to diversify the services they provide. For instance, LME Clear Ltd offers the possibility of clearing indirect clients[47] contracts; they are the clients of the clearing member's own clients. Clearing members are then allowed to open client accounts for them, and those accounts can be omnibus, when multiple indirect clients are allocated to the same account, or individual accounts. In both types of accounts, specific porting procedures would be in place and, as with the other forms of segregation, the rules governing these obligations are contained in the CCP rulebook and its Accounts Disclosure Document.

The foregoing explanation of the different types of accounts clearing members hold in CCPs is detailed here to illustrate the dynamics of the relationship between CCPs and clearing members. The content of the contractual agreements, as well as the exercise of discretion of CCPs, might be a source of litigation. We will now consider whether the recognition of the existence of a duty of care of CCPs could help to solve some of these issues.

4.2.2 Should UK regulators care about CCPs' duty of care?

Section 291 of the FSMA 2000 clearly states the liability in relation to a recognised body's regulatory functions. The statutory provision limits the liability

---

47 LME Clear Disclosure: disclosure under EMIR Art 39 (7), 17.

for recognised bodies, among them CCPs. Hence, CCPs 'are not to be liable in damages for anything done or omitted in the discharge of the recognised body's regulatory functions unless it is shown that the act or omission was in bad faith'. In turn, regulatory function refers to 'functions of the recognised body so far as relating to, or to matters arising out of, the obligations to which the body is subject under or by virtue of this Act'. It follows that CCPs may act according to their own discretion, regardless of the effects this might have for others' rights, and the only limit upon them is not to act in 'bad faith'. Accordingly, CCPs' rule-books include several clauses delimiting the scope of the CCPs' liability.

As might be anticipated from the previous section, the dynamics of the contractual relationship between CCPs and clearing members prompt several potential sources of litigation – particularly when some of the rules are not observed or when, in exercising their discretion, CCPs adversely affect the rights of clearing members and their clients. Thus, we argue the importance of recognising a duty of care[48] in the contractual relationship between CCPs and clearing members. The recognition of such a duty would imply a regulatory reform and subsequently could be constructed under the parameters of common law negligence.

The seminal case regarding the establishment of a duty of care is *Hedley Byrne v Heller & Partners*,[49] where the duty of care was recognised in the provision of information and advice. The two most significant developments of *Hedley Byrne* were the recognition of liability for negligent misstatements and where the injury suffered was pure economic loss.[50] However, the concern in the relationship between CCPs and clearing members is not in the area of advice given;[51] rather, it refers to financial service providers or intermediaries, in this case CCPs, acting as providers of clearing services.

In order to argue the existence of a duty of care in the CCP-clearing member relationship, it is adequate to review the imposition of duties of care in novel situations, as presented in *Bank of Credit & Commerce International (Overseas) Ltd (in Liquidation) v Price Waterhouse (N2)*.[52] Sir Brian Neill identified three tests applied in early authorities.[53] These are: 'the three-stage test of foreseeability, proximity, and justice and reasonableness;[54] assumption of responsibility;[55] and the incremental approach'.[56] The development of the incremental approach in

---

48 Andrew Twigger, 'Sophisticated Investors: Do They Have Any Rights?' (2010) 9 *Journal of International Banking and Financial Law*, 515.

49 [1964] AC 465.

50 Gerard McMeel, and John Virgo, *McMeel and Virgo on Financial Advice and Financial Products* (3rd ed, Oxford University Press 2014), 171.

51 Twigger, 'Sophisticated Investors: Do They Have Any Rights?' (n48), 515.

52 [1998] EWCA Civ 236, (1998) PNLR 564, [1998] Lloyd's Rep Bank 85).

53 BCCI [1998] PNLR 583.

54 *Caparo Industries plc v Dickman* [1990] 2AC 605.

55 It was first recognised in *Hedley Byrne* and reinterpreted in *Junior Books Ltd v Veitchi Co Ltd* [1983] 1 AC 520.

56 High Court of Australia *Sutherland Shire Council v Heyman* [1985] 157 CLR 424, 481. Approved by the House of Lords in *Murphy v Brentwood District Council* [1991] 1 AC 398, 461.

the twentieth century[57] allowed the recognition of liability in tort for negligent acts[58] and negligent omissions.[59] We would now open the discussion on the content of the duty of care of CCPs in front of their clearing members and their clients as a form of expansion of liability in the tort of negligence.

Although the existence of a duty of care of CCPs has not been recognised in courts, some recent cases elucidate the importance of reviewing its potential content. The first is *MF Global UK Ltd (In Special Administration) v LCH Clearnet Ltd*.[60] In this case, the Joint Special Administrators of MF Global applied for an order under the Insolvency Act 1986 s236 or s237 (3) against the respondent French and UK companies, seeking the production of documents and a full description of the sales or auction process by which the respondents' close-out of MF Global open positions with the defendants. LCH Clearnet (respondents) operated the clearing houses in different jurisdictions, including the UK and France. When MF Global went into administration in 2011, it had a number of open positions with LCH Clearnet, including European Sovereign Debt. Since the appointment of MF Global administrators constituted a default event, LCH Clearnet exercised the right to close out MF Global's open positions. The MF Global administrators allege that the value of the losses suffered was significantly larger than it should have been. In particular, the administrators calculated that 'if all the open positions had been closed at or around the prices quoted by Bloomberg, on the relevant termination dates, the discount suffered would have been €241 million, as opposed to €422 million'.[61] According to the MF Global administrators, it is not clear why there were such significant differences between the Bloomberg prices and the close-out prices. The discussion was, therefore, whether LCH Clearnet exercised its right to close out the positions of its client in accordance with the duty of care. In this case, it was sought to understand the process that LCH Clearnet would close out the open positions, including the selection of the participants in the sale process, as well as the explanation of how bids were obtained and reviewed. LCH Clearnet made all the relevant information available. Although the application was dismissed, there is an important consideration to highlight from this case: the limited liability of LCH Clearnet to bad faith acts that clearly diminish their counterparties' rights. Under the current regime, clearing houses – more specifically CCPs – are allowed by statute to limit their responsibility. Their counterparts can seek access to the information about how diligent CCPs have been in performing their obligations or exercising their contractual rights. However, once the information is received, the only cause of action would be acts of bad faith, fraud, or gross negligence. In other

---

57 Gerard McMeel, and John Virgo, *McMeel and Virgo on Financial Advice and Financial Products* (n50).
58 *Donoghue v Stevenson* [1932] AC 562.
59 *Home Office v Dorset Yacht Co Ltd* [1970] AC 1004.
60 *MF Global UK Ltd (In Special Administration), Re*, also known as *Fleming v LCH Clearnet Ltd* [2015] EWHC 2319 (Ch).
61 *MF Global UK Ltd (In Special Administration)*.

words, CCPs can act as negligently as possible and the only limit is the utmost negligence or wilful default.

The second case that offers an interesting perspective regarding the management and value of clients' assets is *MF Global UK Ltd (In Administration), Re.*[62] In this case, the joint administrators of MF Global UK sought a direction from the court relating to the distributions to be made to clients of an insolvent investment bank. Similar to the obligation of CCPs, investment firms were required to segregate money received from or held for their clients and hold it in a trust for them; that money is called 'client money'. According to the Client Assets Sourcebook (CASS) Chapters 7 and 7A, in the event of administration or liquidation of the firm amongst other circumstances, client money had to be distributed among the clients pro rata according to their entitlements. The value of the client's entitlement was to be established as at the date when the obligation arose – the primary pooling event (PPE).

The dispute in the case was whether that calculation in the event of administration or liquidation was to be done with the market value, as at the PPE, or with the prices at which the trades were subsequently closed out,[63] whether at the contractual settlement date or at an earlier date in accordance with applicable default provisions.[64] The Court held that the client's money entitlement had to be valued by reference to market value as at the PPE, rather than by reference to the subsequent closed out prices. Moreover, it clarified that the hindsight principle only operates as a default mechanism to fill gaps in relevant regulation and that it was not applicable to the determination of claims to client money for the purposes of a distribution under CASS 7A.

This case is illustrative, because it explains how the client assets regime contributes to determine the valuation methodology during the normal course of business, as well as in the event of insolvency. Although the CASS regime is not applicable to CCPs operating in the OTCDM, the discussions in the case show the importance of having such a regime in place. The existence of a client assets regime does not prevent litigation but seeks to enhance the certainty regarding the process of valuation of assets and provides an additional layer of protection of clients and clearing members' rights. The absence of regulatory guidance related to the management and valuation of assets leaves these issues, as is the case with CCPs, to the discretion of the dominant counterparty.

Against this background, we emphasise the need to review the statutory and contractual limits to the liability of CCPs. The restriction of CCPs' liability to acts in bad faith, gross negligence, and wilful default have a substantial impact on the ability of clearing members and their clients to enforce their rights. One way to assist the review of the regime is to construct a 'duty of care' applicable to CCPs when performing their obligations. Such a duty of care should comprise, in particular, the duty of CCP to act fairly and professionally in accordance with

---

62 [2013] EWHC 92 (Ch).
63 Ibid.
64 Ibid.

the best interests of clearing members and clients. The standards of conduct contained in MiFID I, MiFID II, and EMIR are a useful framework to build up the scope of the duty and would complete the UK regime.[65]

This study anticipates some shortcomings of the proposal to review the limited liability regime. Even if UK regulators consider the reform of the statutory provision that allows recognised bodies to restrict its liability in the terms of s291 of FSMA 2000, the courts may be reluctant to the recognise CCPs' liability beyond bad faith. English courts tend to adopt a certain approach in cases concerning the interpretation of contractual clauses, as described in some of the arguments of McMeel in 'Myth of Contractual Estoppel'. According to McMeel,[66] until 2006, English judges would always consider the written contract, but they were generally prepared to recognise that what was set down in writing did not always reflect the realities of the relevant transaction. However, in the 2006 *Peekay*[67] case and the 2010 *Springwell* case,[68] the Courts interpreted that where parties had agreed to enter into a contract on a certain basis, they could not then claim at a later stage that the reality of the situation was something different. Applied in the context of the clauses limiting the liability of CCPs, this means that, whatever the reality of the situation, the strict wording of the original contract is upheld.[69] Thus, along with the reform of the statutory limitation of liability, regulators should develop the scope and content of CCPs' liability. Otherwise, CCPs would continue to include clauses with a similar content that are likely to be upheld in English courts.

Similarly, English courts have been reluctant to recognise the existence of a duty of care when the counterparties are 'sophisticated investors'.[70] However, the interpretation in those cases has been focused on the extent to which

---

65 House of Lords European Union Committee 5th Report of Session 2014, The Post-Crisis EU Financial Regulatory Framework: Do the Pieces Fit? 15; see *The Select Committee on the European Union Sub-Committee A (Economic and Financial Affairs) Inquiry on Review of the EU Financial Regulatory Framework Evidence Session No 13 Tuesday 21 October 2014 Witnesses: Sue Lewis and Colin Tyler* <http://data.parliament.uk/writtenevidence/committeeevidence.svc/evidencedocument/eu-sub-a-economic-and-financial-affairs-committee/review-of-the-eu-financial-regulatory-framework/oral/14797.html> accessed 15th October 2015. For all retail clients and all clients engaged in MiFID. In the COBS 2, there is a new MiFID-inspired rule that a firm must act 'honestly, fairly and professionally in accordance with the best interests of its client'. This rule will be actionable by private persons in accordance with section 138D of FSMA 2000 (as substituted by s 24 of FSA 2012).

66 Gerard McMeel, 'Documentary Fundamentalism in the Senior Courts: The Myth of Contractual Estoppel' (2011) *Lloyd's Maritime and Commercial Law Quarterly*, 185.

67 *Peekay Intermark Ltd v Australia and New Zealand Banking Group Ltd* [2006] 2 Lloyd's Rep 511.

68 *Springwell Navigation Corporation v JP Morgan Chase Bank & Ors* [2010] EWCA Civ 1221.

69 A practitioner's opinion on contractual estoppel, 'Contractual Estoppel – Testing the Banks' Position (November 2011) <www.enyolaw.com/news/contractual-estoppel-testing-the-banks-position-november-2011> accessed 23rd October 2015.

70 Ibid.

sophisticated counterparties understand the content of contracts[71] and the riskiness of the investments.[72] Our approach here is different: the scope of the duty of care of CCPs is not restricted to giving advice to their counterparties – it is centred on the standard of diligence in the holding and management of assets and positions of clearing members. It is a duty applicable to the normal course of business of CCPs, as well as the insolvency of a CCP.

In the area of acting fairly and professionally in the best interests of clearing members and their clients, the regulators would have the opportunity to dictate solutions to the conflicting interests, designing a system of rules and guidance that articulates the interests of CCPs, clearing members, and their clients along with public policy objectives. This would present a formidable challenge to any regulator. However, the recognition of the duty of care would rebalance the relationship between CCPs and clearing members, and could potentially benefit more complex or indirect relationships (clearing members' clients).

In developing the content of duty of care, regulators might be assisted by CCPs; the motivation behind introducing a duty of care is not to attack CCPs, but to facilitate the normal course of business and execution of contractual obligations. The enhancement of a culture of cooperation between the contractual parties reduces the causes of future litigation and increases the certainty and reliability of contractual terms.

4.3 Absence of a special resolution regime for CCPs

The third shortcoming of the UK's regime of CCPs in the OTCDM is the absence of an SRR. The Bank has focused its prudential regulation on the development of loss-allocation and recovery rules, aiming to ensure that CCPs have in place efficient rules to allocate the losses arising from clearing members' default and losses originated in a different cause (losses originated in the normal course of business or those triggered by investment). The strengthening of recovery rules has occupied the supervision in the first years of the regime. Although the expectation is that CCPs will be robust enough not to enter into any type of insolvency, failure is still a possibility. Therefore, supervisors should have a complete regulatory framework to conduct CCPs' insolvency proceedings in an orderly manner, seeking to ameliorate the consequences of the CCPs' default and to ensure the continuity of services.

CCP insolvency occurs when the default and recovery rules have not been sufficient to manage the financial distress. The recovery of a CCP comprises a wide range of measures, including the allocation of the uncovered losses caused by

---

71 J. Mance said in *Bankers Trust International Plc v Dharmala Sakti Sejahtera* [1996] CLC 518; Lord Hoffmann said in *Commissioners of Customs and Excise v Barclays Bank plc* [2007] 1 AC 181, 'the law of negligence does not impose liability for mere omissions'.

72 See for example, *IFE Fund v Goldman Sachs International* [2007] Lloyds Rep 449 (CA) and *Titan Steel Wheels Ltd v Royal Bank of Scotland plc* [2010] EWHC 211 (Comm), in *Peekay Intermark Ltd v ANZ Banking Group* Ltd [2006] CLC 582.

participant default,[73] liquidity shortfalls,[74] tools to replenish financial resources,[75] tools for a CCP to re-establish a matched book, and mechanisms to allocate losses not related to participants' default.[76] In the UK, the Bank has devoted the regulatory efforts towards the design of strong recovery rules.[77] As we have noted before, the UK recovery regime goes beyond the EMIR requirements and imposes an additional obligation to CCPs: requiring them to have in place rules to allocate losses arising from different reasons than clearing members' default (e.g. investment losses).

According to the structure of the key elements upon which the Bank focuses its assessment of CCPs, the recovery and resolvability rules are allocated as structural mitigation of risk. The Bank announced in 2013[78] that the areas of risk identification and mitigation represent the most important and fundamental requirements for CCPs. Hence, the supervision would cover both the design of CCPs' rules and the use of management discretion in the application of those rules. The Bank classifies the mitigating factors into three categories: operational mitigants, financial mitigants, and structural mitigation.[79] The operational mitigants include the promotion and maintenance of standards, management and governance, risk management and controls, and disaster recovery plans. The financial mitigants involve the rules concerning collateral, margins and default funds, liquid resources, and capital requirements. The structural mitigation comprises recovery and resolvability regimes. This range illustrates the various tools and mechanisms that CCPs have to protect themselves against counterparty credit risk and other potential sources of losses. Therefore, the resolution regime only applies after all the fences of the CCP have been insufficient to allocate and absorb losses.

Recovery and resolvability regimes are a tool for the effective management of participants' default, and the provision to ensure that CCPs have adequate financial resources to contain losses or liquidity shortfalls, whilst minimising the disruption to the system and the products they clear. These regimes are closely linked to risk management practices that CCPs should observe in order to comply with the PFMI.[80] Under this rationale, the Bank follows the guidance of the PMFIs[81] to structure its approach. In particular, CCPs are required to have clear

---

73 Key Consideration 7 of Principle 4 of the PFMI. CPMI-IOSCO, 'Recovery of Financial Market Infrastructures' (October 2014) <www.bis.org/cpmi/publ/d121.pdf> accessed 5th November 2015 (hereinafter CPMI-IOSCO Recovery of FMIs 2014).

74 Key Consideration 10 of Principle 7 of the PFMI, Ibid.

75 For instance, obtain liquidity from participants to replenish financial resources by means of cash calls and/or raise additional equity capital, CPMI-IOSCO Recovery of FMIs 2014.

76 These are extraordinary one-off loss or recurring losses from general business, custody, and investment risks, Ibid.

77 Ibid.

78 Bank of England, 'The Bank of England's Approach to the Supervision of Financial Market Infrastructures' (April 2013) 5 (hereinafter the Bank's approach to FMIs' Supervision, 2013).

79 Ibid 7.

80 CPMI-IOSCO Recovery of FMIs 2014.

81 Principle 4, Key Consideration 7 of the PFMI (n73).

rules on how any losses in excess of loss-absorbing resources would be allocated (as well as the use of contractual procedures of tear-up contracts as a last-resort mechanism); the design of loss-allocation rules should be sensitive to the incentives given to participants and intended to maintain the continuity of services. Also, the loss-allocation rules should ensure that losses fall on participants and shareholders. Beyond the hypothesis of participants' default, the Bank requires CCPs to have in place rules to allocate the losses that directly reduce their capital resources;[82] for instance, when the CCP invests the margin or part of the default fund it received from participants and suffers investment losses.

Regarding the resolution regime of CCPs, the Bank announced that certain rules and proceedings of CCPs would have implications for the Bank's resolution options.[83] For instance, the segregation requirement is a mechanism that, as explained earlier, contributes to isolate the impact of a participant's default and may facilitate the resolution of both CCPs and clearing members. Also, the transfer of full ownership of the assets that constitute the collateral provide the CCP with a high level of flexibility in liquidity management.[84] Moreover, if the margin received by the CCP is not bankruptcy remote, it could be subject to a reduction in its value (a write down) in line with the 'no-creditor-worse-off' safeguard,[85] which in the Bank's opinion would broaden the set of potential resolution strategies.

The design of a UK special resolution regime for CCPs would be in line with international OTCDM reform. One of the safeguards to support a resilient and efficient framework for central clearing is to have in place 'resolution and recovery regimes that aim to ensure the core functions of CCPs are maintained during times of crisis'.[86] Following this objective, the FSB, in consultation with CPMI-IOSCO, issued guidance on FMI Resolution and the Key Attributes of Effective Resolution Regimes.[87] The objective is that SRRs attend to the particularities of

---

82 Adding to the recognition requirements, the July 2013 amendments also required CCPs, by February 2014, to put in place rules to allocate losses arising from CMs' default that exceed the pre-funded resources. And by May 2014, arrangements to allocate insolvency-threatening losses arising other than as a result of a clearing member's default (non-default losses). *The Bank of England's supervision of Financial Market Infrastructures, Annual Report*, March 2015 (hereinafter the Bank's supervision of FMIs 2nd Annual Report 2015) 13–14. See David Elliott, 'Central Counterparty Loss-Allocation Rules' (Bank of England, Stability Paper No 20, 2013) <www.bankofengland.co.uk/financialstability/Documents/fpc/fspapers/fs_paper20.pdf> accessed 5th November 2015.

83 The Bank's approach to FMIs' Supervision, 2013, 9.

84 Ibid 10.

85 Katy Stone, 'Three-Step Strategy for Resolution of Failed Institutions'. Opinions of Andrew Wilkinson and Alexander Wood, and Kate Stephenson Weil, Gotshal & Manges LLP, Lexis-Nexis Blog. (6th November 2014) <http://blogs.lexisnexis.co.uk/randi/three-step-strategy-for-resolution-of-failed-institutions/> accessed 5th 2015.

86 FSB, 'OTC Derivatives Market Reforms – Eight Progress Report on Implementation' (7 November 2014).

87 FSB, 'Key Attributes of Effective Resolution Regimes for Financial Institutions' (15 October 2014) <www.financialstabilityboard.org/wp-content/uploads/r_141015.pdf> accessed 2nd November 2015.

each type of FMI, among them CCPs. The design of the SRR will help to overcome the shortcomings rising from applying general laws or, in the case of the UK, banking insolvency laws to the defaulted clearing house.[88]

The first step towards ruling CCPs' insolvency in the UK was to extend the insolvency regime of the Banking Act 2009 to CCPs. On 24th February 2015, secondary legislation[89] was enacted which amends the FSMA Regulations 2013.[90] The amendment[91] sought to ensure that the SRR under the Banking Act 2009 was applicable to CCPs based in the UK; this came into force on 18th March 2015.

The Code of Practice[92] explains how the Banking Act 2009 applies to CCPs.[93] In particular, it delimits the circumstances in which the Bank, acting as the Resolution Authority, will use the stabilisation powers. The Code provides guidance as to how the SRR applicable to CCPs achieves the objectives[94] to protect and enhance financial stability and public confidence, protect public funds, and avoid interfering with property rights. The Bank will have regarded those objectives in using the stabilisation powers with respect to CCPs.[95] Such stabilisation powers include the power to transfer some or all the business of a CCP or its group undertaking to a commercial purchaser, the power to transfer some or all the business of a CCP or its group undertaking to a bridge CCP (a company wholly owned and controlled by the Bank), and the power to transfer the ownership of the CCP to any person. According to the FSA 2012, in the first two events the Bank is allowed to transfer membership agreements, which preserve the position of each member together with the rules of operation of the failed CCP.

88 CPSS-IOSCO (CPSS (now CPMI)-IOSCO), 'Consultative Report: Recovery of Financial Market Infrastructures' (August 2013) <www.bis.org/cpmi/publ/d109.pdf> accessed 18th January 2018.
89 Regulations 2015 make an amendment to the transitional provision included in the Financial Services and Markets Act 2000 (Over the Counter Derivatives, Central Counterparties, and Trade Repositories) Regulation 2013 (SI 2013/504) ('the Principal Regulations'). Regulation 25 of the Principal Regulations made amendments to Part 1 of the Banking Act 2009 (hereinafter BA 2009) to the effect that the special resolution regime provided for in Part 1 of the 2009 Act will apply to 'recognised central counterparties', i.e. those CCPs which are subject to, and recognised pursuant to, the requirements of Regulation (EU) 648/2012 of the European Parliament and of the Council of 4th July 2012 on OTC Derivatives, Central Counterparties, and Trade Repositories (OJ No L 201, 27 17 2012, 1).
90 FSMA 2000, Regulations 2013 govern OTC Derivatives, CCPs and TRs.
91 'The FSMA 2000 (OTC Derivatives, Central Counterparties, and Trade Repositories) (Amendment) Regulations 2015' <www.legislation.gov.uk/uksi/2015/348/pdfs/uksi_20150348_en.pdf> accessed 2nd November 2015.
92 HM Treasury, 'Banking Act 2009: Special Resolution Regime Code of Practice' (March 2015) Chapter 13: SRR for Central Counterparties (hereinafter BA CoP 2015) <www.gov.uk/government/uploads/system/uploads/attachment_data/file/411563/banking_act_2009_code_of_practice_web.pdf> accessed 2nd November 2015.
93 The authorities are legally obliged to have regard to the Code under s5(4) of the Act.
94 Special Resolution Objectives are set out in s4 of the BA 2009.
95 S 4 (2) BA 2009.

In October 2017, the Bank reaffirmed its position about the applicability of the Banking Act 2009 as the resolution regime for CCPs. It clarified, however, that the only resolution powers inapplicable to CCPs are the bail-in tool and the asset management vehicle tool.[96]

As might be anticipated, the Bank's first aim is to exercise the stabilisation powers to maintain the continuity of CCP clearing services[97] – an objective that is also relevant for the protection of financial stability and public confidence. The special attention given to the continuity of CCPs' services is in line with the recognition of the systemic importance of CCPs in the OTCDM and in the financial system. This is to understand that there are wider systemic risks posed by a failure of a CCP and that any action or omission of regulators in such an event will also have systemic impact.[98] Moreover, the prominent position of CCPs as systemic risk managers highlights the role of CCPs as *de facto* regulators and supervisors for the markets they clear.[99] By protecting themselves, CCPs impose market discipline on their clearing members and clients. Thus, default management, recovery, and resolution rules for CCPs are part of their necessary armour to contribute to systemic stability.

Although the UK is one of the jurisdictions leading the regulatory advances on CCPs resolution,[100] by anticipating how the Bank would exercise the stabilisation powers, it is equally important that it goes beyond this and designs a special resolution regime for CCPs. The main focus of the Bank as prudential regulator is to ensure the safety and soundness of CCPs, making them robust institutions – but a core feature of a stable financial system requires recognising that financial institutions are resolvable.[101] This, indeed, is the key shortcoming of the current UK regime for CCPs in the OTCDM. It seems that the Bank is reluctant to recognise that CCPs might fail,[102] and in consequence it has been strictly focused on developing recoverability rules, leaving the resolution regime aside. Recovery and loss-allocation rules are certainly an important part of the prudential regulation

96 Bank of England, 'The Bank of England's approach to resolution' (October 2017) <www. bankofengland.co.uk/-/media/boe/files/news/2017/october/the-bank-of-england-approach-to-resolution> accessed 24th December 2017.

97 S 4 (6) BA 2009.

98 BA CoP 2015, 81.

99 Paul Tucker, 'Clearing Houses as System Risk Managers' (Bank of England, Speech at the DTCC-CSFI Post Trade Fellowship Launch, London (1 June 2011) <www.bankofen gland.co.uk/archive/Documents/historicpubs/speeches/2011/speech501.pdf> accessed 4th November 2015.

100 FSB, *Progress and Next Steps Towards Ending 'Too-Big-To-Fail: Report of the Financial Stability Board to the G-20* (2 September 2013) <www.financialstabilityboard.org/wp-con tent/uploads/r_130902.pdf?page_moved=1> accessed 4th November 2015.

101 Bank of England, 'Consultation Paper: The Bank of England's Powers to Direct Institutions to Address Impediments to Resolvability' (May 2015).

102 Arshadur Rahman, 'Over-The-Counter (OTC) Derivatives, Central Clearing and Financial Stability' (Bank of England, Bank's Financial Market Infrastructure Directorate, *Quarterly Bulletin* 2015 Q3), 291 <www.bankofengland.co.uk/quarterly-bulletin/2015/over-the-counter-derivatives-central-clearing-and-financial-stability> accessed 9th November 2015.

of CCPs, but the regime must be completed with efficient resolution rules.[103] The delay in developing a special resolution regime for CCPs is in principle attributable to the EU in not issuing the relevant regulation or guidance – only on 28th November 2016 the first EU legislation proposal was issued[104] – but also to the international perception[105] that the CCPs' default must be maintained at essentially zero.[106] Therefore, we aim here to discuss some of the aspects to be considered in the resolution of CCPs and to justify a different regime to that of the Banking Act 2009, which was designed for banks.

4.3.1 CCP failure is a possibility

Earlier in the chapter, we discussed how UK regulators seem to perceive that the failure of a CCP is not going to happen and, as a result, the regulatory action does not include the design of a resolution regime that attends to the particularities of CCPs. Some scholars argue that regulating CCPs is less complicated than regulating banks, and that the regime can be designed so that CCPs are almost 'default-free'.[107] Indeed, Hull proposes that the key element to achieve a CCP free from default is a regime that ensures CCPs have in place good practices regarding the choosing of members, valuation of transactions and determination of initial and variation margins, and default fund contributions. Moreover, he explains that the content of the contract between CCPs and clearing members can contribute to achieving the objective.[108] However, this would seem to be a simplistic approach to CCP regulation, restricted to transactional issues, ignoring

---

103 Matt Gibson, 'Recovery and Resolution of Central Counterparties' *Reserve Bank of Australia Bulletin* December Quarter (2013) 39 <www.rba.gov.au/publications/bulletin/2013/dec/pdf/bu-1213-5.pdf> accessed 4th November 2015; see Financial Services and the Treasury Bureau, the Hong Kong Monetary Authority, the Securities and Futures Commission and the Insurance Authority, 'An Effective Resolution Regime for Financial Institutions in Hong Kong: Consultation Paper' (January 2014) <www.fstb.gov.hk/fsb/ppr/consult/resolution_e.pdf> accessed 4th November 2015.

104 Proposal for a Regulation of the European Parliament and of the Council on a Framework for the Recovery and Resolution of Central Counterparties and Amending Regulations (EU) No 1095/2010 (EU) No 648/2012, and (EU) 2015/2365 <http://eur-lex.europa.eu/legal-content/EN/TXT/?uri=CELEX%3A52016PC0856> accessed 11th December 2017 (hereinafter EU Proposal CCPs Recovery and Resolution).

105 'Federal Reserve Bank of New York President Says Post-Crisis Derivatives Clearinghouses Must Be Bulletproof', Michael Mackenzie, 'Call for 'Bulletproof' Clearing Houses' *FT* (22 March 2012) <www.ft.com/cms/s/0/eacb29cc-7451-11e1-9e4d-00144feab49a.html#axzz3r5s4KjUu> accessed 10th November 2015.

106 BIS, 'Macroeconomic Impact Assessment of OTC Derivatives Regulatory Reforms' *BIS*, Macroeconomic Assessment Group on Derivatives (August 2013) 15 <www.bis.org/publ/othp20.pdf> accessed 4th November 2015.

107 John C. Hull, 'The Changing Landscape for Derivatives' (April 24, 2014), Rotman School of Management Working Paper No 2428983 <http://ssrn.com/abstract=2428983> or <http://dx.doi.org/10.2139/ssrn.2428983> accessed 4th November 2015.

108 John Hull, 'CCPs, Their Risks, and How They Can Be Reduced' (Fall 2012) 20 (1) *Journal of Derivatives*, 26–29.

the complexities of the CCPs' functioning and failing to understand the systemic importance of these institutions. In the words of Duffie, 'the bulk of the financial risk of a CCP is not represented by conventional assets and liabilities',[109] as is the case with banks, broker-dealers, and insurance companies. CCPs involve a nexus of multiple contracts that clearing members use to net and mutualise their credit risk. Thus, the management of CCPs' failure requires a regime designed, amongst other aspects, to minimise the distress costs of all market participants, clearing members, third parties, and taxpayers that could suffer the spill-over costs.[110]

This is not the place to discuss the benefits and limits of CCPs in the OTCDM, but it is worth noting the vulnerable nature of these systemically important financial institutions.[111] A comprehensive insolvency regime is the armour that ensures CCP robustness and resilience, which in turn benefits the stability of the OTCDM and the financial system. A special resolution regime might counter the argument that clearing houses are weak bulwarks against financial contagion,[112] financial panic, and systemic risk.[113] The updating of the insolvency regime[114] will enhance the use of tools available to provide a better management of CCPs' failure and will prevent difficulties similar or even greater than those faced during the GFC from arising again.

Despite the fact that the resolution of a CCP is, indeed, a rare scenario,[115] it cannot be denied that CCPs are subject to a number of risks that could threaten their viability.[116] CCPs centralise the credit risk of a large part of the OTCDM; as a result, it is possible that they may fail.[117] The systemic importance of CCPs and the impact of their potential or actual failure is not merely a theoretical

---

109 Darrell Duffie, 'Resolution of Failing Counterparties' (2014) Stanford University Working Paper N 3256, 17 December <www.gsb.stanford.edu/gsb-cmis/gsb-cmis-get-alfresco-doc/382301/notcase> accessed 5th November 2015.

110 Ibid.

111 Scott Farrell, 'Too Important to Fail: Legal Complexity in Planning for the Failure of Financial Market Infrastructure' (2014) 29 (8) *Journal of International Banking Law & Regulation*, 461.

112 Hal S. Scott, 'Interconnectedness and Contagion' Committee on Capital Markets Regulation (November 2012) <http://capmktsreg.org/app/uploads/2014/11/2012.11.20_Interconnectedness_and_Contagion.pdf> accessed 10th November 2015.

113 Mark J. Roe, 'Clearinghouse Overconfidence' (2013) 101 *California Law Review*, 1641 <http://ssrn.com/abstract=2224305> accessed 10th November 2015.

114 Mark J. Roe, and Stephen D. Adams, 'Restructuring Failed Financial Firms in Bankruptcy: Learning from Lehman' Harvard John M. Olin Center for Law, Economics and Business, 32 *Yale Journal on Regulation* 363 <www.law.harvard.edu/programs/olin_center/papers/pdf/Roe_796.pdf> accessed 4th November 2015.

115 See Tracy Alloway, 'A Glimpse at Failed Central Counterparties' FT Alphaville (2 June 2011) <http://ftalphaville.ft.com/2011/06/02/583116/a-glimpse-at-failed-central-counterparties/> accessed 4th November 2015.

116 CPMI-IOSCO Recovery of FMIs 2014.

117 Nikil Chande, Nicholas Labelle, and Eric Tuer, 'Central Counterparties and Systemic Risk' (Reports Bank of Canada Financial System Review, 2010).

discussion.[118] The GFC showed the prominent role that FMIs have in the midst of financial crises[119] and inspired the regulatory movement towards the adoption of CCPs in the OTCDM.[120] Therefore, prudential regulators are called to have in place a comprehensive legal framework to resolve CCPs in an orderly manner, avoiding the disturbance of clearing services. When attending to the size of the UK OTCDM,[121] national regulators have an important commitment to put in place a complete regime to ensure CCP resilience: one that manages the resolution of CCPs.

Our first argument in calling for a special resolution regime for CCPs is historical. The failures of clearing houses in the exchange market show that their systemically important role puts them in a very fragile position and that, like other big financial institutions, they can fail. The most notorious cases of CCPs' failure are Caisse de Liquidacion, Paris (1974), Kuala Lumpur Commodity Clearing House (1983), and Hong Kong Guarantee Corporation (1987).[122] Moreover, in the wake of the 1987 crash, both Chicago Mercantile Exchange (CME) and the Options Clearing Corporation (OCC) encountered severe difficulties in receiving margin and were near failure.[123]

Caisse de Liquidacion, the French clearing house, was closed down in 1974. In the period prior to the failure, the prices in the Paris white sugar market were extremely volatile. One of the primary causes of the clearing house failure was that the clearing house did not increase margin requirements in response to such volatility. Many participants defaulted on margin calls, in particular Nataf Trading House, which held a very large position. Due to the losses of the Nataf Trading House, the Ministry of Commerce closed the sugar market and ordered that any contract would be settled at the average price; the price was higher than when trading was suspended. The Ministry's decision was challenged in court

---

118 Paul Tucker, 'Central Counterparties in Evolving Capital Markets: Safety, Recovery and Resolution' in OTC Derivatives: New Rules, New Actors, New Risks' Banque de France – Financial Stability Review No 17 (April 2013) <www.bankofengland.co.uk/publications/Documents/speeches/2013/speech650.pdf> accessed 2nd November 2015.

119 'In recent history, CCPs globally have proved themselves to be robust over a set of market-wide events including extreme price volatility and participants default. In terms of participant events, major global CCPs have skilfully managed the crises that involved such as Drexel Burnham Lambert (1990), Barings (1995), Griffin (1998), Enron (2001), Refco (2005) and Lehman Brothers (2008)' Marcus Zickwolff, 'The Role of Central Counterparties in Financial Crisis Recovery' (World Federation of Exchanges, 2010) <www.world-exchanges.org/insight/views/role-central-counterparties-financial-crisis-recovery> accessed 5th October 2015.

120 Nikil Chande, Nichola Labelle, and Eric Tuer, 'Central Counterparties and Systemic Risk' (n117).

121 Arshadur Rahman, 'Over-The-Counter (OTC) Derivatives, Central Clearing and Financial Stability' (Bank of England) (n102), 286.

122 Jon Gregory, *Central Counterparties: Mandatory Clearing and Bilateral Margin Requirements for OTC Derivatives* (Wiley Finance Series 2014), 268.

123 IMF, 'Making OTC Derivatives Safer: The Role of Central Counterparties' FMI, Global Financial Stability Report (April 2010).

and two of Nataf's guarantors refused to cover the sums they owed, resulting in the insolvency of the Caisse de Liquidacion.

The case of the Kuala Lumpur Commodity Clearing House in Malaysia was the consequence of a crash in palm oil futures. In this case, six clearing members defaulted on a total of US$70 million, which led to the complete suspension of trading. National regulators blamed the impact on the market on the CCP, arguing that the CCP stopped operations when there were severe changes in market prices and with the default of the first clearing member.

The third case of CCP failure occurred with the Hong Kong Guarantee Corporation in the midst of the 1987 stock market crash. After a period of growth, the prices in the equity market of Hong Kong stock market dropped by almost 50 percent ('Black Monday').[124] The market was closed for four days and THE Corporation had to be bailed out. The bailout decision was motivated by the fears of unmet margin calls on purchased equity future positions[125] and serious concerns about the ability of the CCP to absorb the losses.

There have been other cases of CCPs' severe financial distress that, although they did not end in their failure, demonstrated their vulnerability. In the US, the CME,[126] OCC, and the Chicago Board of Trade (CBoT) were very close to failure.[127] According to the report of the SEC,[128] on several occasions during the week of Black Monday, OCCs' clearing members had inadequate funds in their clearing banks to satisfy OCC debit instructions. Thus, clearing banks were forced to decide whether to allow clearing members to overdraft on their accounts or to refuse to pay to the OCC. The large moves in and around Black Monday created interlinked problems concerning difficulties in receiving variation margins, extraordinary increases in volumes of trade, unexpected price volatility, and a lack of interoperability clearing arrangements.

Finally, the latest case of a CCP in financial distress involved *Bolsa de Valores, Mercadorias & Futuros de Sao Paulo* (BM&FBOVESPA).[129] In 1999, the president of Brazil decided to release control over the exchange rate, and the resulting mass devaluation of the Brazilian Real in respect to the US dollar was around

---

124 Alan Greenspan, Statement and Comments of Alan Greenspan, Chairman of the Federal Reserve, on Black Monday, The Stock Market Crash of October 19, 1987 US Congress Senate. Committee on Banking, Housing, and Urban Affairs, Hearing, 100 Congress 1 Session (Washington).

125 Mark Carlson, 'A Brief History of the 1987 Stock Market Crash with a Discussion of the Federal Reserve Response' (2007) <www.federalreserve.gov/pubs/feds/2007/200713/200713pap.pdf> accessed 2nd November 2015.

126 Chicago Mercantile Exchange, Committee of Inquiry (1987): Preliminary Report of the Committee of Inquiry, Merton Miller (Chairman), Chicago, Chicago Mercantile Exchange.

127 Ben Bernanke, 'Clearing and Settlement During the Crash' (1990) 3 (1) *The Review of Financial Studies*, 133–151 <www.jscc.co.jp/en/data/5.pdf> accessed 2nd November 2015.

128 US Securities and Exchange Commission (1988) The October 1987 Market Break.

129 Jon Gregory, *Central Counterparties: Mandatory Clearing and Bilateral Margin Requirements for OTC Derivatives* (n122), 270.

50 percent. The consequence was the failure of two large banks that were clearing members. The collapse was prevented with the bailout of the defaulting banks.

There are some common factors that can be identified from the cases described earlier. In particular, we should note the insufficiency of margins and default funds to absorb losses in the event of prices and market volatility, as well as shortcomings in the monitoring of positions of risk. Also, we observe the absence of mechanisms to control excessive exposure of one of the clearing members, as in Caisse de Liquidacion, and inefficient measures to manage clearing members' default, along with liquidity strains arising from operational issues faced by CCPs. Recognising that the insolvency of CCPs – although undesirable – can still occur,[130] current regulatory reforms draw several lessons from these historic failures or near-failures of clearing houses. The IMF highlights three lessons:[131] the regulation of margin requirements and the frequent adjustment to secure contract performance; the importance of market surveillance and the authority to manage destabilising exposures; and the coordination within the clearing house to monitor clearing members' positions.

The second argument for an SRR relates to the prominent position CCPs hold from a risk perspective. CCPs interpose themselves between the two clearing members and, as such, assume contractual rights and obligations. From the risk perspective, the most important function of CCPs is to collateralise every transaction. CCPs usually publish a standard methodology for collateralised transaction, calculated according to the risk model of the underlying asset, but it does not consider the creditworthiness of the counterparty,[132] as would be the case in a bilateral transaction.[133] The CCP protects itself and mutualises losses by requiring all clearing members to post collateral. The collateral is comprised of initial and variation margins, and the default fund contribution whose purpose is to absorb losses. The mutualisation of losses under the CCP structure improves the safety and soundness of the market, whilst at the same time the increased use of central clearing increases the systemic importance of the CCP. Thus, the CCP occupies a prominent position in the management of clearing members' default, to the extent that all the debts and credits of any insolvent member become subject to insolvent set-off in the hands of the CCP.[134]

Additionally, we can further emphasise the systemic role played by CCPs in the OTCDM when we consider that CCPs mitigate clearing members' credit

130 Bob Hills, 'Central Counterparty Clearing Houses and Financial Stability' (June 1999) *Financial Stability Review*, 129.

131 IMF, 'Making OTC Derivatives Safer: The Role of Central Counterparties' (n123).

132 Silla Bush, 'Dodd-Frank Swap-Clearing Rule Gets CFTC Final Approval' (Bloomberg 29 November 2012) <www.bloomberg.com/news/articles/2012-11-28/cftc-said-to-have-votes-to-complete-swap-clearing-requirement> accessed 10th November 2015.

133 Simon Gleeson, *International Regulation of Banking: Capital and Risk Requirements* (Oxford University Press 2012), 386.

134 Edward Bailey, and Hugo Groves, *Corporate Insolvency: Law and Practice* (4th edn, LexisNexis 2014), 1409.

risk by transferring that risk to creditors outside the CCP.[135] This is why CCPs *transfer* but do not *eliminate* systemic risk.[136] In this scenario, derivatives dealers are largely interconnected and only part of their transactions are centrally cleared. That the imposition of risk outside of the CCP may have systemic consequences[137] is precisely due to the fact that SIFIs enter into non-centrally cleared transactions.

4.3.2 *Features of CCPs' insolvency regime*

In the area of the insolvency of SIFIs, the most recent discussions come from the failure of Lehman Brothers.[138] Although Lehman is not a CCP, it is a case that demonstrates some common features affecting SIFIs in financial distress[139] in the OTCDM,[140] and from which regulators might draw some lessons. In the event of SIFI insolvency, it must be possible to stabilise the existent contracts effectively.[141] Hence, the SRR should allow the resolution authority to market the contracts of the portfolio at their fundamental value; note that this is different to the fire sale prices. Moreover, it is also recommended that the resolution authority hold the entire portfolio together and sell it along its product lines,[142] which is challenging due to the large size of such portfolios. Particularly in the case of CCPs,[143] the

---

135 Franklin R. Edwards, and Edward R. Morrison, 'Derivatives and the Bankruptcy Code: Why the Special Treatment?' (2005) 22 *Yale Journal on Regulation*, 91.

136 Craig Pirrong, 'The Clearinghouse Cure' (2008) 31 *Regulation*, 44, 48, 51.

137 Mark J. Roe, The Dodd-Frank Act's Maginot Line: Clearinghouse Construction 36 (5 March 2013) (unpublished working paper) <http://ssrn.com/abstract=2224305> in Sean J. Griffith, 'Clearinghouse Hope or Hype? Why Mandatory Clearing May Fail to Contain Systemic Risk' (2013) 3 *Harvard Business Law Review*, 160 <www.hblr.org/?p=326> accessed 10th November 2015.

138 'The commencement of LBHI's bankruptcy case – the largest by far in U.S. history, with claims well exceeding $300 billion – provided a contractual basis for a large majority of Lehman's derivatives counterparties to terminate their transactions with Lehman. As a result, more than 80 percent of Lehman's derivatives positions terminated as of, or soon after, the date of the bankruptcy filing' Report of Anton R. Valukas, Examiner, March 11, 2010 (*The Lehman Examiner's Report*).

139 Solomon J. Noh, 'Lessons from Lehman Brothers for Hedge Fund Managers: The Effect of a Bankruptcy Filing on the Value of the Debtor's Derivatives Book' (2012) 5 *The Hedge Fund Law Report* 7, 1 <www.shearman.com/~/media/Files/NewsInsights/Pub lications/2012/08/Lesson-from-Lehman-Brothers-for-Hedge-Fund-Manag__/Files/ View-full-article-Lesson-from-Lehman-Brothers-fo__/FileAttachment/BR_080112_Les sonfromLehmanBrosforHedgeFundManage__.pdf> accessed 10th October 2015.

140 Kimberly Summe, 'Misconceptions About Lehman Brothers' Bankruptcy and the Role Derivatives Played' (2011) 64 *Stanford Law Review*, 16, 18.

141 Mark J. Roe, and Stephen D. Adams, 'Restructuring Failed Financial Firms in Bankruptcy: Selling Lehman's Derivatives Portfolio' 32 *Yale Journal on Regulation* (2015) <http:// digitalcommons.law.yale.edu/cgi/viewcontent.cgi?article=1414&context=yjreg> (n114).

142 Howell E. Jackson, and Stephanie Massman, 'Options for Resolving Distressed Financial Conglomerates' Harvard Law School Working Paper (3 May 2015).

143 Sean J. Griffith, 'Clearinghouse Hope or Hype? Why Mandatory Clearing May Fail to Contain Systemic Risk' (n137).

authorisation for sales along product lines is a good place to start.[144] The rationale is to structure the insolvency regime to close out and liquidate positions in such a way that the portfolio is coherently sold when possible.

The design of an SRR should address some basic questions concerning how to efficiently allocate losses, how to mitigate fire sales,[145] and how to ensure the continuity of the clearing services.[146] In this regard, the industry shares the concern of the consequences of a CCP failure and has advised certain elements that a CCP resolution plan should include. In particular, JP Morgan[147] emphasises the importance that a resolution regime for CCPs effectively limits contagion, avoids pro-cyclicality,[148] and ensures the continuity of services. The first recommendation is that regulators design a credible recapitalisation strategy that seeks to favour recapitalisation over liquidation. The benefits of recapitalisation include the reduction of fire sale risk on collateral and preventing the creation of potential asymmetry of risk across participants, which in turn results in extreme volatility.

In the opinion of JP Morgan, the current framework of loss allocation in cases of clearing members' default is inefficient, hence the need for regulators to design a recapitalisation strategy. The shortcoming of the loss-allocation rules could be overcome by implementing standard stress tests; EMIR mandates CCPs to conduct stress tests, but at the same time foresees that CCPs apply different sets of stress tests in order to ensure safe and sound risk management.[149] The Bank has not designed a standard stress test, but to guide the bespoke stress tests developed by each CCP.[150] Therefore, although the international bodies will propose some minimum elements of CCPs' stress tests[151] that will be necessarily followed by the Bank, it has not included the standardisation of these tests within its regulatory priorities. Although the adoption of standardised stress tests is debated, there have been some private initiatives[152] proposing best practices CCP should

---

144 Mark J. Roe, and Stephen D. Adams, 'Restructuring Failed Financial Firms in Bankruptcy: Selling Lehman's Derivatives Portfolio' (n114).
145 JP Morgan Chase & Co, 'What Is a Resolution Plan for CCPs?' (September 2014) <www.jpmorganchase.com/corporate/About-JPMC/document/resolution-plan-ccps.pdf> accessed 9th November 2015.
146 Darrell Duffie, 'Resolution of Failing Counterparties' (n109).
147 JP Morgan Chase & Co, 'What Is a Resolution Plan for CCPs?' (n145).
148 BIS, 'The Role of Margin Requirements and Haircuts in Procyclicality' (CGFS Papers No 36, March 2010) <www.bis.org/publ/cgfs36.pdf> accessed 10th November 2015.
149 According to EMIR article 42(3) and 43(2), CCPs should perform stress tests to quantify whether they have sufficient resources to cover the losses from the default of at least one or two clearing members.
150 Interview with Mr Paul Brione Head of Central Counterparty Supervision, Bank of England, London, 25 September 2015.
151 CPMI-IOSCO started the review of CCPs stress tests in March 2015, BIS, Press Release (11 March 2015) <www.bis.org/press/p150311.htm> accessed 9th November 2015. A CPMI-IOSCO report for public consultation on all CCP resilience and recovery issues is expected to be published by mid-2016.
152 European Association of CCP Clearing Houses (EACH), 'Best Practices for CCPs Stress Tests' (April 2015) <www.eachccp.eu/wp-content/uploads/2015/07/EACH-paper-Best-practices-for-CCPs-stress-tests-April-2015.pdf> accessed 9th November 2015 (hereinafter, EACH Best Practices).

observe when conducting stress tests and, in that way, achieve a certain level of standardisation. The objective of the European CCPs' initiative in this matter is to clarify the meaning of 'extreme-but-plausible market conditions' – the parameter referred to in EMIR when conducting stress tests. In order to achieve a degree of standardisation, CCPs propose a set of best practices for stress tests, which include principles[153] and risk management areas where best practices are needed.[154]

These recurrent discussions[155] and concerns indicate that there is an important pending task regarding the design and implementation of CCPs' stress tests, and one in which it would be advisable for the Bank to be more proactive. Indeed, the FSB recognises that one of the substantive priorities with respect to CCP resilience is the review of existing stress testing policies.[156] Accordingly, the recommendation of the FSB is to implement a 'supervisory stress test' as a complement to the CCPs' internal stress tests. The adoption of a common framework would enhance confidence in the adequacy of CCPs' resources and allow the comparison of those resources among CCPs.[157] Similarly, the implementation of a stress test framework would assist regulators in the identification of macroprudential risks[158] arising from CCPs in stressful scenarios.

Duffie recommends the use of different techniques to crystallise the losses to counterparties and to contractually restructure their clearing payment obligations to clearing members.[159] One is the procedure known as Variation Margin Gains Haircutting (VMGH).[160] According to this technique, when the default fund is insufficient to absorb losses, the CCP can 'reduce ("haircut") pro rata across all clearing members the variation margin payments that it is due to make to clearing members whose positions (in the relevant clearing services) have increased in value since the default'.[161] The shortfall of the VMGH might be the unexpected consequences regarding the potential reaction of end-users liquidating assets in order to raise funds. This could result in a decrease of the assets value and the creation of a pro-cyclical scenario that further destabilises the market.[162]

---

153 Principles of Relevance, Structure, Governance and Transparency, EACH Best Practices Ibid.

154 Stress test scenarios, period of risks, stress positions and practices, stress liquidity, aggregation, collateral, and disclosure, among others. EACH Best Practices, Ibid.

155 Here, Khalique considers the need for CCPs to make their stress test data more transparent, Farah Khalique, 'Countdown Begins to Clearing House Resilience Rules' (2015) 13 (5) *Global Risk Regulator*, 14–15.

156 FSB, 'Progress Report on the CCP Workplan' (22 September 2015) <www.financialstability board.org/wp-content/uploads/Progress-report-on-the-CCP-work-plan.pdf> accessed 9th November 2015.

157 Ibid.

158 Ibid.

159 Darrell Duffie, 'Resolution of Failing Counterparties' (n109).

160 Craig Pirrong, 'ISDA The Economics of Central Clearing: Theory and Practice' (University of Houston, May 2011) <www2.isda.org/attachment/MzE0Ng==/ISDAdiscus sion_CCP_Pirrong.pdf> accessed 9th November 2015.

161 David Elliot at the Bank describes the process for VMGH and the potential advantages over insolvency, David Elliott, 'Central Counterparty Loss-Allocation Rules' (n82).

162 JP Morgan Chase & Co, 'What is a Resolution Plan for CCPs?' (n145).

The second contractual restructuring approach is a 'tear-up'. The tear-up technique is used in very extreme scenarios to return to a matched book and consists of 'cash settlement and cancellation without reopening open contracts'.[163] The price might be based on the price used to calculate the most recent variation in margin requirements.[164] Although this technique might encourage clearing members to reduce the size of their positions with weak CCPs, the problem with tear-ups is that they share losses unpredictably, which is not efficient, and discourages clearing members who expect to suffer moderate and predictable losses.[165]

However, as might be anticipated, VMGH and tear-ups are more recovery than resolvability techniques. Along with them, CCPs have the default fund, or 'guarantee fund', that receives contributions from all clearing members and is called to meet the losses in the case that they exceed a defaulting member's initial margin.[166] Thus, only when all the available resources and contractual proceedings are inadequate and insufficient will a resolution be the alternative. In this matter, JP Morgan suggests that one alternative to ensure that all market participants are fully funded is to enforce their liability. The rationale behind this proposal is to use the standard stress tests to measure the upfront obligation of each participant and, in that way, remove all the uncertainty regarding the sufficiency of funds in extreme circumstances. JP Morgan's approach is to ensure the adequacy of resources to mutualise losses and take the regime closer to achieving the 'default-free' expectation. However, the drawbacks of such a proposal are the heavy burden put on clearing members and the hurdles imposed by the conditions to meet such requirements. Indeed, there are already complaints and critiques regarding the higher margin requirements that the reforms have brought for both cleared and uncleared derivatives. Therefore, a reform seeking to increase the pre-funding of all loss-absorbency resources would be even more rejected by market participants and by regulators that are interested in supervising the market but do not want to squeeze it by making central clearing even more costly.

Despite the critiques that the imposition of higher or additional contributions from clearing members to common or recapitalisation funds might have, it seems to be the predominant alternative. The joint 2015 CCP workplan called for the FSB Resolution Steering Group (ReSG) to 'assess the need for additional prefunded financial resources (including capital) and liquidity arrangements in resolution and to develop a proposal'.[167] The aim is to create a fund that will operate only when the recovery mechanisms have been exhausted and the CCP is

163 David Elliott, 'Central Counterparty Loss-Allocation Rules' (n82), 8.
164 Ibid.
165 Darrell Duffie, 'Resolution of Failing Counterparties' (n109).
166 Fergus Cumming and Joseph Noss, 'Assessing the Adequacy of CCPs' Default Resources' (Bank of England, Financial Stability Paper No 26, November 2013) 4 <www.bankof england.co.uk/financialstability/Documents/fpc/fspapers/fs_paper26.pdf> accessed 9th November 2015.
167 FSB, 'Progress Report on the CCP Workplan' (2015) (n156).

not viable anymore. The fund will include contributions from clearing members and CCPs, and will be triggered when the resolution authority considers it to be pertinent. Such recapitalisation funds will be the new default funds while the CCP recovers stability. Additionally, CCPs can opt to obtain liquidity through financing. In this case, it is advisable to grant a security over the non-cash assets. Duffie[168] explains that such securities can grant over initial margins or the default fund, as well as to claims to future contributions of clearing members.

Similarly, the resolution authority needs to be allowed to intervene quickly[169] and to step in the current contract. At the same time, the special resolution regime for CCPs should ensure that there are client asset rules that protect clearing members and their clients' rights. The FSB advises[170] that segregation rules applicable during a crisis and resolution of the CCP allow for the rapid return of segregated assets to their clients or the transfer to a third party or bridge institution.

Additionally, the CCPs' insolvency regime should be consistent with international efforts to deal with cross-border issues.[171] The FSB have published guidance pursuing its commitment to develop policy proposals on how legal certainty in cross-border resolutions can be further enhanced.[172] Hence, the FSB published the Principles for Cross-Border Effectiveness of Resolution Actions[173] that set out statutory and contractual mechanisms that jurisdictions should consider including in their legal framework to give cross-border effect to resolution actions in accordance with the Key Attributes[174] and its FMI Annex.

In this regard, the ReSG agreed to establish by the end of 2015 a working group called Cross-Border Crisis Management Group for FMIs (fmiCBCM). The fmiCBCM will monitor progress in the development of resolution strategies and operational resolution plans for CCPs and of institution-specific cross-border cooperation agreements (COAGs), as well as the establishment of CMGs for

---

168 Darrell Duffie, 'Resolution of Failing Counterparties' (n109).
169 Squam Lake Working Group on Financial Regulation, 'Improving Resolution Options for Systemically Relevant Financial Institutions' (Working Paper Centre for Geoeconomic Studies, October 2009) <www.cfr.org/financial-crises/improving-resolution-options-sys temically-relevant-financial-institutions/p20558> accessed 5th November 2015.
170 Annex 3: Client Asset Protection in Resolution, FSB, 'Key Attributes of Effective Resolution Regimes for Financial Institutions' (n87).
171 FSB, 'Progress Report on the CCP Workplan' (2015) (n156).
172 At the St Petersburg G20 summit in 2013 the FSB made the commitment FSB, *Progress and Next Steps Towards Ending 'Too-Big-To-Fail'* (n100).
173 FSB, 'Principles for Cross-Border Effectiveness of Resolution Actions' (3 November 2015) <www.financialstabilityboard.org/2015/11/principles-for-cross-border-effectiveness-of-resolution-actions/> accessed 5th November 2015.
174 FSB, 'Key Attributes of Effective Resolution Regimes for Financial Institutions' (n87). The Key Attributes consultative document incorporates guidance on their application to non-bank financial institutions and on arrangements for information sharing. The first annex sets out guidance on resolution of FMIs including CCPs and resolution of systemically important FMI participants, and the third annex sets out guidance on client asset protection in resolution.

CCPs. The Bank has set up two CMGs for two CCPs in order to facilitate information exchange among CCPs and CMs' supervisors.[175] Similarly, the fmiCBCM will clarify how the resolution powers of the Key Attributes consultative document and their FMI Annex would be exercised. The FSB anticipates some of the issues that will be further analysed by the fmiCBCM. These relate to legal structures, the arrangement of clearing activities or other services, relationships and interdependencies between the CCP and participants, links with other FMIs, CCP rules including default management and recovery procedures, and financial resources including liquidity arrangements.

It might be highly anticipated that the final proposal of the fmiCBCM and CPMI-IOSCO will involve additional pre-funded resources and arrangements, as well as further guidance about resolution planning. The FSB has worked towards setting standards on the essential aspects of CCP resolution planning.[176] On 16th August 2016, the FSB together with the BCBS, the CPMI, and IOSCO agreed on a joint workplan to enhance resilience, recovery, and resolvability of CCPs. The FSB Key Attributes would guide the standard-setting process in order to ensure CCPs can be resolved with no need of government bailout.[177] The FSB discussion note of 2016 seeks to develop effective strategies on the objectives of CCP resolution, timing of entry into resolution, adequacy of financial resources, non-default losses, application of the 'no-creditor-worse-off' safeguard, and cross-border cooperation and resolution actions.[178]

After a consultation period, on 5th July 2017, the FSB issued Guidance on Central Counterparty Resolution and Resolution Planning.[179] The Guidance complements the Key Attributes and the FMI Annex, and intends 'to assist authorities in their resolution planning and promote international consistency'.[180] The Guidance sets that CCPs resolution plans should maintain market and public confidence, as well as control the systemic consequences and disruption that contagion might bring. It also emphasises the relevance of the powers granted to resolution authorities,[181] which include the ability to enforce any outstanding contractual obligations, return the CCP to a matched book, write down the equity of the CCP, and transfer critical function to a 'bridge CCP', among others.

It is worth noting that some considerations discussed in this chapter of what a CCPs resolutions regime should include were also covered in the FSB Guidance. As its implementation is still ongoing, the effectiveness of the proposed reforms will have to be assessed in the coming years.

---

175 Bank of England, 'The Bank of England's approach to resolution' (October 2017) (n96), 19.
176 FSB, 'Essential Aspects of CCP Resolution Planning' (Discussion Note, 16th August 2016).
177 Ibid.
178 Ibid.
179 FSB, Guidance on Central Counterparty Resolution and Resolution Planning' (5 July 2017) <www.fsb.org/wp-content/uploads/P050717-1.pdf> accessed 11th December 2017. (Hereinafter FSB Guidance)
180 Ibid 1.
181 Ibid 3.

Finally, in the process of regulating the insolvency of a CCP, it is advisable that UK regulators consider the risks that CCPs face in the event of clearing members' insolvency[182] and how this might threaten the stability of the CCP.[183] The relevant insolvency rules governing the contracts in which a clearing house is a part are contained in the Companies Act 1989 Part VII (CA 1989 Part VII). These rules apply to the insolvency of clearing houses and their counterparts in the exchange markets, as well as to the counterparts of CCPs operating in the OTCDM.[184] CA 1989 Part VII operates in conjunction with the Recognition Requirements for Investment Exchanges and Clearing Houses of the FSMA 2000 and Recognition Regulations 2001. CA 1989 Part VII disapplies the general law of insolvency from the operation of the default rules of recognised investment exchanges and clearing systems.[185] These default rules are the clearing house rules which provide for taking action in the event of a person appearing unable, or likely to be unable, to meet his/her obligations in respect of one or more market contracts connected with the exchange or clearing house.[186] According to s188 (2) of CA 1989, in the event of a person's default, the clearing house concerned must close out on the defaulter's position and realise the defaulter's property prior to any action, which an insolvency office-holder may take under general law.

The aim of CA 1989 is to safeguard the operations of financial markets; hence, the Act rules the insolvency, winding up, or default of a counterparty to transactions in the market.[187] It also rules the effectiveness or enforcement of certain charges given to secure obligations in connection with market transactions – these are market changes.[188] Regarding market property, CA 1989 includes the rights and remedies[189] in relation to assets provided as margin or default fund contribution in relation to such transactions or subject to such a charge.

In this regard, in CME Clearing Europe Ltd's Accounts Disclosure Document,[190] some of the consequences and foreseeable issues arising from clearing members' insolvency were noted. The first concern is the operation of the automatic

182 The Insolvency of Clearing Members is ruled by Part VII Companies Act (CA) 1989, or if the clearing member is a Bank, the SRR of the Banking Act 2009.
183 LCH Clearnet, CCP Risk Management, Recovery and Resolution' (LCH Clearnet, Whitepaper 1.2 Policy Issues) <www.lchclearnet.com/documents/731485/762448/final+white+paper+version+three.pdf/1d1700aa-a1ae-4a6c-8f6f-541eec9b7420> accessed 22nd December 2017.
184 FSA, 'Cooperation Guidance Between Recognised Bodies and Insolvency Practitioners to Assist Management of Member Defaults by Recognised Bodies (Recognised Clearing House Version)' <www.bankofengland.co.uk/financialstability/Documents/fmi/Insolvency%20practitioners.pdf> accessed 6th November 2015.
185 Edward Bailey, and Hugo Groves, *Corporate Insolvency: Law and Practice* (n134), 1411.
186 Companies Act 1989 (CA 1989), s188 (1).
187 CA 1989, ss155–172.
188 CA 1989, ss173–176.
189 CA 1989, ss177–181.
190 CME Clearing Europe Ltd Accounts Disclosure Document (n36).

set-off[191] that under English law does not allow the distinction between the various client accounts and will most likely set off amounts across all those accounts and against the clearing members' house account. The CCP will not be able to calculate net sums per client account and the porting system will not operate as expected. When porting has not been possible, in the event of the insolvency of a clearing member, it is probable that any payments made to them for their client's account get trapped in the insolvency proceedings.[192] As a result, the client will be an unsecured creditor of the amounts owed to it by the clearing member, assuming the risk of not being repaid at all. The second potential issue concerns the rules of transaction avoidance and claw-back – these include transactions at undervalue and preferences.[193] The claw-back provision[194] would allow the liquidator or administrator of the clearing member to challenge transactions entered into by the company property.

Finally, a third cause of concern is the applicability of the protection included in CA 1989 Part VII. CME Clearing Europe Ltd[195] considers that it is not clear whether Part VII eliminates the risk that an insolvency official might challenge the close-out after completion of the default proceedings, which is a challenge that is allowed in English insolvency law. One possible interpretation is to understand that the protection of Part VII benefits the CCPs' porting arrangements, because they are part of the settlement of a clearing member's client positions under the default rules.

4.3.3 Shortcomings of the CCPs' insolvency regime

Up to this point, this chapter has explored the importance of designing an SRR for CCPs and recommendations regarding its content. We will now go on to explore the shortcomings that such a regime may have concerning the rights of clearing members and their clients.

4.3.3.1 Enforcement of clearing members' rights

Regulators need to be particularly careful when adopting rules that restrict the possibility for clearing members and clients to enforce their rights in front of the defaulting CCP, particularly when the regime restricts the right to terminate

---

191 Philip Wood, *Set-off and Netting, Derivatives, Clearing Systems* (Sweet & Maxwell 2007), 5.

192 CME Clearing Europe Ltd Accounts Disclosure Document (n36).

193 Ibid.

194 'Can a liquidator or an administrator challenge or unwind transactions entered into by the company before it was wound up or entered into administration?' LexisNexis Practice Notes <www.lexisnexis.com/uk/lexispsl/restructuringandinsolvency/document/393783/55MK-MBW1-F18D-T2XC-00000-00/Can+a+liquidator+or+an+administrator+challenge+or+unwind+transactions+entered+into+by+the+company+before+it+was+wound+up+or+entered+into+administration%3F> accessed 20th October 2015.

195 CME Clearing Europe Ltd Accounts Disclosure Document (n36).

contracts in the case of a CCP's insolvency, as suggested by the FSB.[196] Analysing the Australian experience, Farrell[197] argues that the adoption of special resolution regimes for CCPs could lead to a competition between recovery and resolution rules. This is, for instance, the competition between the close-out netting rights of participants and the restrictions imposed on this matter in a new insolvency regime. The challenge is for regulators to design a resolution regime that interferes to a lesser extent with the existent recovery regime.

In the EU, one obstacle to the effective resolution is the risk that counterparties exercise termination rights in derivatives contracts[198] according to the Financial Collateral Arrangements Directive (FCAD).[199] As the exercise of such rights would be greatly disruptive and bring the risk of contagion,[200] it is advisable to remove this obstacle in a resolution regime for CCPs.[201] However, the experience of the Banking Resolution Regime shows that the implementation of suspension of rights provisions might be problematic in a cross-border scenario.[202] The FSB[203] recommended the use of contractual mechanisms to achieve cross-border recognition and, following this recommendation, ISDA developed a Resolution Stay Protocol.[204] The protocol enables counterparties to opt voluntarily[205] into the stay and suspension provisions by agreeing on a change to their ISDA derivatives contracts.

The form of the collateral also raises some concerns that affect the relationship between the clearing member and the CCP.[206] If the collateral is provided in cash

196 FSB, 'Application of the Key Attributes of Effective Resolution Regimes to Non-Bank Financial Institutions: Consultative Document' <www.financialstabilityboard.org/wp-con tent/uploads/r_141015.pdf> accessed 4th November 2015. 'In 2013 the FSB announced that one of its tasks was to develop proposals for contractual or statutory approaches to prevent early termination of financial contracts', FSB, *Progress and Next Steps Towards Ending 'Too-Big-To-Fail'* (n100).

197 Scott Farrell, 'Too Important to Fail: Legal Complexity in Planning for the Failure of Financial Market Infrastructure' (n109), 467.

198 BCBS-IOSCO Final Report on Margin for Derivatives (September 2013).

199 Directive on financial collateral arrangements (2002/47/EC). Implemented in the UK by the Financial Collateral Arrangements (No. 2) Regulations 2003.

200 Paul Tucker, 'Central Counterparties in Evolving Capital Markets: Safety, Recovery and Resolution' Resolution' in OTC derivatives: new rules, new actors, new risks' (n118).

201 For banks, Chapters V and VI of the RRD confer the power to authorities to suspend termination rights.

202 Financial Services and Markets Group Baker McKenzie, 'Bank Recovery And Resolution – Ending the Spectre of 'Too Big To Fail'' (May 2015) <www.bakermckenzie.com/files/ Uploads/Documents/Alumni/Legal%20Alert.pdf> accessed 5th November 2015.

203 FSB, 'Cross-border Recognition of Resolution Action' (FSB, Consultative Document, 29 September 2014).

204 ISDA 2014 Resolution Stay In Protocol <https://www2.isda.org/functional-areas/pro tocol-management/protocol/20> accessed 5th November 2015.

205 Financial Services and Markets Group Backer McKenzie, 'Bank Recovery and Resolution – Ending the Spectre of "Too Big to Fail"' (n202); ISDA designated a cut-off date under the protocol of 2 November 2015.

206 Joanne Braithwaite, 'Private Law and the Public Sector's Central Counterparty Prescription for the Derivatives Markets (LSE Legal Studies Working Paper No 2/2011) <http://ssrn. com/abstract=1791740> accessed 13th January 2016.

there is a transfer of ownership from the clearing member to the CCP, and therefore the clearing member would assume the category of the CCP's unsecured creditor. In contrast, when collateral is in non-cash assets, clearing members may retain property rights; they transfer the non-cash assets to an account of the CCP and grant a security interest over those assets. As a result, CCP takes first fixed charge to secure the clearing members' performance of its obligations; but as the clearing member keeps the proprietary rights, those assets are protected in case of the CCP's insolvency.

4.3.3.2 CCP bailout?

Moreover, one of the fundamental principles that regulators have made clear from the beginning is that they do not allow the use of public sources[207] to bail out CCPs.[208] Therefore, the development of a comprehensive special resolution regime for CCPs is pivotal to complete the regime. Such a regime will take into account the specific factors that constitute CCPs and that make the regime different from the regulation of banks' resolvability. At the time of writing, the Bank is waiting expectantly for the European Commission to give guidance regarding the resolvability of CCPs.

The EU legislation proposal of November 2016[209] – that has not been yet approved[210] – includes some rules related to prevention and preparation tools. This is a preliminary stage to allow national supervisors to assess the measures and defences in place to manage CCP crisis. It then bestows resolution authorities with early intervention powers to act pre-emptively when a CCP is at risk to reach the point of failure. Finally, it proposes a set of resolution tools to orderly manage CCP insolvency. The EU proposal seems to be guided, almost to the letter, by the measures already implemented in the UK.

The advances regarding the Bank's intervention powers as the resolution authority for CCPs help to prevent the bailout scenario. Firstly, the existence of a resolution authority ensures that all recovery and resolution measures are exhausted before considering the use of public sources to save the CCP. Secondly, the existence of a resolution authority deters CCPs from thinking that they are too important to be intervened in or restructured, and that the solution at hand is to bail them out. Thus, the fact that the Bank is equipped with the powers to restructure a CCP prevents the CCP from taking excessive risks that could lead to its failure. Moral hazard in this context would arise if a CCP believes that it will automatically receive an emergency liquidity or bailout if it

---

207 George Walker, 'Systematically Important Institution Too Big to Fail' (Financial Regulation International 26 October 2012).
208 FSB Guidance, Ibid (n179) 12.
209 EU Proposal CCPs Recovery and Resolution, Ibid (n104).
210 European Parliament, 'Briefing EU Legislation in Progress Recovery and resolution of central counterparties (CCPs)' (30 March 2017) <www.europarl.europa.eu/RegData/etudes/BRIE/2017/599345/EPRS_BRI(2017)599345_EN.pdf> accessed 11th December 2017.

becomes insolvent.[211] The UK authorities have been reluctant to accept that, even in a very extraordinary event, CCPs would be bailed out, and that they should invest the Bank as the authority to make that decision. However, given the extreme circumstances, it is still unclear whether a bailout would be provided. The House of Lords published a report questioning CCPs about their interest in having access to the Bank's liquidity line.[212] Whilst the general opinion of CCPs, particularly that of LCH Clearnet, noted that there were times when central bank liquidity would be beneficial, there were also arguments supporting the idea that the CCPs' business model should never rely on central banks' liquidity assistance,[213] because of the moral hazard issues this might raise.

The approach of the Bank is that liquidity is primarily a concern for the CCP. However, the Bank accepts that there should be no technical obstacles to the provision of liquidity[214] to a CCP that temporarily and exceptionally needs it. Hence, as explained earlier, in November 2014 the Bank widened access to its sterling facilities to include CCPs.[215] Having access to the Sterling Monetary Framework (SMF) means that, in the event of a clearing member default, the CCP can use the margin posted by that clearing member or other assets as collateral to obtain sterling liquidity from the Bank.[216]

4.3.3.3 Clearing members – the ultimate underwriters

We will now consider the role played by clearing members, as the 'ultimate underwriters' of CCP default risk. The recognised and authorised structure of CCPs in the UK is that of the demutualised CCPs, where ownership is separated from the clearing participation. Clearing members are not the owners of the CCP, but they

211 Christian Chamorro-Courtland, 'The Trillion Dollar Question: Can a Central Bank Bail-Out a Central Counterparty (CCP) Clearing House which is 'Too Big To Fail'?' (Spring–March 2012) *Brooklyn Journal of Corporate Financial & Commercial Law*.

212 House of Lords, 'The Future Regulation of Derivatives Markets: Is the EU on the Right Track? European Union Committee' Ch 5 The EU Regulation of CCP Clearing Houses (2009) <www.publications.parliament.uk/pa/ld200910/ldselect/ldeucom/93/9308.htm> accessed 5th November 2015.

213 'Roger Liddell, CEO of LCH Clearnet, commented that personally he believed businesses should never rely on the central bank providing liquidity as a last resort, because of the moral hazard issues this raised. The business models of businesses should assume that they would receive no support in the event of a crisis (QQ 137–9)' House of Lords, 'The Future Regulation of Derivatives Markets: Is the EU on the Right Track? European Union Committee', Ibid.

214 In line with other central banks' work in 2012. See the FSB's 'OTC Derivatives Market Reforms: Third Progress Report on Implementation', (FSB, 'Third Progress Report' (June 2012) <www.financialstabilityboard.org/wp-content/uploads/r_120615.pdf> accessed 9th November 2015.

215 The Bank of England is widening access to its Sterling Monetary Framework (SMF) to accept broker-dealers and Central Counterparties (CCPs) (Bank of England, *News Release*, 2014) <www.bankofengland.co.uk/publications/Pages/news/2014/144.aspx> accessed 9th November 2015.

216 Arshadur Rahman, 'Over-The-Counter (OTC) Derivatives, Central Clearing and Financial Stability' (Bank of England) (n102), 291.

participate in the mutualisation of losses. As was explained, the default waterfall varies according to the CCP's default rules, but in general it starts with the initial margin of the defaulting member; it then moves to the default fund contribution of the member, followed by default fund contributions of other members as the last resort for the equity of the CCP. When all these resources are exhausted, the CCP becomes insolvent. At this point, one alternative is to ask clearing members for additional funds to prevent the closure of the CCP and, in this scenario, clearing members become underwriters of the CCP.

This demutualised structure and its relationship with the waterfall default raise some questions that are only partially solved by UK regulators. For instance, in the event a CCP cannot effectively manage the risk of insolvency, clearing members would have to assume such a risk themselves. Hence, clearing members might want to see more CCP capital committed to the default resources, arguing that CCPs are not properly incentivised to manage risk.

Ben Bernanke argues that the requirement for the surviving participant to provide more funds to the insolvent CCP, as a measure to contribute to its recovery, does not extend to the CCP's failure.[217] However, the international standards of the FSB, CPMI, and IOSCO seem to be moving towards creating an additional fund, which will be largely formed with clearing members' contributions. Indeed, in recent discussions, clearing members have argued that there is a need to review clearing membership requirements, collateral eligibility, the availability of certain recovery tools, and the bespoke nature of CCP rulebooks.[218] At first sight it seems that, while regulators are privileging the stability of CCPs and re-insuring that these 'too-big-to fail' institutions are not going to be bailed out, they are indirectly transposing the burden to clearing members. The problem with such an approach is that, instead of promoting the use of central clearing, which is one of the initial objectives of the post-GFC reforms, it is discouraging market participants from trading in the OTCDM.

If the tendency of the coming regulation is to impose further funding requirements to clearing members, it will be necessary that regulators intervene to rebalance the relationship between CCPs and their members. In order to achieve such symmetry, regulators are expected to design more rigorous stress tests, with complete disclosure of results. Lastly, clearing members and clients want to see all default management actions available to CCPs defined *ex ante*, arguing that this should eliminate the need for CCPs to have emergency powers.[219]

Trying to reconcile the interests involve, the 2017 FSB Guidance establishes that the resolution authority should have the power to compensate clearing

---

217 Ben Bernanke, 'Clearing and Settlement During the Crash' (1990) 3 (1) *The Review of Financial Studies*, 133.
218 FIA, 'FIA Global CCP Risk Position Paper' (April 2015) <https://fia.org/articles/fia-global-issues-recommendations-central-clearing-risks> accessed 5th October 2015. These issues were also discussed at the Federal Reserve Bank of Chicago's 2015 Clearing Symposium.
219 Ibid.

members that have contributed financial resources in excess of their obligations. Such compensation might be on equity or other types of ownership or convertible debt instruments.[220]

4.3.3.4 CCP ring-fencing?

Let us now address the question of ring-fencing as a regulatory solution to manage CCPs' financial distress. We will explore what type of OTCDM failures ring-fencing could help to solve, and consider the benefits and limitations tied to the adoption of ring-fencing for SIFI CCPs.

4.3.3.4.1 TAXONOMY OF RING-FENCING

Ring-fencing is usually defined according to the functions it performs. In a regulatory context, ring-fencing refers to the legal deconstruction of a firm in order to more optimally reallocate and reduce risks.[221] It is a regulatory device that helps to protect the firm from becoming subject to liabilities and other risks associated with bankruptcy.[222] Hence, ring-fencing is one tool regulators tend to use to mitigate systemic risk[223] and to manage the too-big-to-fail problem[224] related to SIFIs.

There are multiple functions and uses of ring-fencing, classified by Schwarcz[225] at firm-level and market-level. He argues that, at firm-level, ring-fencing might be used to make a firm bankruptcy remote, to help a firm operate on a standalone basis, to preserve a firm's business and assets, and to limit a firm's risky activities and investments. At market-level, ring-fencing might contribute to correct market failures and to protect against systemic risk.

4.3.3.4.2 FUNCTIONS OF RING-FENCING AT FIRM-LEVEL

To make a firm 'bankruptcy remote' is to protect it from becoming subject to liabilities and risks derived from bankruptcy. This practice is commonly used in securitisation[226] and covered bond transactions.[227] In these transactions, the ring-fenced firm is the Special Purpose Vehicle (SPV) whose creditworthiness is

---

220 FSB Guidance, Ibid (n179), 6.

221 Steven L. Schwarcz, 'Ring-Fencing' *Southern California Law Review* (November 2013).

222 Steven L. Schwarcz, 'The Conundrum of Covered Bonds' (2011) 66 *Business Law*, 567.

223 Daniel K. Tarullo, 'Regulation of Foreign Banking Organizations' (Yale School of Management Leaders Forum, New Haven, CT, 28 November 2012) <www.federalreserve.gov/newsevents/speech/tarullo20121128a.htm> accessed 31st January 2016.

224 Charles Randell, 'The Great British Banking Experiment: Will the Restructuring of UK Banking Show Us How to Resolve G-SIFIs?' (2012) 6 (1) *Law and Financial Markets Review*, 39.

225 Steven L. Schwarcz, 'Ring-Fencing' (n221).

226 Thomas J. Gordon, 'Securitization of Executory Future Flows as Bankruptcy Remote True Sales' (2000) 67 *University of Chicago Law Review*, 1317.

227 Steven L. Schwarcz, ' The Conundrum of Covered Bonds' (n222).

protected. As a result, the SPV is able to issue securities at lower costs than if the affiliated firm issued them.[228] For CCPs, bankruptcy remoteness would mean that their own assets are protected in case of financial distress or insolvency. This is possible when there is a separation of the CCP's assets related to clearing services and other business, and may occur if CCPs are legally structured as SPVs.[229] In a group of CCPs, operated in a silo-by-silo basis, the bankruptcy remoteness is predicable to the assets of the CCP parent or SPV. These assets are not designated for loss-sharing of subsidiaries of CCPs. One example of a CCP operating under this structure is LCH Clearnet, currently operating seven different CCPs.[230] The principal benefit of using ring-fencing to achieve bankruptcy remoteness is to protect CCPs from voluntary or involuntary bankruptcy proceedings.[231]

The CCP's bankruptcy remoteness is different from the bankruptcy remoteness of clearing member clients' positions and assets as mandated in the CRR.[232] According to Section 305 (2) of the CRR, clients' assets will not be available to cover losses of the clearing member or other clients following the default of the clearing member or one or more of its other clients – this is because clearing members' clients' assets are bankruptcy remote.

Ring-fencing can help the firm to operate on a standalone basis, ensuring that the ring-fenced firm is able to operate alone, even if its affiliated firms fail.[233] This function of risk-fencing could be adapted to CCPs, but the question here is whether ring-fencing is required to ensure the stability of CCPs in the event of clearing members' insolvency? The current regime of CCPs in the OTCDM includes some requirements concerning the capability of CCPs to stay solvent and manage clearing members' default. According to the PFMI, the Key Attributes consultative document,[234] and EMIR, CCPs must be able to manage the default of the two last clearing members. This means that, although clearing members are not exactly 'affiliates' of the CCP, in the sense of a corporate group structure, there is a connection between clearing members' solvency and the CCP's management of clearing members' default. Therefore, the role of ring-fencing in this area would be secondary and duplicative, as a reinforcement of the protection of CCPs in case of clearing members' insolvency.

228 Steven L. Schwarcz, 'Securitization Post-Enron' (2004) 25 *Cardozo Law Review*, 1539 in Steven L. Schwarcz, 'Ring-Fencing' (n221), 6.
229 Darrell Duffie, 'Resolution of Failing Central Counterparties' in Kenneth E. Scott, Thomas H. Jackson and John B. Taylor (eds.), *Making Failure Feasible: How Bankruptcy Reform Can End 'Too Big to Fail'* (Hoover Institution Press, Stanford University, 2015), 97.
230 Ibid 97.
231 Steven L. Schwarcz, 'Ring-Fencing: Functions and Conceptual Foundations' *Columbia Law School Blue Sky* (Blog) (28 March 2013) <http://clsbluesky.law.columbia.edu/2013/03/28/ring-fencing/> accessed 31st January 2016 'Ring-Fencing' (n208) 8.
232 CRR (Regulation 575/2013): Recitals (81) to (86); Arts 107, 300–311 and 497; Annex II; Basel III contains, and CRD IV implements, a framework for calculating the counterparty credit risk associated with exposures to CCPs. According to s305 CCR, the client would 'bear no losses on account of the insolvency of the clearing member or its other clients.
233 Steven L. Schwarcz, 'Ring-Fencing: Functions and Conceptual Foundations' (n231).
234 FSB, 'Key Attributes of Effective Resolution Regimes for Financial Institutions' (n87).

The function of ring-fencing to preserve a firm's business and assets prevents affiliated firms from taking advantage of the ring-fenced firm.[235] In the context of CCPs offering clearing services to clearing members and their clients, the structure of the legal relationship between CCPs and clearing members neglects the possibility that clearing members could take advantage of CCPs' business and assets. In particular, the rules of segregation and portability of clearing members' positions and assets determine a clear dividing line between CCPs' assets and those of clearing members. As we discussed earlier, to meet these goals, EMIR and UK regulators must address some issues. The first source of concern is that the legal segregation of EMIR works in an ideal scenario where the records of the CCP and the clearing members coincide, but if they are different there is a potential source of litigation. Similarly, legal segregation does not necessarily mean that collateral is also operationally segregated,[236] where collateral is held in different segregated accounts. Thus, the formality of the segregation obligation is a step towards clearing members' and clients' asset protection, but it does not ensure the actual separation of assets. Therefore, in the event that ring-fencing was adopted for CCPs, this is not one of the functions it would perform.

The last function of ring-fencing at a firm-level is to limit a firm's risky activities and investments.[237] The objective is to reduce the probability and impact of systemic financial crisis originated in specific activities, as exemplified in the new UK ring-fencing regime for retail banking.

The most recent ring-fencing initiative in the UK regime seeks to ring-fence banks by legally separating some of their risky assets from retail banking operations. The PRA[238] is in charge of developing the policy to implement the ring-fencing of core UK financial services and activities.[239] The adoption of ring-fencing in the UK was recommended by the Independent Commission on Banking (ICB)[240] in 2011 as a measure to improve financial stability. The purpose of

---

235 Steven L. Schwarcz, 'Ring-Fencing' (n 221) 10.
236 Tariq Zafar Rasheed, and Bas Zebregs, 'Can a House Divided Between Itself Stand? Segregation in Derivatives Clearing' (2012) 5 *Journal of International Banking and Financial Law*, 293.
237 Steven L. Schwarcz, 'Ring-Fencing' (n 221), 11.
238 .Bank of England – Prudential Regulation Authority, 'The Implementation of Ring-Fencing: Consultation on Legal Structure, Governance and the Continuity of Services and Facilities' (Consultation Paper CP19/14, October 2014).
239 More detail on the definition of core activities, ring-fenced banks (RFBs), and the activities which RFBs can and cannot undertake is set out in two pieces of secondary legislation made by HM Treasury in 2014, *The Ring-Fenced Bodies and Core Activities Order 2014.*
240 Independent Commission on Banking, 'Final Report' (September 2011) <http://webarchive.nationalarchives.gov.uk/20131003105424/https:/hmt-sanctions.s3.amazonaws.com/ICB%20final%20report/ICB%2520Final%2520Report%5B1%5D.pdf> accessed 31st January 2016; this formed the basis of draft legislation which was reviewed by the Parliamentary Commission on Banking Standards (PCBS). The government's response to the PCBS and its impact assessment were published in February 2013; also see HM Treasury/Department for Business, Innovation and Skills, 'Banking

ring-fencing is to isolate those banking activities where continuous provision of service is central to the economy and to a bank's customers in order to ensure the continuity of services even in the event of the bank's failure without government solvency support.[241] As we can see, the reform of the FSA 2013 added at least one measure to promote the safety and soundness of firms by reducing the effect that failure of firms might have on the stability of the UK financial system.[242]

The PRA's policy to implement ring-fencing from January 2019 considers the legal structure arrangements of banking groups subject to ring-fencing,[243] the government arrangements of ring-fenced institutions,[244] and the arrangements to ensure the continuity of services[245] to ring-fenced institutions.[246] As proposed by the PRA, ring-fencing is implemented to contribute to recovery and resolution scenarios. A ring-fenced bank (RFB) has its business restricted, and as such it has a degree of protection from shocks originating in other parts of the financial system. When an RFB fails, ring-fencing also facilitates orderly resolutions and supports the continuous provision of services.[247] Along with the PRA's policy, the FPC is required to issue a framework for a systemic risk buffer (SRB) for ring-fenced banks and large building societies.[248]

For CCPs, a ring-fencing regime would have to be adapted and designed according to the risks the CCP failure may pose to financial stability. Duffie explains that one feature that distinguishes CCPs from other SIFIs, including banks, is that its balance sheet is different[249] – it does not reflect assets and

---

Reform: A New Structure for Stability and Growth' (February 2013) <www.gov.uk/gov ernment/uploads/system/uploads/attachment_data/file/228995/8545.pdf> accessed 31st January 2016.

241 Independent Commission on Banking, *Final Report* (n240).

242 Bank of England – Prudential Regulation Authority, 'The Implementation of Ring-Fencing: Consultation on Legal Structure, Governance and the Continuity of Services and Facilities' (Consultation Paper CP19/14, October 2014) <www.bankofengland.co.uk/ pra/Documents/publications/cp/2014/cp1914.pdf> accessed 31st January 2016.

243 Ibid.

244 'Rules in the areas of governance, risk management, internal audit, remuneration and human resources policy. Such functions underpin how RFBs make decisions and devise strategy which is critical, in particular, in enabling an RFB to take decisions independently of other group members', Ibid.

245 'Rules governing how RFBs can receive services and facilities from other intragroup entities or third parties outside their group. These are intended to mitigate risks to the ability of the RFB to perform its core services arising from the acts, omissions, or the failure of other group entities', Ibid.

246 Ibid.

247 Ibid.

248 Bank of England, 'The Framework of Capital Requirements for UK Banks' (Bank of England, Financial Policy Committee, December 2015) <www.bankofengland.co.uk/ publications/Documents/fsr/2015/fsrsupp.pdf> accessed 31st January 2016; see Bank of England, 'The Financial Policy Committee's Framework for the Systemic Risk Buffer: A Consultation Paper' (January 2016) <www.bankofengland.co.uk/financialstability/ Documents/fpc/srbf_cp.pdf> accessed 31st January 2016.

249 Darrell Duffie, 'Resolution of Failing Central Counterparties' in Kenneth E. Scott, Thomas H. Jackson, and John B. Taylor (eds.), *Making Failure Feasible: How Bankruptcy Reform Can End 'Too Big to Fail'* (n229), 88.

liabilities. Instead, a CCP balance sheet represents a nexus of contracts that allows clearing members to net and mutualise their credit risk. As the daily payment obligations of a CCP sum become zero, CCPs have small amounts of equity and conventional debt and a large potential of clearing obligations.[250] Therefore, the range of risks posed by the potential failure of a CCP are also different – mainly comprising the contagion of default to non-defaulted clearing members, fire sales of collateral or derivatives contracts, exacerbating market volatility, and loss of continuity of clearing services. In deciding to adopt ring-fencing rules for CCPs, we must consider these risks and how to better manage them.

4.3.3.4.3 FUNCTIONS OF RING-FENCING AT MARKET-LEVEL

Ring-fencing can contribute to solving market failures.[251] In particular, in this study we consider information failure – the issue regarding the asymmetry of information is a common concern in financial markets, especially in markets led by complexity and innovation, as in the OTCDM. The level of complexity of markets and transactions undermines disclosure;[252] it is not uncommon that market participants cannot fully understand the risks of their transactions and still decide to invest.[253] But even complete disclosure is not always sufficient to mitigate information failures that might cause systemic risk.[254] When market participants understand the risks involved in their transactions and products, they tend to protect themselves but not the system as a whole.[255] Moreover, complexity also affects regulators, because it makes it difficult for them to understand the evolution of the market they regulate. The lack of specialised knowledge and expertise diminishes the effective design and implementation of financial regulation.

These considerations are relevant in our understanding of the dynamics of the OTCDM: complexity and innovation are central to the role of CCPs and the services they provide to clearing members and their clients. Hence, CCPs have specialised knowledge and expertise regarding the clearing services and the products thereof. However, the extent to which clearing members and regulators have access and fully understand this information is likely to be limited. Similarly, information

---

250 Ibid.
251 Steven L. Schwarcz, 'Ring-Fencing' (n208).
252 Steven L. Schwarcz, 'Regulating Complexity in Financial Markets' (2009/2010) 87 *Washington University Law Review*, 211.
253 John D. Finnerty, and Kishlaya Pathak, 'A Review of Recent Derivatives Litigation' (2011) 16 *Fordham Journal of Corporate & Financial Law*, 73–74 (observing that court records reveal investors' misunderstandings about the nature of derivative financial instruments).
254 Steven L Schwarcz, 'Systemic Risk and the Financial Crisis: Protecting the Financial System as a "System"' (Macroprudential Regulation, 12 February 2014) <www.law.berkeley.edu/files/bclbe/Schwarcz_Paper.pdf> accessed 30th January 2016; also see Steven L. Schwarcz, 'Controlling Financial Chaos: The Power and Limits of Law' (2012) 3 *Wisconsin Law Review*, 815; Steven L. Schwarcz, 'Regulating Shadows: Financial Regulation and Responsibility Failure' (2013) 70 *Washington and Lee Law Review*, 1781.
255 Steven L. Schwarcz, 'Systemic Risk and the Financial Crisis: Protecting the Financial System as a "System"' (n254).

failure also affects the relationship between CCPs and clearing members. Clearing members and clients know their positions and exposures, and the quality of the assets serving as collateral to their transactions. Indeed, clearing members are required to report the information to CCPs, which in turn use that information to comply with segregation and portability obligations. And yet, CCPs have a purely administrative function to keep the register of positions, assets, and value related to collateral; in carrying out this function, they rely completely on the information clearing members give them relating to their clients' types of assets and value related to collateral. As a result, it is possible that the information clearing members report is not accurate and, as such, affects the efficient functioning of the CCP, particularly when complying with portability requirements.

Schwarcz argues that ring-fencing contributes to solving information failure by simplifying the investments that certain financial firms can make.[256] However, this argument would be debatable in the area of the OTCDM and CCPs. The role of regulators is to control the risk originating in the market and, in so doing, they impose certain prudential requirements that market participants and transactions must meet. For instance, the introduction of mandatory clearing for a large portion of OTCDM is ruled in order to enhance the counterparty credit risk, as well as to increase the stability of the market. The rationale is to ensure the safety and soundness of CCPs, which in turn improves their resilience. Therefore, the regime of CCPs in the OTCDM is not exclusively protecting the CCPs as individual institutions, but also aiming at strengthening the OTCDM as a whole, and thereby controlling systemic risk.

In this sense, although the use of CCPs enhances the standardisation of products and processes, and this could be regarded as a simplification of the derivatives trading, the introduction of mandatory central clearing is also introducing complexity to the market. Therefore, it is not clear how the introduction of ring-fencing rules could effectively help to solve an information failure that – in the form of complexity – the regime is itself introducing to the OTCDM. Thus, the key element for ring-fencing rules to achieve this objective is to clearly identify the events of information failure affecting CCPs and the provision of clearing services, as well as to propose coherent solutions. These solutions should have regard to the sources of complexity in the market; namely market practices and those manufactured by the regime.

The second function of ring-fencing at market-level is to protect against systemic risk, which is particularly important due to the SIFI nature of CCPs.

4.3.3.4.4 BENEFITS AND LIMITATIONS OF RING-FENCING FOR CCPS

Attending to the well-known systemic implications of CCP failure,[257] the discussion concerning the use of ring-fencing for CCPs is closely connected to the

---

256 Steven L. Schwarcz, 'Ring-Fencing' (n208).
257 Andrew Cornford, 'The Failure of Cross-Border Financial Firms: New Thinking in the Aftermath of the Financial Crisis' (Observatoire de la Finance, Geneva, July 2010)

issues of how to manage the 'too-big-to-fail' (TBTF) problem.[258] Before the GFC, the TBTF doctrine[259] was mostly associated with the size of the institution. However, the events of Bear Stearns and Lehman Brothers broadened the theory to consider that some institutions are too *interconnected* to fail.[260] CCPs in the OTCDM occupy a prominent and systemic position as they concentrate and manage the risk of transactions that were traditionally traded on a bilateral basis. The enhancement in the use of central clearing reflects the high level of interconnectedness between CCPs and OTCDM participants. CCPs are linked directly with clearing members and indirectly with clearing members' clients. These interconnections become channels of communication and transmission of default. Hence, the financial difficulties of CCPs might rapidly spill over to a large number of other institutions, or even to the entire financial system.

The understanding of the systemic importance of CCPs would be incomplete without considering that CCPs, as SIFIs, are usually cross-border financial firms. In the area of insolvency of cross-border financial firms, the fundamental debate is between the adoption of a universal approach and a territorial approach.[261] The adoption of a universal set of cross-border policies might sometimes be better suited to manage SIFIs' insolvency than territorial policies, such as ring-fencing.

On the one hand, the defenders of the universal approach assert that one of the main limits of ring-fencing is that the resulting restrictions on capital flows might exacerbate problems elsewhere, and they might lead to inefficient capital and liquidity management.[262] Moreover, universal approach proponents argue that ring-fencing measures (e.g. prohibition of intra-group transfers) increase financial stress and impede other national authorities' crisis management efforts.[263] When national regulators seize domestic assets for the benefit of national creditors,[264] orderly resolution is inefficient[265] and it affects the rights of creditors of other jurisdictions. Ring-fencing assets might increase the possibility of group-wide failure, because it critically affects the continuity of certain functions.

<http://fsbwatch.org/pdf/failure_of_crossborder_financial_firms_cornford.pdf> accessed 31st January 2016.

258 FSB, 'Reducing the Moral Hazard Posed by Systemically Important Financial Institutions' (FSB, Interim report to G20 Leaders, 18th June 2010).

259 The origin of the term can be traced to the open bank assistance offered to Continental Illinois in 1984.

260 Thomas F. Huertas, and Rosa Lastra, 'The Perimeter Issue: To what Extent should *Lex Specialis* be extended to Systemically Institutions? An Exit Strategy from Too Big To Fail' in Rosa Lastra (ed.), *Cross-Border Bank Insolvency* (Oxford University Press 2011), 273.

261 Jonathan Edwards, 'A Model Law Framework for the Resolution of G-SIFIs' (2012) 7 (2) *Capital Markets Law Journal,* 122.

262 Basel Committee, Cross-Border Bank Resolution Group (CBRG) 2010 Section III.

263 HS Scott, 'Supervision of International Banking Post-BCCI' (1992) 8 Ga St U L Rev 487, 504.

264 Bank of Credit and Commerce International (BCCI).

265 Hons SL Bufford, 'Global Venue Controls Are Coming: A Replay to Prof LoPucki' (2005) 79 Am Bank LJ 105, 136.

On the other hand, proponents[266] of a territorial approach argue that ring-fencing allows national authorities to apply their own insolvency laws to the entities, operations, and assets of the firms in their jurisdiction. The main benefit of ring-fencing is that it encourages early intervention by national authorities when it is necessary, even if the insolvent firm is a cross-border entity.[267]

A regime for CCPs must be designed to efficiently protect against their failure and against systemic risk. Considering the benefits and limitations of ring-fencing, we can see the need to structure rules suitable for combining with cross-border measures designed to enhance resilience[268] of the OTCDM. Moreover, a ring-fencing regime should consider the twin realities of cross-border arbitrage[269] deeply embedded in the interconnections of CCP with other financial entities. Similarly, as the cost of using ring-fencing might be duplicative,[270] because there are other solutions to systemic risk (e.g. bailouts), regulators should decide whether the regime would bring additional benefits to the management of CCP failure – for instance, the inclusion of ring-fencing rules in the Dodd-Frank Act is justified as a measure that could help to mitigate the TBTF problem.

4.4 Conclusion

The shortcomings of the UK regime of CCPs in the OTCDM that we have discussed in this chapter illustrate how the use of a risk-based approach to regulation by UK regulators is creating manufactured risks. Regarding the insufficient legal framework underpinning CCPs' operations, these manufactured risks stem from the lack of protection of clearing members and clearing members' clients' rights from the imposition of unfair contract terms, as well as the lack of clarity related to the standard of diligence that CCPs should observe when performing their contractual obligations.

Along with the creation of manufactured risks, the inadequacy of the insufficient legal framework underpinning CCPs' operations also reveals the absence of an organisational culture in implementing risk-based regulation. The role of regulators – the Bank or the FCA – is unclear in implementing rules for CCPs related to the management of clearing members' assets and positions.

Regarding the shortcoming of the insufficient legal framework underpinning CCPs' operations, we argue that the robustness of a CCP is not limited to prudential matters but should also pursue the robustness of its clearing members. Hence, our central argument is that making CCPs safe and sound does not justify

---

266 LM LoPucki, 'The Case for Cooperative Territoriality in International Bankruptcy' (2000) 98 Mich L Rev 2216.

267 Some members of the CBRG share this view, Basel Committee, Cross-Border Bank Resolution Group (CBRG) (n262).

268 Basel Committee, Cross-Border Bank Resolution Group (CBRG) (n262).

269 James L. Bromley, and Tim Phillips, 'International Lessons from Lehman's Failure: A Cross-Border No Man's Land' in Rosa Lastra (ed.), *Cross-Border Bank Insolvency* (Oxford University Press 2011) (n260).

270 Steven L. Schwarcz, 'Ring-Fencing' (n208).

the imposition of excessive restrictions on the clearing members' contractual rights, and indirectly on clearing members' clients' rights. One area of particular concern in the relationship between CCPs and clearing members is the limitation of CCPs' liability allowed by Section 291 of FSMA 2000. This regime prevents clearing members from exercising their contractual rights when the CCPs are acting negligently. CCPs can only be held responsible when they act in bad faith, fraudulently, or in gross negligence. There is no standard of diligence applicable to CCPs when they perform contractual obligations.

In order to illustrate how problematic might be the current limitation of CCPs' liability in practice, we have highlighted the rules of CCPs' rulebooks operating in the UK and the related issues, including the CCPs' management of clearing members' assets and the effectiveness of segregation requirement as was conceived in EMIR. In particular, UK regulators should design a regime that goes beyond legal segregation and ensure the actual segregation of collateral. The development of additional rules would also impose a duty on CCPs to verify the accuracy of the information provided by clearing members concerning their clients' positions, types of assets, and value related to collateral. Moreover, CCPs' rulebooks almost exclusively rule the CCPs' 'obligations related to clearing members' positions, including recording positions and margin, management and liquidation of collateral, portability, management of mutualisation of risks, and, in some types of accounts, the management of clearing members' clients' default. The content of these rules and the high level of discretion granted to CCPs when performing their obligations allow for potential sources of litigation. There is a need to review the statutory and contractual limits to the liability of CCPs. There must be a recognition of a duty of care in the contractual relationship between CCPs and clearing members, which would contribute to rebalance the relationship between CCPs and their members, and thereby strengthen the protection of clearing members' rights.

The discussion concerning the absence of an SRR for CCPs reveals another weakness in the UK regime of CCPs in the OTCDM. During the first years of the regime, the Bank has been focused on strengthening the loss-allocation and recoverability rules; however, this approach is incomplete. Strengthening the resilience of CCPs implies a comprehensive regulatory framework that allows supervisors to conduct CCPs' insolvency proceedings in an orderly manner and, more importantly, ensures the continuity of services. Both recovery and resolvability regimes are tools for the effective management of clearing members' default and seek to guarantee that CCPs are sufficiently solvent to contain losses and liquidity shortfalls. Moreover, recovery and resolution rules aim to ensure that the core functions of CCPs are maintained in times of financial distress and crisis.

We call UK regulators to design a resolution regime that attends to the particularities of CCPs. The systemic importance of CCPs and the impact of their failure is not merely a theoretical discussion. Although it is a very rare scenario, CCPs can actually fail and regulators need to have rules and enforcement powers to resolve CCPs avoiding the disturbance of clearing services. As CCPs are the centre of multiple contracts that net positions and mutualise credit risk, their resolution regime should minimise the distress costs of all market participants, clearing members, third parties, and taxpayers that could suffer spill-over costs.

Furthermore, the design of an SRR for CCPs should address questions related to the efficient allocation of losses, how to mitigate fire sales, and how to ensure the continuity of services. The international regulatory trend seems to be moving towards the design of a credible recapitalisation strategy that seeks to favour recapitalisation over liquidation. Despite the critiques to this method, the rationale is to create a fund that will operate only when all the recovery tools have been exhausted and the CCP is not viable any more. Stress tests should also be developed as a complement to the CCPs' internal stress tests. Another recommendation is to use techniques to crystallise losses to counterparties and to contractually restructure their clearing payment obligations to clearing members. These contractual restructuring measures include VMGH and tear-ups.

Similarly, the resolution authority should be equipped with powers that facilitate early intervention. In this matter, the advances in the UK are in the Code of Practice that explains how the Banking Act 2009 applies to CCPs. In particular, it delimits the circumstances in which the Bank would exercise its stabilisation powers, which include the power to transfer some or all the business of a CCP to a 'bridge CCP' that is owned or controlled by the Bank, and the power to transfer the ownership of the CCP to any other person. Ruling the early intervention powers of the Bank – as the resolution authority of CCPs – is one step forward. However, there are other aspects that are still to be developed. The CCPs' insolvency regime should be consistent with international efforts to deal with cross-border issues (e.g. the work of the fmiCBCM in cooperation with IOSCO). In the process of regulating the insolvency of CCPs, UK regulators should consider the risks that CCPs face in the event of clearing members' insolvency and how that might threaten the stability of the CCP.

We have considered some of the challenges an SRR for CCPs might face in practice. Regulators need to be especially careful when adopting rules that limit the possibility for clearing members and clients to enforce their rights in front of a defaulting CCP (e.g. the right to terminate contracts in the case of a CCP's insolvency suggested by the FSB Key Attributes consultative document, or termination rights in derivatives contracts in the FCAD). Moreover, the design of an SRR for CCPs will be the opportunity to clarify whether CCPs could be bailed out. Although one of the fundamental principles that regulators have made clear from the beginning is that they do not allow the use of public sources to bail out CCPs, there is still debate whether the principle would remain under exceptional circumstances.

Furthermore, we have considered the issue related to the role clearing members play as the ultimate 'underwriters' of the CCP default risk. If the tendency of the coming regulation is to impose further funding requirements onto clearing members, as a measure to contribute to the CCPs' recovery, it will be necessary for regulators to intervene to 'rebalance' the relationship between clearing members and CCPs. This could be achieved by means of designing more rigorous stress tests and enhancing the disclosure of CCPs' management actions *ex ante*, so clearing members are sufficiently informed about the functioning of the CCP.

Finally, in our discussion concerning the SRR for CCPs, we considered whether ring-fencing could be used as a regulatory solution to manage CCPs' financial distress. If applied by UK authorities, the ring-fencing of CCPs should be designed as a complementary tool to strengthen protection against their failure and against the concretion of systemic risk. However, the challenge is to make ring-fencing rules suitable for application alongside cross-border measures designed to enhance the resilience of the OTCDM.

5 Shortcomings – failure to rule innovation risk

5.1 Introduction

The last shortcoming of the UK regime of CCPs in the OTCDM is that it fails to rule on innovation risk. The focus of the Bank is on the management of credit, liquidity, and operational risks. Although this tripartite interest of the regime tackles the primary concerns of the functioning and stability of CCPs, as well as deals with one of the fundamental areas of the CCPs regulation, there are other types of manufactured risks that are not being considered. In this chapter, we argue that the current UK regime of CCPs is fractured, because it disregards one of the most traditional characteristics of the OTCDM – [1]innovation risk.[2] Since the origins of the OTCDM, innovation has boosted the continuity, expansion, and growth of the market. For the purpose of this study, 'innovation risk' covers the alternative innovative mechanisms[3] that CCPs and their members might use to avoid regulatory burdens, while at the same time complying with the new regulatory requirements, an approach of 'creative compliance'. Therefore, if the Bank's objective is to regulate CCPs to ensure the safety and soundness of the OTCDM, the regime of CCPs should include the risk that innovation[4] repre-

---

1 Randal Kroszner, 'Can the Financial Markets Privately Regulate Risk? The Development of Derivatives Clearinghouses and Recent Over-the-Counter Innovation' (2009) 31 (3) *Journal of Money, Credit and Banking*, 614 <http://faculty.chicagobooth.edu/randall.kroszner/research/pdf/Kroszner%20JMCB%20Clearinghouses.pdf> accessed 5th October 2015.

2 Adam Waldam, 'OTC Derivatives & Systemic Risk: Innovative Finance or the Dance into the Abyss?' (1993–1994) 43 *American University Law Review*, 1023.

3 Defining financial innovation: 'Financial innovation is the act of creating and then popularizing new financial instruments, as well as new financial technologies, institutions and markets'. J. Lerner, and P. Tufano (2011) 'The Consequences of Financial Innovation: A Counterfactual Research Agenda, Annual Review of Financial Economics 3', in World Economic Forum: Rethinking Financial Innovation: Reducing Negative Outcomes While Retaining The Benefits (2012) <www.oliverwyman.com/content/dam/oliver-wyman/v2/publications/2012/apr/Rethinking_Financial_Innovation.pdf> accessed 19th December 2017.

4 Panagiotis Delimatsis, 'Transparent Financial Innovation in a Post-Crisis Environment' (2012) 16 (1) *Journal of International Economic Law*, 159.

sents to the achieving of regulators' objectives.[5] Moreover, the regime should consider the role of CCPs as 'co-regulators' to the extent that they impose market discipline.

This chapter starts with a brief explanation of the events where innovation risk might take place. It then presents an overview of the governance rules of EMIR and the role that the UK Senior Managers and Certification Regime (SM&CR) could have if applied to individuals who work in CCPs. We discuss how the demutualised structure of CCPs operating in the UK puts conflict of interest issues at the forefront and, in particular, refer to the convergent interests of CCPs' owners, clearing members, and the public interests. As the Bank's approach is yet to be developed, there then follows a section devoted to highlighting the need for CCPs' governance rules and how those rules might contribute to partially solve some of the innovation risk-related concerns. Finally, we explain how innovation is likely to lead to some of the unintended consequences of the CCP regime, referring to the potential dangers coming from the innovative financial techniques OTCDM participants will use to meet the high-quality collateral requirements of CCPs. We also explore how the 'innovative' use of portfolio compression diminishes the effectiveness of CCPs as managers of counterparty credit risk in the OTCDM, as well as the impact this practice might have on triggering systemic risk.

5.2 Innovation to avoid central clearing

Innovation can take different forms: one of them is the use of derivatives transactions that dealers want to keep in bilateral trading, to avoid central clearing. Major dealers will seek to protect their profitability by participating in the higher margin bilateral trading and, to that end, they are likely to engage in faux customisation of clearing-eligible products and to influence the governance of CCPs. Griffith,[6] when studying the issues related to the governance of CCPs, emphasises the interest that major dealers might have in keeping clearing-eligible derivatives off the CCPs.

The regulation of the governance of CCPs could help to overcome one part of the shortcoming related to innovation risk. It is not possible to control the creativity of market participants when it comes to bespoke transactions; neither is it possible for regulators to anticipate the forms derivatives transactions might take. However, what is achievable is to control the power that major derivative dealers might have over the governance of CCPs. This is to control the self-interest that

---

5 Rosa Lastra, and Andrea Miglionico, 'The House of Lords Report on the Post-Crisis EU Regulatory Framework: Where Does the UK Stand?' (2015) 5 *Journal of International Banking and Financial Law*, 303, 304C.
6 Sean J. Griffith, 'Governing Systemic Risk: Towards a Governance Structure for Derivatives Clearinghouses', (2012) 61 *Emory Law Journal*, 1153, 1195 <http://law.emory.edu/elj/_documents/volumes/61/5/articles/griffith.pdf> accessed 4th November 2015.

major dealers might exert to 'escape' the clearing requirement by convincing the CCP that certain clearing-eligible products, disguised as bespoke instruments, should not be cleared through the CCP. The debate is closely related to the line – continuously stepped by regulators – between the imposition of clearing eligibility requirements that constrain the freedom of CCPs to decide what products to clear and the consequences it has in terms of liquidity, and to open the discretion for CCPs to decide as it is most convenient to them. The scenario allowing the CCP to use its discretion is vulnerable to the self-interest of major dealers, and this is the point that should be urgently considered by regulators in the design and implementation of a CCP's governance regime.

The position adopted in the European regulation is restrictive.[7] EMIR and complementary legislation clearly instruct CCPs about the requirements that derivatives transactions shall meet in order to be cleared.[8] ESMA develops the scope of classes of clearing-eligible transactions[9] through RTS;[10] therefore, any change to the scope must go through the process of an amendment of the RTS. Similarly, EMIR lacks a mechanism to temporarily suspend the clearing obligation. The process to suspend or revoke a clearing obligation could take months since it would require a change in EU legislation. Recognising the lack of flexibility of the current regime in the latest review of EMIR,[11] the ESMA advised the European Commission[12] to 'streamline the process for determining clearing

7 Art 4 (1) EMIR requires certain OTC derivatives as determined by ESMA to be subject to mandatory clearing.
8 Art 5 EMIR establishes the Review Process for Mandatory Clearing. It includes two processes, implemented by ESMA, for assessing the eligibility of a class of OTC derivatives transactions for mandatory clearing: 'bottom-up' and 'top-down' procedures.
9 EMIR does not include exceptions from clearing mandate for particular types of OTC derivatives. However, it includes certain relaxations for FX Contracts and Covered Bonds in Recital 19 and 24 EMIR, respectively.
10 On 6 August 2015, the European Commission adopted a delegated regulation that makes it mandatory for certain over-the-counter (OTC) interest rate derivative contracts to be cleared through Central Counterparties; this delegated regulation entered into force on 21st December 2015; on 1st March 2016, the European Commission adopted a delegated regulation that makes it mandatory for certain over-the-counter (OTC) credit default derivative contracts to be cleared through Central Counterparties. This regulation entered into force on the twentieth day following that of its publication in the *Official Journal of the European Union*. Afterwards, the clearing obligation will progressively take effect according to the categories of OTC derivatives, as classified in the Annex to the delegated regulation.
11 EMIR Review Report no 4 ESMA input as part of the Commission consultation on the EMIR Review 13 August 2015 | [ESMA/2015/1254 4] 1 *Improvements to the Clearing Obligation Procedure* <www.esma.europa.eu/system/files/esma-2015-1254_-_emir_review_report_no.4_on_other_issues.pdf> accessed 4th November 2015.
12 European Commission Directorate General Financial Stability, Financial Services and Capital Markets Union. Public Consultation of Regulation [EU NO 648/2012] on OTC Derivatives, Central Counterparties, and Trade Repositories (21st May–13th August 2015) <http://ec.europa.eu/finance/consultations/2015/emir-revision/docs/consultation-document_en.pdf> accessed 4th November 2015.

obligations and to introduce tools allowing the suspension of the clearing obligation when certain conditions arise'.[13]

In response to the latest Consultation of EMIR Review, the UK[14] and the ECB[15] advised the adoption of a quicker mechanism in attending to the difficulties that CCPs might face when being compelled to clear less liquid products. The Bank's proposition in this matter is helpful and seeks to boost the efficient functioning of clearing services, but it needs to be accompanied by strong governance rules for CCPs.

The foregoing description of the rules concerning eligibility of central clearing and the discussion thereof lead us to argue for the relevance of the governance rules of CCPs. When the regime includes a prescriptive list of clearing-eligible derivatives, as EMIR does, the concern is that this might adversely affect the liquidity of the CCP, which would be obliged to clear less liquid transactions. However, if the prescriptive list approach is reformed to allow CCPs to decide when to except the clearing eligibility for certain products, the clearing eligibility system would be more flexible and efficient. The downside of this discretionary approach is that it might open the opportunity for major dealers to influence the CCP to not clear certain type of derivatives that, in principle, would be subject to the clearing obligation. In order to control the self-interest of major dealers, regulators might use governance regime.

As we saw in Chapter 3, the Bank has not yet developed the governance principles of CCPs, but it is one of the regulatory priorities according to the second report of May 2015.[16] The current regime is comprised of the governance rules in EMIR and the self-regulatory codes adopted by CCPs. We will now explore the governance rules in EMIR and introduce the individual accountability regime of the UK financial services.

---

13 ESMA, 'ESMA recommends changes to EMIR framework' [ESMA/2015/1260] (Press Release 13 August 2015) <www.esma.europa.eu/system/files/2015-1260_esma_recommends_changes_to_emir_framework.pdf> accessed 4th November 2015.

14 It was discussed in the interview at the Bank (interview with Mr Paul Brione Head of Central Counterparty Supervision, Bank of England, London, 25 September 2015).

15 'Regarding the *clearing obligation*, the ECB wishes to reiterate and support the points made by the European Systemic Risk Board in its own response to the public consultation, namely that a swift process to remove or suspend the clearing obligation should be established when the relevant market situation so requires (e.g. certain instruments become illiquid; a CCP is under recovery or resolution procedures), and that systemic risk issues should be more explicitly taken into account when identifying the categories of products suitable for mandatory clearing'. (emphasis added) ECB response to the European Commission's consultation on the review of the European Market Infrastructure Regulation (EMIR) [ECB-02] (September 2015) <www.ecb.europa.eu/pub/pdf/other/ecb_reply_to_commission_public_consultation_emiren.pdf?d2d149511414150aa03972c156c5e9d9> accessed 4th November 2015.

16 The Bank of England's supervision of Financial Market Infrastructures Annual Report March 2015 (hereinafter the Bank's supervision of FMIs 2nd Annual Report 2015).

5.2.1 Governance rules

5.2.1.1 EMIR

EMIR seeks to serve as a framework for the safe and sound functioning of the CCPs as the new intermediaries in the OTCDM. That is why the internal organisation and governance of CCPs occupies a large part of EMIR. Title IV rules, among other aspects, the organisational requirements of CCPs.

Regarding the organisational requirements, the general provision establishes the obligation for the CCPs to have robust governance arrangements, including a 'clear organisational structure with well-defined, transparent and consistent lines of responsibility, effective processes to identify, manage, monitor and report the risks to which it is or might be exposed, and adequate internal control mechanisms, including sound administrative and accounting procedures'.[17] CCPs' internal control structure facilitates internal and external monitoring by providing access to relevant data. Such access to information seeks to effectively enhance the transparency of CCPs' operation; consequently, this enhances the ability of regulators to access accurate information, which in turn benefits the process of supervision.

As might be anticipated, this provision reflects one of the characteristics of the risk-based approach to regulation and supervision, which is the reliance on the internal control system and how it contributes to achieving regulators' objectives. The rationale is that the CCPs' internal organisation and management is the first tool to achieve the efficient functioning of the CCP, in the pursuance of financial stability. To that end, CCPs adopt policies and procedures to ensure compliance with the relevant regulation.

According to regulatory requirements, CCPs are also compelled 'to maintain and operate an organisational structure that ensures continuity and orderly functioning in the performance of its services and activities'.[18] The continuity of services in times of financial distress is a concern of regulators from a recovery and resolution perspective, as well as from the governance and internal organisation point of view.

EMIR rules the internal governance of CCPs and have provided that, similar to other financial institutions, senior managers should be sufficiently skilled and experienced 'so as to ensure the sound and prudent management of the CCP'.[19] The members of the board of a CCP shall have adequate expertise in financial services, risk management, and clearing services – these organisational requirements, included in the governance of CCPs, demonstrate another element of the risk-based approach to regulation. The internal system of control and, in general, the internal structure and governance of the regulated firm are established in such a manner that will contribute to the achievement of the regulatory objectives.

---

17 Art 26 EMIR.
18 Ibid.
19 Art 27 EMIR.

The rationale is to ensure that the system of internal control works. These rules governing the senior management and governance arrangements of the CCP should contribute to the safety and soundness of the CCP itself, and thereby help to achieve financial stability.

Moreover, a CCP will establish a risk committee, consisting of representatives of its clearing members, independent members of the board, and representatives of its clients; this committee shall be completely independent from the management of the CCP. The risk committee advises on several matters; mainly, 'any arrangements that may impact the risk management of the CCP, such as a significant change in its risk model, the default procedures, the criteria for accepting clearing members, the clearing of new classes of instruments, or the outsourcing of functions'.[20]

It is still unclear whether the UK regime of individual accountability would be automatically applicable to senior managers and employees of CCPs; hence, the applicable regime, at the time of writing, is contained in EMIR. However, it is useful to explain the role of individual accountability regimes in the context of governance of CCPs.

5.2.1.2 UK individual accountability regime

5.2.1.2.1 THE CONTEXT OF INDIVIDUAL ACCOUNTABILITY

Here we emphasise the importance of individual accountability regimes as part of governance rules, in particular in the context of financial regulation, and conduct of business rules and governance.

Along with the elements already examined, a governance regime should also include a system of effective oversight of senior management and employees. This is an accountability regime that ensures individuals are of sufficiently good repute and possess the required knowledge, expertise, and skills to perform their functions. This regime adopts standards of conduct as criteria to authorise individuals to perform significantly important functions; these standards also assist the assessment of the actions and behaviour of those individuals. Hence, such a regime usually includes the 'fit and proper' standard, which allows regulators to consider honesty, integrity, reputation, competence and capability, and the financial soundness of the individuals performing significant functions within the firm. Moreover, once these individuals have been authorised, there are some standards of conduct related to the way functions should be performed: the duty to act with integrity; to act with due skill, care, and diligence; to observe proper standards of market conduct; to deal with regulators in an open and cooperative way; and to take reasonable steps to ensure that the business of the firm is organised and complies with the relevant requirements and standards of the regulatory system.

---

20 Art 28 EMIR.

The rationale of individual accountability regimes is primarily focused on identifying the responsibilities that each individual has within the firm. The clear determination of such responsibilities assists both regulators and firms in implementing systems of control to ensure that individuals perform their functions following the standards of conduct and that they act in the best interest of the firm and the market. In the event of non-observance, firms and regulators bring into operation a system of control, i.e. firm internal disciplinary proceedings, and administrative or criminal sanctions imposed by regulators.

In financial services regulation, the adoption of individual accountability rules is seen as an extension of its reach 'downwards' into the level of the firm to impose specific responsibilities on individuals.[21] The importance of adopting rules that link individual responsibility with the due care and skill in the conduct of business, as well as proper internal organisation, was initially recognised in the UK by the Securities and Futures Authority in 1998.[22] The detailed evolution of individual accountability in UK financial services is beyond the scope of this book; however, it is relevant to emphasise that the standard of 'fitness and propriety', guidance on adequate management controls, and standards and rules on how to perform functions in the carrying on of regulated activities have all been common elements to all regimes. They have been included in the Approved Persons Regime (APR) of FSMA 2000, as well as the New Senior Managers and Certification Regime (SM&CR).

As explained in Chapter 1, the adoption of firms' internal control systems is a key component of the risk-based approach to regulation. The aim is to determine that all mechanisms of internal control are adequate and sufficient. Hence, in order to ensure that regulators' decision-making is objective and based on pre-established standards (e.g. fitness and propriety), there should be a continuous review and assessment of the firm's internal controls. In particular, the implementation of individual accountability regimes reflects one of the elements of risk-based regimes – the reliance on the firm's internal control as a way of transplanting risk-based supervision at a firm-level, which also minimises the regulator's exposure to risk. In this case, the risk is that a breach of standards of conduct affects the public interest.

It is also important to clarify that prudential supervision does not necessarily reduce the likelihood of collapse, fraud, or non-compliance of conduct rules and standards, mainly because it is concerned with the stability of firms and markets. This is why the development of individual accountability regimes is an important part of governance regimes and why, therefore, it is necessary to adopt systems of internal controls other than financial,[23] which are effective on the basis

---

21 Joanna Gray, and Jenny Hamilton, *Implementing Financial Regulation: Theory and Practice* (John Wiley & Sons Ltd 2006), 55.

22 SFA Board of Notice 473, May 1998, Ibid.

23 The Hampel Report emphasised that financial controls are only one part of the whole framework of internal control systems. Committee on Corporate Governance, Report of the Committee on Corporate Governance, London, Gee & Co (1998) *Hampel Report.*

of cooperation between regulators and firms. Achieving effective cooperation requires that firms value its importance. Only then are regulators in the position to deliver their objectives. The firm's internal control comprehends several mechanisms, which we will briefly highlight in this section, as they are not the core of the discussion. Internal control includes rules of corporate governance,[24] which for financial firms have a broad scope. Such governance goes beyond the shareholders to include debt holders, insurance policy holders, and other creditors, called debt governance.[25] Moreover, internal auditing[26] is also a key component of internal control systems.[27] Its terms and conditions[28] follow the Institute of Internal Audit International Professional Practices Framework (IPPF), which includes the International Standards for the Professional Practice of Internal Auditing (the IIA Standards).[29] In the particular case of financial firms, internal auditing assists regulators in the process of regulation and supervision[30] because it is performed on the basis of risk analysis, where the audit is to identify internal and external risks.[31] Such an identification of risk contributes to the effective design and implementation of risk-based regimes, as an effective risk-based

24 See Committee on the Financial Aspects of Corporate Governance, *Report of the Committee on the Financial Aspects of Corporate Governance, London Gee & Co* (1992) (*Cadbury Report*); Financial Reporting Council, 'The UK Corporate Governance Code' (September 2012) <www.slc.co.uk/media/5268/uk-corporate-governance-code-september-2012. pdf> accessed 1st March 2016.

25 Klaus J. Hopt, 'Better Governance of Financial Institutions' (Max Planck Institute for Private Law, ECGI Working Paper Series in Law, Working Paper No 207/2013 Hamburg, Germany, April 2013) <http://personal.lse.ac.uk/schustee/hopt%20governance.pdf> accessed 27th January 2016. The OECD identifies three special factors of corporate governance of banks: systemic risk, high leverage, and dispersed non-experts as claim holders. See OECD, 'Corporate Governance and the Financial Crisis: Key Findings and Main Messages' *OECD* (June 2009) <www.oecd.org/corporate/ca/corporategovernanceprinciples/43056196. pdf> accessed 27th January 2016.

26 Under FSMA 2000, internal audit is a 'controlled function'.

27 Auditing is part of effective governance in banking systems. Basel Committee on Banking Supervision, 'Framework for internal control systems in banking organisations' BCBS (1998).

28 It does not have a statutory basis.

29 Chartered Institute of Internal Auditors, 'Consultative Document: Effective Internal Audit in the Financial Services Sector Draft recommendations to the Chartered Institute of Internal Auditors' (11 February 2013) <www.iia.org.uk/media/212348/effective_internal_ audit_in_fs_consultation_document_for_web.pdf> accessed 27th January 2016.

30 Basel Committee on Banking Supervision (BCBS), Internal Audit in Banking Organisations and the Relationship of the Supervisory Authorities with Internal and External Auditors, July (2000). See BCBS Consultative Document, 'The Internal Audit Function in Banks', December 2011) <www.bis.org/publ/bcbs210.pdf> accessed 27th January 2016; also see BCBS Consultative Document, 'The Internal Audit Function in Banks' (BCBS, June 2012) <www.bis.org/publ/bcbs223.pdf> accessed 27th January 2016.

31 Tomas Hrebik, 'Internal Audit in Financial Institutions' (2015) University of Economics in Prague, 9 *Journal of International Scientific Publications, Economy & Business*, 6 <www.scientific-publications.net/get/1000012/1431690554840972.pdf> accessed 27th January 2016.

regime integrates the multiple perceptions and attitudes towards risks, i.e. the perception of firms and regulators.

5.2.1.2.2 THE RELEVANCE OF ADOPTING AN INDIVIDUAL
        ACCOUNTABILITY REGIME

The importance of developing a regime of individual accountability for financial firms lies in the implementation of narrower parameters to assess whether directors and other individuals performing controlled and authorised functions might be held accountable. The regime is stricter than the traditional company law set of Directors' Duties[32] that, although illustrative to understand their duties and responsibilities,[33] does not reach the level of specificity required in financial firms. As financial firms operate in regulated markets, the Directors' Duties are not limited to benefit the company, shareholders, and third parties deemed as 'stakeholders'. Instead, financial firms are obliged to promote the interest of consumers and meet high public expectations. Especially after a period of financial crisis and scandals in the banking sector, financial regulators are committed to enhancing conduct in the market.

The discussion is particularly relevant because the UK government and financial regulators are introducing a range of reforms to increase individual accountability within the financial sector.[34] The PCBS recommended bringing forward reforms in relation to individual conduct and standards in banking.[35] Such a reform was included in the Financial Services Act 2013 amending the FSMA 2000. The reforms replaced the APR[36] of Part V of FSMA 2000 for individuals who work in banking. The Banking Act 2013 introduced the SM&CR that came into effect on 7th March 2016. Although the SM&CR was initially conceived to

---

32 Companies Act 2006 and Insolvency Act 1986 are the statutory basis of Directors' Duties in the UK. 'It maintains a primary duty on directors to act in the interests of shareholders. Directors are bound by fiduciary duties at general law in relation to the Company. However, it also requires that, in fulfilling this duty, directors specifically have regard to a number of other matters, including: the likely consequences of any decision in the long term; the interests of the company's employees; the need to foster the company's business relationships with suppliers, customers and others; and the impact of the company's operations on the community and the environment'. See John Birds, and Anthony J. Boyle (eds.), *Boyle and Birds' Company Law* (Jordan Publishing 2014), 110.

33 In company law, directors' general duties are based on certain common law rules and equitable principles. The relationship between statutory duties and the previous duties based on case law is recognised in s 170 (3) (4) 171–174 Companies Act 2006.

34 See FCA website <www.the-fca.org.uk/improving-individual-accountability> accessed 25th January 2016.

35 See the PCBS Final Report *Changing Banking for Good* (HL Paper 27, HC 175, published 19 June 2013), and the Government's response (Cm 866, published 8 July 2013).

36 Under the APR, financial services firms ('authorised persons' under FSMA 2000) may not employ a person to perform a 'controlled function', unless that person has been approved by the PRA or the FCA, following an application by the firm concerned.

rule conduct in the banking sector,[37] the government is proposing to extend the regime to all sectors of the financial services industry.[38] To that end, HM Treasury introduced a bill to Parliament on the extension of the regime, which is likely to be implemented in 2018.[39]

Although it could be assumed that the SM&CR will be applicable to senior managers and employees of CCPs in the OTCDM, this study argues that the SM&CR would not be automatically applicable to them, as it has been said that neither the FCA nor the PRA supervise CCPs. The Bank will have to clarify which is the competent regulator in this area, whether that be the Bank or, as we would recommend, the FCA. Thus, if the appropriate regulator is the Bank, it will have to issue rules regarding the individual accountability of senior managers and employees of CCPs operating in the OTCDM. If the appropriate competent regulator is the FCA, the SM&CR will be directly applicable to all individuals who work in the CCPs by 2018.

To develop this argument, we will next address several questions concerning the legal framework governing the responsibility and accountability of senior managers and employees. In this section, we will explain the generalities of the former APR and how it illustrates the new SM&CR, as well as explore the SM&CR's key features and how its implementation would contribute to building up the governance and conduct of business regime of CCPs.

5.2.1.2.3 THE APPROVED PERSONS REGIME (APR)

The regulation of directors and managers was initially included in the APR. These individuals could be deemed 'approved persons' if their role within the organisation is considered a 'controlled function'.[40] In order to perform a controlled function,[41] the individual must perform an activity that is significant to the regulatory process and assist the regulator to fulfil its regulatory objectives[42] – meaning

---

37 'The rules apply to banks, building societies, credit unions, the largest investment banks that are regulated by the PRA, branches of foreign banks operating in the UK', see FCA website <www.the-fca.org.uk/improving-individual-accountability#sthash.JLCYEDGU.dpuf> accessed 25th January 2016.

38 HM Treasury, 'Senior Managers and Certification Regime: Extension To All FSMA Authorised Persons' (October 2015) <www.gov.uk/government/uploads/system/uploads/attachment_data/file/468328/SMCR_policy_paper_final_15102015.pdf> accessed 25th January 2016.

39 FCA website <www.the-fca.org.uk/improving-individual-accountability#sthash.JLCYEDGU.dpuf> accessed 25th January 2016.

40 FSA, 'Factsheet for All Firms: Becoming an Approved Person' (August 2011) 1 <www.fca.org.uk/static/fca/documents/fsa-factsheet-approved.pdf?trk=profile_certification_title> accessed 25th January 2016.

41 'A Complete List of FCA Controlled Functions' <www.handbook.fca.org.uk/handbook/SUP/10A/4.html> accessed 25th January 2016.
  'A Complete List of PRA Controlled Functions' <www.prarulebook.co.uk/rulebook/Content/Chapter/271670/19-10-2015> accessed 25th January 2016.

42 FSA, Factsheet for All Firms: Becoming an Approved Person (n40).

that only approved persons can perform controlled functions.[43] The criteria for approval is that the individual meet and maintain the requirements of the fit and proper test (FIT) and that he/she performs the controlled function in accordance with a set of standards called Statements of Principle and Code of Practice for Approved Persons (APER).

5.2.1.2.4 THE FIT AND PROPER TEST (FIT)[44]

The main criteria used by regulators to assess whether an individual is fit and proper to perform controlled functions includes the following: i) honesty, integrity, and reputation;[45] ii) competence and capability;[46] and iii) financial soundness.[47] The inclusion of these criteria strengthens the approved persons' responsibility and the accountability regime. The appropriate regulator considers that a person is fit and proper when he/she is suitable to be approved by the appropriate regulator and thereby perform controlled functions.[48] The approval decision[49] implies the assessment of the individual's character and the complexity of the activities and business of the regulated firm where the individual works.[50] Similarly, the appropriate regulator shall assess the risks[51] that the individual poses to consumers and confidence in the financial system.[52] The approval can be withdrawn when the appropriate regulator considers that the individual is no longer fit and proper to take up the controlled function for which he/she was approved. However, the withdrawal of approval would only occur when there is a blatant disregard of conduct standards as probity,[53] competency, and the standard of care and skill. The intervention of the appropriate regulators is not always justified;[54] for instance, in the event of minor indiscretions,[55] the firm is expected to use its internal disciplinary proceedings to make the individual accountable.

43 S 59 FSMA 2000. A function is 'controlled' when it fulfils the general conditions of s 59 (5)-(7) of the FSMA 2000. They are: s 59 (5) where the individual has significant influence over the conduct of the approved person; s 59 (6) where the individual deals with customers; s 59 (7) where the individual deals with the property of its customers.

44 FIT 1.3.1 FCA, 'Fit and Proper Test for Approved Persons' <www.handbook.fca.org.uk/handbook/FIT.pdf> accessed 25th January 2016.

45 FIT 2.1.

46 FIT 2.2.

47 FIT 2.3.

48 Joanna Gray, and Jenny Hamilton, *Implementing Financial Regulation: Theory and Practice* (n21), 71.

49 FSMA 2000 s 59.

50 Dalvinder Singh, 'Corporate Governance and Banking Supervision' in Dalvinder Singh, *Banking Regulation of UK and US Financial Markets* (Ashgate Publishing 2007), 100.

51 Joanna Gray, and Jenny Hamilton, *Implementing Financial Regulation: Theory and Practice* (n21), 76.

52 Dalvinder Singh, 'Corporate Governance and Banking Supervision' (n50), 103.

53 'Probity refers to an individual's uprightness and honesty', Ibid 101.

54 Joanna Gray and Jenny Hamilton, *Implementing Financial Regulation: Theory and Practice* (n21), 72.

55 Ibid.

5.2.1.2.5 STATEMENTS OF PRINCIPLE AND CODE OF PRACTICE
　　　　FOR APPROVED PERSONS (APER)

The Statements of Principle are high-level standards that apply to approved persons for the controlled functions they perform.[56] The Code of Practice for Approved Persons is a guide that explains, through examples, whether an approved person's conduct complies with the Principles.[57]

APER applies to FCA and PRA controlled functions in relation to approved persons (Accountable Functions). It also applies to the performance of any other functions related to a regulated activity.[58] The Statements of Principle include the duty of approved persons to act with integrity; to act with due skill, care, and diligence; to observe proper standards of market conduct; to deal with regulators in an open and cooperative way and disclose appropriately any information; to take reasonable steps to ensure that the business of the firm is organised so that it can be controlled effectively; and to take reasonable steps to ensure that the business of the firm complies with the relevant requirements and standards of the regulatory system.[59]

In order to determine whether an approved person's conduct complies with the Statements of Principle, regulators issue the Code of Practice for Approved Persons.[60] The purpose of the Code is to set out descriptions of conduct[61] which, in the regulator's opinion, do not comply with the relevant Statements of Principle. Moreover, the Code sets out certain factors[62] to assess an approved persons' conduct. (For instance, to take into account whether the approved person exercised reasonable care when considering the information available to him/her or the knowledge he/she had, or whether he/she reached a reasonable conclusion upon which he/she acted, or the nature, complexity of the firm's business.)[63] The Code also includes specific conducts to each one of the principles.[64]

5.2.1.2.6 ENFORCEMENT POWERS IN THE APR

According to the APR, approved persons must comply with the Statements of Principle, which are a series of binding standards of professional conduct issued by the FCA and PRA. Regulators were bestowed with enforcement powers when approved persons breached the Statements of Principle, or were knowingly

---

56　FSA, Factsheet for All Firms: Becoming an Approved Person (n40).
57　FCA Handbook, 'Statements of Principle and Code of Practice for Approved Persons (APER)' <www.handbook.fca.org.uk/handbook/APER/1/> accessed 25th January 2016.
58　APER 1.1A2 P <www.handbook.fca.org.uk/handbook/APER.pdf> accessed 25th January 2016.
59　APER 2.1A3 P.
60　Code of Practice for Approved Persons is issued under s 64 of the Act.
61　APER 3.1A1.
62　APER 3.3.1E.
63　ibid.
64　APER 4.1.1A G.

concerned in a breach of regulatory requirements by the firm. The regulators can take a variety of enforcement actions against an approved person,[65] such as withdrawing approval or prohibiting an individual from undertaking controlled functions,[66] imposing a fine,[67] or naming and shaming by publishing a statement of the misconduct.[68] The FCA could also issue a private warning.[69]

5.2.1.2.7 THE SENIOR MANAGERS AND CERTIFICATION REGIME (SM&CR)

The multiple misconduct events in the UK financial services showed the need to reform the existing approved persons' regime.[70] The PCBS stated that the APR was a 'complex and confused mess', and that it failed to give senior managers clear expectations as to their responsibilities.[71] The PCBS recommended the design of a regime – the new SM&CR – that includes three pillars and is applicable to all 'relevant authorised persons' (RAP).[72]

The first pillar is the Senior Persons Regime (SPR) that focuses on individuals authorised to perform key roles and responsibilities in regulated firms called senior management functions (SMFs). SMFs are performed by persons responsible for managing one or more aspects of the authorised person's affairs, so far as relating to the activity, and those aspects involve, or might involve, a risk of serious consequences – for the authorised person or for business or other interests in the UK.[73]

The FCA or the PRA must approve all individuals who will perform SMF (referred to as senior managers). Senior managers specified by the PRA will require pre-approval by the PRA with the FCA's consent and senior managers specified by the FCA will require pre-approval by the FCA only. The regulatory pre-approval requires the submission of Statements of Responsibilities and the assertion that the candidate is a fit and proper person to perform the respective SMF.[74] The PRA and the FCA might include any additional conditions they deem appropriate and, if necessary, order the review of the Statement of Responsibilities. Moreover, regulators can vary existing approvals either at the

65 FSMA 2000 s 66 (2).
66 FSMA 2000 s 63 (1) and (1A) and s 56 (1).
67 FSMA 2000 s 66 (3), s 206.
68 FSMA 2000 s 66 (3), s 205.
69 FCA, 'Enforcement Guide' (FCA 7.10–7.17) (2014) <www.handbook.fca.org.uk/hand book/document/EG_Full_20140401.pdf> accessed 25th January 2016.
70 'Senior Managers and Certification Regime – Individual Accountability in The Banking Sector', Practice Notes, LexisNexis <www.lexisnexis.com/uk/lexispsl/financialservices/ document/393814/5DGP-02W1-F18F-P416> accessed 25th January 2016.
71 Parliamentary Commission on Banking Standards, 'Changing Banking for Good' (Final Report, para 564) (2013/2014) <www.publications.parliament.uk/pa/jt201314/jtselect/ jtpcbs/27/2704.htm> accessed 25th January 2016.
72 According to FSMA 2000, s71A, a bank, a building society, a credit union, or a PRA-designated investment firm.
73 FSMA 2000 s 59ZA.
74 FSMA 2000 s 60A.

firm's initiative or their own.[75] Along with the control of regulators, firms are legally required to assess the fitness and propriety of their senior managers at least annually.

The second pillar is the Certification Regime, applicable to anyone working in banking, whose actions or behaviour could seriously harm the bank, its reputation, or its customers.[76] The regime requires RAP to take reasonable care to ensure that such harmful actions are avoided, or that the firm has certified employees as fit and proper to perform 'significant-harm functions'. Senior managers are responsible for conducting and reviewing the certification process.[77]

The third pillar is that of the conduct rules. The rules replace the existing APER statements and code contained in the FCA Handbook and PRA Rulebook,[78] and will include standards of behaviour that all those covered by the new regimes will be expected to meet. Hence, firms must ensure that members of staff are aware of the conduct rules applicable to them.

5.2.1.2.8 SENIOR MANAGEMENT FUNCTIONS (SMFS)

The FCA and the PRA set out 17 SMFs. It is necessary that firms identify the members of staff holding SMFs, as well as the relevant regulator that will pre-approve the fitness and propriety of them. There is a transition regime called 'grandfathering' – according to this regime, an individual who was authorised under the current APR, and who is not changing their role, would not need to go through the authorisation process in order to continue as approved for the equivalent SMF.

5.2.1.2.9 MANAGEMENT RESPONSIBILITY MAP (MRMAP)

The SM&CR requires firms to present a document describing its management and governance arrangements. The aim is to maintain a clear organisational structure as required by Senior Management Arrangements, Systems, and Controls (SYSC). The purpose of the SYSC is to encourage firms' directors and senior managers to take appropriate practical responsibility for their firms' arrangements on matters likely to be of interest to the appropriate regulator, to increase certainty about how firms must take reasonable care to organise and control its affairs responsibly and effectively, with adequate risk management systems.[79] The SYSC also seeks to encourage firms to vest responsibility for effective organisation

---

75 FSMA 2000 s 63ZA, s 63ZB, s 63ZC, s 63ZD, and s 63ZE.
76 Senior Managers and Certification Regime – Individual Accountability in The Banking Sector. Practice notes, LexisNexis (n69).
77 FSMA 2000 s 63E and s 63F.
78 FSMA 2000 s 64A and s 64B.
79 FCA Handbook, 'Senior Management Arrangements, Systems and Controls' (January 2016) SYSC 1.2.1. <www.handbook.fca.org.uk/handbook/SYSC.pdf> accessed 25th January 2016.

in specific directors and senior managers, as well as to create a common platform of organisational systems and controls requirements for all firms.[80]

The implementation of the MRMAP implies access to clear and transparent information about the internal organisation of the firm and lines of responsibility.[81] For the first time, qualitative information[82] concerning the delegation of responsibilities among senior managers and other employees will be available to supervisors.

5.2.1.2.10 STATEMENTS OF RESPONSIBILITY (SOR)

The Statements of Responsibility (SoR) must clearly describe the SMFs allocated to each senior manager and follow the FCA[83] and PRA[84] requirements. The SoR are limited to the accountability rules of the SM&CR.

5.2.1.2.11 CONDUCT RULES TO NON-EXECUTIVE DIRECTORS (NEDS)

The FCA issued guidance on how conduct rules would apply to NEDs. In the consultation paper and policy statement,[85] the FCA announces that the parameter applicable to NEDs is the standard of care, skill, and diligence of a reasonably diligent person with the general knowledge and performing the NEDs' functions.[86] The PRA[87] considers that the conduct rules, as regards the duty to act with integrity, will apply in the same way for senior managers and NEDs, while other rules regarding the duty of care, skill, and diligence will only apply to the NEDs' prescribed responsibilities.

5.2.1.2.12 PRESCRIBED RESPONSIBILITIES (PRS)

The FCA and PRA published a list of 30 prescribed responsibilities (PRs).[88] These responsibilities must be assigned to individuals who perform SMFs to ensure that

---

80 SYSC 1.2.1
81 Deloitte, 'Individual Accountability in UK Banking | Details of Senior Management and Certification Regimes Emerge' (31 July 2014) <http://blogs.deloitte.co.uk/financialservices/2014/07/individual-accountability-in-uk-banking.html> accessed 30th March 2016.
82 Ibid.
83 FCA Handbook, SUP 10C.11.23–28, 32 (2016) <www.handbook.fca.org.uk/handbook/SUP/10C/11.html?date=2016-03-07> accessed 25th January 2016.
84 AR2 <www.prarulebook.co.uk> See Bank of England, 'Strengthening Individual Accountability in Banking' (Supervisory Statement SS28/15 July 2015) <www.bankofengland.co.uk/pra/Documents/publications/ss/2015/ss2815.pdf> accessed 25th January 2016.
85 FCA, 'Changes to the Approved Persons Regime for Solvency II Firms: Final Rules' (Policy Statement: PS15/21) including feedback on CP14/25, CP15/5 and CP15/16), and consequential relating to CP22/15 on strengthening accountability in banking, August 2015 <www.fca.org.uk/static/documents/policy-statements/ps15-21.pdf> accessed 25th January 2016.
86 Ibid.
87 Bank of England, 'Strengthening Individual Accountability in Banking: UK branches of Non-EEA banks' (Policy Statement PS/20/15, August 2015).
88 FCA, Annex 4 to CP 15/22.

they will be accountable in the event of a breach. The distribution of the PRs must be done between executives and NEDs; however, the extent to which such responsibilities are assigned to regulated firms varies, according to the type of firm. As a result, PRs can be divided into four groups.[89] The first group of PRs is applicable to all firms: they relate to SMR and CR and the responsibility for financial crime. The second group comprises the PRs that apply to small firms (firms that have assets of £250 million or less), and the third group of PRs is applicable to large firms. In all groups, the PRs cover risk management, systems and controls, financial resources, and legal and regulatory obligations[90] according to the size of the firm. The last group comprises the PRs that only apply to specific types of firms.

As might be anticipated, the core features of the SM&CR represent a step forward in terms of individual accountability. Under the previous regime, the assessment of individual actions within the firm was a difficult task for supervisors. Although the new regime might be seen as an improvement, it does not necessarily prevent the diffusion of collective responsibility. Access to information concerning internal organisation and governance arrangements, delegation of responsibilities, and a system of prescribed responsibilities is part of the regime – it is also important to ensure that supervisors can rely on the accuracy of the information, and that they are in the position to take disciplinary actions against senior managers and employees.

5.2.1.2.13 ENFORCEMENT POWERS IN THE SM&CR

In the event that senior managers cease to be 'fit and proper', are knowingly concerned in a breach of other requirements, or have personally failed to comply with the conduct rules, the PRA and/or the FCA can take enforcement actions.[91] The SM&CR adds a new hypothesis in which regulators might take enforcement actions. Along with the hypotheses of the former APR, the SM&CR allows regulators to take enforcement actions against senior managers when the firm breaches regulatory requirements, the breach takes place in an area of business for which the senior manager was responsible, and the individual failed to take reasonable steps to prevent the regulatory breach. Once again, the criteria to attribute responsibility to senior managers will be determined by the reasonableness of the actions taken to avoid contravention of the regime.

In this area, the new SM&CR is under reform. Initially, the SM&CR included a reverse burden of proof. Senior managers were responsible when an ARP did not comply with a relevant requirement and they were unable to prove that they took 'reasonable steps to prevent or stop the non-compliance event'. However, this 'presumption' has been replaced with the Duty of Responsibility. According

---

89 Senior Managers and Certification Regime – Individual Accountability in Banking, Practice Notes, LexisNexis (n69).
90 Ibid.
91 FSMA 2000 s 66A and s 66B.

to this duty, where there has been a breach in the area for which senior managers are responsible, the burden will no longer be on senior managers to prove that they took reasonable steps to prevent regulatory breaches. Instead, if regulators want to bring disciplinary proceedings, they will have to prove that senior managers did not take such reasonable steps. Although the reform has been positively perceived by senior managers,[92] regulators emphasise that, in practice, this is merely a change of process, not substance.[93]

From regulators' perspective, the adoption of the Duty of Responsibility makes clear that they will hold somebody accountable only when personal culpability on the part of the individual is established.[94] This is when the conduct of the individual falls below the standards of reasonableness for someone in his position.[95] Until now, it is still unclear whether the PRA will use the presumption of responsibility in some cases.[96] Paul Fisher emphasised that the PRA will consider each situation on its merits, and that there may be situations where senior managers may be guilty under the Presumption of Responsibility.[97] He strongly denied that the presumption will only be used in significant cases or cases of last resort.[98]

The FCA has said that it will use its enforcement powers 'proportionally and fairly'.[99] The purpose of the FCA is to establish whether senior managers have adequate governance arrangements and control frameworks,[100] i.e. they have implemented adequate training and have communicated to staff their responsibilities and whether systems of control have been improved. Furthermore, s 36 of the Banking Act 2013 created a new criminal offence, applicable to senior managers, relating to a reckless decision causing a financial institution to fail.[101]

---

92 Elisabeth Bremner and others, 'Senior Managers' Regime: Individual Accountability and Learning Lessons' (Compliance Officer Bulletin 2015) 2.

93 Andrew Bailey, Chief Executive of the PRA, Ibid 3.

94 Tracey McDermott, 'Speech on Personal Accountability' (FCA, 2nd December 2015) <www.fca.org.uk/news/speeches/personal-accountability> accessed 26th January 2016.

95 Tracey McDermott, Acting Chief Executive FCA, in her evidence to the PCBS.

96 Andrew Bailey, Chief Executive of the PRA, in Elisabeth Bremner, and others, 'Senior Managers' Regime: Individual Accountability and Learning Lessons' (n92) 4.

97 Ibid.

98 Paul Fisher, 'The Financial Regulation Reform Agenda: What Has Been Achieved and How Much is Left to Do?' (Bank of England 30th September 2015) <www.bankofengland.co.uk/speech/2015/the-financial-regulation-reform-agenda-what-has-been-achieved-and-how-much-is-left-to-do> accessed 26th January 2016.

99 FCA, 'Statement From The Financial Conduct Authority Following the Announcement By HM Treasury of Changes to the Senior Managers' Regime' (October 2015) <www.fca.org.uk/news/hm-treasury-changes-to-the-senior-managers-regime> accessed 26th January 2016.

100 FCA, 'Strengthening Accountability in Banking: Final Rules (Including Feedback on CP14/31 and CP15/5) and Consultation on Extending the Certification Regime to Wholesale Market Activities' (CP15/22 July 2015) <www.fca.org.uk/static/documents/consultation-papers/cp15-22.pdf> accessed 26th January 2016.

101 This provision applies only to senior managers working in banks, building societies, and PRA-designated investment firms. It does not extend to senior managers in credit unions.

This overview of the SM&CR is an outline for us to understand how its implementation would complement governance rules of CCPs, as well as the conduct of business regime. It would solve the absence of an individual accountability regime for senior managers and employees of CCPs. The question is whether the former APR, replaced by the SM&CRs, is applicable to CCPs' senior managers and employees. The reason to question the applicability of the regime is that the FSMA 2000 bestows the PRA and the FCA – but not the Bank – with certain powers and responsibilities over individuals who carry controlled functions within UK financial services firms.

Hence, the first impediment to apply the SM&CR to individuals who work in CCPs is that neither the PRA nor the FCA are acting as CCPs regulators. It could be argued, however, that Part V of FSMA 2000 uses the word 'authority' to indicate the regulator that carries out the approval proceedings. Therefore, a literal interpretation of these statutory provisions could lead us to understand that 'authority' is not restricted to PRA and FCA – it also might refer to the Bank of England, when it acts as regulator (e.g. regulator of CCPs). Nonetheless, the next difficulty is that the Bank does not have further guidance regarding approval proceedings and rules governing the regime of approved persons and controlled functions, as the PRA and FCA do.

Along with the difficulties concerning the lack of clarity regarding the implementation of the SM&CR, there is the fact that CCPs are not explicitly required to have in place standards of conduct or fitness and propriety tests. As was explained earlier, the process of authorisation and recognition requires CCPs to meet the requirements of s 288 of FSMA 2000 and Article 17 of EMIR. Also, any applicant for recognition must comply[102] with all the requirements established by the MiFID,[103] as prescribed by s 290 (1A).[104] However, none of these requirements make express reference to standards of conduct that should be observed by individuals who work in the CCP. In this scenario, it is the national authority – the Bank – in charge of developing a regime that enhances the standards of conduct and distribution of responsibilities to all levels within the CCP, and this is not a regulatory priority of the Bank.[105]

This study argues that including rules of individual accountability applicable to senior managers and employees of CCPs would benefit and complete, at least

---

102 FSMA 2000 Part XVIII Recognised Investment Exchanges and Clearing Houses (hereinafter FSMA Part XVIII) Section 286 (6).

103 Commission adopts proposals for a Directive on markets in financial instruments repealing Directive [2004/39/EC] of the European Parliament and of the Council, and for a regulation on markets in financial instruments and amending regulation [EMIR] on OTC derivatives, Central Counterparties, and trade repositories.

104 FSMA pt XVIII s 290 Recognition orders (. . .) (1A) (. . .) See HM Treasury Consultation Paper: A New Approach to Financial Regulation: The Blueprint for Reform (Cm 8083), (June 2011).

105 Ch 3 of this book.

partially, the governance and conduct of business regime. It will contribute to making clear that senior managers and employees of CCPs are not only obliged to follow internal codes of conduct, corporate governance rules,[106] and fiduciary duties, but they also must observe the rules and standards that the SM&CR imposes to individuals working in financial firms.

5.2.1.2.15 THE RELEVANCE OF THE REGIME

The claimed benefits that the SM&CR brings to the banking sector could be replicated for the CCPs in the OTCDM. Hence, the importance of adopting the SM&CR lies on the clarification of the roles and responsibilities of senior managers and all other individuals who work in the CCP. The effective implementation will require the engagement of all regulated individuals. In particular, senior managers should be satisfied that the governance structures of the CCP are compatible with the spirit of the regime and the responsible management of their business.[107] This is consistent with idea that CCPs should be managed in a manner consistent with public interest.[108]

The spirit of the regime is to protect the system, hereby public interests, by preventing and sanctioning any type of misconduct of individuals who work in the financial services industry. This consideration is especially relevant to the role CCPs have in the OTCDM. As explained in Chapter 2, CCPs are nodes of concentration of risk and interconnectedness; their systemically important position in the market requires, besides the effective design and implementation of prudential rules, the adoption of high standards of conduct that apply to all individuals who work in CCPs.

The aim of the SM&CR to raise the standards of individual conduct would enhance the governance structure of CCPs. The SM&CR, as an improvement of the earlier APR, is designed to fit with the realities of complex financial services firms,[109] as are CCPs. The system of responsibilities of all regulated individuals is reinforced with a variety of changes. These changes include clarity of reporting lines and responsibilities, a recruitment that selects the fit and proper person for the job, a performance management that ensures staff are properly trained and equipped for their roles, and considering consumer and market outcomes as part of everyday decision-making.[110]

---

106 Interview Grant Elliot (Senior Analyst Clearing and Business Development), Matthew Gravelle (Government Relations Team) and Huong Auduc (Legal Department) CME Clearing Europe Ltd, London, 12 June 2014.

107 Martin Wheatley, 'From Accountability to Reality' (Speech by CEO of the FCA (14 July 2015) <www.fca.org.uk/news/accountability-from-debate-to-reality> accessed 26th January 2016.

108 Bank of England, 'The Bank of England's Approach to the Supervision of Financial Market Infrastructures' (April 2013) 5 (hereinafter the Bank's approach to FMIs' Supervision, 2013).

109 Wheatley, 'From Accountability to Reality' (Speech by CEO of the FCA, 14th July 2015) (n107).

110 Ibid.

All these features of the SM&CR would help to overcome, at least partially, one of the shortcomings identified in this book. It will complement the governance regime for CCPs, which has the potential to ameliorate the issues coming from innovation risks. The adoption of an individual accountability regime will also help to solve the shortcoming of the regime, explained in Chapter 2, concerning the lack of conduct of business regime. As individual accountability regimes, such as the SM&CR, are a part of conduct of business rules, the shortcoming would be partially solved with SM&CR adoption and with the explicit adoption of fitness and propriety standards and parameters of conduct applicable to senior managers and employees of the CCP.

Assuming that by 2018 the SM&CR is going to be extended to all firms authorised under FSMA 2000, the CCPs might be covered by the regime. However, the challenge is to see whether and how the Bank will further develop the rules of CCPs' senior managers' and employees' responsibility. The extension of the SM&CR does not automatically solve the problem of the lack of individual accountability rules in the CCPs regime, as neither the FCA nor the PRA supervise CCPs. Although the extension of the regime does not solve the issue, the fact that the SM&CR will be applicable to all firms authorised under FSMA 2000 stresses the need to solve the question concerning the individual accountability regime of CCPs in the OTCDM. The Bank will have to clarify which is the conduct regulator of CCPs – whether it is the Bank or, as we would argue, the FCA. In the first case, the Bank will have to issue rules regarding individual accountability of senior managers and employees of CCPs operating in the OTCDM. In the event that the FCA is the conduct regulator, the SM&CR will be directly applicable to individuals who work in the CCPs.

5.2.2 CCPs' demutualised structure

It has been suggested that the governance of CCPs is key to ensuring that moral hazard problems at the level of the CCP are mitigated.[111] The recommendation is that CCPs should be organised as cooperatives or mutual organisations, whose users are its owners.[112] The benefit of this type of organisation is that CCPs' and clearing members' interests coincide: both parties will benefit from profits or will assume losses. Hence, both CCPs and clearing members have incentives to participate in CCP default management and on the overall resilience of central clearing arrangements.[113]

---

111 Bruno Biais, Florian Heider, and Marie Hoerova, 'Incentive Compatible Centralised Clearing' in 'OTC Derivatives: New Rules, New Actors, New Risks' (Banque du France-Financial Stability Review N 17 April 2013) <www.banque-france.fr/fileadmin/user_upload/banque_de_france/publications/Revue_de_la_stabilite_financiere/2013/rsf-avril-2013/16-BIAIS_Bruno.pdf> accessed 12th November 2015.

112 Ibid.

113 Former Federal Reserve Governor Randall S. Kroszner notes that risk mutualisation 'creates incentives for all of the exchange's members to support the imposition of risk controls that limit the extent to which the trading activities of any individual member expose all of

However, as was the case of exchanges,[114] CCPs followed the trend of demutualisation.[115] The term 'demutualisation' is used with different meanings; however, here it refers to the phenomena of changing the ownership structure of the CCP from being solely owned by users to being owned by investors on a for-profit basis.[116] Accordingly, clearing members participate in the mutualisation of losses, whilst the owners of the CCP receive the profits. Under the demutualised structure, CCPs might have part of their capital committed to the default resources. Despite this, the governance of the CCP allows the clearing members to have a voice in matters related to risk management, as is contemplated in EMIR. Eurex, the clearing houses of the Intercontinental Exchange, Inc (ICE), and the CME Clearing House Division are examples of demutualised CCPs.

5.2.2.1 Conflicting interests

The demutualised structure of CCP brings to the forefront the divergent interests present in the risk management governance of the CCP. These are the tensions[117] between the interests of the CCP's owners and the interests of the clearing members. Recognising the conflicting interests of CCPs and clearing members, Paul

---

[the] other members to losses from defaults', Federal Reserve Bank of Chicago, 'Central Counterparty Clearing: History, Innovation, and Regulation' (Fed, *Economic Perspectives* 4th Quarter), 38.

114 The International Federation of Stock Exchanges (Federation Internationale des Bourses Valeurs, or FIBV) surveyed exchanges in October 2000: '78% of exchanges said that they either had approval to demutualize or were actively considering demutualization', 'Demutualisation: The Challenges Facing Global Exchanges' <www.mondovisione.com/exchanges/handbook-articles/demutualisation-the-challenges-facing-global-exchanges/> accessed 12th November 2015.

115 See Ruben Lee, *Running the World's Markets, The Governance of Financial Infrastructure* (Princeton University Press 2011) and sources cited therein. Also see, e.g. Alfredo Mendiola, and Maureen O'Hara, 'Taking Stock in Stock Markets: The Changing Governance of Exchanges' (Working Paper, Cornell University, 2003) <http://ssrn.com/abstract=431580> Also see Benn Steil, 'Changes in the Ownership and Governance of Securities Exchanges: Causes and Consequences' (Wharton Financial Institutions Center, Working Paper No 02–15 February 2002), <http://fic.wharton.upenn.edu/fic/papers/02/0215.pdf> accessed 12th November 2015.

116 Ruben Lee, *Running the World's Markets: The Governance of Financial Infrastructure*, Ibid.

117 FIA, 'FIA Global CCP Risk Position Paper' (April 2015) <https://fia.org/sites/default/files/content_attachments/FIAGLOBAL_CCP_RISK_POSITION_PAPER.pdf> The Clearing House, 'Central Counterparties: Recommendations to Promote Financial Stability and Resilience' (Clearing House Banking Brief White Paper Series, December 2012) <www.theclearinghouse.org/~/media/files/association%20documents/20121217%20tch%20white%20paper%20on%20central%20counterparty%20risk.pdf> accessed 5th October 2015.

Jeff Stehm, 'Clearance And Settlement Systems For Securities: Critical Design Choices in Emerging Market Economies' (World Bank Discussion Papers No WDP 321, Washington, DC, 1996) <www-wds.worldbank.org/external/default/WDSContentServer/WDSP/IB/1996/04/01/000009265_3961219102438/Rendered/PDF/multi_page.pdf> accessed 5th October 2015.

Tucker observed, 'the *quid pro quo* has to be involvement in risk policies and practices'. This means access to information and risk management at the same time. The efficiency of governance rules relies on the coordination of CCPs' and clearing members' interests, which in turn should be articulated with the risk management practices. Therefore, the question is whether allowing the responsible and significant participation of clearing members in CCP governance would solve the tensions of conflicting interests, and to what extent.

The conflict of interest within the demutualised CCP comprises three types of interests: CCPs' owners, clearing members, and prominently the public interest. In a demutualised CCP, owners of the CCP are external investors – they are 'external' because they are not involved with the CCPs' clearing service. Their interest is therefore limited to the 'operation on normal commercial for-profit basis';[118] they seek to obtain an adequate return on their investment.[119] The issue here is that those external investors, as owners of the CCP, have no interest in managing systemic risk,[120] because the majority of the CCP's losses are mutualised amongst clearing members. Here, 'moral hazard' refers to the fact that, as external investors are largely protected from CCPs' losses, they are likely to overexpose the CCP to certain risks in order to maximise their profits. In this scenario, it has been argued that owners and managers[121] might be tempted to engage in correlation-seeking that increases the risks for the CCP, and thereby systemic risk. Correlation-seeking comprises the practices whereby managers 'correlate their firm's contingent debt obligations with insolvency risk'.[122] This practice benefits shareholders at unsecured creditors' expense.[123]

'Shareholder opportunism', or the practice of correlation-seeking, has implications, which we identify in the three most famous bailouts in the history of the US market: AIG, Fannie Mae, and Freddie Mac. Squires argues that, in these three cases, managerial decisions not only caused deep losses, but may have been consistent with the managers' duty to maximise shareholder value.[124] AIG's case is an example of 'reverse correlation-seeking', consisting of AIG reallocating its investment portfolio into assets[125] that increased internal correlations on the firm's contingent debts. Fannie[126] and Freddie used a type of correlation-seeking

---

118 Ruben Lee, *Running the World's Markets: The Governance of Financial Infrastructure* (n115) 233.
119 Ibid 265.
120 Sean J. Griffith, 'Governing Systemic Risk: Towards a Governance Structure for Derivatives Clearinghouses' (n6), 1209.
121 'Correlation-seeking tends to occur when managers have the duty to act in shareholders' best interest' Richard Squire, 'Shareholder Opportunism in a World of Risky Debt' (2010) 123 *Harvard Law Review*, 1183.
122 Ibid.
123 Ibid 1184.
124 Ibid 1153.
125 John W. Cioffi, *Public Law and Private Power: Corporate Governance Reform in the Age of Finance Capitalism* (Cornell University Press 2010), 3.
126 See Fannie Mae, Quarterly Report (Form 10-Q) (31 March 2009).

that occurs when a firm has passed the 'tipping point' where its contingent debts are large enough in themselves to cause insolvency, and the firm piles on additional correlated debts that pose no downside risk to shareholders. In all three cases, the use of correlation-seeking reduced equity volatility and simultaneously increased shareholder returns.[127] That is why this practice might adversely affect solvent firms. Therefore, this book argues that a regime of governance for CCPs would contribute to enhance clarity regarding ownership structure, disclosure, and control over the internal process of decision-making process, especially the decisions concerning prices and conditions of contingent debts.

The governance regime is only one tool regulators have available.[128] The discussion regarding the role of corporate governance[129] to enhance director-manager accountability to firms' owners-shareholders is beyond the scope of this book. Indeed, it has been argued that 'more effective corporate governance' may not be a serious part of the solution.[130] This is because any corporate governance system has some constraints that are better solved with robust government regulation. Following this line of thought, the adoption of governance rules for CCPs would contribute to identify and solve the potential conflicts originating from actions taken by CCPs owners.

The interests of clearing members are related to the risk management of the CCP because they will be the first to assume losses. Clearing members are interested in maintaining the operation of the CCP because they trade through it, but also because the failure will directly affect them. Nonetheless, clearing members' interests might conflict with the CCP in two ways: firstly, when clearing members seek to keep certain derivatives transactions off the CCP, which this study classifies as innovation risk. Secondly, in the clearing members' privileged position in front of the CCP, since they dominate the amount of trading and they have the most accurate information about the transactions subject to clearing. The clearing members' influence over the amount of trading has been explained as clearing members influencing the CCP to increase their market share and exclude competitors.[131] Accordingly, clearing members will exert influence over the CCP to impose excessively high margin collateral requirements and thereby limit membership to the largest financial institutions.[132] At this point, this study argues that, although such influence is possible, in the UK the limits on clearing membership are imposed by the regime itself. Access to clearing is one of the issues affecting competition among CCPs; however, regulators have already recognised that only

---

127 Richard Squire, 'Shareholder Opportunism in a World of Risky Debt' (2010) (n121), 1153.
128 Richard Squire argues that regulators should remove obstacles to creditor monitoring and reconsider executive pay rules that exacerbate shareholder creditor conflict, Ibid 1213.
129 Dalvinder Singh, 'Corporate Governance and Banking Supervision' (n50), 80.
130 Nicholas Calcina Howson, 'When "Good" Corporate Governance Makes "Bad" (Financial) Firms: The Global Crisis and the Limits of Private Law' (2009) 108 *Michigan Law Review* First Impressions, 44.
131 Sean J. Griffith, 'Governing Systemic Risk: Towards a Governance Structure for Derivatives Clearinghouses' (n6), 1197.
132 Ibid.

the largest financial institutions are in the position to meet clearing membership requirements. As a result, the current concern is in developing relevant rules on indirect or client clearing.

There is also a potential conflict between the CCP and clearing members concerning the asymmetry of information related to cleared transactions. Clearing members have access to all the relevant and accurate information about clearing members' and clients' positions, assets, collateral, value of assets, and so on. In an ideal scenario, that information is made available in a timely manner to the CCP – as we have seen, however, under the current regime CCPs perform a purely administrative role regarding such information, because they do not have the duty to confirm the accuracy of the information provided by clearing members. There is a potential source of conflict in the event of differences between the information reported by clearing members and the information recorded by CCPs.[133]

Litigation regarding information asymmetries in the OTCDM is not in this case limited to the traditional causes, such as misunderstanding of the instruments,[134] disagreements concerning the interpretation of contractual terms,[135] the formation of the contract,[136] or fraudulent use of derivatives.[137] In this area, litigation would take place as a result of the issues related to the 'legal segregation' contained in EMIR. CCPs' liability is limited because they rely on the information clearing members give to comply with segregation and portability requirements. For instance, when clearing members use an omnibus client account, they do not always provide information about the identity of their clients. Any delay in receiving information or inaccuracy in such information could jeopardise the CCP's ability to port positions and collateral;[138] a conflict issue would arise if clearing members or clients claim that they suffered losses as a result of the delay. Litigation might also be caused by disagreements regarding the value of the assets provided as collateral by clearing members. If those assets are lost or damaged when deposited in the custodian, or if the custodian becomes insolvent, the

---

133 'If investors believe that some companies do not publish accurate information, but cannot distinguish between these companies and those that are truthful, they might accordingly reduce their investments in all companies', JW Kuan, and SF Diamond, 'Ringing the Bell on the NYSE: Might a Nonprofit Stock Exchange Have Been Efficient?' (Bepress Legal Series Paper 1451, Santa Clara University School of Law, 13 July 2006).

134 *Metropolitan West Asset Management v Shenkman Capital Management* 2005 US Dist LEXIS 17003 (SDNY 2005).

135 *The Joint Administrators of Lehman Brothers International (Europe) v Lehman Brothers Finance SA* Case No: A2/2012/1247 Court of Appeal (Civil Division) 14 March 2013 [2013] EWCA Civ 188 2013 WL 617550.

136 *Lehman Brothers Commercial Corp v Minmetals International Non-Ferrous Metals Trading Co* 179 F Supp 2d 159 (SDNY 2001).

137 *Caiola v Citibank* 295 F3d 312, 312 (2d Cir 2002).

138 CME Clearing Europe Ltd Accounts Disclosure Document, 5 <www.cmegroup.com/europe/clearing-europe/membership/files/CMECE-Account-Disclosure-Document.pdf> accessed 20th October 2015.

responsibility of the CCP is restricted to having used appropriate skill, care, and diligence when choosing the custodian.

The third type of interest is the public interest – financial stability. This reflects the systemic importance of CCPs in the OTCDM, and in the financial system as a whole. Regulatory authorities primarily preserve the public interest; hence, the Bank received the mandate to regulate CCPs as means of making the OTCDM safer, and to prevent it from becoming a source of systemic risk. However, the protection of the public interest also concerns the CCP as an entity. Although CCPs are private entities that, as any other financial institution, participate in the market to obtain profits, they play a fundamental role in contributing to market and financial stability along with the 'co-regulatory functions'. (The co-regulatory functions of CCPs are explained in the next section.)

The restrictions imposed by EMIR to CCPs' investment policies are a good example of the conflict of interest between CCPs as individual financial firms and the pursuit of overall financial stability. Although the restrictions are in place, the topic is currently under debate; as part of EMIR Review there is consultation on reassessing the restrictions on CCPs' investments. In particular, the consultation considers three restrictions: firstly, the prohibition for CCPs to invest in money market funds subject to certain conditions.[139] The CCPs' position in this area is that similar transactions are authorised in the US. Therefore, this restriction appears problematic when CCPs collect and cash collateral from clients and clearing members intraday throughout international markets in different time zones, and therefore need safe, liquid, and reliable outlets to securely invest the late cash flows.[140]

The second restriction under consideration is allowing CCPs to treat regulated and highly creditworthy buy-side firms (e.g. pension funds and insurance undertakings) as potential investment counterparties. CCPs would be able to repo cash balances with high-quality liquid assets;[141] they claim that these investments would allow CCPs to diversify their counterparty risk profile, while simultaneously provide additional liquidity in the repo market for the buy-side.[142]

The third restriction of EMIR is to prohibit the use of derivatives by CCPs for the purpose of hedging interest rate risk.[143] Under EMIR, CCPs invest the cash collateral received by clearing members into highly liquid financial instruments; a significant percentage is invested at fixed rate. CCPs ask EU regulators to consider that a prudent and regulated use of derivatives would allow CCPs to protect themselves from variations of interest rates in their investments. Moreover, CCPs recognise that, if allowed, the use of specific interest rate derivatives for

---

139 The restriction is on Annex II of the ESMA RTS No 153/2013.
140 LCH Clearnet Response to the European Commission Consultation on EMIR August 2015; LSEG Response to European Commission Consultation on the Regulation (EU) No 648/2012 on OTC Derivatives, Central Counterparties, and Trade Repositories.
141 LCH Clearnet Response to the European Commission Consultation on EMIR August 2015.
142 Ibid.
143 Annex II para 2 of the ESMA RTS No 153/2013.

hedging of investment risks should be prudent and compliant with Article 47(1) of EMIR, and subject to board and risk committee approval.[144]

As might be anticipated, the restrictions on CCPs' investment policies were designed considering the need to control the type and levels of risk CCPs take when acting as investors. However, these measures can simultaneously be undermining the ability of CCPs to participate in the market and benefit from the products and services available, as other financial firms do. Therefore, the regulators' challenge is to find the right balance between the protection of financial stability and the interest of CCPs as individual financial firms.

5.3 The need for CCPs' governance rules

The Bank announced that, during 2015, it would develop governance rules for CCPs.[145] As with other areas of the regime, the Bank will follow EMIR and the PFMIs – although such a regulatory framework provides guidance on how to design CCPs' governance rules, in this section we recommend some areas that the regulator should consider. The core argument is that rules of boards' and risk committees' membership are not enough to ensure the active participation of all stakeholders in the governance of the CCP.

The discussion of the conflicting interests that converge in the CCP illustrates a key area that can be regulated with governance rules. A regime of governance could contribute to mitigating the possible influence of clearing members over the CCP to benefit their own interests. This book calls regulators to design a regime of CCPs' governance that is not limited to ruling the boards' and risk management committees' composition and voting rights, as they are broadly defined in EMIR. The CCP governance regime should instead seek to balance the convergent interests surrounding the functioning of the CCP. Board composition and voting rights and caps[146] have been criticised as insufficiently effective mechanisms for efficient CCP corporate governance.[147] Instead, the governance rules should add several means to prevent, or at least reduce, clearing members' influence over the CCP aligning control and risk.[148]

Pursuing the balance of convergent interests in the CCP requires ensuring representation of all stakeholders in the governance structure. CPMI and IOSCO

---

144 Ibid.
145 The Bank's supervision of FMIs 2nd Annual Report 2015.
146 'Voting caps conflict with the basic corporate law premise that voting interests should be aligned with ownership interests' Letter from Ernest Goodrich Jr, Legal Department Managing Director Deutsche Bank AG, and Marcelo Riffaud, Legal Department Managing Dir, Deutsche Bank AG, to David A Stawick, Secretary, CFTC, and Elizabeth M Murphy, SEC 2–3 (8 November 2010) <www.sec.gov/comments/s2-27-10/s72710-9.pdf> accessed 16th November 2015.
147 Sean J Griffith, 'Governing Systemic Risk: Towards a Governance Structure for Derivatives Clearinghouses' (n6), 1209.
148 Darrell Duffie, and Haoxiang Zhu, 'Does a Central Clearing Counterparty Reduce Counterparty Risk?' (December 2011) *Review of Asset Pricing Studies*, 74.

recommend that the governance arrangements of CCPs should be designed to fulfil public interest and promote objectives of owners and users.[149] This means that the Bank should firstly delimit who has the category of stakeholder[150] and how the composition of groups of stakeholders might vary. Such changes would need to be reflected in the boards' and committees' composition.[151]

The lack of CCPs' independence, with respect to their clearing members, might be solved with corporate governance rules. As Griffin explains, this scenario is different to the traditional principal-agent conflict that corporate law tries to solve in the manager-shareholder relationship.[152] Here, the issue is that the clearing members might seek to gain profits by imposing excessive risk on the clearing house, and in turn to increase the systemic risk.[153] Therefore, the design and implementation of CCPs' governance rules that balance the convergent interests within the CCP will protect stakeholders' rights, whilst at the same time clarify the parameters of accountability of board and risk committee members.

Similarly, the CCP governance regime should consider the role that CCPs have as 'co-regulators'. In the UK, the Bank in 2013 recognised that CCPs would become the leading voice of the industry in the OTCDM.[154] Following this line of thought, CCPs act as co-regulators by imposing market discipline. The contribution of CCPs is to promote high levels of disclosure and transparency about market participants and transactions. The level of discretion attributed to CCPs allows them to play a double role in helping regulators to achieve their objectives. Firstly, the role of CCPs as 'regulated firms', complying with the authorisation and recognition requirements and the provision of clearing services. Secondly, the role of CCPs in imposing minimum requirements for clearing members and their clients to participate in the market. The issue of rulebooks and corporate governance shows the scope of rulemaking and enforcement attributed to CCPs. The co-regulatory role of CCPs requires rules that solve the internal conflict of interests, so that the CCP is free from stakeholders' influence. In this sense, some suggestions might include the limitation of ownership participation[155] and the

---

149 The second PFMI states: 'Principle 2: Governance. An FMI should have governance arrangements that are clear and transparent, promote the safety and efficiency of the FMI, and support the stability of the broader financial system, other relevant public interest considerations, and the objectives of relevant stakeholders'.

150 Donna M. Nagy, 'Playing Peekaboo with Constitutional Law: The PCAOB and its Public/Private Status' (2005) 80 (3) *Notre Dame Law Review*, 975.

151 Group of Thirty, 'Global Clearing and Settlement: A Plan of Action' (2003) <http://aecsd.org/upload/iblock/a61/Global_Clearing_Settlement_2003.pdf> accessed 19th December 2017.

152 Adolf A. Berle, and Gardiner C. Means, *The Modern Corporation and Private Property* (Transaction Publishers 1991), 1932.

153 Mark Roe, 'Derivatives Clearinghouses Are No Magic Bullet' *Wall Street Journal* (6 May 2010) <www.wsj.com/articles/SB10001424052748703871904575216251915383146> accessed 16th November 2015.

154 The Bank's approach to FMIs' Supervision, 2013.

155 Examples of ownership restrictions are set out in IOSCO, Technical Committee (2006, Table 2) 16 in Ruben Lee, *Running the World's Markets: The Governance of Financial Infrastructure* (n115).

imposition of fit and proper standards to those involved in the governance of the CCP. Although these recommendations have been proposed to enhance investor protection,[156] such standards also strengthen the robustness of the CCP's functioning. To sum up, if the objective is to ensure that CCPs act as co-regulators in line with the Bank's objective, then it is first important to strengthen the internal structure and governance rules of CCPs.

5.4 Innovation leading the unintended consequences of the regime

The process of financial regulation faces the challenge of meeting market needs alongside public expectations. Regulators are usually compelled, particularly after periods of crisis, to react and control the sources of systemic risk. History and the hypothetical scenarios that are in some way foreseeable illustrate the task for regulators when they design the regime. The downside of this process is, however, that almost always post-crisis regulation is exclusively focused on the most prominent areas of concern – the risks that have already crystallised – whilst at the same time it overlooks less probable risk. Hence, risk-based regulation approaches allow the regulator to fall into this cycle, where several types of risks (i.e. innovation risks) are ignored and only those risks regulators perceive to be more prominent are regulated.

This weakness in the UK regime of CCPs in the OTCDM concerns the double role the Bank has when regulating and supervising CCPs, OTCDM, and UK financial stability. The Bank is not only the prudential regulator of the CCP, but also the guardian of stability of the UK financial system, and as such this should be reflected in a coherent regulatory framework. The regime of CCPs in the OTCDM should contribute not only to the safety and soundness of CCPs, and in turn the OTCDM, but should be coherent with the wider objective of financial stability. The Bank is expected to oversee the potential risks that the new regulation of CCPs might bring to the stability of the system, with reference to the persistent interconnections between CCPs, OTCDM participants, and other sectors of the financial system.

5.4.1 Innovation concerning collateral requirements

Certainly, it cannot be denied that any type of regulation comes with a wave of innovation[157] and creative compliance. As we discussed in Chapter 1, creative compliance describes 'using the law to escape legal control without actually violating legal rules'[158] – a reaction from regulated firms to the content of certain

---

156 Ibid 342.
157 Edward J. Kane, 'Good Intention and Unintended Evil: The Case Selective Credit Allocation' *Everett Reese Recognition Lectures* <https://fraser.stlouisfed.org/docs/meltzer/kangoo77.pdf> accessed 15th November 2015.
158 Doreen McBarnet, 'Law and Capital: The Role of Legal Form and Legal Actors' (1984) 12 *International Journal of the Sociology of Law*, 233; Doreen McBarnet, 'Law, Policy and

regulation. In the particular case of the OTCDM and the regulation incentivising the use of CCPs, one of the ways in which innovation takes form is derived from the collateral and margin requirements imposed on clearing members. Parties involved in OTC derivatives contracts are dealing with the potential default of their counterparties, and here, clearing (the function by which credit risk is managed) can be carried out centrally, by CCPs or bilaterally. Before the GFC, the vast majority of the contracts were cleared bilaterally with an inadequate collateralisation, prompting instability to the market and being more vulnerable to the concretion of systemic risk. As a result, regulators decided to promote the use of CCPs, procuring the enhancement and protection of financial market stability.

Collateral and margin requirements are regulated in Chapter 3 of EMIR, which rules over exposure management, margin requirements, default funds, liquidity risk controls, the so-called default waterfall, collateral requirements, investment policy, default procedures, reviews of models, stress testing, and back testing settlement. Regarding the margin requirements, CCPs shall impose, call, and collect margins from their clearing members and, exceptionally, from CCPs with which it has interoperability arrangements.[159] The function of margins is the protection against counterparty credit risk – that is why the required margins shall be sufficient to cover potential exposures that the CCP estimates will incur until the liquidation of the relevant positions. This means that margins should be collected and remain during the entire life of each transaction. Additionally, margins shall be enough to 'cover losses that result from at least 99% of the exposures movements'.[160] Regular monitoring of margins is carried out by the CCP, which in turn shall collateralise all of its exposures with all its clearing members.

Furthermore, better protection against exposures and risks is achieved through the design, supervision, and regular review[161] of models and parameters to measure initial and variation margins. The aim is that margin models capture the risk characteristics of the products subject to clearing and the market liquidity, as well as the possible variation over the duration of the transaction.[162] The specificities

---

Legal Avoidance' (1988) 1 *Journal of Law & Society*, 13; Doreen McBarnet, 'It's Not What You Do But The Way That You Do It: Tax Evasion, Tax Avoidance and the Boundaries of Deviance' in D. Downes (ed.), *Unraveling Criminal Justice* (Macmillan 1991); Doreen McBarnet, and Christopher Whelan, 'Beyond Control: Law Management and Corporate Governance' in Joseph McCahery, Sol Picciotto, and Colin Scott (eds.), *Corporate Control and Accountability* (1992); Doreen McBarnet, and Christopher Whelan, 'The Elusive Spirit of the Law: Formalism and the Struggle for Legal Control' (November 1991) 54 (6) *The Modern Law Review*, Law and Accountancy, 848.

159   EMIR recognises the multiple CCPs that will be providing services in the European market by regulating the interoperability arrangements that will facilitate the joint participation of these intermediaries. The interoperability arrangements will ensure non-discriminatory access to the data and the settlement system. Art 51 EMIR.

160   Art 41 EMIR.

161   Art 49 EMIR.

162   Art 41 EMIR.

of margins' calculation, including the specification of the appropriate percentage and time horizons for the liquidation period, is done by ESMA consulting EBA and the ESCB, according to the RTS.

Besides the margin requirements, EMIR also regulates the default fund, which will cover losses that exceed the losses covered by margin requirements. CCPs use the fund only when margins, both initial and variation, are not sufficient to cover the losses of one or more clearing members. The risk management rules require CCPs to establish a minimum amount below which the size of the default fund is not to fall under any circumstances.[163] The fund receives resources of single clearing members, and the amount of the contribution shall be proportional to the exposures of each clearing member. The design of stress tests allows CCPs to pre-empt scenarios of extreme market conditions[164] that might threaten the continuity of clearing services.

Moreover, EMIR includes a third level of protection as 'other financial resources'. These resources will be used by the CCP to cover potential losses exceeding the losses covered by the margins and the default fund. The requirement is that these financial resources 'shall include dedicated resources, shall be freely available to the CCP, and shall not be used to meet the capital requirement of Article 16'.[165] The orderly use of margin, default funds, and other financial resources is regulated as the default waterfall.[166] These are the instructions to be followed by the CCP when one or more clearing member defaults.

Regarding the liquidity risk, the objective of EMIR is to ensure CCPs at all times have access to adequate liquidity to provide the clearing services. To that end, the CCP is expected to obtain credit lines or similar arrangements to cover their liquidity needs when necessary.

In order to cover the initial and ongoing exposures to its clearing members, 'a CCP shall accept highly liquid collateral with minimal credit and market risk'.[167] The terms and the quality of the collateral depend on the type of counterparty (financial or non-financial counterparty), and the conditions included in the RTS.[168]

This brief description of the margin requirements in EMIR illustrates their relevance for clearing members to be able to trade in the OTCDM and for the risk management of the CCP. The current regime greatly relies on compliance with these prudential rules to ensure the safety and soundness of CCPs and, in turn, the stability of the OTCDM. Moreover, the system of margins and default fund contributions is implemented to tackle the underlying incentive problems

---

163 Art 42 (1) EMIR.
164 Art 42 (3) EMIR.
165 Art 43 EMIR.
166 Art 45 EMIR.
167 Art 46 EMIR.
168 RTS propose setting the thresholds to limit the operational burden and a threshold for managing the liquidity impact associated with initial margin requirements.

of clearing members.[169] As a result, clearing members need to use high liquid assets[170] to meet collateral and margin requirements.

Questions concerning the substantial legal issues arising from collateralisation have already been addressed in the literature.[171] This book goes beyond the current discussion and calls the attention to the potential dangers coming from the innovative financial techniques that market participants will use to meet the high-quality collateral.[172] These are some unintended consequences of the regime with profound systemic implications; in particular, how clearing members are likely to use a practice known as 'collateral transformation' or 'upgrading collateral'.[173] When a market participant wants to trade in the OTCDM, and is interested in benefiting from central clearing, he/she will be subject to the margin and collateral regime described earlier. In the rather common scenario that the market participant does not have assets that comply with the required high-quality collateral, the alternative is to go to other markets and gain access to high-quality assets. One option is to enter into a repo transaction, which allows the transformation of this collateral into 'acceptable assets' or 'acceptable collateral'. The counterparty of the repo transaction – a dealer or bank – might be a direct counterparty or intermediary for such a contract. Until this stage, the rehypothecation is allowed for some of the lower-quality assets. This means that the consequences of the rehypothecation are still present, though not directly affecting the collateral transferred to the CCP.

Although collateral transformation benefits market participants (the counterparty in the repo transaction, and the CCP receiving high-quality assets), the weakness here is the systemic impact such activity might have. The sum of the imposition of central clearing, the concomitant collateral requirements, and the resulting innovation of collateral transformation prompts the transmission of credit risk from the OTCDM to the repo market. The credit risk, initially

169 'Regarding the incentive problems: since the CCP insures its members against credit risk, they could become imprudent and fail to monitor the credit risk of their counterparties. [For this reason] The CCP should limit the amount of insurance it provides to CMs'. Bruno Biais, and Florian Heider, and Marie Hoerova, 'Incentive Compatible Centralized Clearing' in 'OTC Derivatives: New Rules, New Actors, New Risks', Banque de France Financial Stability Review No 17, April 2013 (n111).

170 This type of collateral is ineligible for rehypothecation, International Capital Markets Association <www.icmagroup.org/Regulatory-Policy-and-Market-Practice/short-term-markets/Repo-Markets/frequently-asked-questions-on-repo/10-what-is-rehypothecation-of-collateral/> accessed 26th October 2015.

171 Some works discussing the impact of collateralisation in the CCPs: Joanne Braithwaite, 'Private Law and the Public Sector's Central Counterparty Prescription for the Derivatives Markets (March 21, 2011) LSE Legal Studies Working Paper No 2/2011 <http://ssrn.com/abstract=1791740> accessed 17th October 2015.

172 Isobel Wright, and Nora Bullock, 'Key interactions between EMIR and AIFMD' (2014) 9 JIBFL 589, 590.

173 Paula Tkac, 'Reducing Systemic Risk or Merely Transforming It?' (Federal Reserve Bank of Atlanta, July 2013) <www.frbatlanta.org/cenfis/publications/notesfromthevault/1307.cfm> accessed 5th October 2015.

originated in the OTCDM, is now shared between the CCPs and the counterparties of the repo contracts. The high level of interconnection between the OTCDM and other markets remains as a channel of communication of financial distress.

To illustrate this point further, before the GFC, the concern was that the failure of OTCDM market participants could result in the failure of the OTCDM and its systemic consequences. One of the causes that contributed to the near-failure of AIG was collateral calls. The use of 'collateral transformation', which replaces the collateral call, concerns a run in the repo market. If suppliers of high-quality collateral retreat from the market, this might force the liquidation of derivative positions and/or lower-quality collateral assets. In consequence, the risk of potential fire sales is increased, which in turn might substantially reduce the asset value.

5.4.2 Compression is a form of innovation

The innovative use of compression diminishes the effectiveness of CCPs as managers of counterparty credit risk in the OTCDM, and CCPs' role in front of systemic risk. The use of compression, a service increasingly being offered by CCPs, might reduce the capital that a bank, as a clearing member (bank/CM), must hold against its default fund contribution to the CCP.[174]

The role of CCPs as efficient managers of counterparty credit risk has been widely accepted. Their efficiency is attributed to the implementation of several prudential mechanisms that ensure the safety and soundness of the CCP. In this discourse, the robustness of the CCP and the management of clearing members' defaults have been central. Indeed, a regulatory priority, in Europe and in the UK, is to ensure that CCPs have enough resources available to mutualise losses in the event of a clearing member's default. However, the objectives of the CCPs regime might find a shortcoming when integrated with other regimes and innovative practices; in particular, the consequences that the innovative use of compression by banks/CMs might bring to the management of a clearing member's default. This is how the Basel III leverage ratio has increased the incentives for compression, and how the impact of compression on capital requirements for banks' exposures to CCPs might imply a reduction of the amount of collateral available in the event of a clearing member's default.

In order to develop the argument, we will consider compression in three parts, beginning with examining the process of compression, objectives, and innovative uses following the regulatory requirements of EMIR. We will then explore the role of two prudential tools included in Basel III: leverage ratio and capital requirements for banks' exposures to CCPs. Finally, we will highlight the benefits that compression brings to banks/CMs and CCPs. We also address how

---

174 Thomas Murray Data Services, 'CCP in Focus – Compression and its Effect On Bank Capital Requirements and Leverage Ratios' (19 May 2014) <http://ds.thomasmurray.com/opinion/ccp-focus-compression-and-its-effect-bank-capital-requirements-and-leverage-ratios> accessed 28th January 2016.

innovative compression affects the calculation of both leverage ratio and capital requirements, as well as diminishes the effectiveness of CCPs as managers of counterparty credit risk in the OTCDM.

5.4.2.1 Taxonomy of compression

The OTCDM is led by innovation in different ways. Innovation might take form through the use of new mechanisms and processes, or by the novel use of well-known practices. The use of compression in the context of the clearing relationship between banks/CMs and CCPs falls into the second category. It is also an example of the uncertainties that are 'unknown but knowable', as was explained in the first chapter. In the case of compression, what is unknown is not the process itself, but the use of it. To clarify this point further, compression is not a new practice; it has been used as tool to enhance operational efficiencies and in the derivatives market. It emerged as a way for derivatives users to manage operational risks in 2003, with the launch of TriOptima's triReduce service.[175] However, as a result of the new capital and leverage ratio requirements of Basel III,[176] compression is now being used to reduce the size of the bank's balance and derivatives portfolio.[177]

In the context of the OTCDM, compression is a process by which OTC derivatives transactions in the standardised same contract offset, or partially offset, and as a result it might be possible for the client and/or clearing member to net these trades.[178] One of the objectives of compression is to reduce the notional outstanding amount by creating a new replacement contract that removes the offsetting exposure, without affecting the market risk of the portfolio.[179] ESMA[180]

---

175   TriOptima, 'TriReduce: Key Benefits Optimizing Leverage Ratios, Reducing Risk' <www.trioptima.com/services/triReduce/benefits.html> accessed 27th January 2016.
176   BIS, 'International Regulatory Framework for Banks: Basel III' <www.bis.org/bcbs/basel3.htm> accessed 28th January 2016.
177   ISDA, 'The Impact of Compression on the Interest Rate Derivatives Market' (ISDA Research Note, July 2015).
178   Thomas Murray Data Services, 'CCP in Focus – Compression and its Effect on Bank Capital Requirements and Leverage Ratios' (n174).
179   'Activity in global OTC derivatives markets fell in the first half of 2015. The notional amount of outstanding contracts declined from $629 trillion at end of December 2014 to $553 trillion at end of June 2015. Even after adjustment for the effect of exchange rate movements on positions denominated in currencies other than the US dollar, notional amounts were still down by about 10 percent. Trade compression to eliminate redundant contracts was the major driver of the decline' (emphasis added) BIS, 'Statistical release: OTC Derivatives Statistics at end-June 2015' Monetary and Economic Department (November 2015) <www.bis.org/publ/otc_hy1511.pdf> accessed 28th January 2016.
180   ESMA, 'Final Report ESMA's Technical Advice to the Commission on MiFID II and MiFIR' (Final Report ESMA/2014/1569 19 November 2014) <www.esma.europa.eu/sites/default/files/library/2015/11/2014-1569_final_report_-_esmas_technical_advice_to_the_commission_on_mifid_ii_and_mifir.pdf> accessed 28th January 2016.

explains that the process of compression with a CCP would allow counterparties to reduce the notional value of contracts in their books against that CCP.[181]

This service is used in cleared and uncleared derivatives and is increasingly being offered by CCPs.[182] Indeed, EMIR and the Dodd-Frank Act require the use of compression, the former for non-clear derivatives and the latter for major swaps participants. Although compression has been offered in the derivatives market for more than a decade, it had a downside that previously discouraged participants from using it.[183] This was the 'linking of trade records' that required both parties to agree for a trade to be compressed – this changed in 2014, with the 'unlinking' of trade records at LCH Clearnet.[184] Now each counterparty can compress the transactions that it has cleared through the CCP, without the involvement of its original counterparty.[185] This change prepared the market to the introduction of 'blended rate compression',[186] the latest form of compression available for OTC derivatives. By using blended rate compression, participants can compress transactions with different interest rates but the same remaining cash flow dates.[187] The use of this type of compression will significantly increase the eligible trades.[188]

EMIR contemplates the use of compression for financial counterparties and non-financial counterparties with 500 or more OTC derivative contracts outstanding with a counterparty, which are not cleared through CCPs. They are required, at least twice a year, to analyse the possibility and/or to conduct portfolio compression in order to reduce their counterparty credit risk. Moreover, counterparties must be able to explain if they have concluded portfolio compression is not suitable. Thus, the rule on EMIR is not a mandate to conduct portfolio compression, because it is not always in the interest of the counterparties.[189]

181 European Union Emissions Trading Scheme, 'Legal definition, economic sense and significance of portfolio compression' (2015) <www.emissions-euets.com/risk-mitigation-techniques-emir/portfolio-compression-emir> accessed 28th January 2016.
182 LCH Clearnet and CME Clearing Ltd.
183 ISDA, 'The Impact of Compression on the Interest Rate Derivatives Market' July 2015 (n177).
184 Risk, 'LCH Clearnet, Clearing House of the Year' (Risk.Net News, January 2015) <www.lchclearnet.com/documents/731485/762444/Risk+Awards+PDF.pdf/> accessed 27th January 2016.
185 Ibid.
186 ISDA, 'The Impact of Compression on the Interest Rate Derivatives Market' July 2015 (n177).
187 LCH Clearnet, 'LCH Clearnet's SwapClear Launches New Blended Rate Compression Service' (LCH Clearnet News, 17 September 2014) <www.lchclearnet.com/news-events/news/swapclear-launches-new-blended-rate> accessed 28th January 2016.
188 Ibid.
189 'Portfolio compression may carry some disadvantages specific to a party's legal, tax, accounting and/or operational status and may therefore not be appropriate in all circumstances', IOSCO, 'Risk Mitigation Standards for Non-Centrally Cleared OTC Derivatives' (IOSCO, FR01/2015, 28 January 2015) <www.iosco.org/library/pubdocs/pdf/IOSCOPD469.pdf> accessed 18th January 2018.

Although EMIR includes compression as a risk mitigation tool for uncleared derivatives, it is possible that counterparties of centrally cleared derivatives use this mechanism. The voluntary character of compression allows cleared and uncleared derivatives participants to decide how to use different methods of compression. According to the number of parts compressing their trades with each other, the method of compression is bilateral or multilateral; in multilateral compression, its main benefit is that it 'enables a bigger pool of positions to be offset, resulting in higher compression ratios'.[190]

The claimed benefits of compression include a reduction in gross notional value of outstanding trades without affecting market risks, a reduction in operational risks, and a possible reduction of counterparty credit risk in bilateral derivatives, as well as a simplified default management process. The simplification and reduction of trades and processes is the main argument in favour of compression, as it is perceived as a mechanism for controlling systemic risk. However, the real impact that compression has in the reduction of the OTCDM size is debatable. Even though portfolio compression reduces the size of the market, the increase in the use of central clearing through CCPs has exactly the opposite effect: each bilateral transaction is divided into two new transactions when they are cleared through a CCP, which in turn doubles the notional amount.[191]

5.4.2.2 Basel III: leverage ratio and capital requirements for bank exposures to CCPs

In order to understand how compression is linked to the leverage ratio and capital requirements for banks' exposures to CCPs, this section explores the rationale of the leverage ratio imposed by the BCBS[192] in Basel III Section 227.

5.4.2.2.1 LEVERAGE RATIO

Leverage is defined as the practice that 'allows a financial institution to increase the potential gains or losses on a position or investment beyond what would be possible through a direct investment of its own funds'.[193] The excessive leverage by banks was identified as one of the causes that contributed to the GFC.[194] As a

---

190 European Union Emissions Trading Scheme, 'Legal Definition, Economic Sense and Significance of Portfolio Compression' (2015) (n181).

191 Ibid.

192 'The Basel-III framework included a more restrictive definition of Tier I capital, pro-cyclical capital, additional capital for the so-called Global Systemically Important Banks (G-SIBs) and a minimum simple leverage ratio', Karim Pakravan, 'Bank Capital: The Case Against Basel' (2014) 22 (3) *Journal of Financial Regulation and Compliance*, 208–218.

193 International Financial Corporation – World Bank Group, 'The New Leverage Ratio' (Crisis Response: Public Policy for the Private Sector, Note Number 11, December 2009) 1 <www.worldbank.org/financialcrisis/pdf/levrage-ratio-web.pdf> accessed 18th January 2018.

194 Adrian Blundell-Wignall, and Paul Atkinson, 'The Subprime Crisis: Causal Distortions and Regulatory Reform' (Lessons from the Financial Turmoil of 2007 and 2008, 2008) <www.

result, the G20 leaders[195] and FSB[196] proposed the introduction of a leverage ratio, as an additional prudential tool, to complement capital adequacy requirements. Despite the multiple critiques[197] to the leverage ratio of Basel III,[198] it will be completely introduced in Pillar I before 1st January 2018.

Leverage ratio is designed to offer a non-risk-based ratio that can be used as a 'credible' supplementary measure to the risk-based capital requirements.[199] The rationale behind the adoption of leverage ratio is to provide supervisors with an additional mechanism to validate the banks' risk assessments.[200] As a result, regulators would have a better understanding of banks' risks[201] and be able to restrict the leverage practice within the banking sector.[202] Moreover, it is said to contribute to avoid the destabilising deleveraging process that can damage the wider financial system.[203]

---

rba.gov.au/publications/confs/2008/pdf/blundell-wignall-atkinson.pdf> accessed 28th January 2016.

195 G-20 Declaration of April 2009 on Strengthening the Financial System states that 'risk-based capital requirements should be supplemented with a simple, transparent, non-risk based measure which is internationally comparable, properly takes into account off-balance sheet exposures, and can help contain the build-up of leverage in the banking system'. G20, 'London Summit – Leaders' Statement' (2 April 2009) <www.imf.org/external/np/sec/pr/2009/pdf/g20_040209.pdf> accessed 28th January 2016.

196 The Financial Stability Board report on pro-cyclicality (FSB 2009) 2 recommends that 'the Basel Committee should supplement the risk-based capital requirement with a simple, non-risk based measure to help contain the build-up of leverage in the banking system and put a floor under the Basel II Framework', FSB, 'Recommendations for Addressing Pro-cyclicality in the Financial System' (2 April 2009) <www.fsb.org/2009/04/report-of-the-financial-stability-forum-on-addressing-procyclicality-in-the-financial-system/> accessed 28th January 2017.

197 Adrian Blundell-Wignall, and Paul Atkinson, 'Thinking Beyond Basel III: Necessary Solutions for Capital and Liquidity' (2010) OECD Journal: Financial Market Trends 1.

198 Bill Allen, and others, 'Basel III: Is the Cure Worse than the Disease?' (2012) 25 *International Review of Financial Analysis*, 159; Peter Miu, Bogie Ozdemir, and Michael Giesinger, 'Can Basel III Work? Examining the New Capital Stability Rules by the Basel Committee: A Theoretical and Empirical Study of Capital Buffers' (20 February 2010) <http://ssrn.com/abstract=1556446> accessed 28th January 2017.

199 Murray, 'CCP in Focus – Compression and its Effect on Bank Capital Requirements and Leverage Ratios' (n174).

200 Jurg M. Blum, 'Why 'Basel II' May Need a Leverage Ratio Restriction' (2008) 32 *Journal of Banking and Finance*, 1699.

201 Adrian Blundell-Wignall, Paul Atkinson, and Caroline Roulet, 'Bank Business Models and the Basel System: Complexity and Interconnectedness' (2014) 2013/2 *OECD Journal: Financial Market Trends*, 2.

202 Thomas Curry, 'Statement on Basel II: Capital Changes in the US Banking System and the Results of the Impact Study', before the Subcommittee on Financial Institutions and Consumer Credit and Subcommittee on Domestic and International Monetary Policy, Trade, and Technology of the Committee on Financial Services, US House of Representatives Hearing (11 May 2005), in Heidi Mandanis Schooner, and Michael W. Taylor, *Global Bank Regulation: Principles and Policies* (Academic Press 2009), 159.

203 Thomas Murray, 'CCP in Focus – Compression and its Effect on Bank Capital Requirements and Leverage Ratios' (n174).

The formula to calculate the leverage ratio is:

Leverage Ratio = Tier 1 Capital/Total Exposure

The total exposure amount includes on- and off-balance sheet assets, including derivatives. The method used to measure the bank's exposure to a CCP is the Current Exposure Method (CEM).[204] The objective of the CEM is 'to capture the current replacement costs by marking contracts to market and the adding a factor (add-on)'.[205] For OTC derivatives, the add-on factor is an adjusted sum called Potential Future Exposure (PFE).[206] Although the BCBS announced the replacement of the CEM with the standardised approach for measuring derivatives exposure (SA-CCR),[207] the PFE remains as one factor in the SA-CCR formula. In both methods (CEM and SA-CCR), the PFE is calculated by multiplying the effective notional amount of the OTC derivative contract by an appropriate conversion factor.[208] The add-on is developed for each asset class – similar to the five asset classes used for the CEM, i.e. interest rate, foreign exchange, credit, equity, and commodity.[209]

This formula illustrates the existence of a relationship between the value of leverage ratio and total exposure. This relationship emphasises the effect that compression practices have in the amount of total exposure.

5.4.2.2.2 CAPITAL REQUIREMENTS FOR BANK EXPOSURES TO CCPS

Basel III's objective in introducing the capital requirements for bank exposures to CCPs, called 'Qualifying CCPs',[210] is to capture the risks CCPs pose to banks/

---

204 'Basel III allows 3 methods in estimating the exposure of a bank to any counterparty: The Internal Model Method (IMM); the Standardised Method (SM) and the Current Exposure Method (CEM). However, Basel III only allows the CEM when estimating a bank's exposure to a CCP', Antonie Kotzé, 'Current Exposure Method for CCP's under Basel III' (Discussion Document, Johannesburg Stock Exchange, Equity Derivatives, May 2012) <www.quantonline.co.za/documents/Safcom%20Current%20Exposure%20Method.pdf> accessed 18th January 2018; also see Antonie Kotzé and Paul du Preez, 'Current Exposure Method for CCP's Under Basel III' (2013) 3 (2) *Risk Governance & Control: Financial Markets & Institutions*, 7.

205 Thomas Murray, 'CCP in Focus – Compression and its Effect on Bank Capital Requirements and Leverage Ratios' (n174).

206 BCBS, 'The Standardised Approach for Measuring Counterparty Credit Risk Exposures' (BIS, March 2014 (Rev April 2014) <www.bis.org/publ/bcbs279.pdf> accessed 28th January 2016.

207 Standardised Approach (SA-CCR) for measuring exposure at default (EAD) for counterparty credit risk (CCR).

208 BCBS, 'The Standardised Approach for Measuring Counterparty Credit Risk Exposures' (n206); see Andrew S. Fei, 'Overview of Basel Committee's Standardized Approach for Measuring Derivatives Exposure' (SA-CCR, formerly known as NIMM) (31 March 2014) <http://blog.usbasel3.com/basel-committee-standardized-approach-for-calculating-counterparty-credit-risk-exposure-nimm-sa-ccr/> accessed 18th January 2018.

209 BCBS, 'The Standardised Approach for Measuring Counterparty Credit Risk Exposures' (n206).

210 Criticising the contradictions between Basel III and EMIR and CRD IV: 'Basel III is written into EMIR (European Market Infrastructure Regulation) via CRD IV (Capital

CMs.[211] Accordingly, banks must capitalise their trade exposures, as well as their default fund contribution. In order to calculate a bank/CM exposure to the default fund, and the amount of capital a bank/CM must hold, one of the methods (Method 1) requires the calculation of a CCP's hypothetical capital requirement (Kccp).[212] One of the factors needed to calculate the Kccp is Exposure before Risk Mitigates (EBRM), which is calculated using the method CEM.[213]

5.4.2.3 Compression influences leverage ratio and capital requirements

In order to understand how compression is related and affects leverage ratio and capital requirements for a bank's exposures to CCPs, it is important to emphasise the objective of compression. Compression is the reduction of gross notional amounts without affecting market risk. Gross notional amount[214] is one of the factors of the CEM method, which is used to calculate leverage ratio and capital requirements. This means that if there is a reduction in gross notional amounts, there is also a reduction in total exposures. As a result, there is a reduction of the capital a bank/CM is obliged to hold against its default fund contribution to the CCP. Similarly, the reduction in the total exposure will impact the calculation of the leverage ratio. Therefore, banks/CMs will benefit from using compression services.

The successful experience of LCH Clearnet Ltd shows that CCPs can gain competitive advantage over other CCPs operating in the market when they offer innovative compression services, as banks/CMs are in constant search of solutions to optimise collateral.[215] Nonetheless, the use of compression in the OTCDM brings risks, including the risk that in the event of clearing members' default banks/CMs will have less collateral available to close out their positions. This

---

Requirements Directive IV). CRD IV defines a [Qualifying] QCCP as one that has been authorised under Article 14 or is recognised under Article 25 of EMIR. Neither of these articles, or indeed any other part of EMIR, makes any mention of a QCCP or the relevant requirements to becoming one'. Thomas Murray, 'CCP in Focus – When is a QCCP not really a QCCP?' (Thomas Murray Data Services, 17 February 2014) <http://ds.thomasmurray.com/opinion/ccp-focus-when-qccp-not-really-qccp> accessed 18th January 2018.

211 BCSC, 'Capital Requirements for Bank Exposures to Central Counterparties' (BIS, April 2014) <www.bis.org/publ/bcbs282.htm> accessed 18th January 2018.

212 Ibid.

213 Thomas Murray, 'CCP in Focus – Compression and its Effect on Bank Capital Requirements and Leverage Ratios' (n174).

214 'The notional amount of outstanding OTC derivatives contracts determines contractual payments and is an indicator of activity. Nominal or notional amounts outstanding are defined as the gross nominal or notional value of all deals concluded and not yet settled on the reporting date'. BIS, 'OTC Derivatives Statistics at End-June 2014' *BIS*, Monetary and Economic Department, Statistical Release (November 2014) <www.bis.org/publ/otc_hy1504.htm> accessed 28th January 2016.

215 Thomas Murray, 'CCP in Focus – Compression and its Effect on Bank Capital Requirements and Leverage Ratios' (n174).

scenario directly increases risk and affects the management of clearing members' default – the actual removal of collateral from CCPs might become a source of systemic risk.[216] CCPs are safe and sound only when they have sufficient resources and risk management mechanisms to absorb losses. Thus, the use of compression is proven to be an innovation in the form of creative compliance, since while regulators seek to increase the capital requirements in the OTCDM, banks/CMs introduce a solution to mitigate this increase and as such affect the achievement of regulators' objectives. By using compression in the way explained earlier, clearing members are 'using the law to escape legal control without actually violating legal rules'.[217]

5.4.2.4 A way forward

The foregoing potential issues are forms of innovation and examples of the issues that interconnectedness between SIFIs (banks and CCPs) brings to financial stability. The Bank (at the time of writing) has not considered the issues and, therefore, there is no solution in the current regime. However, the FPC conducted a full review of the OTCDM in 2016.[218] The review was an opportunity to identify not only issues concerning the regime of CCPs, but also how the interconnectedness of CCPs with other systemically important financial institutions, such as banks, might negatively affect the objective of financial stability. The findings emphasised the importance of CCPs in the process of making OTCDM safer.[219] The FPC highlights that post-crisis reforms, and in particular the adoption of CCPs, have 'reduce[d] the aggregate counterparty risk in the financial system and [increased] the transparency of derivatives exposures'.[220] The study of the OTCDM recognises that although interconnections between CCPs and other systemically important institutions exists, they do not pose prominent risks to the financial stability because the largest global CCPs are 'expected to hold sufficient pre-funded resources'.[221] However, the FPC is cautious and recommends further enhancement of CCPs' resolution rules and supervisory stress tests.

The role of the FPC in the area of interconnectedness is of central importance. It is directly linked to the FPC's primary aim to contribute to achieving the Bank's stability objective. The responsibility of the FPC is to identify, monitor, and take

---

216 Ibid.

217 Doreen McBarnet, 'Law and Capital: The Role of Legal Form and Legal Actors' (n158) 233.

218 Bank of England, 'Financial Stability Report 2015' (Issue No 37, July 2015) <www.bankofengland.co.uk/publications/Pages/fsr/2015/jul.aspx> accessed 28th January 2016.

219 Bank of England, 'Financial Stability Report 2016' (Issue No 39, July 2016) 25 <www.bankofengland.co.uk/-/media/boe/files/financial-stability-report/2016/july-2016.pdf> accessed 20th December 2017.

220 Ibid.

221 Bank of England, '2017 Financial Stability Report 2017' (Issue No 42, November 2017) 60 <www.bankofengland.co.uk/-/media/boe/files/financial-stability-report/2017/november-2017.pdf> accessed 20th December 2017.

action to remove or reduce systemic risks.[222] One of the sources of systemic risk is attributable to 'structural features of financial markets, such as connections between financial institutions'[223] – hence, the balance sheet interconnectedness is one of the core factors that the FPC uses to monitor systemic risks.[224] In the UK, since 2011, prudential regulators have collected the information on exposure of UK banks to other financial institutions (e.g. CCPs). Moreover, regulators have tightened limits on direct exposures between systemically important financial institutions, and the level of interconnectedness is a factor to determine whether an institution is a global systemically important bank (G-SIB).

As the Bank explains, the analysis of the interconnectedness between banks and CCPs includes reforms to both markets.[225] On the one hand, the banking system has adopted the ring-fencing[226] of banks and recovery and resolution plans. On the other hand, the principal policy in the area of CCPs has been the introduction of recovery and resolution tools for CCPs.[227] However, as we explained in Chapter 4, the resolution regime of CCPs is still in the process of being built. Thus, the FPC is in the position to identify issues, such as the ones explained earlier, and give advice to the Bank in identifying potential sources of systemic risk.

The findings of the 2016 review showed that enhancement in initial margin is an important tool to strengthen CCPs resilience. However, this might put excessive pressure on firms to post additional highly liquid assets at the times when is very difficult (i.e. the risk of pro-cyclicality). Therefore, such a tool must be implemented with caution and any potential systemic negative effects should be prevented. Hence, the FPC is focusing its efforts in improving the methodology applicable to supervisory tests that identify the linkages between CCPs and their clearing members.[228] Moreover, the FPC commitment is to further develop resolution rules for CCPs according to international standards.

222 Paul Tucker, Simon Hall, and Aashish Pattani, 'Macroprudential Policy at the Bank of England' (Bank of England, Quarterly Bulletin 2013 Q3) <www.bankofengland.co.uk/publications/Documents/quarterlybulletin/2013/qb130301.pdf> accessed 28th January 2016.

223 Bank of England, 'The Financial Policy Committee's Review on the Leverage Ratio' (October 2014) 8 <www.bankofengland.co.uk/financialstability/Documents/fpc/fs_lrr.pdf> accessed 28th January 2016.

224 Zijun Liu, Stephanie Quiet, and Benedict Roth, 'Banking Sector Interconnectedness: What Is It, How Can We Measure It and Why Does It Matter?' (Bank of England, *Quarterly Bulletin* 2015 Q2) <www.bankofengland.co.uk/publications/Documents/quarterlybulletin/2015/q2prerelease_1.pdf> accessed 28th January 2016.

225 Ibid.

226 Financial Services Act 2013 (Banking Reform); see Bank of England, 'Structural Reform' <www.bankofengland.co.uk/pra/Pages/supervision/structuralreform/default.aspx> accessed 28th January 2016; also see Prudential Regulation Authority, 'The Implementation of Ring-Fencing: Legal Structure, Governance and the Continuity of Services and Facilities' (Policy Statement PS10/15 May 2015) <www.bankofengland.co.uk/pra/Documents/publications/ps/2015/ps1015.pdf> accessed 28th January 2016.

227 Chapter 3.

228 Financial Stability Report 2016 (Issue No 39, July 2016) (n219).

As a central complementary measure, in the 2017 Financial Stability Report[229] the Bank announced its commitment to design options for supervisory stress tests[230] and to improve systems of cooperation and information sharing with other regulators. The objective of the Bank's stress tests is to capture those risks that are not considered in the CCPs' own stress tests (e.g. a clearing member's default affecting multiple types of products in different jurisdictions).[231]

5.5 Conclusion

This chapter explained the failure to rule innovation risk in the UK regime of CCPs in the OTCDM, emphasising that the safety and soundness of the OTCDM requires regulators to consider the risk that innovation[232] represents to the achieving of their objectives. Innovation is certainly difficult to define. However, our discussion began by making reference to the use of innovation to avoid the clearing obligation for certain types of derivatives. Although the regime establishes the list of transactions that are subject to central clearing, there is a debate calling for allowing CCPs a certain level of discretion when deciding what derivatives should be cleared. As there might be market participants that are interested in avoiding the clearing obligation, one way to achieve this is to influence the decision of the CCP regarding what products should be centrally cleared. In order to avoid this situation, regulators can control the power that major derivative dealers might have over the governance of CCPs by controlling the self-interest that major dealers might exert to 'escape' the clearing requirement, by convincing the CCP that certain clearing-eligible products, disguised as bespoke instruments, should not be cleared through the CCP. Therefore, the regulation of the governance of CCPs could help to overcome one part of the weakness related to innovation risk.

The governance rules to be further developed by the Bank in the UK follow the relevant provisions of EMIR; in fact, one of the Bank's regulatory priorities is to design governance principles of CCPs. In line with the recent regulation on individual accountability in the UK financial services, this chapter explored the SM&CR, arguing that including rules of individual accountability applicable to senior managers and employees of CCPs would benefit and complete, at least partially, the governance and conduct of business regime. It will contribute to making clear that senior managers and employees of CCPs are not only obliged to follow internal codes of conduct, corporate governance rules, and fiduciary

---

229 Bank of England, Financial Stability Report 2017 (n221), 57.
230 See BIS, 'Framework for Supervisory Stress Testing of Central Counterparties (CCPs)' (Consultative Report, June 2017) <www.bis.org/cpmi/publ/d161.pdf> accessed 20th December 2017.
231 Ibid 60.
232 'Financial innovation is a continuous, dynamic process that entails the creation and subsequent popularization of new financial instruments', Panagiotis Delimatsis, 'Transparent Financial Innovation in a Post-Crisis Environment' Journal of International Economic Law Vol 16 1 1 March 2013 (n4) 159.

duties, when appropriate, but they also must observe the rules and standards that the SM&CR imposes to individuals working in financial firms.

Although one might assume that the SM&CR will be applicable to senior managers and employees of CCPs in the OTCDM, in fact it will not be automatically applicable to them, as neither the FCA nor the PRA supervise CCPs. The Bank will have to clarify which is the competent regulator in this area, whether that be the Bank or, as we propose, the FCA. If the appropriate regulator is indeed the Bank, it must issue rules regarding the individual accountability of senior managers and employees of CCPs operating in the OTCDM. If the appropriate competent regulator is named as the FCA, the SM&CR will be directly applicable to all individuals who work in the CCPs by 2018.

Another area that could be solved with the design and implementation of governance rules concerns the conflict of interests that might occur within CCPs. This chapter discussed how the demutualised structure of CCPs operating in the UK puts conflict of interest issues in the spotlight, in particular, the convergent interests of CCPs' owners, clearing members, and the public interests. A governance regime might contribute to mitigating the influence that clearing members might have over the CCP to benefit their own interests; we would call for regulators to design a regime of CCPs' governance that is not limited to ruling the boards' and risk management committees' composition and voting rights, as they are broadly defined in EMIR. The CCP governance regime should instead seek to balance the convergent interests surrounding the functioning of the CCP, amongst other considerations; pursuing the balance of convergent interests in the CCP requires ensuring representation of all stakeholders in the governance structure. The Bank should firstly delimit who has the category of stakeholder and how the composition of groups of stakeholders might vary; such changes would need to be reflected in the boards' and committees' composition.

The CCP governance regime should consider the role that CCPs have as co-regulators, imposing market discipline. The contribution of the CCP is to promote high levels of disclosure and transparency about market participants and transactions; they enjoy a level of discretion which allows them to play a double role in helping regulators to achieve their objectives. The co-regulatory role of CCPs requires rules that solve the internal conflict of interests, so that the CCP is free from stakeholders' influence. In this sense, some recommendations might include the limitation of ownership participation and the imposition of fit and proper standards to those involved in the governance of the CCP. These standards not only promote investor protection, but also strengthen the robustness of the CCP's functioning. To sum up, if the aim is to ensure that the CCP acts as co-regulator, in line with the Bank's objective, then it is first important to strengthen the internal structure and governance rules of CCPs.

Finally, in this chapter we explored how innovation in the form of creative compliance is likely to lead to some of the unintended consequences of the CCP regime. We referred to the potential dangers coming from the innovative financial techniques OTCDM participants will use to meet the high-quality collateral requirements of CCPs, as well as explored how the 'innovative' use of portfolio compression diminishes the effectiveness of CCPs as managers of counterparty credit risk in the OTCDM and its role in front of systemic risk. Therefore, the Bank, assisted by the FPC, and attending to its role as macro- and microprudential regulator, is expected to oversee the potential risks that the new regulation of CCPs might bring to the stability of the system. This is especially because the 'innovative' techniques explained are a form of innovation and exemplify the issues that interconnectedness between SIFIs (banks and CCPs) brings to financial stability.

6 Comments on the US derivatives market regulation for CCPs[1]

6.1 Introduction

The purpose of this chapter is to identify the shortcomings in adopting a risk-based approach to regulation of CCPs in the US. Although this is not a comparative study, it is first important to emphasise the well-known differences between both systems. While the US framework is characterised by a powerful supervisor and concomitant functions assigned to SROs,[2] the UK has a clearly different regulatory structure. In the UK, CCP regulatory functions are attributed almost exclusively to the Bank, while self-regulatory organisations have more limited powers. Another relevant difference between the two regimes is that the UK has unified regulation, as opposed to several[3] and fragmented regulations and supervisors in the US.[4] The historical[5] tiered US supervisory structure may result in regulatory overlaps, which is indeed one of the shortcomings of the Dodd-Frank Wall Street and Consumer Protection Act (DFA), which we will study in this chapter.

1 We use the term CCPs to include clearing entities and designated clearing entities (DCEs). DCEs are commonly classified according to the functions they perform: a Central Counterparty is an entity that interposes itself between counterparties to contracts traded in financial markets, becoming the buyer to each seller, and seller to each buyer, to ensure the performance of open contracts.

2 Tanja Boskovic, Caroline Cerruti, and Michel Noel, 'Comparing European and US Securities Regulations: MiFID versus Corresponding US Regulations' World Bank Working Paper No 184 (December 2010), 1.

3 See Alejandro Komai, and Gary Richardson, 'A Brief History of Financial Regulation in the United States from the Beginning Until Today: 1789 to 2009' NBER Working Paper 17443 (2011).

4 The US securities regulations and oversight are organised in three different layers: 1. federal laws and a federal regulator (the SEC); 2. state laws and regulators; and 3. self-regulatory organisations including NYSE, Chicago Climate Exchange, Nasdaq Stock Market. See World Bank, 'Regulatory Framework and Oversight' (Comparing European and US Securities Regulations, WB Working Paper' (2011) <http://siteresources.worldbank.org/ECAEXT/Resources/258598-1256842123621/6525333-1263245503321/Regulation_ch1.pdf> accessed 22nd December 2017.

5 Government Accountability Office, GAO-05–61, 'Financial Regulation: Industry Changes Prompt Need to Reconsider US Regulatory Structure' (October 2004), 4.

Our discussion will argue the existence of different shortcomings of the US regime for clearing houses in the derivatives market. In such a context, we will highlight the limits triggered by the incomplete implementation of risk-based regulation as a regulatory strategy, using the concept coined by Power[6] about the new 'politics of uncertainty'. This notion provides us with the framework to understand the risk-based approach to regulation and how it facilitates the integration of multiple perceptions of risk within the regulatory process, features lacking in the current US regime for CCPs. The integration of varied perceptions of risk proposed in this book would include the point of view of 'those who regulate, those who are regulated and those for whose benefit regulation exists'.[7]

Precedent chapters addressed discussions about the shortcomings of the UK regime governing CCPs in the OTCDM. However, attending to the notorious volume of OTC derivatives traded in the US, it is necessary to consider potential flaws that, in terms of regulation and supervision, affect the current regime of the OTCDM – mainly the provisions contained in Titles VII and VIII of the DFA.

In this chapter, we seek to throw some light on the most relevant concerns related to the implementation of risk-based approach to regulation by US regulatory agencies. Our central question is whether the implementation of an incoherent risk-based regime has contributed to the exacerbation of the flaws revealed in the regulatory structure adopted in the US derivatives market. In order to address this, we will first briefly summarise the rules governing the OTC derivatives markets and, in particular, rules applicable to CCPs. We will then explore the shortcomings of the DFA regarding the regulation and supervision, as well as how an incomplete adoption of the risk-based approach has contributed to accentuate such flaws. The inadequacies of the US regime of CCPs include: the absence of a determined resolution regime for CCPs, the inconvenient extraterritorial implications of the US regime, the failure to respond to future innovations, and the negative effects of a bifurcated regulatory structure.

6.2 Overview of the US regime for CCPs

The rhetoric surrounding financial regulation and the call for reform after crises[8] is usually inspired by the detection of serious malfunctions[9] and the need for correction of certain market failures. It might be expected that regulatory reforms come as a natural response to events of financial distress; however, this

---

6 Michael Power, *Organised Uncertainty* (Oxford University Press 2007).
7 Joanna Gray, 'What Next for Risk-Based Financial Regulation?' in Ian McNeil, and Justin O'Brien (eds.), *The Future of Financial Regulation* (Hart Publishing Ltd 2010), 139.
8 Larry E. Ribstein, 'Bubble Laws' 40 *Houston Law Review*, 77–98 (2003) cited by Niamh Moloney, 'Financial Services and Markets' in Robert Baldwin, Martin Cave, and Martin Lodge (eds.), *The Oxford Handbook of Regulation* (Oxford University Press 2010), 438.
9 Howard Davis, and David Green, *Global Financial Regulation: The Essential Guide* (Polity 2008).

is in fact a heavily contested territory.[10] The debate[11] moves between the two extremes, from those who advocate the necessity of a rigid strict control to those who prefer no state regulatory interference whatsoever.[12] Moreover, the development and reform in financial regulation usually involves the use of incentive structures,[13] striving to induce the regulated to adjust their own actions and responses. Some authors affirm that regulatory reform post-GFC is particularly interesting, because it is said to respond 'to the reactive quality of regulatory reform, which has characterised the last thirty years'.[14] However, such a reactive character can be hardly distinct in the post-GFC reforms, if compared to the previous process of reform in financial markets. In general, financial regulation reforms are almost always driven to deliver a paradigmatic and radical response to crisis conditions.

All these considerations are relevant to justify the content of the post-GFC regulatory reform. Particularly in the case of the OTC derivatives market, the GFC demonstrated a regulatory failure in a fragile market infrastructure, along with several market failures. In essence, the OTC derivatives market lacked regulatory practices and risk management tools that kept pace with the complexities and hidden risks of certain financial instruments.[15] Indeed, the US government accepted that by 2008 the 'regulatory framework with respect to derivatives was manifestly inadequate';[16] regulators were incapable of managing the consequences of the crisis.[17] Similarly, in the UK, George Osborne accepted that the

---

10 Ibid.

11 Joanna Gray, 'Financial Regulation Before and After Northern Rock' in Joanna Gray and Orkun Akseli (eds.), *Financial Regulation in Crisis? The Role of Law and the Failure of Northern Rock* (Edward Elgar 2011), 72.

12 'Indeed, many "liberal" academic economists, e.g. supporters of free banking such as Dowd and Benston and Kaufman, would attribute many of [the] crises and problems to the (indirectly malign) effects of regulatory efforts – perhaps the most extreme example of iatrogenesis (medically induced illness) ever known'. Charles Goodhart, and others, 'Financial Regulation: Why, How and Where Now?' (Routledge and Bank of England 1998), 2.

13 Ibid 44.

14 Niamh Moloney, 'Financial Services and Markets' in Robert Baldwin, Martin Cave, and Martin Lodge (eds.), *The Oxford Handbook of Regulation* (Oxford University Press 2010), 439.

15 Jack Selody, 'The Nature of Systemic Risk' in John Raymond LaBrosse, Rodrigo Olivares-Caminal, and Dalvinder Sing (eds.), *Managing Risk in the Financial System* (Edward Elgar Publishing Ltd 2011), 29.

16 Financial Crisis Inquiry Commission, *The Financial Crisis Inquiry Report* (Public Affairs New York 2011), 49.

17 The IMF highlights the limited role of regulators and supervisors in the midst of the GFC: 'Financial liberalization and deregulation constitute a fourth commonly identified contributor to crisis conditions. Observers have emphasized such moves as the removal of barriers between commercial and investment banking in the United States and the greater reliance of banks on internal risk management models, all of which occurred without a commensurate buildup in supervisory capacity. Conversely, regulation and supervision were slow again to catch up with new developments, in part due to political processes and capture, and failed to restrict excessive risk-taking. Risks, notably in the 'shadow banking system' but also at large,

crisis 'globally as well as in the UK was caused both by failures in the financial sector, and by failures in regulation of the financial sector'.[18]

Recognising the need for regulation and supervision of OTC derivatives markets, in September 2009 (Pittsburgh Summit), the G20 leaders set out the fundamental guidance, stating:

> All standardised OTC derivative contracts should be traded on exchanges or electronic trading platforms, where appropriate, and cleared through central counterparties by end-2012 at the latest. OTC derivative contracts should be reported to trade repositories. Non-centrally cleared contracts should be subject to higher capital requirements. We ask the FSB and its relevant members to assess regularly implementation and whether it is sufficient to improve transparency in the derivatives markets, mitigate systemic risk, and protect against market abuse.[19]

This commitment was endorsed by the November 2010 Seoul Summit, when G-20 Leaders asked the FSB to monitor OTCDM reform on a regular basis. There have been subsequent reports informing about the advances made.[20] Additionally, the role of standardisation through CCPs was encouraged at the G20 London Submit 2009. During the crisis period, IOSCO's standard-setting functions moved towards the risk regulation agenda.[21] IOSCO reviewed[22] its objectives and principles,[23] and added eight new principles, including two focused on the efficient management of systemic risk.[24] Amongst other initiatives,[25] IOSCO is committed to promoting transparency and soundness in the OTCDM. To that end, IOSCO formed a Task Force on OTC Derivatives Regulation, with the objective to coordinate regulators' efforts to work together in the development of supervisory and oversight structures related to the OTCDM.[26] IOSCO has

---

internationally active banks, were permitted to grow without much oversight, leading eventually to both bank and nonbank financial instability'. IMF, 'The Regulatory Responses to the Global Financial Crisis: Some Uncomfortable Questions' WP/14/46 (March 2014), 6.
18 HM Treasury-FCA (2011b), 'A New Approach to Financial Regulation: The Blueprint for Reform' CM8083 (June 2011), 3.
19 G20, 'Leaders' Statement The Pittsburgh Summit' (September 24–25, 2009), 9.
20 FSB, OTC Derivatives Market Reforms: FSB Report Implementing OTC Derivatives Market Reforms 25th October 2010 The Ninth Progress Report on Implementation (24 July 2015).
21 Eilís Ferran, and others, *The Regulatory Aftermath of the Global Financial Crisis* (Cambridge University Press 2012), 152.
22 'IOSCO was persuaded that its Objectives and Principles were not designed to prevent systemic risk and were therefore insufficient', Roberta S Karmel, 'IOSCO's Response to the Financial Crisis' Brooklyn Law School, Legal Studies Paper No 268 (16 March 2012) <https://papers.ssrn.com/sol3/papers.cfm?abstract_id=2025115> accessed 12th December 2017.
23 IOSCO, 'Objectives and Principles of Securities Regulation' (September 1998). These principles were designed in response to the Asian Financial Crisis of 1998.
24 IOSCO, 'Mitigating Systemic Risk: A Role for Securities Regulators' IOSCO Discussion Paper OR01/11 (February 2011).
25 Ibid.
26 IOSCO, 'IOSCO Forms Task Force on OTC Derivatives Regulation' Press Release, IOSCO/MR/11/2010 (2010) <www.iosco.org/news/pdf/IOSCONEWS191.pdf> accessed 18th January 2016.

issued international standards for the regulation of market participants that are in the business of dealing, making a market or intermediating transactions in OTC derivatives ('OTC derivatives market intermediaries' or 'DMIs').[27] Moreover, IOSCO and CPSS published the Principles for Financial Market Infrastructures that are applied to CCPs and TRs.[28]

Consequently, there have been progressive regulatory reforms following the guidance of the G20 and IOSCO. In the US, the reforms to the OTCDM are part of the DFA, which established a comprehensive framework for regulating the OTC swaps markets.[29] One of the upheavals of the GFC was the realisation that large financial institutions and markets, as OTC derivatives, can generate systemic risk. Hence, the DFA was meant to be a framework to implement measures designed to identify, quantify, and control that risk. Ideally, the measures adopted by virtue of the DFA would be timely, capture well-identified mechanisms, and be used as an input for regulatory tools.[30] Part of the OTCDM reforms introduced standards to strengthen the regulation and supervision of CCPs.

However, the Trump administration has clearly stated their intention to reform and substantially modify the content of such regulation as part of the Financial Choice Act 2017,[31] which seeks to significantly amend the DFA.[32]

6.2.1 Dodd-Frank Act

The DFA imposes the most consequential change to derivatives regulation, which is mandatory central clearing for swaps[33] and for security-based swaps.[34] In the aftermath of the GFC, and following the international trend of reform of the derivatives market, Gary Gensler, former chairman of the CFTC, announced

---

27 IOSCO, International Standards for Derivatives Market Intermediary Regulation, Final Report Technical Committee IOSCO, FR03/12 (June 2012) <www.iosco.org/library/pubdocs/pdf/IOSCOPD381.pdf> accessed 18th January 2016; also see IOSCO, 'Review of Implementation Progress in Regulation of Derivative Market Intermediaries' IOSCO, FR15/2015 (July 2015) <www.iosco.org/library/pubdocs/pdf/IOSCOPD497.pdf> accessed 18th January 2016.
28 CPSS-IOSCO Pfmi
29 Arthur E. Wilmarth Jr, 'Dodd-Frank Act: A Flooded and Inadequate Response to the Too-Big-To-Fail Problem' (2011) 89 (3) *Oregon Law Review*, 952.
30 Sylvain Benoit, and others, *Where the Risks Lie: A Survey on Systemic Risk* (Review of Finance, Oxford University Press 2017), 110.
31 On 9th June 2017, the US House of Representatives passed the 'CHOICE Act', a Republican proposal that would substantially restructure the post-crisis regulatory framework.
32 H. Rodgin Cohen, and Samuel R. Woodall III, 'Financial CHOICE Act of 2017' (2017) *Harvard Law School Forum on Corporate Governance and Financial Regulation*.
33 'In Dodd-Frank a Swap includes a list of 'commonly known' swaps such as CDS, currency swaps, and total-return swaps (. . .) there is an exclusion in Dodd-Frank for "any sale of a nonfinancial commodity or security for deferred shipment or delivery, so long as the transaction is intended to be physically settled" ', Alan N. Rechtschaffen, *Capital Markets, Derivatives and the Law: Evolution After Crisis* (Oxford University Press 2014), 219.
34 A 'security-based swap' is defined in the Securities Exchange Act 1934. It included swaps that are based on an index, a single security, or loan, or the occurrence or non-occurrence of an event of an issuer or group of issuers if that event affects the finances of the issuer.

'[t]he Wall-Street Reform bill would bring comprehensive regulation to the swaps market place. Swap dealers would be subject to robust oversight. Standardized derivatives would be required to trade on open platforms and be submitted for clearing to central counterparties'.[35] Moreover, Gensler reaffirmed the CFTC's aim to implement the reform, in order to lower risk, promote transparency and protect the American public.[36]

In the midst of the reform, senator Chris Dodd articulated the key areas needing urgent regulatory intervention. He argued that the coming Act would bestow the CFTC and the SEC with regulatory powers over the OTCDM and that, following the G20 statement, more transactions would be centrally cleared and traded on organised exchanges. Likewise, those transactions exempted from the clearing obligation – the uncleared swaps – would be subject to higher margin requirements. The reform would also impose new capital and registration requirements to swap dealers[37] and major swap participants.[38] The registration requirements should be fulfilled with the CFTC since, in order to enhance transparency, the Act would impose reporting obligations to all trades.

The principal and interrelated areas of focus of the DFA are similar to those set by the G20 summit: increased transparency in OTCDM for both market participants and regulators, and reduced counterparty risk and systemic risk arising from OTC derivatives contracts.[39] The mechanisms implemented by the CFTC and the SEC to manage counterparty and systemic risk include the mandatory use of central clearing for certain types of derivatives, as well as the adoption of higher capital and margin requirements for uncleared derivatives.[40] The purpose, as it is in EMIR, is to encourage greater standardisation of derivatives and move towards the voluntary use of central clearing. Concerning DCOs, the DFA requires that those entities in charge of clearing swap trades will be registered with the CFTC, while CAs that clear security-based swap trades will be registered

---

35 Gary Gensler, 'Chairman of the CFTC' <www.cftc.gov/LawRegulation/DoddFrankAct/index.htm> accessed 12th December 2017
36 Ibid.
37 'A swap dealer is a person who: 1) holds itself out as a dealer in swaps; 2) is a market-maker; 3) enters into swaps for its own account with counterparties "regularly"; or 4) is known as a dealer or market-maker'. CFTC, 'Final Rules Regarding Further Defining "Swap Dealer," "Major Swap Participant" and "Eligible Contract Participant"' (This is a joint rulemaking with the SEC) <www.cftc.gov/idc/groups/public/@newsroom/documents/file/msp_ecp_factsheet_final.pdf> accessed 12th December 2017.
38 'A major swap participant is a person who: 1) has a "substantial position" in swaps, excluding those entities holding positions for hedging commercial risks; 2) has outstanding swaps that "create substantial counterparty exposure" with potentially systemic concerns for the financial system; or 3) is a "highly leveraged" institution not subject to capital requirements and has a substantial position in swaps', Ibid 1.
39 Alan N. Rechtschaffen, *Capital Markets, Derivatives and the Law: Evolution After Crisis* (n32), 227.
40 Ibid.

with the SEC.[41] The path of implementation of these reforms started early in August 2010.[42]

6.2.1.1 Regulation of financial derivatives and central clearing

The DFA provides that the SEC will regulate 'security-based swaps', the CFTC will regulate 'swaps', and the CFTC and SEC will jointly regulate 'mixed swaps'.[43] Title VII of the DFA requires that both the SEC and CFTC, in consultation with the Board of Governors of the Federal Reserve System (the Board), jointly define the terms swap, security-based swap, and security-based swap agreement.[44] Title VII further provides that the SEC and CFTC shall together establish such regulations regarding 'mixed swaps',[45] as may be necessary to carry out the purposes of swap and security-based swap regulation under Title VII.[46] In addition, Title VII requires the SEC and CFTC to jointly adopt rules governing the way in which books and records must be kept for security-based swap agreements.[47]

Title VIII of the DFA provides the regulation and supervision for clearing and settlement systems. Entities authorised to provide clearing services which the US regime broadly includes are the DCOs and CAs. On the one hand, DCOs are supervised by the CFTC and function as CCPs for financial and commodity futures contracts, options on futures, and swaps. On the other hand, CAs are subject to the supervision of the SEC and function as securities depositories, securities settlement systems, and CCPs that variously clear and settle trades of securities, including options and security-based swaps. Both types of entities, the DCOs and the CAs, are FMUs and, when regarded as systemically important by the FSOC, they are classified as designated financial market utilities (DFMUs), and at the same time designated clearing entities (DCEs)[48] overseen by the Board, along with the respective supervision of either the CFTC or the SEC. The following graph helps us to understand the place of DCEs in the US financial system.

41 Ibid 219.
42 Ibid 221.
43 Arthur E. Wilmarth, Jr, 'Reforming Financial Regulation to Address the Too-Big-to-Fail Problem' (2010) 35 *Brooklyn Journal of International Law*, 707.
44 Charles L. Hauchi, 'Dodd-Frank's Swap Clearing Requirements and Systemic Risk' (Winter 2013) 30 (1) Yale *Journal on Regulation*, 279; also see David Skeel, *The New Financial Deal: Understanding the Dodd-Frank Act and Its Unintended Consequences* (John Wiley & Sons 2010).
45 R. Kroszner, and R Shiller, *Reforming US Financial Markets: Reflections Before and Beyond Dodd-Frank* (The MIT Press 2011).
46 Willa E. Gibson, 'Clearing and Trade Execution Requirements for OTC Derivatives Swaps Under the Frank-Dodd Wall Street Reform and Consumer Protection Act' (2011) 38 *Rutgers Law Rec*, 227, 229 <https://papers.ssrn.com/sol3/papers.cfm?abstract_id=1710822> accessed 12th December 2017.
47 Dodd-Frank Wall Street Reform and Consumer Protection Act, Pub L No 111–203, 124 Stat 1376 (2010).
48 DCEs are a subset of DFMUs.

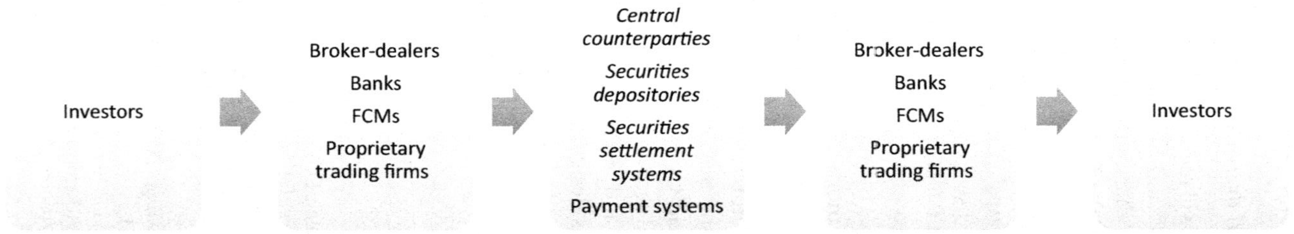

Investors → Broker-dealers
Banks
FCMs
Proprietary
trading firms
→ *Central
counterparties*

*Securities
depositories*

*Securities
settlement
systems*

Payment systems
→ Broker-dealers
Banks
FCMs
Proprietary
trading firms
→ Investors

Figure 6.1 DCEs and the US financial system

As central to financial stability reform as it was acclaimed in the aftermath of the GFC, the DFA still reveals the issues associated with the phenomenon called 'delegated legislation'.[49] Such a phenomenon allows many laws passed by Congress to delegate authority to certain agencies to produce rules to administrate these statutes.[50] The issue and implementation of such delegated legislation is key to ensure the enforcement of laws. Although the DFA is regarded as a comprehensive and complete body of legislation, the discretion given to regulatory agencies to promulgate complementary rules has proved to be one of the limits of the DFA in accomplishing its objectives. Indeed, in a recent report of the US Department of the Treasury to President Donald Trump,[51] the Treasury informed the status quo of the implementation of the derivatives market rules contained in the DFA. It asserts that whilst the CFTC has finalised all of its major rulemakings required under Title VII, and has implemented the major reforms for the swaps market – although many such rules have been implemented smoothly, several are the subject of exemptive, no-action, and interpretive letters, or are under review by the CFTC – the SEC has finalised most of its major rulemakings required under Title VII, although it has not finalised certain key Title VII derivatives reforms for security-based swaps.[52]

Moreover, the dual structure of regulatory authorities of the DFA is also problematic.[53] The split jurisdiction between SEC and CFTC has posed challenges for market participants.[54] Sometimes the differences in approach might not be completely incompatible, but might be inconsistent with or duplicative of one another, increasing the cost and complexity of compliance programmes.[55] Therefore, the Treasury recommends that the CFTC and the SEC give priority to reviewing and harmonising their respective rulemakings, to minimise to the extent of inconsistent compliance burdens on market participants.[56] Likewise, the Treasury recommends that Congress should consider further intervention to achieve a harmonised regulation of swaps and security-based swaps. Similar consideration might be predicable of the regulation and supervision of clearing and

---

49 Sean Speer, 'Regulatory Reform Should Be About Strengthening Legislative Responsibility' The Regulatory Review (23 October 2017) <www.theregreview.org/2017/10/23/speer-strengthening-legislative-responsibility/> accessed 23rd October 2017.

50 Ibid.

51 US Department of the Treasury, A Financial System That Creates Economic Opportunities Capital Markets Report to President Donald J Trump, Executive Order 13772 on Core Principles for Regulating the United States Financial System (September 2017) (hereinafter, US Treasury Report to President Trump (September 2017)).

52 US Treasury Report to President Trump (September 2017), 109.

53 Saule T. Omarova, 'One Step Forward, Two Steps Back: The Institutional Structure of US Financial Services After the Crisis of 2008' in Robin Hui Huang, and Dirk Schoenmaker (eds.), *Institutional Structure of Financial Regulation: Theories and International Experiences* (Routledge Taylor and Francis Group 2014), 137.

54 US Treasury Report to President Trump (September 2017) (n50), 127.

55 Ibid.

56 Ibid.

settlement systems, where the supervisory inquiry is shared among the Board, the SEC, and the CFTC.

To provide some context to the regulatory reforms of the OTCDM, the following sections briefly introduce the rules governing swaps and security-based swaps. We then move onto the analysis of Title VIII, on the supervision of CCPs.

6.2.1.2 Title VII regulates swaps and security-based swaps

The DFA set a dual regime for derivatives. Whilst standardised derivatives with sufficient liquidity must be cleared by a clearing house and traded on an organised exchange, customised derivatives are exempt from clearing and exchange mandate and are subject to margin and capital requirements.[57] In the event of security-based swaps, the central clearing is carried out by a clearing agency.[58]

In contrast to the European Regime for CCPs, the DFA establishes the five criteria that the relevant authority takes into account for determining whether a swap or a security-based swap is subject to the clearing requirement. These factors are: 1) outstanding notional exposures, liquidity, and pricing data; 2) availability of framework, capacity, expertise, and infrastructure to clear the trade; 3) the effect on mitigating systemic risk; 4) the effect on competition; and 5) reasonable legal certainty in the event of insolvency. Moreover, recognising that DCOs and clearing agencies are the ones in the best position to judge whether certain types of swap are apt to be centrally cleared, all swaps must be submitted to the CFTC and the SEC for clearance approval.

Trading of swaps and security-based swaps is an area of special interest in the DFA. The exchange trading requirement is imposed to swaps that are required to be centrally cleared. Such swaps shall be executed on a 'board of trade designated as a contract market' or on a 'swap execution facility',[59] and security-based swaps subject to the clearing requirement must be executed on an exchange or on a 'security-based swap execution facility'.

According to this mandate, on 16th May 2013, the CFTC voted to establish a swap execution facility (SEF), as a new and more transparent trading venue. One of the advantages of the SEF is that they execute trades that can be cleared in different clearing houses, as opposed to the traditional way future exchanges operate, which are tied to a single clearing house.[60] Moreover, for the first time,

---

57 Alan N. Rechtschaffen, *Capital Markets, Derivatives and the Law: Evolution After Crisis* (n32), 217.

58 A clearing agency is an intermediary in making payments or deliveries or both in connection with transactions in securities. See s 3(a)(23)(A) of the Exchange Act.

59 'A Swap Execution Facility is a trading system in which multiple participants have the ability to execute or trade swaps by accepting bids and offers made by multiple participants', see 'Core Principles and Other Requirements for SEF' 78 Fed Reg 33476 at 33481 (4 June 2013) Also see 76 Fed Reg 1214, 1219 (7 January 2011).

60 Scott D. O'Malia, 'Core Principles and Other Requirements for SEF' Speech, CFTC (16 May 2013) <www.cftc.gov/PressRoom/SpeechesTestimony/omaliastatement051613c> accessed 12th December 2017.

SEFs offer a trading platform where the public is able to gain access to and participate in the market.

Despite the benefits attributed to clearing and exchange requirements, the DFA gives the option to invoke the well-known 'end-user exception'.[61] Thus, if one of the counterparties to a swap is not a 'financial entity',[62] or is using swaps to hedge or mitigate commercial risk, they must notify the CFTC as to how they use swaps – and as a result, the transaction will not be subject to clearing and exchange requirements. The differential treatment for swaps used for hedging risk (as opposed to those merely speculative swaps), is a key feature of the DFA. It recognises that hedging is a more legitimate or fair use of derivatives, and as such, legislators decided to give them a preferential treatment, freeing these transactions from mandatory central clearing and organised exchange trading: the 'end-user exception'.

6.2.1.3 Title VIII regulates central clearing

Regarding the regulation applicable to CCPs in the US, the DFA aims to increase the resilience of these systemically important financial institutions, as well as to encourage their growth and development as they are regarded as central to the improvement in the management of counterparty credit risk in the OTCDM. CCPs become new centres for risk concentration and, as such, need to be carefully protected against severe financial shocks. Although the final push towards the use of central clearing had to be implemented through mandatory regulation, the willingness of market participants to use CCPs was evidenced long before the GFC. It has been reported that the growth of the market of IRS led to the creation of a clearing house in 1999. Similarly, the Federal Reserve Bank of New York, along with other regulators, had put in place some arrangements to further the use of central clearing for CDS.

The decision to bring CCPs to the OTCDM put regulators on task to ensure the stability of the market. According to Section 802 of the DFA, Congress was compelled to provide the background to enhance the regulation and supervision of systemically important FMUs and the conduct of systemically important payment, clearing, and settlement activities by financial institutions. The objectives were essentially to provide consistency, to promote robust risk management and safety and soundness, to reduce systemic risks, and to support the stability of the broader financial system.

---

61 Yaron Nili, 'End-User Exception from Dodd-Frank Clearing Mandate and Trade Execution Requirement' HLS Forum on Corporate Governance and Financial Regulation (23 August 2014) <https://corpgov.law.harvard.edu/2014/08/23/end-user-exception-from-dodd-frank-clearing-mandate-and-trade-execution-requirement/> accessed 12th December 2017.

62 S 723(a) (3) defines financial entity to include major swap and security-based swaps participants, as well as firms engaged in banking.

To accomplish such goals, Title VIII provides the FSB, the SEC, and the CFTC with new authority to promulgate risk management standards for designated FMUs, as well as to set standards for the conduct of systemically important payment, clearing, and settlement activities of financial institutions.[63]

Furthermore, the first step is to rule the capital, liquidity, and operational requirements that CCPs,[64] as FMUs,[65] shall meet and to design effective clearing member default procedures. The DFA reflects the need to strengthen the financial infrastructure in the derivatives market. Thus, Title VIII[66] addresses several prudential issues associated with clearing and settlement. Among other areas, the DFA bestows US regulators – FSOC, Board of Governors, the Federal Deposit Insurance Corporation (FDIC), CFTC, and SEC[67] – with the power to set enhanced risk management standards[68] for systemically important institutions, as CCPs[69] might be regarded.[70] The multi-agency rulemaking and supervising

63 Andrce Owens, and Bruce Newman, 'Dodd-Frank Title VIII: The Devil is in the Details' WilmerHale (7 September 2010) <www.wilmerhale.com/pages/publicationsandnewsdetail. aspx?NewsPubId=92206> accessed 17th October 2017.

64 'Section 804 of the DFA provides the Financial Stability Oversight Council (the 'Council') the authority to designate a financial market utility ('FMU') that the Council determines is or is likely to become systemically important because the failure of or a disruption to the functioning of the FMU could create, or increase, the risk of significant liquidity or credit problems spreading among financial institutions or markets and thereby threaten the stability of the US financial system'. FSCO, 12 CFR Chapter XIII and Part 1320 'Authority to Designate Financial Market Utilities as Systemically Important' (27 July 2011) <www.gpo.gov/ fdsys/pkg/FR-2011-07-27/pdf/2011-18948.pdf#page=11> accessed 17th October 2017.

65 Financial market utilities are multilateral systems that provide the infrastructure for transferring, clearing, and settling payments, securities, and other financial transactions among financial institutions or between financial institutions and the system.

66 Title VIII of the DFA is entitled the Payment, Clearing, and Settlement Supervision Act of 2010.

67 Dodd-Frank Act s 805, s 803(8).

68 Including risk management procedures, margin and collateral requirements, participant default policies, timely completion of clearing and settlement activities, and capital requirements, Dodd-Frank Act s 805.

69 To date, the Council has designated the following FMUs as systemically important (the supervisory agency – i.e. the federal agency that has primary jurisdiction over a designated FMU under federal banking, securities, or commodity futures laws – is indicated in parentheses):

   • The Clearing House Payments Company, LLC, on the basis of its role as operator of the Clearing House Interbank Payments System – (Board);
   • CLS Bank International – (Board);
   • Chicago Mercantile Exchange, Inc – (CFTC);
   • The Depository Trust Company – (SEC);
   • Fixed Income Clearing Corporation – (SEC);
   • ICE Clear Credit LLC – (CFTC);
   • National Securities Clearing Corporation – (SEC); and,
   • The Options Clearing Corporation – (SEC).

70 FSOC, 12 CFR Chapter XIII and Part 1320 RIN 4030 – AA01, 'Final Rule Authority to Designate Financial Market Utilities as Systemically Important' <www.gpo.gov/fdsys/pkg/ FR-2011-07-27/pdf/2011-18948.pdf#page=11> Last accessed 17th October 2017.

mandate[71] to oversee CCPs seeks to encourage a more intensive supervision of clearing houses,[72] aiming at implementing a more effective and compliance-based oversight[73] of these market infrastructures. Like the regime in the UK, the DFA allows CCPs to open accounts[74] at the central bank,[75] and to obtain access to emergency credit facilities, in case of financial distress. This would be subject to authorisation by the Board, in consultation with the Secretary of the Treasury. Additionally, the Board[76] has the ability to exempt or modify the requirements for capital reserves that would apply under Section 19 of the Federal Reserve Act.

6.2.1.3.1 GOVERNANCE OF DCOS AND CAS

One important area of progress for the US regime is that of the rules concerning the governance fitness standards and the composition of governing bodies.[77] On 1st October 2010, the CFTC identified some areas of conflict of interest that might affect the functioning of DCOs, DCMs, or SEFs. By issuing a set of rules, the CFTC seeks to ensure that DCOs have in place and enforce rules to minimise conflicts of interest in its decision-making process and establish a process for resolving such conflicts.

To address the governance-related issues,[78] the CFTC proposed changes in structural governance requirements by imposing limits on ownership of voting equity and exercise of voting power ('Conflict of Interests NPRM').[79]

The structural governance requirements require that each DCO, DCM, or SEF must have a Board of Directors with at least 35 percent, but not less than two, public directors. Also, they must have a nominating committee with at least 51 percent public directors, and one or more disciplinary panels, with a public participant as chair. Moreover, each DCO must have a risk management

---

71 Dodd-Frank Act s 811.
72 Dodd-Frank Act s 812.
73 Dodd-Frank Act s 807, s 808. Title VIII also authorises those same organisations to conduct examinations of FMU operations and to exercise enforcement powers to compel compliance with new rules and standards.
74 Regulation HH s 234.5 sets out minimum conditions and requirements for a Federal Reserve Bank to establish and maintain an account for, and provide services to, a designated FMU.
75 Dodd-Frank Act s 806.
76 The Board adopted Regulation HH (12 CFR Part 234) to implement certain statutory provisions of Title VIII of the Dodd-Frank Wall Street Reform and Consumer Protection Act (Dodd-Frank Act).
77 CFTC, 17 CFR Parts 1, 37, 38, 39, and 40 RIN 3038 – AD01, 'Governance Requirements for Derivatives Clearing Organizations, Designated Contract Markets, and Swap Execution Facilities; Additional Requirements Regarding the Mitigation of Conflicts of Interest'. <www.cftc.gov/idc/groups/public/@lrfederalregister/documents/file/2010-31898a. pdf> accessed 1st November 2017.
78 75 FR 63732 (18 October 2010).
79 The Conflicts of Interest NPRM primarily aims to implement s 726 and s 725(d) of the Dodd-Frank Act. Along with those provisions, the CFTC seek to implement s 725(c), 10, s 735(b), 11, and s 733.

committee (RMC), with at least 35 percent public directors and 10 percent customer representatives.[80] Going beyond the mere composition of the RMCs, the rules of the CFTC require DCOs to report to the Commission when its Board of Directors rejects a recommendation from or supersedes an action of the RMC.[81] Similarly, the DCO will report to the Commission should its RMC reject a recommendation from or supersede an action of a subcommittee of the RMC.[82]

Furthermore, according to the Conflicts of Interest NPRM, no DCM or SEF member (and related persons) may beneficially own more than 20 percent of any class of voting equity, or directly or indirectly vote an interest exceeding 20 percent of the voting power of any class of equity.[83]

It was debated that independency of DCOs from market participants was central in achieving the regulatory objective of incentivising the use of central clearing in the swaps market. The tendency of market participants to exert some influence over the DCO, seeking to minimise the number of swaps subject to central clearing, underlines the importance of guaranteeing that the governance and control of the DCO is free from any external influence.

Likewise, rules to manage conflict of interest should include a framework that allows DCOs to determine whether a product is capable of being cleared, the minimum criteria that an entity must meet in order to become and remain a clearing member, and whether a particular entity satisfies such criteria.[84]

Both sets of rules – structural governance and Conflict of Interests NPRM – are designed following the parameters of the Governance NPRM, incorporating certain elements of the Proposal for a Regulation of the European Parliament and of the Council on OTC Derivatives, Central Counterparties, and Trade Depositories, and the Recommendations for Central Counterparties, drafted by the Committee on Payment and Settlement Systems of the Bank for International Settlements and the Technical Committee of the International Organisation of Securities Commissions of November 2004 (the 'CCP Recommendations').

The CFTC's Regulatory Program for Governance NPRM establishes that DCOs must maintain and enforce a set of procedures to ensure the adequate management of actual and potential conflict of interests. Therefore, DCOs are required to identify and review existing and potential conflicts of interests, as well as make fair decisions in the event such conflicts occur. One important element of this system of assessment of conflict of interest is that it incorporates a typical element of risk-based regimes – the early identification of circumstances that might represent the concretion of a specific risk (in this case, a conflict-of-interest

---

80 See generally 75 FR 63732 (18 October 2010).
81 CFTC, 17 CFR Parts 1, 37, 38, 39, and 40 RIN 3038 – AD01, 'Governance Requirements for Derivatives Clearing Organizations, Designated Contract Markets, and Swap Execution Facilities; Additional Requirements Regarding the Mitigation of Conflicts of Interest' <www.cftc.gov/idc/groups/public/@lrfederalregister/documents/file/2010-31898a. pdf.> accessed 1st November 2017 (hereinafter CFTC, 17 CFR Parts 1, 37, 38, 39, and 40).
82 Ibid.
83 Ibid.
84 Ibid.

event). Moreover, the identification of such risks is not restricted to the primary stages of DCOs' activity. It also attempts to assess the risk on an ongoing basis, recognising that the proliferation of new events of conflict of interests might change as the swap market evolves and that regulators are not always able to foresee all of them. Thus, DCOs are required to design and enforce a regulatory programme to monitor these events as they occur and they are allowed to hire this service from third parties.

One primary concern is the level of transparency governance arrangements must have.[85] It is contested whether regulators, market participants, and the public should learn of decisions that have systemic importance (for instance, the determination of whether a specific type of swap is capable of being cleared). Similarly discussed[86] is the importance of identifying the governing bodies responsible for making such decisions, in particular, the role and internal process of RMCs. The CFTC rules impose upon DCOs the duty to disclose certain information and some decisions deemed relevant to the public and regulators, and to ensure such information is clear, complete, accessible, and accurate. However, attending to the nature of clearing services, DCOs are autonomous in their decision to disclose 'non-public information'.[87]

Besides the transparency requirements, DCOs shall establish and enforce appropriate fitness standards[88] for directors, members of disciplinary committees, clearing members, and any other individual with direct or indirect access to the clearing services. The enforcement of these standards is reinforced by the role assigned to DCOs, as they are required to include, as one of membership requirements, the mandate to their members to agree to become subject to the jurisdiction of the DCO and, as such, comply with fitness standards. Like the UK regime, the US regulation relies on the role DCOs should play in imposing market discipline as self-regulatory entities.

Similar to the CFTC government standards for DCOs, the SEC has worked towards implementing enhanced standards for the operation and governance of those CAs[89] registered with the Commission.[90] Among other areas related to prudential standards, CAs registered with the SEC must ensure 'the rules of the

---

85 S 725(c) of the DFA.

86 See, e.g. comments from Jason Kastner, Vice Chairman, International Swaps and Derivatives Markets Association, CFTC Roundtable Tr at 74–75 <www.gpo.gov/fdsys/pkg/FR-2011-01-06/pdf/2010-31898.pdf> accessed 20th December 2017.

87 'The Governance NPRM proposes to define "non-public information" as any information that the DCO, DCM, or SEF owns or any information that such entity otherwise deems confidential, such as intellectual property belonging to (A) such registered entity or (B) a third party, which property such registered entity receives on a confidential basis'. CFTC, 17 CFR Parts 1, 37, 38, 39, and 40 Ibid (n80).

88 S 735(b) of the DFA.

89 S 17A(b)(3) provides that a clearing agency shall not be registered unless the Commission determines that the clearing agency's rules are consistent with the Exchange Act.

90 Securities and Exchange Commission, 17 CFR Part 240 [Release No 34–78961; File No S7–03–14] RIN 3235-AL48 'Standards for Covered Clearing Agencies' www.sec.gov/rules/final/2016/34-78961.pdf accessed 5th November 2017 (hereinafter SEC 17 CFR Part 240).

clearing agency assure a fair representation of its members and participants in the selection of its directors and administration of its affairs'.[91]

The SEC primarily conducts the enforcement of statutory requirements, using on-site inspections.[92] Such examinations allow the assessment of existing/ emerging risks and level of compliance. These rules also facilitate the evaluation of a CA's oversight of participants' compliance.[93] This part of the supervisory task reaffirms the role that CCPs have in imposing market discipline and their key contribution to the effective supervision of the market in which they operate. Regulators, in this case the SEC, rely upon the control CCPs might have over their members. The cooperation of CCPs might lower the burden of supervision and could help to reduce the number of resources destined to oversee and enforce regulation.

In 2012, the SEC issued Rule 17Ad-22 to strengthen the supervision of CAs.[94] The rule aimed to promote the safe and reliable operation of CAs and improve transparency and access to these entities. To further develop the implementation of the relevant provisions of Title VIII of the DFA, the SEC issued Rule 17Ad-22(b) to establish certain requirements for CAs that provide CCP services and Rule 17Ad-22(d) to introduce requirements for the operation and governance of CAs.

6.2.1.3.2 OPERATIONAL RISK

In a similar trend to that of the Bank in the UK and the guidance of the PFMIs, one of the regulatory priorities of UK regulators is to strengthen the supervision of different sources of operational risk, e.g. cyber risk. To contribute to the soundness of the US technology financial infrastructure, the SEC adopted Regulation Systems Compliance and Integrity ('Regulation SCI').[95] The objective of Regulation SCI[96] is to set policies and procedures to ensure that certain systems have adequate levels of capacity, integrity, resiliency, and security to maintain their operations without any disruption. SCI systems regarded as 'critical'[97] are subject to heightened requirements. Those systems include services that are central to the operation of markets and cannot be interrupted at any time.

6.2.2 The proposed reform

Surprisingly, breaking with its trend towards financial de-regulation,[98] the Trump administration has anticipated the need to heighten regulation for clearing

---

91 15 USC 78q-1(b)(3)(A), (C), (D), (F).
92 S 21(a) of the Exchange Act.
93 SEC 17 CFR Part 240, Ibid (n89)
94 CCA Standards proposing release, supra note 5, at 29513.
95 Exchange Act Release No 34–73639 (19 November 2014); 79 FR 72252 (5 December 2014) ('Regulation SCI') adopting release.
96 17 CFR 242 1001.
97 17 CFR 242 1000 (providing definitions of 'SCI systems' and 'critical SCI systems').
98 'The new administration's goal is to reduce the financial burden on banks by repealing and reducing various provisions of the Dodd-Frank Act and replacing them with new policies

houses[99] and the call to limit the scope of clearing.[100] The US Treasury report highlighted that, given the systemic importance of clearing houses, it is necessary to increase their regulatory and supervisory scrutiny.[101] The focus seems to be on reconciling the differences with the European Regime for CCPs.

In particular, the Treasury highlights the need to put in place a central clearing regime with 'tailored and targeted capital requirements'.[102] Accordingly, regulators are expected to deduct the initial margin for centrally cleared derivatives from the SRL denominator and to adjust capital rules to reflect the exposure more accurately. In line with the issue studied in Chapter 5, discussing innovation risk and the interactions between central clearing rules and banking capital requirements, the Treasury also recommends the move from CEM to an adjusted SA-CCR as a calculation variable of initial margin. Moreover, it invites regulators to seek a coherent assessment concerning the interaction between capital and liquidity rules and the incentives to use central clearing in the derivatives market.

The proposed changes are likely to reflect the well-established discussion related to the use of central clearing as a method to enhance stability, and better risk management in the derivatives market. They also emphasise the importance of ensuring the intended move towards central clearing is not being affected by incoming regulation applicable to some clearing members, i.e. capital and liquidity requirements for the banking sector. Moreover, the call for a more stringent regulation for clearing houses brings to the forefront the concern about the systemic importance of these entities and the concomitant need to ensure they are sufficiently stable and resilient.

Although illustrative about the approach US regulation will take, the Treasury report leaves several areas uncovered – for instance, the completion of an insolvency regime not solely focused on recovery, but also involving a bulletproof

---

to encourage growth and job creation. Congressional Republicans have similarly suggested repealing or significantly changing the Dodd-Frank Act as well as modifying the structure and authorities of the Consumer Financial Protection Bureau (CFPB or Bureau), the Office of the Comptroller of the Currency (OCC), and the National Credit Union Administration (NCUA); delaying or eliminating altogether the Department of Labor's Fiduciary Rule; repealing the Volcker Rule; and exempting certain banking organizations from Basel capital requirements and/or the Enhanced Prudential Standards'. KPMG, 'Ten Key Regulatory Challenges Facing the Financial Services Industry in 2017' Americas FS Regulatory Center Of Excellence (2017) <https://assets.kpmg.com/content/dam/kpmg/sg/pdf/2017/02/Ten-key-regulatory-challenges-facing-the-financial-services-industry.pdf> accessed 23rd October 2017.

 99 Barney Jopson, and Joe Rennison, 'Trump Administration Calls for Heightened Regulation of Clearing' *Financial Times* (6 October 2017).

100 Gary Cohn, President Donald Trump's chief economic adviser, about the role of clearing houses asserts: 'Like every great modern invention, it has its limits, and I think we have expanded the limits of clearing probably further beyond their useful existence', Jeanna Smialek, 'Gary Cohn Calls Clearinghouses a "New Systemic Problem"' Bloomberg (15 October 2017) <www.bloomberg.com/news/articles/2017-10-15/white-house-s-cohn-calls-clearinghouses-a-new-systemic-problem> accessed 17th October 2017.

101 US Treasury Report to President Trump (September 2017) (n50)

102 Ibid 138.

strategy to manage the insolvency of clearing houses. Also (similar to the UK regime), the regulation and supervision of conduct of business issues affecting the relationship between clearing houses and clearing members seems to be perceived as a secondary area of concern. Despite such similarities between the UK and the US approaches, the most prominent justification seems to be that both regimes are following the regulatory patterns set by international standard-setting organisations, i.e. IOSCO, CPMI, and so forth. Those patterns are undoubtedly centred on ensuring the stability and resilience of CCPs, and to incentivise the move towards central clearing in the OTC derivatives market.

6.2.3 Regulatory agencies for CCPs in the US

The Federal Reserve, as supervisor and regulator of certain financial institutions, is the primary federal banking regulator for several payment, clearing, and settlement systems.

The Commodity Futures Trading Commission is the primary regulator of DCOs, which are clearing houses for futures contracts, options on futures contracts, and swaps. To be registered or maintain registration as a DCO, a clearing house must comply with the CFTC's Core Principles as established in the CEA. Recently, the DFA amended the CEA to re-adopt and amend 14 existing core principles and add four new ones.

The Securities and Exchange Commission is the primary regulator of securities clearing agencies (e.g. CCPs, securities settlement systems, and central securities depositories). The SEC's Standards for the Registration of Clearing Agencies are a set of guidelines that the SEC applies in considering whether to grant or deny registration of a clearing agency. The Standards also serve as guidance to assist clearing agencies in assessing whether their organisations, capacities, and rules comply with the clearing agency registration provisions of the Securities Exchange Act 1934 (SEA).

Title VII of the DFA broadens the authority of the CFTC and the SEC when including a mandate for the central clearing of standardised swaps. To assist the oversight of the financial system, the DFA established the FSOC.[103] Its main task is to identify emerging risk to financial stability across the system; regarding payment, clearing or settlement services, the FSOC is bestowed with the power to identify and designate an FMU. Such a designation allows the appropriate

---

103 The FSOC comprises ten voting members: the treasury secretary (who serves as chairperson of the FSOC); the chairman of the Federal Reserve Board; the heads of the Consumer Financial Protection Bureau (CFPB), Office of the Comptroller of the Currency, SEC, Federal Deposit Insurance Corporation (FDIC), CFTC, Federal Housing Finance Agency (FHFA), and National Credit Union Administration (NCUA); and an independent member with insurance expertise appointed by the president and confirmed by the US Senate. The FSOC also includes five non-voting members who serve in an advisory capacity: the directors of the Treasury Department's Office of Financial Research and the Federal Insurance Office, a state insurance commissioner, a state banking supervisor, and a state securities commissioner.

supervisory agency – the CFTC or the SEC, and sometimes the Board – to impose enhanced risk management standards. However, the function conferred to the FSOC by the DFA is likely to be removed by the Financial Choice Act.[104] Congressional Republicans have anticipated the withdrawal of the FSOC authority to designate non-bank SIFIs; this would remove the role that the Board currently has over FMUs.

6.3 Improvements to the risk-based approach to regulation of CCPs in the US regime

Despite the fact that DFA expands government oversight of the financial system by broadening parties and the subjects of regulation,[105] its implementation has revealed several serious shortcomings related to regulatory structure and approach to regulation. Like the UK regime, the DFA fails to efficiently respond to future market innovations and deliberately targets certain groups,[106] leaving some other business entities out of the scope of the regulation. Recognising the potential implications of such flaws of the DFA, the implementation of a more functional approach to financial regulation has been proposed.[107] Such an approach 'acknowledges the limits of legislation and leaves discretion to administrative bodies and the courts to identify specific abusive acts'.[108] The gap of such an approach is, however, that a functional regulation might be extremely broad, resulting in a lack of clarity that triggers what is known as 'rulemaking by enforcement',[109] where the rules end up being defined in litigation, instead of in analysis or public and open debate.

Building on this idea, it is advisable to propose the use of risk-based approach to regulation, as an effective strategy that allows the integration of the multiple and evolving perspectives of risk. In this context, the benefits of adopting a risk-based regime are the recognition of the limits regulators face when designing and implementing regulation, and the concomitant need to integrate regulated firms' perspective of risk. As we saw in Chapter 2, risk-based regimes facilitate the inclusion of regulators, supervisors, and regulated firms' notions of risk, as well

104 KPMG, 'Ten Key Regulatory Challenges Facing the Financial Services Industry in 2017' *Americas FS Regulatory Center of Excellence* (2017) (n97).
105 Larissa Smith, and Victor M Muñiz-Fracticelli, 'Strategic Shortcomings of the Dodd-Frank Act' (Winter 2013) 58 (4) *The Antitrust Bulletin*.
106 The Dodd-Frank Act standards apply to five different categories of financial institutions: large bank holding companies, large foreign banking organisations, intermediate holding companies, systemically important non-bank financial institutions, and financial market utilities.
107 Larissa Smith, and Victor M Muñiz-Fracticelli, 'Strategic Shortcomings of the Dodd-Frank Act' (n104).
108 Ibid.
109 Paula S. Greenman, Anthony Mechcatie, and John W. Osborn, 'Derivatives Under Dodd-Frank' *Sakdden* (7 August 2015) <https://files.skadden.com/newsletters%2FFSR_A_Regulation_of_Over-the-Counter_Derivatives.pdf> accessed 12th December 2017.

as the early identification of potential sources of new unforeseen risk and some types of uncertainties.

A preliminary consideration must be that supervision is broadly focused on enhancing the regulatory tools to prevent the realisation of systemic risk. An effective supervisory programme facilitates the identification and assessment of the most prominent types of risks and risk profiles of regulated firms. The risk-based approach to regulation enables supervisors to evaluate their objectives against the threat certain firms and types of risks may pose. Hence, the three authorities must design a sufficiently comprehensive risk management framework.

We would argue in favour of a risk-based approach to regulation based on principles, solving the critiques to the DFA regulation of derivatives and central clearing, notions that in the context of our argument reflect the nature of the OTCDM and its regulation as a hub of manufactured risks. The adoption of a complete risk-based approach will also help to recognise that regulators face an inherent impossibility in measuring all the risks arising from the functioning of the OTCDM, because contemporary derivatives trading cannot be fully under stood by quantifiable knowledge.[110] Among the criticisms of the DFA rules on derivatives and central clearing are the regulatory infeasibility,[111] and the related incapability of the multiple regulatory agencies to implement the required regulatory oversight. Also, the unintended consequences of the DFA reflected firstly on the creation of 'too-big-and-too-interconnected-to- fail'[112] institutions, i.e. CCPs, and secondly, the unforeseen effects of collateral requirements.[113]

6.4 Shortcomings of the US regime for CCPs

6.4.1 US regulation fails to respond to future innovations

The US regime's first shortcoming is that it is responsive to past market innovations, without being sensitive to future innovations. Similar considerations to those included in the study of the UK regime seem to be relevant in the context of the US, in terms of addressing the innovation risk. We will now explore the impact of FinTech and, in particular, DLT in the role of CCPs in the OTCDM, as well as how the DFA fails to address the potential disruption coming from such a foreseeable scenario. We will see how the US regime for CCPs, like the UK's, is affected by the undesirable consequences of collateral transformation.

110 Craig Pirrong, 'The Clearinghouse Cure' (2009) 44 *Regulation*, 45.
111 Dan Awrey, 'The Dynamics of OTC Derivatives Regulation: Bridging the Public-Private Divide' (2010) 11 *European Business Organization Law Review*, 155, 185–87. Also see Kristin Johnson, 'Things Fall Apart: Regulating the Credit Default Swap Commons' (2011) 82 *University of Colorado Law Review*, 167, 239–42.
112 Darrell Duffie, and Haoxiang Zhu, 'Does a Central Clearing Counterparty Reduce Counterparty Risk?' (2011) 1 *Review of Asset Pricing Studies*, 74; Craig Pirrong, 'The Economics of Central Clearing: Theory and Practice' ISDA Discussion Paper Series, No 1 (2011), 4.
113 See discussion on collateral transformation in Chapter 5.

6.4.1.1 *The disruptive role of FinTech and DLT*
in central clearing services

The year 2016 can be identified as the year in which FinTech[114] occupied the debate in financial regulation. Regulators around the world have been especially focused on identifying the potential revolutionary effects it might have for financial markets' functioning and structure. The other post-GFC regulatory reforms are not embedded with innovations, and so it is the DFA which has brought FinTech to the forefront recently.

In this section, we will examine the roles that FinTech and DLT, in particular, play in central clearing services, as well as discover that the DFA is insufficient to tackle such innovative developments. We shall see that although there have been few regulatory developments in some states (e.g. the incorporation of blockchain rules in Delaware's company law), the US regime needs to implement a risk-based approach to regulation based on principles to design an effective FinTech regime.

Before going through the specifics of blockchain regulations in the US, it is first important to agree on a simple definition of blockchain. Blockchain entails an algorithm encoding information, allowing amendments of a historical record (called the 'chain'), by means of subsequent transactions (known as 'blocks'), almost eliminating the possibility of altering such information.[115] Distributed ledgers achieve high-level security, as each ledger keeps copies of a record on computers of all system participants. Any differences in the information held by individuals and the system are reconciled and corrected in the system's units' processor power.[116] Blockchains are built up on the basis of three fairness advantages: 1) they use a de-centralised system, and as such individuals' locations are completely irrelevant; 2) this decentralisation facilitates a high level of cyber security; and 3) the system is operated by a 'fair consensus which makes all participants equally responsible and equally capable'.[117] Blockchains can be either

---

114 'Financial technology, commonly called "fintech", is now a highly used buzzword. Startups competing with traditional financial services, offering customer-centric services capable of combining speed and flexibility, are spreading throughout the world'. Bernardo Nicoletti, 'The Future of Fintech: Integrating Finance and Technology in Financial Services' (Palgrave Studies in Financial Services Technology 2017), 1.

115 Joanna Diane Caytas, 'Blockchain in the US Regulatory Setting: Evidentiary Use in Vermont, Delaware, and Elsewhere' The Columbia Science and Technology Review (30 May 2017) <http://stlr.org/2017/05/30/blockchain-in-the-u-s-regulatory-setting-evidentiary-use-in-vermont-delaware-and-elsewhere/> accessed 23rd October 2017.

116 David Yermack, 'Corporate Governance and Blockchains' Harvard Business Review (6 January 2016) <https://corpgov.law.harvard.edu/2016/01/06/corporate-governance-and-blockchains/> accessed 23rd October 2017.

117 World Government Summit, 'Building the Hyperconnected Future of Blockchains' The Internet of Agreements by Hexayurt Capital (February 2017) 6 <http://internetofagreements.com/files/WorldGovernmentSummit-Dubai2017.pdf> accessed 23rd October 2017.

public or private,[118] depending on whether government or private individuals administer and control the system.

The use of blockchain technology has grown swiftly during the past ten years[119] and, at the moment, almost every large financial institution is conducting research on how such technology could affect the services they provide.[120] The OTCDM and its central clearing services are no exception; the ISDA has led the discussion about the role of smart contracts in the context of OTC derivatives.[121]

The role of the distributed ledger in the negotiation of financial derivatives is mainly associated with the better management of operational deficiencies and reduction of transactional costs.[122] The use of 'smart contracts' in the derivatives market does not equate to the concept of a legal contract, which would be defined according to the applicable law, but in short, it comprehends any agreement between two or more parties generating rights and obligations to either one or all parties involved. The concept of smart contract, however, requires the existence of a legal contract, but with some element of such a contract being electronically automated. Moreover, the contract is regarded as a smart one[123] when some contractual terms are automatic and self-executed in accordance to pre-existing conditions.[124]

The ISDA has developed a programme that seeks to identify the benefits Fin-Tech might bring to derivatives trading and post-trading. The industry-led initiative aims at reducing cost and complexity, as well as at increasing efficiency. The new proposal is the implementation of the ISDA Common Domain Model (CDM).[125] The CDM is designed to systematise and streamline representation of data, events, and actions that occur during the life of any derivative transaction. The aim is to simplify and make less costly each stage of derivatives trade and post-trade; in so doing, the CDM will harmonise processes between regulated firms and platforms. In particular, it will provide a framework to facilitate the use of DLT and smart contracts across market actors and international markets.

The benefits of adopting the CDM are related to a high aspiration of reaching efficient interoperability among execution and post-trade management of

---

118 See David Lee Kuo Chuen, and Robert H. Deng, *Handbook of Blockchain, Digital Finance, and Inclusion: Cryptocurrency, FinTech, InsurTech, Regulation, ChinaTech, Mobile Security, and Distributed Ledger* (Academic Press 2017).

119 Vinay Gupta, 'A Brief History of Blockchain' *Harvard Business Review* (28 February 2017) <https://hbr.org/2017/02/a-brief-history-of-blockchain> accessed 23rd October 2017.

120 Lucinda Shen, 'Blockchain Will Be Used By 15% of Big Banks By 2017', 28 September 2016 <http://fortune.com/2016/09/28/blockchain-banks-2017/> accessed 23rd October 2017.

121 ISDA and Linklaters, Whitepaper, Smart Contracts and Distributed Ledger – A Legal Perspective (August 2017) 3 (hereinafter, ISDA & Linklaters, Whitepaper, SC and DL)

122 Ibid 5.

123 'At its core, intelligence can be viewed as a process that converts unstructured information into useful and actionable knowledge', Demis Hassabis, 'The mind in the machine: Demis Hassabis on artificial intelligence' *Financial Times* (22 April 2017).

124 ISDA & Linklaters, Whitepaper, SC and DL (n130)

125 ISDA Common Domain Model Version 1.0 Design Definition Document (October 2017).

Figure 6.2 Opportunities for interoperability (of Central Counterparties)[126]

derivatives transactions. The following graph illustrates the opportunities of such interoperability.

The adoption of blockchain and DLT across capital markets and in the OTCDM, however, faces several challenges.[127] The issues associated with operational risk are at the core of this new technology. The technical difficulties and higher costs of implementing DLT, as well as the cyber risk and the potential for fraudulent use of the system to facilitate money laundering, could jeopardise the disruptive[128] effect blockchain and DLT seek to have in the financial sector.

126 For a more detailed graphic, see ISDA, Whitepaper: The Future of Derivatives Processing and Market Infrastructure (September 2016).

127 Angelos Delivorias, Briefing: 'Distributed Ledger Technology and Financial Markets, PE 593.565 EN, European Parliamentary Research Service' (November 2016) <www. europarl.europa.eu/RegData/etudes/BRIE/2016/593565/EPRS_BRI(2016)593565_ EN.pdf> accessed 23rd October 2017.

128 ' "Disruption" describes a process whereby a smaller company with fewer resources is able to successfully challenge established incumbent businesses', Clayton Christensen, and Michael Raynor, and Rory McDonald, 'What is Disruptive Innovation?' *Harvard Business*

The concept of DLT has evolved to include the emerging applications[129] of the technology. The CPMI understands that 'DLT refers to the processes and related technologies that enable nodes[130] in a network (or arrangement) to securely propose, validate and record state changes (or updates) to a synchronized ledger that is distributed across the network's nodes'.[131]

Moreover, the fact that one of the principles backing the progress of blockchain is open access to any individual interested in trading certainly contradicts the parameters surrounding the rationale of central clearing in the OTCDM. Despite the principle of democratic access to central clearing found in the US and UK regimes, it is true that the implementation of central clearing mandate has revealed that only certain financial institutions, in the position to comply with membership requirements, have actual access to CCPs. Indeed, the process to broaden clearing services to their clients, known as indirect or client clearing, is still a controlled form of access. In other words, the use of central clearing is restricted only to those that are considered sufficiently stable and sound (and under certain conditions the benefits of central clearing are being extended to their clients). However, in our view, it is unrealistic to think that the implementation of DLT as a system replacing current CCPs will uncontestably allow any individual to get access to central clearing services – especially since DLT developers are already working on designing technology that limits access to the data recorded and how to grant access to certain market participants, regulators, and supervisors.[132]

Open or restricted access to a DLT providing clearing services would necessarily go beyond traditional concerns about cyber security. At the basic level, the need to restrict access to a DLT is justified, due to information security issues and scalability when access is granted to a large number of participants. However, when the discussion is brought to clearing services, we should consider the effects open or limited access might have for the stability of the clearing services. As explained earlier, CCPs are willing to comply with central clearing mandates and to clear those transactions that regulators determine need central clearing, understanding that such a determination would not pose excessive risks to the stability

---

Review (December 2015) <https://hbr.org/2015/12/what-is-disruptive-innovation> accessed 29th October 2017.

129 Initially DLT was conceived as a system to allow the production of cryptocurrencies, such as Bitcoin. However, other parts of the financial market are researching new forms of adopting the technology across capital markets. The CPMI reports among others the use of DLT on 'platforms that could be programmed to store and manage records, and transfer any digital asset, instrument or information on a shared ledger', CPMI, 'Distributed Ledger Technology in Payment, Clearing and Settlement: An Analytical Framework' (February 2017) 3 <www.bis.org/cpmi/publ/d157.pdf> accessed 25th October 2017.

130 In computer science, a node is the basic computing unit of a network.

131 CPMI, 'Distributed Ledger Technology in Payment, Clearing and Settlement: An Analytical Framework' (February 2017) (n138).

132 Andrea Pinna, and Wiebe Ruttenberg, 'Distributed Ledger Technologies in Securities Post-Trading: Revolution or Evolution?' European Central Bank – Occasional Paper Series No 172 (April 2016).

and functioning of the CCP itself. In other words, when regulators decide which transaction should be subject of central clearing, they should be careful not to put extra pressure on CCPs, for instance by making them insufficiently liquid products.

In particular, the adoption of distributed ledger and blockchain technologies in the services traditionally provided by FMIs (i.e. payment, settlement, and clearing) reflects how FMIs are entrusted by their participants with upgrading and preserving the integrity of a central ledger and, in the particular case of CCPs, managing certain risks on behalf of participants.[133] Indeed, the role of a DLT in the context of FMIs is that it would allow such entities to carry out their transactions with no need to rely on a unique and centralised ledger.[134] The CPMI must continuously attempt to find the balance between the adoption of new technology and maintaining the safety and soundness of FMIs.

Usually, the benefits predicable of the use of DLT in capital markets are associated with simplification of processes, improving information flows, reducing operational costs, increasing efficiency, and reducing fraud.[135] It has been argued that the adoption of DLT could result in more efficient post-trade process,[136] as many of the shortcomings affecting post-trade markets could be overcome in this way. A DLT would allow competing financial institutions to share information about assets holdings and keep track of the execution, clearing, and settlement of securities transactions, without the need to be involved in a central database management system. The success of DLT will depend, however, on two areas: the level of standardisation in the different types of technology and whether market participants are subject to similar conduct of business rules and governance arrangements.[137] The introduction of different types of DLTs, such as smart contracts, is still in the early stages and responds more to a process of evolution than a revolution of the mainstream post-trade markets.[138] The predominant line of thought[139] considers that certain post-trade functions that are heavily regulated (e.g. clearing) will remain carried out by institutions. Moreover, there are some concerns associated with lack of interoperability arrangements between proprietary databases. As a result, every entity is controlling its own databases that are not automatically updated with the information recorded by the counterparties.

133 CPMI, 'Distributed Ledger Technology in Payment, Clearing and Settlement: An Analytical Framework' (February 2017).
134 Ibid.
135 UK Government Office for Science, Distributed Ledger Technology: Beyond Block Chain, December 2015 <www.gov.uk/government/uploads/system/uploads/attachment_data/file/492972/gs-16-1-distributed-ledger-technology.pdf> accessed 25th October 2017.
136 Andrea Pinna, and Wiebe Ruttenberg, 'Distributed Ledger Technologies in Securities Post-Trading: Revolution or Evolution?' European Central Bank – Occasional Paper Series No 172 (April 2016), 3.
137 Ibid 4.
138 Ibid 4.
139 Ibid 3.

The related operational issues increase operational risks and prevent the efficient use of collateral.[140]

DLT have the potential to allow both trading and settlement to take place instantaneously. This is possible when multiple trading platforms are connected to an integrated DLT system, which unfortunately is not feasible with the current separated databases. If implemented the instant settlement would directly affect the role of clearing for cash transactions. Liquidity and credit risk would be eliminated, as any trade would be executed immediately. In contrast, if the execution of the trade happened at a later stage, as with derivatives contracts, clearing would still be required to hedge the risk until the execution takes place. In this context, smart contracts might facilitate the netting, and when collateral management systems are affiliated to the same DLT, also margin calls. The relevance of DLT will therefore depend on the extent such technology is implemented and the role that regulators give to smart contracts in the clearing process.

Furthermore, smart contracts can also have a central function when clearing is necessary before settlement, because it could change the way netting and collateral are managed.[141] Smart contracts would allow CCPs to make automatic margin calls to its clearing members.

The rationale behind faster processing of transactions is that more transactions would occur in real time or nearly real time in certain markets. As a result, the use of DLTs might affect credit and liquidity needs associated with clearing activity.[142] The increased speed of trading would reduce credit exposures, placing higher demand on liquidity.[143] The impact of these changes will depend upon the type of DLT arrangement and the associated behavioural changes it might induce[144] in clearing services. Therefore, the design of such DLT arrangements might better achieve its effectiveness objective by integrating one of the central elements of risk-based regulation: the integration of the different perspectives of risk held by market participants, DLT providers, regulators, and supervisors.

6.4.1.1.1 THE STATUS QUO OF THE US REGULATION OF FINTECH

Although there is an increasing interest of federal agencies[145] and the Office of Financial Research (OFR) carries out studies on innovation risks,[146] the US

---

140 Ibid 6.
141 Ibid.
142 CPMI, 'Distributed Ledger Technology in Payment, Clearing and Settlement: An Analytical Framework' (February 2017), 13.
143 Ibid.
144 Ibid.
145 Notice of Filing of Proposed Rule Change, 81 Fed Reg 45, 554 (14 July 2016) 'FTC Announces Agenda for March 9 FinTech Forum on Artificial Intelligence and Blockchain Technology' *Fed Trade Commission* (27 February 2017) <www.ftc.gov/news-events/press-releases/2017/02/ftc-announces-agenda-march-9-fintech-forum-artificial> accessed 23rd October 2017.
146 Douglas D. Evanoff, and others, Achieving Financial Stability: Challenges to Prudential Regulation 61 (World Scientific Studies in International Economics) (World Scientific Publishing Company 2017), 244.

federal government has not exercised its power to regulate blockchain.[147] However, some states have important developments and attempts to regulate it.[148] The pioneers, at the time of writing, are Arizona,[149] California,[150] Delaware,[151] Hawaii,[152] Illinois,[153] Maine,[154] Nevada,[155] Vermont,[156] and (though not with state-wide legislation) New York.[157] The progress for blockchain regulation and implementation in the US began in Arizona with the recognition of smart contracts, Vermont in accepting blockchain as evidence in judiciary proceedings, Chicago in implementing real estate records, and most recently Delaware, with authorising share registration of Delaware companies in blockchain form.[158]

In January 2017, J. Christopher Giancarlo, the CFTC commissioner, called the commission to be more focused on the future of the derivatives market, the role of the DLT, and the importance of enhancing cyber security.[159] It is expected that the 'do-no-harm' CFTC's approach will follow the five elements outlined by Giancarlo. The first element is a system of cooperation between regulators and FinTech companies to address the issues of the current regulatory framework. Then, emulating the UK's approach, the second element is to create an

---

147 There have been some unsuccessful attempts in blockchain regulation, e.g. Congress held altogether seven hearings involving blockchain and digital currencies – all between 2013 and 2017. One federal bill on blockchain, regarding virtual currencies, was proposed: on 1st December 2014 and 2nd January 2015, Congressman Steve Stockman (R-TX) proposed, within a month of each other, two virtually identical bills, the Cryptocurrency Protocol Protection and Moratorium Act [22] and the Online Market Protection Act 2014. Another federal legislative attempt mentioning blockchain was a Congressional Resolution proposed 14th July 2016 HR Res 835, 114th Cong (2016).

148 Joanna Diane Caytas, 'Blockchain in the US Regulatory Setting: Evidentiary Use in Vermont, Delaware, and Elsewhere' *The Columbia Science and Technology Review* (30 May 2017).

149 HR 2417, 53d Leg, 1st Reg Sess (Ariz 2017), 2017 Ariz Sess Laws 97 (amending Ariz Rev Stat s 44–7003; adding Ariz Rev Stat s 44–7061).

150 AB 1326, Gen Assemb, 2015–2016 Reg Sess (Ca 2015).

151 Delaware Office of the Governor, 'Governor Markell Launches Delaware Blockchain Initiative' PR Newswire (2 May 2016) <www.prnewswire.com/news-releases/governor-markell-launches-delaware-blockchain-initiative-300260672.html> accessed 23rd October 2017.

152 HR 1481, 29th Leg, Reg Sess (Haw 2017).

153 HRJ Res 25, 100th Gen Assemb, Reg Sess (Ill 2017) (creating the Illinois Legislative Blockchain and Distributed Ledger Task Force).

154 SP 305, 128th Leg, 1st Reg Sess (Me 2017).

155 SB 398, 79th Leg Sess (Nev 2017).

156 S 138, 2015–2106 Leg Sess (Vt 2015), 2016 Vt Acts & Resolves No 51.

157 NY Comp Codes Rules and Regs Title 23 s 200.1 et seq, <www.dfs.ny.gov/legal/regula tions/adoptions/dfsp200t.pdf> Last consulted 23rd October 2017.

158 Andrea Tinianow, 'Delaware Blockchain Initiative: Transforming the Foundational Infrastructure of Corporate Finance' *Harvard Law School Forum on Corporate Governance and Financial Regulation* (16 March 2017) <https://corpgov.law.harvard.edu/2017/03/16/delaware-blockchain-initiative-transforming-the-foundational-infrastructure-of-corporate-finance/> accessed 23rd October 2017.

159 Keynote Address of CFTC Commissioner J. Christopher Giancarlo Before SEFCON VII. January 18, 2017 <www.cftc.gov/PressRoom/SpeechesTestimony/opagiancarlo-19> accessed 20th December 2017.

environment[160] to incentivise innovation by understanding FinTech developments. The third element is to develop a regulatory understanding of such innovations. Once there is a common and fluid dialogue, regulators are expected to determine how current rules should be adapted to new technologies and business models. The final element is to implement a global collaboration to avoid the issues associated with regulatory fragmentation at the international level.[161]

During 2016 the CFTC's commissioner recognised the importance FinTech and DLT might have in derivatives market.[162] He stated that DLT has the potential to 'develop hand-in-hand with smart derivatives that can value themselves in real-time, report themselves to data repositories, automatically calculate and perform margin payments, and even terminate themselves in the event of a counterparty default'. Moreover, in its 2017 report, the FSOC glimpses some of the systemic implications that FinTech and DLT might bring to the supervision of certain markets.[163] The FSOC Report noted that such technology developments could lead to issues related to the information stored across distributed networks rather than one centralised hub. Therefore, there is an urgent need to ensure continuous monitoring and coordination in the implementation of new technologies.[164]

As they started to implement these reforms in May 2017, the CFTC revealed a new FinTech initiative – the CFTC 2.0 – and launched 'LabCFTC' as a hub to better connect FinTech firms and financial regulators. On 17th October 2017, the CFTC issued a 'Premier on Virtual Currencies'[165] to explain virtual currencies, DLT, and the potential future uses of these innovations. The Premier also addressed the supervisory roles of the CFTC and the SEC regarding initial coin offerings (ICOs)[166] and virtual tokens. There is, however, a clear inconsistency between the SEC's analysis on ICOs and the CFTC's determination that, whilst

---

160 The FCA's FinTech Hub <www.fca.org.uk/firms/fca-innovate> accessed 20th December 2017.

161 Address of CFTC Commissioner J Christopher Giancarlo to the American Enterprise Institute, '21st Century Markets Need 21st Century Regulation', 21 September 2016 <www.cftc.gov/PressRoom/SpeechesTestimony/opagiancarlo>17 accessed 20th December 2017.

162 Keynote Address of Commissioner J Christopher Giancarlo before the Markit Group, 2016 Annual Customer Conference New York, Blockchain: A Regulatory Use Case (10 May 2016) <www.cftc.gov/PressRoom/SpeechesTestimony/opagiancarlo-15)> accessed 20th December 2017; Special Address of CFTC Commissioner J Christopher Giancarlo Before the Depository Trust & Clearing Corporation 2016 Blockchain Symposium (29 March 2016) <www.cftc.gov/PressRoom/SpeechesTestimony/opagiancarlo-13)> accessed 20th December 2017.

163 FSOC, 'Annual Report' (13 December 2017) <www.treasury.gov/initiatives/fsoc/studies-reports/Documents/FSOC_2017_Annual_Report.pdf> accessed 20th December 2017.

164 Ibid.

165 CFTC, 'Premier on Virtual Currencies (17 October 2017) <www.cftc.gov/idc/groups/public/documents/file/labcftc_primercurrencies100417.pdf> accessed 20th December 2017.

166 SEC, Report of Investigation Pursuant to Section 21(a) of the Securities Exchange Act of 1934: The DAO (Release No 81207, July 25, 2017) <www.sec.gov/litigation/investreport/34-81207.pdf> accessed 20th December 2017.

virtual currencies are commodities, virtual tokens may be regarded as either commodities or derivatives contracts depending on the particular circumstances.[167] Thus, the CFTC emphasises that its supervision will be guided by a substance-over-form approach.

Although the CFTC Premier noted that certain ICO activity might need to be conducted on or through a CFTC-registered market or platform (e.g. DCOs), there are several unsolved questions regarding the future regulatory enforcement of the CFTC and the SEC in the mighty momentum of the ICO market.[168]

Finally, regarding the specific case of clearing houses (at the time of writing), the latest development was the CFTC's recognition and approval of LedgerX as the first federally regulated digital currency options exchange and clearing house in the US.[169]

The foregoing regulatory developments are incipient; we still have to see how both regulators agree on an effective system to oversee and at the same time incentivise the development of technological developments in financial markets.

6.4.1.1.2 THE ROLE OF RISK-BASED REGULATION IN FINTECH

Against this background, we argue that a risk-based approach to regulation is central to the effective adoption of FinTech (e.g. DLT and smart contracts) in the OTCDM, especially in central clearing services. The implementation of FinTech is heavily reliant on enhanced operational risk and continuous assessment of security risks. Hence, a strategy, such as risk-based regulation, that features the early identification and mitigation of risks is central to the management of the unknown risks and uncertainties brought by FinTech innovations. The sound functioning of these technologies would benefit both market participants and regulators and supervisors. On the one hand, market participants would benefit from a common set of data and process standards that could operate across firms, platforms, and markets. The high-level standardisation of process would reduce post-trade costs[170] and would be time efficient. On the other hand, standardisation might assist the achieving of regulatory objectives, because it enhances transparency and access to timely information and is likely to incentivise compliance. If regulated firms find the use of FinTech and the concomitant standardisation as a simplification of trading and post-trading processes, they are motivated to comply with the respective regulation.

167 CFTC, 'Premier on Virtual Currencies (17 October 2017) (n163).
168 Nicholas Losurdo, 'CFTC Reaffirms Stance on Digital Currencies; Expresses View on DLT and ICOs' (24 October 2017) <www.goodwinlaw.com/publications/2017/10/10_24_17-cftc-reaffirms-stance-on-digital#[1]> accessed 20th December 2017.
169 CFTC, 'CFTC Grants DCO Registration to LedgerX LLC' Press Release (24 July 2017) <www.cftc.gov/PressRoom/PressReleases/pr7592-17> accessed 24th October 2017.
170 'Post-trade costs now make up a large slug in investment bank expenditure between 15% and 20% according to Boston Consulting Group' Scott D O'Malia, Welcoming Remarks, ISDA Conference 'Technology & Standards: Unlocking Value in Derivatives Markets' London (30 November 2017).

John Locke's famous maxim, 'Where there is no Law, there is no Freedom'[171] helps to explain the role that risk-based approach to regulation based on principles can have in solving the issues triggered by FinTech innovations in the OTCDM and its clearing services. In this context, the strategy of risk-based regulation would act as an enabler[172] of further technological developments. By that process, it will also incentivise regulated firms to voluntarily comply with the new regulation, as they will see that such rules are facilitating the adoption of technologies that ease their trade. Moreover, as market participants are the ones developing new technologies, regulators would be compelled to have a fluent dialogue with regulated firms and to understand their perceptions of risk (mainly operational and security risks).

The emphasis on the rule of law is particularly relevant in a time when traditional norms and financial market structures are under strain. Regulators are expected to move towards understanding FinTech developments, and to decide the role which regulation will have. This discussion puts in the forefront classic arguments about the meaning of freedom. In the context of FinTech's momentum, Hayck's definition seems to fit perfectly, freedom being: 'a state in which each can use his knowledge for his purposes'.[173] Indeed, current technology developments in financial services are focused on streamlining trading and post-trading process, and on improving transparency and access to information. FinTech innovators are using their knowledge to enhance their market activities. Therefore, financial regulators are expected to support and guide such processes, to enable innovation whilst protecting the stability of the market. A risk-based approach to regulation is sufficiently broad to do so.

6.4.1.2 Issues related to collateral transformation

Regarding the effects of the DFA in terms of collateral transformation, the US regime for CCPs, like that of the UK,[174] creates myriad challenges for managing collateral and fails to anticipate the negative impact the practice might have for systemic risk management. The implementation of Dodd-Frank swaps regulation has created the incentive for innovation. The collateral transformation is one manifestation of 'regulation-induced innovation'[175] and an unintended effect of the DFA rules of collateral CCPs shall require for clearing members.[176] We classify this practice as a source of innovation risk.

---

171 John Locke, *Two Treatises of Government* (Awnsham Churchill 1689), 234.
172 Joseph Singer, *No Freedom Without Regulation: The Hidden Lesson of the Subprime Crisis* (Yale University Press 2015).
173 Friedrich Hayek, *Law, Legislation and Liberty* (University of Chicago 1973), 142.
174 See discussion in Chapter 5.
175 Edward J. Kane, 'The Inevitability of Shadowy Banking' Presented at the Federal Reserve Bank of Atlanta 2012 Financial Markets Conference 'Financial Reform: The Devil's In the Details' Atlanta, Georgia (10 April 2012) 3 <www.frbatlanta.org/-/media/documents/news/conferences/2012/fmc/papers/kane.pdf> accessed 13th December 2017.
176 BIS, 'CGFS Papers No 49 Asset Encumbrance, Financial Reform and the Demand for Collateral Assets' <www.bis.org/publ/cgfs49.pdf> accessed 13th December 2017.

After DFA and Basel III, CCPs have been narrowing collateral requirements[177] and buy-side firms are continuously looking carefully for centralised services to manage their collateral obligations and maximise their efficiency.[178] With the move towards central clearing, buy-side participants are keen to develop systems to deliver accurate and timely segregation of exchanged collateral, to maintain sufficient liquidity, and to set up omnibus or individual segregation accounts.[179] As collateral management has become a key function, the creative or innovative forms of compliance are in the forefront.

Collateral transformation is one of the key services being offered in the market to 'resolve the gap between collateral supply and demand'.[180] It allows market participants to find in the market the high-quality collateral they require to meet regulatory requirements. As we saw in Chapter 5, one of the alternatives is to enter into a repo transaction; however, stock lending and other structured deals[181] can serve the same purpose.

The adoption of a risk-based regime would assist US regulators in their task to consider the cross-market effects of the DFA. In the process of identification and assessment of risk, supervisors can consider the systemic implications of certain regulatory requirements. In the regulation of CCPs in the OTCDM, the level of interconnection between these entities, their clearing members, and clients with other markets is paramount. The systemic character of CCPs not only illustrates the rules of Titles VII and VIII of the DFA, but also should guide the evaluation and prioritisation of risks in the CCPs' supervision. Collateral transformation events prove that regulation can induce innovation and creative compliance. Therefore, the regulatory strategy needs to be sufficiently dynamic to allow continuous review of the risk triggered in the stage of implementation.

6.4.2 US dual regulatory structure hinders efficient supervision

The second weakness in the DFA is related to the dual regulatory structure led by the CFTC and the SEC, and the limited use of deterrence mechanisms. The prevalent enforcement method is the threat of fines. Although the debate about the need to streamline the US regulatory structure[182] has permeated several reforms for decades,[183] here we seek to consider the case of OTC derivatives regulation.

---

177 Paula Tkac, 'Reducing Systemic Risk or Merely Transforming It?' Federal Reserve Bank of Atlanta (July 2013).
178 DTCC, 'Trends, Risks and Opportunities in Collateral Management' A Collateral Management White Paper (22 January 2014) <www.dtcc.com/news/2014/january/22/collateral-management> accessed 20th December 2017.
179 Discussed at the 11th OTC Derivatives Summit, Global Fixed Income Institute, Bagshot, UK (13–14 July 2017).
180 DTCC, 'Trends, Risks and Opportunities in Collateral Management' A Collateral Management White Paper (22 January 2014) (n178) 7.
181 Ibid.
182 Carl Felsenfeld, Banking Regulation in the United States 29–35 (2nd edn, Juris 2006).
183 Saule T. Omarova, 'One Step Forward, Two Steps Back: The Institutional Structure of US Financial Services After the Crisis of 2008' in Robin Hui Huang, and Dirk Schoenmaker

Indeed, there has been a proposal to merge the CFTC and the SEC, aiming at integrating the oversight over the country's capital markets. The new agency would help to close regulatory gaps in areas that were traditionally unregulated, such as the OTCDM. The call for a unified federal regulatory agency was close to becoming a reality in the mid-1990s, coming shortly after a series of scandals related to the derivatives market.[184]

We would disregard the number of regulatory authorities as a significant factor of risk-based regimes.[185] The development of risk-based regimes in jurisdictions such as the UK has brought back the debate surrounding the adoption of regulatory structures of either a single authority or a twin peaks system. It has also been documented how the former FSA was the leading entity in charge of designing a risk-based regime. However, the implementation of a risk-based approach to regulation goes beyond the number of authorities carrying out the supervision. In fact, when there are multiple regulatory agencies and supervisors, the adoption of risk-based regulation as a strategy requires greater collaboration between the regulators and the regulated firms, as well as the highest level of expertise on the part of regulators to identify areas that require the most attention.[186]

Despite the fact the US regulatory architecture has been regarded as effective in reaching the key objectives of financial supervision, the system has been under scrutiny in recent years. Indeed, the US regulatory structure embeds elements of a functional approach[187] as well as some institutional features.[188] Since its origins in the Great Depression of the 1930s, the regulatory model has reflected the 'siloed structure'[189] of the market. This situation has been clearly identified by business leaders,[190] who judge the complex US system as less responsive to industry needs and far more punitive than other jurisdictions' enforcement

(eds.), *Institutional Structure of Financial Regulation: Theories and International Experiences* (Routledge Taylor and Francis Group 2014), 141.

184 Including the infamous bankruptcy of California's Orange County.

185 See Ligia Catherine Arias-Barrera, 'Multiple Strategies of Financial Regulation Adopted in the Colombian Securities Market: The Case of Over-the-Counter Derivatives' in Pedro Fortes, and others (eds.), *Law and Policy in Latin America: Transforming Courts, Institutions, and Rights* (Palgrave Macmillan 2017), 167.

186 International Securities Exchange, 'Proposal for Regulatory Reform for the US Financial Markets' (March 2009), 10.

187 Supervisory oversight is determined by the business that is being transacted by the entity, without regard to its legal status. Each type of business may have its own functional regulator.

188 The 'Institutional Approach' is a legal-entity-driven approach. The firm's legal status essentially determines which regulator is tasked with overseeing its activity both from a safety and soundness and a business conduct perspective. This legal status also determines the scope of the entity's permissible business activities.

189 G30 Working Group on Financial Supervision, The Structure of Financial Supervision Approaches and Challenges in a Global Marketplace (Group of Thirty 2008) 34.

190 The City of New York, Office of the Mayor and United States Senate, 'Sustaining New York's and the US' Global Financial Services Leadership' (2007) <www.nyc.gov/html/om/pdf/ny_report_final.pdf> accessed 9th November 2017.

approaches. Such a perception of the US rule-based regime puts the country at a competitive disadvantage.

Industry calls have been directed to enhance the competitiveness of the US market by means of implementing a principles-based approach to regulation. It has been advised that US regulatory agencies adopt a set of common principles to guide future rulemaking and enforcement actions.[191] The outcome and principles-based approach would help to deliver a more cooperative and coherent supervision, streamlining the regulatory requirements imposed to US and non-US market participants.

The shortcoming related to the dual regulatory structure is aggravated by the role given to the Board for the regulation and supervision of DCEs (DCOs and CAs designated as systemically important by the FSOC). The interaction and cooperation among the three authorities has been a source of concern since the beginning of the implementation of the DFA. Their lack of coordination has clearly prevented them from achieving their statutory goals, as foreseen in section 813 of the DFA.[192] The debate is centred on the need to improve consistency in oversight, to promote robust risk management, and to improve regulators' ability to monitor and control risk.[193] The actions proposed in 2011 (to overcome the issues associated with the absence of coordination among regulatory agencies) had a common element: the need to formalise the consultation process associated with rulemaking and to share understanding about the process of supervision of DCEs.

Illustrative examples of the urgent need for coordination are the rulemakings of the CFTC and the SEC, establishing enhanced risk management standards for DCOs and CAs in consultation with the Board. According to section 806(e), both the CFTC and the SEC are required to consult the Board before making any changes to the pre-established rules, procedures, and operations associated with DCEs' risks. Such consultation should be effective when inter-agency staff adequately conduct a constructive and timely assessment.

Moreover, in light of the priority given to systemic risk management, the SEC, the CFTC, and the Board should implement a consultative mechanism that allows them to build a shared understanding of the potential sources of systemic risk. As their individual mandates might give rise to different emphases in the supervisory process, it is key to structure a process that facilitates the integration of such

---

191 Ibid.
192 Section 813 requires the CFTC, the SEC, and the Board to make recommendations in four areas: (1) improving consistency in the DCE oversight programs of the SEC and CFTC, (2) promoting robust risk management by DCEs, (3) promoting robust risk management oversight by regulators of DCEs, and (4) improving regulators' ability to monitor the potential effects of DCE risk management on the stability of the financial system of the US.
193 Board of Governors of the Federal Reserve System, Securities and Exchange Commission, Commodity Futures Trading Commission, Risk Management Supervision of Designated Clearing Entities Report to the Congress, Washington DC (July 2011) <www.federalreserve.gov/publications/other-reports/files/risk-management-supervision-report-201107.pdf> accessed 17th October 2017.

multiples and diverse perspectives of risk identification, assessment, and management. The continuous review and update of the process will help to improve risk management supervision and, among other considerations, will feature the complete implementation of the risk-based approach to regulation, as explained in Chapter 2.

The expected outcome of the inter-agency coordinated process of supervision is to achieve greater consistency and avoid costly overlapping of the supervisory inquiry. The process is regarded as the most suitable mechanism to coherently applied statutory requirements, agency regulation, supervisory guidance, and international technical standards.

The process of inter-agency cooperation is aided by the review of risk of section 807 (a) of the DFA. According to this provision, both the CFTC and the SEC are required to review and incorporate several risk issues during their annual examination-planning process. The examination will involve separate work with the Board[194] to assess the scope and methodology implemented.

Finally, the inter-agency process would not be completed unless an appropriate information sharing agreement is in place. Title VIII[195] provides the authority for such information sharing in matters related to DCEs, such as examination reports, confidential supervisory information, any information regarding material and urgent concerns, and so on. The agreement may be through an MoU between the CFTC, the SEC, and the Board.

Certainly, the joint effort of US supervisors has followed some of the typical elements of the risk-based approach to regulation. For instance, on 14th August 2017, the US federal banking regulators – the FRB,[196] OCC,[197] and the FDIC[198] – issued an inter-agency guidance on the risk-based capital treatment of certain centrally cleared derivative contracts.[199] The guidance was issued to clarify the treatment of cleared settled-to-market contracts, in light of some changes introduced to the rulebooks of certain CCPs. Those changes resulted in particular types of margin being considered a settlement and transfer of title to the receiving party, rather than a collateral of the clearing member.[200]

The dual or multiple regulatory agencies structure is challenging. The main concerns are associated with coordination mechanisms to ensure that both the CFTC and the SEC adopt a similar approach to risk-based regulation. The

---

194 S 807(d)(2) of the Act.
195 S 809.
196 Federal Reserve Board.
197 Office of the Comptroller.
198 Federal Deposit Insurance Corporation.
199 Office of the Comptroller of the Currency, Board of Governors of the Federal Reserve System, Federal Deposit Insurance, 'Corporation Regulatory Capital Treatment of Certain Centrally-cleared Derivative Contracts Under Regulatory Capital Rules' (14 August 2017).
200 Kathleen Scott, 'US Federal Banking Regulators Issue Risk-Based Capital Guidance for Certain Derivatives' Financial Services: Regulation Tomorrow (22 August 2017) <www.regulationtomorrow.com/us/us-federal-banking-regulators-issue-risk-based-capital-guidance-for-certain-derivatives/> accessed 14th October 2017.

difficulty starts with the different strategies traditionally followed by those authorities: whilst the SEC applies a rules-based approach,[201] the CFTC[202] has worked towards the design and implementation of a risk-based approach, with a focus on principles. The contrast of the two approaches is reflected through their implementation. The SEC takes on the enforcement of the rules issued by Congress and its own rules; therefore the supervision relies heavily on the enforcement of such rules, regardless of the principles guiding the body of regulation. By contrast, the CFTC's risk-based approach is more focused on achieving regulatory objectives. With this approach, the implementation is mainly centred on compliance, as Congress identifies areas of highest risk, and the CFTC supervises how regulated firms establish their rules in line with regulatory objectives.

Guided by regulatory objectives, a coherent adoption of risk-based regulation and supervision would allow the timely identification and management of risk. Supervision, under a risk-based approach, seeks to achieve compliance with objectives, rather than observance of specific sets of rules. In so doing, regulatory agencies must ensure that the same or equivalent standards are applied across market participants and markets. Moreover, all trading and post-trading infrastructures should observe the same set of risk-based objectives, and therefore supervision is sufficiently broad and effective to cover all markets and products according to diverse levels of risk.

The implementation of such a risk-based approach, focused on principles, embeds the idea that the process of regulation and supervision is a cooperative one. It entails the active participation of regulated firms to create their rules within the framework and control of the regulatory authorities. The approach is not regarded as a form of regulation, but as a new style of governance, blurring the divide between public and private.[203]

Additionally, the implementation of a risk-based approach in the US regulatory authorities would help to overcome the limits of the rule-based model.[204] This is embracing a strategy of regulation that seeks to achieve voluntary compliance rather than bringing costly enforcement actions. The adoption of a model focused on compliance instead of intense enforcement would have a positive impact in terms of competitiveness of the US market, and would reduce the need of 'equivalence' assessments between the US and other states and international regimes.[205] It is worth noting, however, that risk-based regimes do not imply

---

201 Under the Securities Exchange Act 1934, the SEC governs broker-dealers and securities exchanges with a rules-based regulatory structure.

202 Under the Commodity Exchange Act, as modified by the Commodities Futures Modernization Act 2000, the CFTC applies a risk-based regulatory approach.

203 Cristie L Ford, 'New Governance, Compliance, and Principles-Based Securities Regulation' (2008) 45 *American Business Law Journal*, 1–60.

204 Joseph Raz, 'Legal Principles and the Limits of Law' *Yale Law Journal* 81 (1972), 823–854. Also see Ronald Dworkin, *Taking Rights Seriously* (Harvard University Press 1977), 22–23.

205 Eilís Ferran, 'Principles-Based, Risk-Based Regulation and Effective Enforcement' in Michel Tison and others (eds.), *Perspectives in Company Law and Financial Regulation* (Cambridge University Press 2009), 427.

the abolition of enforcement, but the strategic use of enforcement actions.[206] This means that the first approach is to seek voluntary observance of regulation, to select the highest risk areas and firms to assess, and, when needed, to impose enforcement actions. The well-known theory of responsive regulation states that an escalation of enforcement actions reveals the failure of poorly implemented compliance strategies.[207]

Although our line of argument defends the coherent implementation of a risk-based approach focused on principles, we do not deny its potential shortcomings. The downside of this approach is the level of discretion granted to regulatory authorities. The judgement entailed in the supervision process would increase the burden of officers assessing whether a principle has been breached.[208] Whereas the verification of breach of rules is a relatively lighter task, where facts are assessed against detailed rules, the determination of violation of principles demands a strict process to identify and prove the breach.

Thus, the design of a unified risk-based approach focused on principles for the SEC and the CFTC must set clear criteria to guide the decision-making process. It must ensure that common parameters are in place to assess the breach of principles. In particular, the approach should establish a common understanding of the identification, assessment, and management of risk; the prioritisation of regulatory actions; and the adoption of either compliance or deterrence mechanisms. In this context, the coordination between both authorities is central to the success of the regulatory strategy.

6.4.3 The inconvenient extraterritorial implications of the US regime

The third challenge to the US regime is the cross-border implementation of US regulations and how they interact with other markets (e.g. in the UK).[209] Although the inconvenient extraterritoriality of the DFA has been a frequent concern to the non-US derivatives market, such extraterritorial reach is sometimes regarded as positive in terms of the rules on capitalisation, collateralisation, and transparency, which are expected to restore stability and integrity to the global derivatives market.[210]

---

206 Julia Black, Martyn Hopper, and Christa Band, 'Making a Success of Principles-Based Regulation' (2007) 1(3) *Law and Financial Market Review*, 191–206.

207 See Ian Ayres, and John Brathwaite, *Responsive Regulation* (Oxford University Press 1992); cited by Eilis Ferran, 'Principles-Based, Risk-Based Regulation and Effective Enforcement' in Michel Tison and others (eds.), *Perspectives in Company Law and Financial Regulation* (Cambridge University Press 2009), 431.

208 M. Hopper and J. Stainsby, 'Principles-Based Regulation – Better Regulation?' (2006) 21 *Journal of International Banking Law and Regulation*, 387–391.

209 Paula S. Greenman, Anthony Mechcatie, and John W. Osborn, 'Derivatives Under Dodd-Frank' *Sakdden* (7 August 2015) (n108).

210 Michael Greenberger, 'The Extraterritorial Provisions of the Dodd-Frank Act Protects US Taxpayers from Worldwide Bailouts' (2012) 80 *University of Missouri-Kansas City Law Review*, University of Maryland Legal Studies Research Paper No 2012–17 (April 2012).

Concerning OTC derivatives transactions (mainly swaps) and central clearing, the DFA[211] mandates registration and regulation of 'swaps-dealers' (SDs) and 'major swap participants' (MSPs), as well as imposes clearing and trade execution requirements on standardised derivative products. Moreover, the DFA requires recordkeeping and data reporting of swaps, including real-time public reporting, and enhances federal agencies' oversight over the swaps industry.

At first sight, it could be considered that the US regime is going to be exclusively applicable to US entities trading and clearing swaps in the US market. However, the DFA authorises US regulators to implement the statute and secondary rules on an extraterritorial basis in order to protect US interests.[212]

To provide a framework of how problematic cross-border implementation of US regulation can be, it is first important to briefly illustrate some key differences between the UK and the US clearing requirements.[213] Both regimes are designed to ensure that standardised derivatives are required to be centrally cleared though a CCP. However, the process to determine which OTC derivative must be cleared is different. Under EMIR, directly applicable to the UK at the time of writing, CCPs are required to obtain permission from the national regulator – the Bank – to clear a particular type of derivative contract. If the approval is granted, then ESMA will determine whether to include the derivative contract on the list of mandatory clearing. By contrast, under Title VII of the DFA, a CCP must submit to the CFTC or the SEC the type of derivative that it wishes to clear, and then the regulator determines if such a derivatives contract will be subject to mandatory clearing.

The CCP or clearing facility will stand between the two initial counterparties of the derivatives transaction and will assume the consequences of default. Hence, it will provide protection to both counterparties. In this context, the CCP have incentives to establish and enforce capital and collateral requirements to its clearing members. The US regime not only allows CCPs to decide which swaps they plan to clear,[214] but also requires CCPs facilitate a 'non-discriminatory' access to clearing.[215] Along with the clearing obligation for certain types of swaps, there is also a reporting requirement DFA imposes on all cleared and uncleared transactions.

It has been widely documented that the DFA attempted to remedy some persistent flaws of the swaps and derivatives regulation, introducing reforms related to jurisdiction, market participants, capital and margin requirements, central clearing, execution, and business conduct standards.[216] However, there are

---

211 Understanding the impact of Dodd-Frank on financial derivatives.
212 Commodity and Futures Trading Commission and the Securities Exchange Commission, Public Roundtable to Discuss International Issues Relating to the Implementation of Title VII of the Dodd-Frank Act (155).
213 Michael Kent, Caird Forbes-Cockell, and Noah Melnick, 'How EMIR compares to Title VII' (June 2012) *International Financial Law Review*, 1.
214 Dodd-Frank Act s 723 (h)(2)(a), s 763 (a)(1).
215 Dodd-Frank Act s 763 (a)(2)(B).
216 David Skeel, *The New Financial Deal Understanding the Dodd-Frank Act and Its (Unintended) Consequences* (John Wiley & Sons 2010), 59.

still several controversial and unsolved areas associated with the extraterritorial implementation of US rules.

One of these is obtaining Qualifying CCP status (QCCP), under EU capital requirements for certain CAs operating in the US, and having bank clearing members affiliated with a EU entity.[217] Such availability depends on the ESMA recognising the US CCP according to the provisions of EMIR.[218] As a result, there would be a dual treatment depending on whether US CCPs are recognised or not. On the one hand, for those US CCPs receiving recognition as a Qualifying CCP, their EU-based clearing members would be allowed to continue to operate and the CCPs would continue to provide clearing services to market participants based in the EU. On the other hand, if EU banks and their subsidiaries clear their products through a US CCP unrecognised by ESMA, they would incur higher capital charges according to the EU's capital requirements regulation.

The European Commission (EC) undertakes the task to issue an equivalence decision following the parameters of Article 25(6) of EMIR. The goal is to determine that the third-country legal and supervisory arrangements ensure that CCPs comply with requirements regarded as equivalent to those of EMIR, and that those CCPs are subject to effective supervision and enforcement. Although the EC's equivalence decision of the CFTC's regulatory framework for CCPs is an important progress, the SEC regime is not covered by such recognition. Moreover, if both the CFTC and the SEC supervise a US CCP, the equivalence would only cover those services that fall within the CFTC's jurisdiction.[219]

One illustrative example of the flaws triggered by the recognition of the CFTC regime for CCPs and not the SEC rules is the adoption of Rule 17Ad-22(e),

---

217 Fiona Maxwell, 'EU Members of US Options CCP Face $30 Billion Capital Hit: OCC Fears Approval Will Be Held Up By Absence Of SEC Clearing Rules' Risk.net (30 November 2015) <www.risk.net/risk-magazine/news/2436901/eu-members-of-us-options-ccp-face-usd30bn-capital-hit> accessed 5th November 2017.

218 On 16th March 2016, the EC issued an equivalence decision stating that the CFTC's regulatory framework for CCPs is equivalent to EU requirements. See 'Commission Implementing Decision (EU) 2016/377 of 15 March 2016 on the Equivalence of the Regulatory Framework of the United States of America for Central Counterparties that are Authorised and Supervised by the CFTC to the Requirements of Regulation (EU) No 648/2012 of the European Parliament and of the Council' <http://eur-lex.europa.eu/legal-content/EN/TXT/?uri=CELEX:32016D0377> accessed 5th November 2017. The EC also adopted EMIR equivalence decision for derivatives transactions in the US, see Commission Implementing Decision (EU) 2017/1857 of 13 October 2017 on the Recognition of the Legal, Supervisory and Enforcement Arrangements of the United States of America for Derivatives Transactions Supervised by the Commodity Futures Trading Commission as Equivalent to Certain Requirements of Article 11 of Regulation (EU) No 648/2012 of the European Parliament and Council on OTC Derivatives, Central Counterparties, and Trade Repositories <http://eur-lex.europa.eu/legal-content/EN/TXT/?uri=CELEX:32017D1857> accessed 12th December 2017.

219 Shearman and Sterling LLP, 'Update on Third Country Equivalence Under EMIR' (17 March 2016) <www.shearman.com/~/media/Files/NewsInsights/Publications/2016/03/Update-on-Third-Country-Equivalence-Under-EMIR-FIAFR-031716.pdf> accessed 10th November 2017.

which might be cause for further consideration by the EC.[220] A registered CA – an ICE EU[221] – had to comply with both new SEC rules and EMIR. During the process of regulating the ICE EU, the SEC reviewed some proposed changes[222] related to segregation and portability of customer positions and margin, risk modelling, back testing, stress testing, default management, and liquidity risk management. Moreover, when a CA is registered, it must comply with the rules of the Exchange Act and the Commission's rules. However, according to rule 17A (b)(1), the SEC has the authority to exempt a CA from 'any provision of Section 17A or the rules or regulation thereunder'. The exemptive relief should be granted on the bases of public interest, the protection of investors, and the purposes of Section 17A itself, such as ensuring the continuity of clearing and settlement services and protection of securities and funds. These exemptions could benefit non-US clearing agencies, and the SEC could consider among other aspects their structure, the nature of their activities, and requirements under the regulatory regime to which clearing entities are subject in their home jurisdiction. The scope of the exemptive relief might be total or partial, depending on whether none of the requirements under Rule 17Ad-22 (e) or some of them need be applied to a non-US CA.

Besides the SEC's decision-making process to grant the exemptive relief, the Exchange Acts permits the SEC and the relevant national competent authority (NCA) of the non-US CA to enter into cooperative arrangements. The cooperation between authorities could facilitate the process of assessment of an exemption of Section 17A of the Exchange Act, could allow information sharing to avoid potential duplication of regulatory requirements, and could ease a coordinated supervision between the SEC and the NCA. The effectiveness of such arrangements, however, varies on case-by-case basis, and as such might not always be the most constructive solution for extraterritoriality issues.

Another controverted area, where extraterritoriality poses problems, is that of the rules concerning segregation of assets.[223] CCPs are required to hold different accounts to ensure the segregation of clearing members' collateral. Although the segregation regime is, as explained before, one that is limited to legal segregation, the process of implementation is different in the US and the UK and European regimen. Initially, the SEC and the CFTC proposed a mandatory segregation of initial margin but not variation margin. In contrast, EMIR along with the relevant dispositions of MiFID I and II, does not distinguish between initial and variation margin when requiring segregation in OTC derivatives transactions.

---

220 Philip Stafford, 'European Banks Face US Capital Hit Unless Rules Converge' *FT.com* (4 April 2016) <www.ft.com/cms/s/0/bbe6678a-f5c5-11e5-803c-d27c7117d132.html#axzz48oFXlFrR> accessed 5th November 2017.

221 Intercontinental Exchange (ICE EU)

222 Each registered clearing agency is an SRO subject to S 19(b) of the Exchange Act, which requires SROs to submit proposed rule changes to the Commission for public comment and Commission review and approval.

223 See discussion about segregation in Chapter 3.

Moreover, the US regime incorporates a dual system of segregation depending on the type of products and the regulatory agency. Hence, the SEC model of segregation requires that securities customer balances should be kept separate from firms' assets and from commodity customer balances. As a result, the assets cannot be used to finance proprietary business activities. Securities customers maintain priority and equal claim over assets and, when securities segregated assets are insufficient to meet claims, customers assume equally in shortfall and become general creditors.

The SEC's style of segregation[224] is called 'Net Segregation'. Accordingly, a broker may use customer cash credit balances to finance margin loans to other customers and may lend or pledge a portion of customer securities purchased on margin to other customers selling short.

By contrast, the CFTC's segregation model[225] entails that commodity customer balances should be maintained separate from the firm's assets, and funds used for trading on non-US commodity exchanges must be kept separate from those used for trading on US exchanges. Similarly, commodity customer balances should remain separate from securities customer balances, even when they belong to the same customer.

Furthermore, commodity customers maintain priority and equal claim over assets in each of their US and non-US segregated pools. The CFTC's style of segregation is gross segregation. It requires the broker not to use the funds of one customer to margin or guarantee the transactions of another, and to segregate assets in an amount equal to the sum of all customer credit balances. Unlike the SEC's model,[226] the CFTC's segregation model does not impose the existence of insurance.

To solve the issues related to extraterritoriality, the first option at hand is to implement a system of mutual recognition. The 'equivalence decision' of the EC seeks to foster such mutual recognition between the European rules and third-country regimes. However, even when the mutual recognition is in place, the differences in regulatory strategies might be problematic after mutual recognition is granted.[227] The hypothesis would imply that US regulatory authorities, particularly the SEC, would tend to implement a stricter, more rule-based approach to supervision, whereas the European Authority would seek to guide

---

224 See 'Financial Responsibility Rules for Broker-Dealers' SEC Release Nos 34–70072 (30 July 2013) and 'Broker-Dealer Reports' SEC Release 34–70073 (30 July 2013).

225 17 CFR 23.702 Requirements for segregated margin. <www.gpo.gov/fdsys/search/page details.action?collectionCode=CFR&browsePath=Title+17%2FChapter+I%2FPart+23%2 FSubpart+L%2FSection+%26sect%3B+23.702&granuleId=CFR-2016-title17-vol1-sec23-702&packageId=CFR-2016-title17-vol1&collapse=true&fromBrowse=true> accessed 20th December 2017.

226 Russell D. Sacks, 'SEC Adopts Changes to Broker-Dealer Rules' *HLS Forum on Corporate Governance and Financial Regulation* (7 September 2013) <https://corpgov.law.harvard.edu/2013/09/07/sec-adopts-changes-to-broker-dealer-rules/#1> accessed 9th December 2017.

227 Donald C. Langevoort, 'Steps Toward the Europeanization of US Securities Regulation, with Thoughts on the Evolution and Design of a Multinational Securities Regulator' in Michel Tison and others (eds.), *Perspectives in Company Law and Financial Regulation* (Cambridge University Press 2009), 560.

its regulatory action on a principles or outcome basis. To avoid such conflicting scenarios, the mutual recognition cannot be limited to assessing whether rules in both regimes are strictly equivalent, but also must consider the approaches of regulation adopted by supervisors and set from the outset a mechanism to reconcile potential differences. It has been suggested that the resolution of those sort of disputes can be better assisted when a third independent party is involved; some proponents[228] have considered IOSCO as the most adequate forum, or alternatively, and not free of shortcomings,[229] a new global administrative body created as a platform to facilitate mutual recognition processes.

We propose going beyond the system of mutual recognition and the adoption of a third independent party, and to model a 'cross-border strategy of regulation'. The design and implementation of a complete risk-based approach to regulation based on principles is the most feasible solution for extraterritoriality concerns. International standard-setting bodies recognise that harmonisation is useful for certain areas of derivatives regulation (e.g. unique transaction identifier,[230] derivatives trading).[231] In others, such as central clearing, it is clear that such alternative is challenging. The current system of mutual recognition is an important progress towards coherent international regulation of derivatives market and central clearing, but it can be improved. Whereas the adoption of a risk-based approach guided by principles as strategy of regulation has the potential to facilitate the cross-border recognition and implementation of derivatives regimes, it will certainly prevent the overlapping of those areas that mutual recognition leaves uncovered (e.g. multiple rules on segregation).

The risk-based approach to regulation based on principles should be guided by the common US and UK – and also EU – regulatory objectives of improving transparency, enhancing financial stability, reducing systemic risk, and combating market abuse. These objectives are achieved by promoting standardisation and the use of central clearing in the OTCDM.[232] Notwithstanding the differences between US and UK regimes associated to products,[233] collateral segregation,[234]

---

228 Ibid 561.
229 Donald C. Langevoort, 'Structuring Securities Regulation in the European Union: Lessons from the US Experience', in Guido Ferrarini and Eddy Wymeersch (eds.), *Investor Protection in Europe: Corporate Law Making, the MiFID and Beyond* (Oxford University Press 2006), 485–506.
230 BIS, 'Technical Guidance Harmonisation of the Unique Transaction Identifier' (February 2017) <www.iosco.org/library/pubdocs/pdf/IOSCOPD557.pdf> accessed 9th December 2017.
231 Barney Jopson, and Philip Stafford, 'EU and US Agree to Accept Each Other's Derivatives Rules' *Financial Times* (13 October 2017) <www.ft.com/content/597f6d24-b02e-11e7-aab9-abaa44b1e130> accessed 12th December 2017.
232 G20 Leaders Statement: The Pittsburgh Summit (24–25 September 2009).
233 In the EU, the products subject to clear are to be determined, but overall, they include: credit, interest rates, FX, equity, and commodity derivatives. In the US, credit and interest rates derivatives are included, while Foreign Exchange (FX) swaps and forwards are exempted.
234 In the EU, omnibus segregation is permitted but clearing members might opt for individual segregation. In the US, there is the legally separated operationally co-mingled model, a mixed model.

exemptions,[235] inter-affiliate trades,[236] and historical contracts,[237] their outcomes are very similar. Therefore, the extraterritorial implementation of any of those regimes should not be problematic if the interpretation and enforcement of their respective rules is assessed through the lens of the objectives they pursue.

6.4.4 Absence of a determined resolution regime for CCPs

One of the main concerns surrounding the adoption of CCPs in the OTCDM is their systemic nature. National and international regulators are committed to ensure the safety and soundness of CCPs. As explained in Chapter 4, recovery and resolvability rules and standards have been issued to ensure that CCPs are resilient. Like the UK, the US regime reflects the trend of enhancing recovery regimes, while overlooking the possibility of failure and the importance of designing a regime for the orderly resolution of CCPs.

Although this shortcoming may be one of the greatest weaknesses[238] of the DFA financial architecture, regulators have overlooked this area. The DFA seems to recognise the major effect of a CCP's failure and authorises the FSOC to designate CCPs as systemically important. In such an event, CCPs are subject to more stringent supervision[239] and – if necessary – will have access to the Fed's accounts and services.[240] For instance, the Fed could provide emergency funding from their discount window.[241] The upcoming Choice Act 2017 plans to repeal these norms, which were designed to prevent a CCP's failure.

The DFA does not clarify, however, the resolution rules that would be applicable to a CCP's failure. Some commentators[242] argue that regulators are likely

---

235 In the EU, there is a three-year exemption for pension funds. Also, non-financial counterparties are exempted if non-hedging trading volume falls below certain thresholds.
236 Whilst the US regime includes a relief from initial margin requirements for inter-affiliate transactions, the EU regime allows the exemption of initial and variation margin.
237 The trades executed before the clearing obligation started must be cleared in the EU, but in the US, such trades are not subject to mandatory clearing.
238 David Skeel, 'What if a Clearinghouse Fails?' Series on Financial Markets and Regulations, Brookings Center on Regulation and Markets (6 June 2017) <www.brookings.edu/research/what-if-a-clearinghouse-fails/> accessed 13th December 2017
239 The Fed imposes higher capital requirements to designated FMUs, but it is still unclear whether their regulation will be similar to the one of systemically important banks. See Financial Market Utilities, 78 Fed Reg 14,024 (proposed 4th March 2013). Discussing the importance of giving systemically important CCPs similar treatment to SIBs, see Li Lin, and Jay Surti, 'Capital Requirements for Over-the-Counter Derivatives Central Counterparties' IMF Working Paper No 13/3 (2013) 5–6 <www.imf.org/external/pubs/ft/wp/2013/wp1303.pdf> accessed 14th December 2017.
240 S 806 (a) of the DFA.
241 Colleen Baker, 'The Federal Reserve's Supporting Role Behind Dodd-Frank's Clearinghouse Reforms' HBLR (20 April 2013) <www.hblr.org/2013/04/the-federal-reserves-supporting-role-behind-dodd-franks-clearinghouse-reforms/#_ftn37> accessed 14th December 2017.
242 Julia Lees Allen, 'Derivatives Clearinghouses and Systemic Risk: A Bankruptcy and Dodd-Frank Analysis' (2012) 64 *Stanford Law Review*, 1079, 1100–1102.

to use the rules of the DFA for the resolution of SIFIs. Title II of the DFA[243] authorises the orderly liquidation authority (i.e. FDIC) to take over failing financial institutions when their failure can have systemic consequences. When a CCP is designated as systemically important, those rules will govern its resolution. The problem of this interpretation, however, is that such a resolution regime was designed for financial companies[244] that perform 'activities that are financial in nature', and according to the FDIC definition, clearing is not explicitly one of those activities. Therefore, it is not certain whether Title II of the DFA would be the resolution regime of systemically important or designated CCPs.

The provisions of Title II establish a preliminary stage where the systemic importance of the financial company is to be determined by the relevant authority.[245] For CCPs, such determination is made by the FSOC. The designation implies assessing whether the company is in danger of default,[246] and that such default would have adverse effects on the stability of the US financial system. It also emphasises that all the other proceedings have been exhausted, and that the orderly resolution is the only remaining option to mitigate such adverse effects.[247] Once the FDIC is appointed as receiver of the troubled financial company, it assumes all the powers over the liquidation process (e.g. may conduct all aspects of the company's business and may liquidate and wind up the affairs of the company). The FDIC will also be authorised to create a 'bridge financial company'[248] that in the case of CCPs is key to avoid disruption in the provision of clearing services.

According to Section 210 of the DFA, derivatives transactions receive a special treatment. The Act provides special protections to parties to certain derivatives agreements, which are called 'qualified financial contracts'. The debtor's counterparties are free to terminate their contracts, and to close-out and liquidate their positions,[249] when the insolvency proceedings have started.

Even if we accept that Title II is the resolution regime for designated CCPs, and the FDIC includes clearing as financial activity, there is still a need to clarify what agency will act as their Resolution Authority. According to Title II, FDIC would be the authority carrying out the CCPs' resolution. However, it does not have the level of expertise and specialisation to rule derivatives or central clearing.

---

243 Title II of the DFA, 'Orderly Liquidation Authority', creates a new federal receivership process pursuant to which the FDIC may serve as receiver for large, interconnected financial companies.

244 There are four categories of financial companies: bank holding companies, non-bank financial companies supervised by the Board of Governors, subsidiaries of the two foregoing categories of financial companies (other than subsidiaries that are insured depository institutions or insurance companies), and brokers and dealers that are registered with the SEC and that are members of the SIPC.

245 S 203 of the DFA.

246 S 203(c)(4) of the DFA.

247 Ibid.

248 S 210 of the DFA.

249 S 210(c)(8) of the DFA, 12 USC s 1821(e)(8), 11 USC s 555, s 556, s 559, s 560 and s 561.

A better-suited solution would be to grant resolution powers to either the CFTC or the SEC, as primary regulators, in coordination with the Fed.

The alternative is to understand that the ordinary bankruptcy laws might be applicable. However, if a CCP opts to file for Chapter 11,[250] it might find out that they are not allowed to do so because CCPs might be categorised as commodities brokers, which are expressly excluded from Chapter 11. Therefore, the option would be to file for liquidation under Chapter 7,[251] but here again the rules were not designed to resolve CCPs, but stock and commodities brokers. Moreover, ordinary bankruptcy laws do not provide a stay on derivatives as a measure that would prevent the immediate termination of derivatives contracts and would facilitate the orderly resolution of a CCP. This complex and uncertain framework of CCPs' resolution suggests that if a CCP fails, the regulators' only option would be to bail out, which was precisely the scenario the DFA aimed to avoid.

Attending to the lack of certainty, contractual approaches seem to provide a more feasible solution. Market participants have designed a 'waterfall system' to manage CCPs' resolution:

Although useful, contractual strategies are far from providing certainty regarding CCPs' resolution. The reason for the uncertainty is twofold: firstly, because non-defaulting clearing members will never be sure about the role they will play, and the total extent of their contributions in the event of a CCP's failure. The risk of suffering margin haircuts or having their contract tiered up might force clearing members to exit the CCP as soon as they anticipate financial problems, behaviour which would exacerbate the CCP's crisis. On the other hand, the effectiveness of the waterfall can only be tested once failure has occurred. Then, the timely and adequate implementation of the system will be central to stabilising the CCP and avoiding the contagion it might trigger.

For CCPs that are not systemically important, the route is to follow ordinary bankruptcy laws.[252] However, the absence of a stay on termination of derivatives contracts, and the impossibility for regulators to initiate bankruptcy cases, emphasises the inadequacy of the regime as the resolution venue.

The US Treasury recognises the shortcoming of the US resolution regime for CCPs. In the latest report of the Office of Financial Research, the Treasury accepts that the tools for orderly resolution of systemic non-bank firms (e.g. CCPs) pose significant challenges to regulators and are not well developed.[253] The balance

---

250 US Code Chapter 11–Reorganization. This chapter of the Bankruptcy Code generally provides for reorganisation, usually involving a corporation or partnership, but individuals can also be covered by Chapter 11 (11 USC s 301, s 303).

251 This chapter of the Bankruptcy Code provides for 'liquidation' – the sale of a debtor's nonexempt property and the distribution of the proceeds to creditors.

252 David Skeel, 'What if a Clearinghouse Fails?' Series on Financial Markets and Regulations, Brookings Center on Regulation and Markets (6 June 2017) (n 240).

253 Office of Financial Research, '2017 Financial Stability Report' (5 December 2017) 2 <www.financialresearch.gov/financial-stability-reports/files/OFR_2017_Financial-Stability-Report.pdf> accessed 13th December 2017.

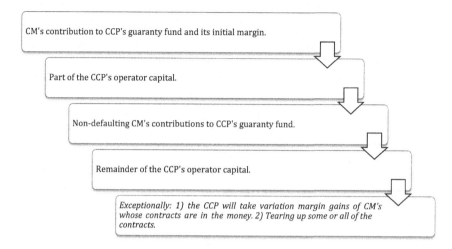

Figure 6.3 The 'waterfall' system to manage CCPs' resolution

of such a regime should be on avoiding contagion against moral hazard concerns. This is to ensure CCPs are sufficiently resilient and have protection against financial distress, without making them 'too-big-to-fail' institutions relying on government bailouts.

As US regulators have not made any progress in this area, the main source of information is scholarship. As we discussed in Chapter 4, Duffie proposes an eclectic approach that allows regulators to use measures similar to those included in the contractual provisions – the waterfall system – to manage CCPs' resolution.[254] The adoption of such an approach would have to be in line with international standards, namely the FSB Key Attributes and the FSB Guidance on Central Counterparty Resolution and Resolution Planning. Hence, it would have to be based on the objectives of adequate allocation of losses and to ensure the continued provision of clearing services. It also would grant clarity about which agency will act as resolution authority and its attendant powers. The regime should also set the criteria to know when to interrupt the operation of contractual provisions of default management to enter into a formal authority-led resolution proceeding.[255]

The adoption of a risk-based regime based on principles would assist the process of designing and implementing a resolution regime for CCPs. But even if US regulators decide not to create a new special regime, the risk-based approach

254 Darrell Duffie, 'Resolution of Failing Central Counterparties' in Kenneth Scott, and others (eds.), *Making Failure Feasible: How Bankruptcy Reform Can End "Too Big to Fail"* (Hoover Institution Press 2015), 87.
255 Ibid.

could help the current regime of Title II of the DFA to be adapted to the particularities of CCPs' failure. In this event, the principles guiding the adaptation would be maintaining critical operations of CCPs and if possible to 'recapitalize CCPs' as a means to avoid liquidation.[256] Moreover, transparency on the resolution rules design and implementation is central to the success of the regime and to enhancing legal certainty. Clearing members will be certain of the extent of their exposure and will be capable of anticipating the future contributions they will have to make in the event of a CCP's failure.[257] The cooperation between regulators, CCPs and clearing members is fostered by the integration of their multiple perceptions of risk. Each interested party would bring to the CCP resolution regime debate the risk such rules might bring to the stability of the regulated firms and the stability of the financial system. As was discussed earlier in this book, multiple interests converge when CCPs default (e.g. financial stability, CCP' resilience, clearing members' contributions to a guaranty fund, and so on), and regulators should try to balance those interests in front of the risk they pose to achieve regulatory objectives. The risk-based approach based on principles is a useful alternative to so doing because it enables cooperation and the timely identification and assessment of the risks prompted by CCP failure.

6.5 Conclusion

Our analysis of the Dodd-Frank Act highlights that the incoherent adoption of a risk-based approach to regulation affects the effectiveness of the US regime for CCPs.

The US regulation does not follow the pace of events of innovation risk. To develop this argument, we first explored the rise of FinTech in the OTCDM and central clearing services. The adoption of new technologies has emphasised the limits regulators face when deciding the risk to control and how to prioritise regulatory actions. The current US regime fails to deal with the changes and risks posed by the use of new developments such as the DLT and smart contracts in the derivatives market, especially in central clearing services. Thus, we argue that a risk-based approach to regulation based on principles, one that features the early identification and mitigation of risks, is central to the management of the unknown risks and uncertainties brought by FinTech innovations. In this context, risk-based regulation would act as an enabler of technology developments.

Similarly, the US regime for CCPs fails to deal with the negative effects of collateral transformation, as a form of 'regulation-induced innovation'. The overlaps between DFA and Basel III bring an excessive burden to market participants to

---

256 JP Morgan Chase & Co, 'What Is the Resolution Plan for CCPs?' *Office of Regulatory Affairs* (September 2014).
257 Darrell Duffie, 'Resolution of Failing Central Counterparties' in Kenneth Scott and others (eds.), *Making Failure Feasible: How Bankruptcy Reform Can End "Too Big to Fail"* (Hoover Institution Press 2015), 96.

have high-quality collateral. In procuring such types of collateral, market participants might enter into subsequent transactions and as a result certain risks traditionally associated with the derivatives are transferred to the other markets (e.g. the repo market). In this context, the adoption of a risk-based regime would assist US regulators in their task to consider the cross-market effects of the DFA and the potential systemic consequences of collateral regulatory requirements.

The second inadequacy of the US regime concerns the dual regulatory structure of the CFTC and the SEC. The bifurcated structure is problematic not only in terms of the duality of regimes applicable to derivatives instruments and participants, in particular to DCOs and CAs, but also concerning the adoption of different and not well-coordinated regulatory strategies. The mixture of strategies features elements of principles-based, rules-based, and risk-based approaches to regulation. Our proposal is that a risk-based approach guided by principles might solve the flaws of the regime. We argue that a coherent adoption of risk-based regulation and supervision facilitates timely identification and management of risks, as well as eases the integration of multiple perceptions of risks. Such a coherent risk-based approach to regulation guided by principles will also incentivise regulated firms to comply voluntarily. We argue in favour of setting a system of equivalent standards for the CFTC and the SEC, applicable across market participants and markets, which in turn might reduce the effects of a dual regulatory structure and the concomitant dual regimes.

We also analysed the cross-border implications of the US regime for CCPs. The extraterritorial implementation of US regulation affects non-US CCPs that provide clearing services to US market participants. To illustrate the extent of this issue, we explored the different regimes of segregation of assets, as well as the flaws of the current system of mutual recognition of CCPs regimes. The adoption of risk-based regulation might be a more feasible solution. We propose that establishing an equivalence strategy that ensures different regimes – e.g. the US and the UK – can find common principles to guide the implementation of cross-border rules. Under such a regime, the coordination between national and third-country authorities would be more effective because the supervision would be guided to achieve similar outcomes, regardless of the content and terms of rules.

Finally, this chapter considers the absence of a defined resolution regime for CCPs. Like the UK, the US regime has put its efforts towards strengthening recovery rules, whilst overlooking the design and implementation of a clear resolution regime for CCPs. We studied the possibility of applying the orderly resolution framework for SIFIs of Title II of the DFA and highlighted the shortcomings of this alternative. In so doing, it is clear that even if Title II is applicable to designated CCPs, there is uncertainty about the resolution authority and the role played by either the CFTC or the SEC, along with the Fed. Moreover, we considered the limits of the alternative provided by US ordinary bankruptcy laws, i.e. Chapters 11 and 7. Finally, we analysed the use of contractual provisions as a means to solve the uncertainty triggered by the lack of clarity of US regulation. We argue that regardless of the decision to use Title II of the DFA, or design a new SRR for CCPs, the risk-based approach to regulation would contribute to ensure that resolution rules are guided by the key principles of maintaining critical operations of CCPs, recapitalising CCPs to avoid liquidation (if feasible), and enhancing transparency of the resolution process. The approach would also facilitate the cooperation among regulators, CCPs, and clearing members in the design and implementation of the regime.

7 Final remarks

This book, for the first time, critically analyses the UK regime of CCPs in the OTCDM. Using a risk-based approach to regulation as a method of analysis to identify the shortcomings and advances of the regime, we have created a foundational discussion about the challenges facing UK regulators, both in design and implementation. We also comment on the US CCPs regime contained in the Dodd-Frank Act and its most notorious shortcomings.

The regimes studied in this book emerged as a result of concerns triggered by the GFC. The crisis highlighted the need for a more formal regulation and supervision of markets that could pose the most prominent risks to financial stability. The role played by the OTCDM within the crisis revealed market and regulatory failures that motivated regulatory reform. The priority of the post-GFC reform has been to strengthen the market infrastructure and, in particular, it has provoked the introduction of CCPs to provide a more efficient management of counterparty credit risks. The implementation of CCPs in the OTCDM has longstanding implications.[1] It represents not only a change in the structure of every transaction, but it also implies the transfer of risk to new intermediaries that are considered to be in a better position to absorb and mutualise the losses coming from participants' default. Although the adoption of CCPs in the OTCDM is not free of shortcomings, we have seen that they increase market safety and integrity, mitigating credit, liquidity, and operational risks as well as contributing to reduce asymmetries of information.

The introduction of mandatory central clearing through CCPs brings benefits to OTCDM supervision: CCPs act as co-regulators by imposing market discipline. Using this rationale, the Bank clearly stated that CCPs would become a forum for the vast majority of OTC derivatives transactions and, as such, CCPs can promote high levels of disclosure about market participants and transactions. The level of discretion attributed to CCPs allows them to play a double role in helping regulators to achieve their objectives. Firstly, CCPs are 'regulated firms', complying with the authorisation and recognition requirements, and providing

---

1 IMF, 'Central Counterparties: Addressing their Too Important to Fail Nature' (IMF Working Paper, WP/15/21, 2015), 4.

clearing services. Secondly, CCPs impose minimum requirements for clearing members and their clients to participate in the market. Moreover, from the regulators' perspective, one of the most attractive benefits of CCPs is that they contribute to enhance standardisation and play an active role in increasing transparency of the OTCDM.

The UK regime of CCPs in the OTCDM has been designed according to the European regulation, i.e. EMIR, and follows the CPMI-IOSCO Principles for Financial Market Infrastructures. Post-GFC, the UK approach to regulation combines some elements of risk-based and judgement-based regimes. Our analysis concludes that risk-based regulation, as it is currently adopted, is a partially efficient approach to regulate CCPs in the OTCDM. One of the most concerning challenges of regulators is efficient source allocation, which risk-based regulation tackles well; moreover, it is broad enough to design and implement a regime for CCPs that contributes effectively to achieve regulators' objectives. In this case, the safety and soundness of CCPs are in line with financial stability. If adequately designed and implemented, risk-based regulation effectively facilitates the integration of multiple perspectives of risks and uncertainties, including those of the regulators and regulated firms. The inextricably intertwined realities of risk and uncertainties expose the limits and opportunities that regulators face in the implementation of the regime.

However, the adoption of a risk-based approach to regulation also brings some shortcomings. We identified two drawbacks for the UK regime of CCPs in the OTCDM: firstly, the absence of an organisational culture to implement risk-based regimes, and secondly, as a result of the prioritisation of risks and regulatory actions, these regimes create manufactured risks. These two drawbacks are exemplified by the shortcomings presented in this book: the absence of a conduct of business regime, the insufficient legal framework underpinning CCPs' operations, the lack of a special resolution regime, and the failure to rule on innovation risk.

The supervision of the Bank has been focused on ensuring the safety and soundness of CCPs. The objective is to ensure that CCPs' rules and policies are designed and applied to monitor, manage, and mitigate risks, especially systemic risk. During the first years of the regime, the Bank progressed in the implementation of new margin models and the enhancement of new arrangement to allocate losses. In general, the advances are focused on the areas of management of credit and liquidity risk, recovery rules, operational risk management, and disclosure. Moreover, the Bank highlights that, according to the FSMA 2000 and the Banking Act 2009, it has a wide range of enforcement powers to require CCPs to provide information, commission independent reports, make on-site inspections, require changes to internal rules, and give directions.

Although we recognise the importance of the areas that have been regulated by the Bank, we must also be aware of other areas where supervision has not been sufficiently developed.

The first abandoned area is the CCPs' conduct of business regime. In pursuing this argument, we considered the misinterpretation of the UK regulators' mandates. In 2013, when the UK introduced reforms to the financial regulatory architecture, the Bank was designated as the regulator and supervisor of financial market infrastructures, within them CCPs. This means that the Bank would perform macro- and microprudential regulation of CCPs and the OTCDM. It was also clearly stated that the Bank would work closely with the FCA, reflecting the FCA's responsibilities for trading infrastructure and market product. A systematic interpretation of the regulators' mandates leads us to the conclusion that, while the Bank carries out the prudential supervision of CCPs, the FCA supervises the conduct of business. However, in practice, regulators and CCPs authorised in the UK perceive that the Bank is the only CCP regulator. The consequence of this misinterpretation is that the current conduct of business rules, implemented by the FCA, do not apply to CCPs in the OTCDM.

From this, we can see that CCPs' standards of conduct are not a regulatory priority, because regulators do not consider this area to pose a significant threat to their regulatory objectives. This imbalance is a consequence of the prioritisation of risks and regulatory actions that features in risk-based regimes: in privileging the prudential supervision over conduct of business rules, regulators are breaking the balance between the two stems of the risk-based approach. This shortcoming also shows that a risk-based approach is not effectively assisting CCPs' supervision in the OTCDM. Although the aim is to ensure the safety and soundness of CCPs, and thereby achieve the stability of the market, regulators are deliberately overlooking the fact that the robustness of CCPs should be built upon prudential as well as conduct of business rules. To address this, regulators need to design and implement a CCP's conduct of business regime that includes areas like consumer protection and competition rules.

Closely connected with the absence of conduct of business rules is the shortcoming concerning the insufficient legal framework underpinning CCPs' operations – specifically, the imbalance affecting the contractual relationship between CCPs and their members. The CCPs' rulebooks and complementary agreements exclusively regulate this relationship. The content of such rulebooks is exclusively and unilaterally drafted by CCPs; therefore, they have a limitlessly high level of discretion to draft contractual provisions, without considering the rights of their counterparties. Our concern should not be limited to the existence of abusive or unfair contractual terms – it also involves the clauses limiting the liability of CCPs to the detriment of clearing members' rights. This issue reveals the need for a broader scheme of protection that would benefit clearing members and their clients. In particular, it calls for the recognition of a duty of care predicable of CCPs in the performance of their contractual obligations related to holding and managing clearing members' assets and positions. We argued that the recognition of such a duty and standards of diligence would imply a regulatory reform of Section 291 of FSMA 2000 and could be constructed under the parameters of the common law.

As noted earlier, the Bank has developed loss-allocation and recovery rules to ensure that CCPs are sufficiently resilient. The Bank's aim is to ensure that CCPs have in place efficient rules to allocate losses arising from clearing members' default and losses originating from a different cause. However, one of the pending tasks is to develop a special resolution regime for CCPs. This is because, although the failure of a CCP is a very rare event, it is still a possibility. The Bank, as the resolution authority, should have a complete regulatory framework to conduct CCPs' insolvency proceedings. The insolvency proceedings will only take place when all the recovery mechanisms have been exhausted and the CCP is not viable anymore. The advances of the Bank in this area are limited to the establishment of early intervention powers.

Nonetheless, the resolvability of a CCP needs to follow a comprehensive and pre-established regime that ensures that the core functions of CCPs are maintained during times of crisis. An SRR of CCPs should address the efficient allocation of losses, the mitigation of fire sales, and how to ensure the continuity of services. The novel contribution of this book in this area is to highlight the potential shortcomings of the resolution regime for CCPs. It is particularly challenging to build up an SRR that can be articulated with the exercise of termination rights in derivatives contracts allowed by the FCAD. The possibility of bailout CCPs and the role of clearing members as the ultimate underwriters of CCPs are also considered in this discussion. Moreover, one of the questions explored in this book is around the suitability of implementing ring-fencing for CCPs. In this regard, the central concern is whether ring-fencing – in essence, a territorial approach to insolvency – could be coordinated with cross-border policies. The argument is relevant because CCPs occupy a prominent and systemic position and provide services in more than one jurisdiction. The ring-fencing regime, if applicable, should consider the twin realities of cross-border arbitrage embedded in the interconnections between CCPs and other entities.

We also explored the role of innovation and the risk it poses to the achieving regulatory objectives. The central argument is that CCPs are providing services in a market led by innovation. The regulated firms' attitude towards risks and regulation is pivotal to anticipate whether they are willing to comply or if, alternatively, they will find innovative forms of compliance. The practice of creative compliance might frustrate the expected outcomes of the regime – the multiple edges of innovation challenge the role of regulators. However, understanding the dynamics of the OTCDM, the conflicting interests that converge within the CCPs, and the interaction between CCPs regime with other regimes are illustrative of how innovation poses a significant risk to the achievement of regulators' objectives. As noted earlier, the regulatory solutions might be as diverse as the issues triggered by innovation. However, this book argued that the design and implementation of governance rules might contribute to solve, at least partially, the issues that stem from the conflicting interests converging within the CCP. The development of governance rules implies the adoption of standards of conduct. We could, therefore, question the importance of having in place an individual accountability regime. It's not clear whether the new SM&CR would be automatically applicable to CCPs by 2018; the Bank must clarify the applicability of the SM&CR and the role of the FCA.

The analysis of the Dodd-Frank Act highlights the failure of the US CCP regime in implementing a coherent risk-based approach to regulation. This lack of coherence is associated with flaws of the bifurcated regulatory structure. The divided jurisdiction between the CFTC and the SEC is problematic, not only in terms of the duality of regimes applicable to derivatives instruments and participants, but, also and perhaps more importantly, concerning the adoption of an amalgam of regulatory strategies. US regulatory agencies have adopted multiple strategies featuring elements of principles-based, rules-based, and risk-based approaches to regulation. We have seen throughout this book that a risk-based approach might solve the flaws of the regime. A coherent adoption of risk-based regulation and supervision facilitates timely identification and management of risks. Moreover, it allows the integration of multiple perceptions of risks, including those of regulators, supervisors, and regulated entities. Thus, the implementation of a coherent risk-based approach to regulation guided by principles will also have an impact on the effective use of voluntary compliance strategies, which are significantly less expensive than the traditional deterrence mechanisms of sanctions. This will defend the design of a system of equivalent standards for the CFTC and the SEC, applicable across market participants and markets. Besides the aim of achieving a high level of coherence, the system of supervision will be sufficiently broad and effective to cover all markets and products according to diverse levels of risk.

As in the UK regime, the US body of regulation is incipient when dealing with events of innovation risk, failing to deal with the unintended consequences of collateral transformation. The direct effect of the intersection between derivatives regulation and capital requirements for Bank's members of CCPs is that the risks traditionally associated with the derivatives market are transferred to other markets (e.g. repo market). Similarly, the rise of FinTech, as a relatively new phenomenon, has emphasised the limits of regulatory agencies when prioritising the risks that will be controlled and managed through regulation. In particular, the status quo of the US regime fails to deal with the changes and risks posed by the use of DLT and smart contracts in the derivatives market, especially in central clearing services.

Finally, the cross-border impact of the US regime for CCPs exacerbates extraterritorial issues affecting non-US CCPs providing clearing services to US market participants. Through our analysis of the phenomena of divergent rules on segregation, and the system of recognition and authorisation of CCPs, we see the importance of establishing an equivalence strategy that ensures different regimes – e.g. the US and UK – can find common principles to guide the implementation of cross-border rules. The key, however, is not to customise the rules to make them similar; instead regimes must move towards the implementation of an outcomes- or principles-based approach. Under such a regime, the coordination between national and third-country authorities would be more effective, because the supervision would be guided to achieve the same results, and not to comply with specific sets of rules.

We recommend the adoption of a risk-based approach to regulation based on principles to bring a more efficient solution to the shortcomings of the US regime for CCPs in the OTCDM. The risk-based approach might facilitate the process of mutual recognition of CCPs regimes, mitigating the negative effects of extraterritoriality. Moreover, risk-based regulation provides the framework for the continuous assessment and review of new developments; this would ensure the timely identification of the risks triggered by market and technological innovation, as well as the integration multiple perceptions of risks. We argue that it could be advantageous to use a risk-based approach to mitigate the differences of the regulatory strategies adopted by the CFTC, the SEC, and the Board. This would enhance coherence and aid the achievement of regulatory objectives. Finally, reaching a high level of cooperation between regulators and regulated firms might assist the process of designing a complete resolution regime of CCPs. Such a regime should embed a balance of the divergent interests of regulators, CCPs, and clearing members that convert in the event of CCPs default.

As the UK and US regimes of CCPs in the OTCDM are being developed, there are some areas for future research; for instance, the strengthening of standard stress tests for CCPs and the role that DLT will have in central clearing services. Moreover, the assessment of CCPs' resolution rules when the current international guidelines are implemented in major markets. Finally, we still have to see the upcoming regulation after the UK agrees to the terms of its withdrawal from the EU.

Bibliography

Books

Adam, B., Beck, U., and van Loon, J. (eds.), *The Risk Society and Beyond, Critical Issues for Social Theory* (Sage Publications 2000).

Adams, J., *Risk* (UCL Press 1995).

Alexander, K., Dhumale, R., and Eatwell, J., *Global Governance of Financial Systems: The International Regulation of Systemic Risk* (Oxford University Press 2006).

Andenas, M., and Chiu, I H-Y., *The Foundations and Future of Financial Regulation: Governance for Responsibility* (Routledge 2014).

Ayres, I., and Braithwaite, J., *Responsive Regulation: Transcending the Deregulation Debate* (Oxford University Press 1992), 39.

Baldwin, R., *Reader on Regulation* (Oxford University Press 1998), 298.

Baldwin, R., and Cave, M., *Understanding Regulation: Theory, Strategy and Practice* (Oxford University Press 1999).

Baldwin, R., Cave, M., and Lodge, M. (eds.), *The Oxford Handbook of Regulation* (Oxford University Press 2010).

Baldwin, R., Cave, M., and Lodge, M., *Understanding Regulation* (Oxford University Press 2012).

Baldwin, R., Hood, C., and Rothstein, H., *The Government of Risk: Understanding Risk Regulation Regimes* (Oxford University Press 2004).

Barnes, B., and Edge, D. (eds.), *Science in Context: Readings in the Sociology of Science* (MIT Press).

Bazley, S., and Haynes. A., *Financial Services Authority Regulation and Risk-Based Compliance* (2nd edn., Tottel 2006).

Beck, U., *Risk Society: Towards a New Modernity* (Sage Publications 1992).

Benoit, S., Colliard, J., Hurlin, C., and Perignon, C., *Where the Risks Lie: A Survey on Systemic Risk* (Review of Finance, Oxford University Press 2017), 110.

Bentham, J., *Introduction to the Principles of Morals and Legislation* (Clarendon Press 1907).

Black, J., 'The Development of Risk-Based Regulation in Financial Services: Just "Modelling Through"?' in Black, J., Lodge, M., and Thatcher, M. (eds.), *Regulatory Innovation: A Comparative Analysis* (Edward Elgar Publishing 2005).

Black, J., 'The Role of Risk in Regulatory Processes' in Baldwin, R., Cave, M., and Lodge, M. (eds.), *The Oxford Handbook of Regulation* (Oxford University Press 2010).

Black, J., Lodge, M., and Thatcher, M., *Regulatory Innovation, A Comparative Analysis* (Edward Elgar Publishing 2005).

Breyer, S., *Breaking the Vicious Circle: Towards Effective Risk Regulation* (Harvard University Press 1993).

Burchell, G., Gordon, C., and Miller, P., *The Foucault Effect: Studies in Governmentality* (Chicago University Press 1991).

Cotterell, R., *The Sociology of Law: An Introduction* (Butterworths 1992).

Davis, H., and Green, D., *Global Financial Regulation: The Essential Guide* (Polity Press, 2008).

Douglas, M., and Wildavsky, A., *Risk and Culture: An Essay on Selection of Technological and Environmental Dangers* (University of California Press 1982).

Downes, D. (ed.), *Unraveling Criminal Justice* (Palgrave Macmillan 1991).

Dworkin, R., *Taking Rights Seriously* (Harvard University Press 1977).

Felsenfeld, C., *Banking Regulation in the United States 29–35* (2nd edn, Juris 2006).

Ferran, E., and others, *The Regulatory Aftermath of the Global Financial Crisis* (Cambridge University Press 2012).

Giddens, A., *Runway World: How Globalization Is Reshaping Our Lives* (Profile Books 1999).

Giddens, A., and Pierson, C., *Conversations with Anthony Giddens: Making Sense of Modernity* (Stanford University Press 1998).

Goodhart, C., and others, *Financial Regulation: Why, How and Where Now* (Routledge and Bank of England 1998).

Govaere, I., Quick, R., and Bronckers, M., *Trade and Competition Law in the EU and Beyond* (Edward Elgar Publishing 2011).

Gray, J., and Akseli, O., *Financial Regulation in Crisis? The Role of Law and the Failure of Northern Rock* (Edward Elgar 2011).

Gray, J., and Hamilton, J., *Implementing Financial Regulation: Theory and Practice* (John Wiley & Sons Ltd 2006).

Gunningham, N., 'Enforcement and Compliance Strategies' in Baldwin, R., Cave, M., and Lodge, M. (eds.), *The Oxford Handbook of Regulation* (Oxford University Press 2010).

Gunningham, N., Grabosky, P., and Sinclair, D., *Smart Regulation* (Clarendon Press 1998).

Hawkins, K., 'Law as Last Resort' in Baldwin, R. (ed.), *Reader on Regulation* (Oxford University Press 1998).

Hawkins, K., and Thomas, J., *Enforcing Regulation* (Kluwer Nijhoff 1984).

Henderson, S., *Henderson on Derivatives* (Lexis Nexis Butterworths 2003).

Hood, C., and Jones, D. K. C. (eds.), *Accident and Design, Contemporary Debates in Risk Management* (UCL Press 1996).

Huang, J., *The Law and Regulation of Central Counterparties* (Hart Publishing Ltd 2010).

Hudson, A., *The Law on Financial Derivatives* (2nd edn, Sweet & Maxwell 1998).

Hudson, A., *Credit Derivatives: Law, Regulation and Accounting Issues* (Sweet and Maxwell 1999), 63.

Johnson, B.B., and Covello, V.T. (eds.), *The Social and Cultural Construction of Risk: Essays on Risk Selection and Perception* (Dordrecht 1987).

Kelman. M., *A Guide to Critical Legal Studies* (Harvard University Press 1987).

Kemshall, H., *Risk, Social Policy and Welfare* (Open University Press 2002).

Kindleberger, C., and Alibe, R.Z., *Manias, Panics and Crashes: A History of Financial Crises* (6th edn, Palgrave Macmillan 2011).

Knight, F., *Risk, Uncertainty and Profit* (Boston 1921).

Kobrak, C., and Wilkin, M. (eds.), *History and Financial Crisis: Lessons from the 20th Century* (Routledge 2013).

Kroszner, R., and Shiller, R., *Reforming US Financial Markets: Reflections Before and Beyond Dodd-Frank* (MIT Press 2011).

LaBrosse, J.R., Olivares-Caminal, R., and Singh, D. (eds.), *Managing Risk in the Financial System* (Edward Elgar Publishing Limited 2011).

Langevoort, D., 'Structuring Securities Regulation in the European Union: Lessons from the US Experience', in Ferrarini, G. and Wymeersch, E. (eds.), *Investor Protection in Europe: Corporate Law Making, the MiFID and Beyond* (Oxford University Press 2006), 485–506.

Lowenstein, R., *When Genius Failed: The Rise and Fall of Long-Term Capital Management* (Fourth Estate 2002).

Luhmann, N., *Risk: A Sociological Theory* (Aldine De Gruyter 1993).

Luhmann, N., Albrow, M., and King-Utz, E. (trs.), *A Sociological Theory of Law* (2nd edn, Routledge 2014).

Lupton, D., *Risk* (Routledge 1999).

McBarnet, D., 'It's Not What You Do But The Way That You Do It: Tax Evasion, Tax Avoidance and the Boundaries of Deviance' in Downes, D. (ed.), *Unraveling Criminal Justice* (Palgrave Macmillan 1991).

McNeil, I., and O'Brien, J., *The Future of Financial Regulation* (Hart Publishing Ltd 2010).

Moloney, N., 'Financial Services and Markets' in Baldwin, R., Cave, M., and Lodge, M. (eds.), *The Oxford Handbook of Regulation* (Oxford University Press 2010).

Nicoletti, B., *The Future of Fintech: Integrating Finance and Technology in Financial Services* (Palgrave Studies in Financial Services Technology 2017).

O'Malley, P., *Risk, Uncertainty and Government* (Routledge 2004).

O'Malley, P., *Governing Risks* (Taylor & Francis 2006).

Omarova, S.T., 'One Step Forward, Two Steps Back: The Institutional Structure of US Financial Services After the Crisis of 2008' in Hui Huang, R. and Schoenmaker, D. (eds.), *Institutional Structure of Financial Regulation: Theories and International Experiences* (Routledge 2014), 137.

Osborne, D., and Gaebler, T., *Reinventing Government: How the Entrepreneurial Spirit is Transforming the Public Sector* (Plume Books 1993).

Parker, C., *The Open Corporation* (Cambridge University Press 2000), 246.

Power, M., *The Risk Management of Everything: Rethinking the Politics of Uncertainty* (Demos 2004).

Power, M., *Organised Uncertainty* (Oxford University Press 2007).

Priest, G.L., 'The New Legal Structure of Risk Control' ch7 in O'Malley, P. (ed.), *Governing Risks* (Taylor & Francis 2006).

Schelling, T., *Arms and Influence* (Yale University Press 1966).

Schrader-Frechette, K., *Risk and Rationality* (University of California Press 1991).

Selody, J., 'The Nature of Systemic Risk' in LaBrosse, J.R., Olivares-Caminal, R., and Singh D. (eds.), *Managing Risk in the Financial System* (Edward Elgar Publishing Ltd 2011).

Singh, D., 'The US Architecture of Bank Regulation and Supervision' in LaBrosse, J.R., Olivares-Caminal, R., and Singh, D. (eds.), *Managing Risk in the Financial System* (Edward Elgar Publishing Ltd 2011).

Skeel, D., and Cohan, W.D., *The New Financial Deal: Understanding the Dodd-Frank Act and Its Unintended Consequences* (John Wiley & Sons 2011).

Smandych, R. (ed.), *Governable Places: Readings in Governmentality and Crime Control* (Advances in Criminology Series, Aldershot, Dartmouth, 1999).

Veljanovski, C., 'Strategic Use of Regulation' in Baldwin, R., Cave, M., and Lodge, M. (eds.), *The Oxford Handbook of Regulation* (Oxford University Press 2010).

Zubler, T., 'Book Note' in Breyer, S. (ed.), *Breaking the Vicious Circle: Towards Effective Risk Regulation* (Fall 1994) 8 *Harvard Journal of Law & Technology*, 1.

Articles

Abken, P., 'Over-the-Counter Financial Derivatives: Risky Business?' (March–April 1994) 79 (2) *Federal Reserve Bank of Atlanta Economic Review*.

Allen, J.L., 'Derivatives Clearinghouses and Systemic Risk: A Bankruptcy and Dodd-Frank Analysis' (2012) 64 Stanford Law Review, 1079.

Anderson, S., 'A History of the Past 40 years in Financial Crises' (2000) *International Financing Review*, issue supplement.

Awrey, D., 'The Dynamics of OTC Derivatives Regulation: Bridging the Public-Private Divide' (2010) *European Business Organization Law Review*, 11.

Awrey, D., 'Regulating Financial Innovation: A More Principles-Based Alternative?' (2011) 5 (2) *Brooklyn Journal of Corporate, Financial & Commercial Law*, 273.

Awrey, D., 'Complexity, Innovation, and the Regulation of Modern Financial Markets' (2012) 2 *Harvard Business Law Review*, 267.

Bazley, S., 'The Financial Services Authority, Risk-Based Regulation, Principles Based Rules and Accountability' (2008) *Journal of International Banking Law & Regulation*, 422, 1.

Beck, U., 'World Risk Society and Manufactured Uncertainties' (2009) 1 *IRIS*, 292.

Becker, B., and Mazur, F., 'Risk Management of Financial Derivatives Products: Who's Responsible for What?' (Fall 1995) 21 (1) *The Journal of Corparation Law*, 177, 183

Biskupic, J., 'Senators Question Breyer's Economics; Biden Calls Cost-Effective Approach to Environmental Protection "Elitist"' (15 July 1994) *Washington Post*, A6.

Black, J., 'Critical Reflections on Regulation' (2002) 27 *Australian Journal of Legal Philosophy*, 1.

Black, J., 'The Development of Risk Based Regulation in Financial Services: Canada, the UK and Australia, A Research Report' (2004) ESRC Centre for the Analysis of Risk and Regulation London School of Economics and Political Science.

Black, J., 'The Emergence of Risk-Based Regulation and the New Public Risk Management in the United Kingdom' (Autumn 2005) *Public Law*, 512–535.

Black, J., 'Tensions in the Regulatory State' (Spring 2007) *Public Law*, 58–73.

Black, J., 'Forms and Paradoxes of Principles-Based Regulation' (2008) 3 (4) *Captal Market Law Journal*, 425.

Black, J., 'Risk and Regulatory Policy: Improving the Governance of Risk' in 'Risk-Based Regulation: Choices, Practices and Lessons Being Learnt' (2010) *OECD*, 185–224.

Black, J., and Baldwin, R., 'Really Responsive Risk-Based Regulation' (2010) 32 *Law and Policy*, 184.

Black, J., and Baldwin, R., 'When Risk-Based Regulation Aims Low: A Strategic Framework' (2012) 6 (2) *Regulation and Governance*, 131.

Black, J., and Baldwin, R., 'When Risk-Based Regulation Aims Low: Approaches and Challenges' (2012) 6 (1) *Regulation and Governance*, 2.

Braithwaite, J., 'Accountability and Governance Under the New Regulatory State' (1999) 58 (1) *Australian Journal of Public Administration*, 90.

Caytas, J., 'Blockchain in the US Regulatory Setting: Evidentiary Use in Vermont, Delaware, and Elsewhere' *The Columbia Science and Technology Review*, 30 May 2017 <http://stlr.org/2017/05/30/blockchain-in-the-u-s-regulatory-setting-evidentiary-use-in-vermont-delaware-and-elsewhere/> Accessed 12th December 2017.

Christensen, C., Raynor, M., and McDonald, R., 'What Is Disruptive Innovation?' *Harvard Business Review*, December 2015 <https://hbr.org/2015/12/what-is-disruptive-innovation> Accessed 12th December 2017.

Cohen, H.R., and Woodall, III S.R., 'Financial CHOICE Act of 2017' (2017) *Harvard Law School Forum on Corporate Governance and Financial Regulation*, June <https://corpgov.law.harvard.edu/2017/06/15/financial-choice-act-of-2017/>.

Daníelsson, J., 'On the Feasibility of Risk Based Regulation' (2003) 49 (2) *Institute for Economic Research*, CESifo Economic Studies, 1.

Day, M., 'Macro-Prudential Regulation' *Financial Regulation International*, 1 October 2010 <www.financialregulationintl.com/regulation/regulatory-reforms/macro-prudential-regulation-1.htm?origin=internalSearch> Accessed 5th December 2017.

Desmond, E., 'Risky Business: Responding to OTC Derivatives Crises' (2002) 40 (677) *Columbia Journal of Transnational Law*, 687.

Dizard, J., 'Clearing House Push Created Unforeseen Systemic Risks' *Financial Times* London, 29 January 2016.

The Economist, 'Assets or Liabilities? Regulators Worry That the Asset-Management Industry May Spawn The Next Financial Crisis' 2 August 2014.

Evanoff, D., Russo, D., and Steigerwald, R.S., 'Policymakers, Researchers, and Practitioners Discuss the Role of Central Counterparties' (2006) (4) *Economic Perspectives*, Federal Reserve Bank of Chicago and European Central Bank.

Feder, N.M., 'Deconstructing Over-the-Counter Derivatives' (2002) 677 *Columbia Bussiness Law Review*, 719.

Fischhoff, B., Watson, S., and Hope, C., 'Defining Risk' (1984) 17 *Policy Sciences*, 123–139.

Fleming, S., 'The Age of the Compliance Officer Arrives' (April 2014) *FT Report*, 24.

Foot, M., 'Delivering Cost-Effective Regulation Through Risk-Based Supervision' (1999) 89 *Journal of International Financial Management*, 2.

Ford, C.L., 'New Governance, Compliance, and Principles-Based Securities Regulation' (2008) 45 *American Business Law Journal*, 1–60.

Gibson, W., 'Clearing and Trade Execution Requirements for OTC Derivatives Swaps Under the Frank-Dodd Wall Street Reform and Consumer Protection Act' (2011) 38 (227) *Rutgers Law Record*, 229 <http://papers.ssrn.com/sol3/papers.cfm?abstract_id=1710822> Accessed 12th December 2017.

Giddens, A., 'Risk and Responsibility' (1999) 62 *Modern Law Review*, 1.

Grabosky, P., 'Regulation by Reward: On the Use of Incentives as Regulatory Instruments' (1995) 17 (3) *Law & Policy*, 257.

Grabosky, P., 'Using Non-Governmental Resources to Foster Regulatory Compliance' (1995) 8 (4) *Governance*, 529.

Gray, J., 'Risk Based Regulation Moves Further Centre Stage' (2006) *Financial Regulation International*, 1 December 2006 <www.financialregulationintl.com/regulation/regulatory-reforms/risk-based-regulation-moves-further-centre-stage-1.htm?origin=internalSearch> Accessed 5th December 2017.

Gray, J., 'Principles-Based Regulation: FSA's Dominant Theme for 2007/2008' *Financial Regulation International*, 1 March 2007 <www.financialregulationintl. com/regulation/fsa-and-cpma-and-boe/principles-based-regulation-fsas-domi nant-theme-for-20072008-1.htm?origin=internalSearch> Accessed 5th December 2017.

Gray, J., 'Principles-Based Regulation Takes Further Shape: New Industry Guidance Is Confirmed'. (2007) *Financial Regulation International*, 1 September 2007 <www.financialregulationintl.com/regulation/fsa-and-cpma-and-boe/principles-based-regulation-takes-further-shape-new-industry-guidance-is-confirmed-1. htm?origin=internalSearch> Accessed 5th December 2017.

Gray, J., 'Northern Rock: Systemic, Liquidity and Credit Risk-Lessons for risk-based regulation?' *Financial Regulation International*, 1 October 2007 <www.finan cialregulationintl.com/financial-industry/financial-crisis/northern-rock-systemic-liquidity-and-credit-risks-lessons-for-risk-based-regulation-1.htm> Accessed 5th December 2017.

Gray, J., 'Is It Time to Highlight the Limits of Risk-Based Regulation?' (2009) 4 *Capital Markets Law Journal*, 1.

Gray, J., and Metzing, P.C., 'Defining and Delivering Judgement-Based Supervision: The Interface with the Legal System' (July/November 2013) 14 (3/4) *Journal of Banking Regulation*.

Greenberger, M., 'The Extraterritorial Provisions of the Dodd-Frank Act Protects US Taxpayers from Worldwide Bailouts' (2012) 80 *University of Missouri-Kansas City Law Review*, University of Maryland Legal Studies Research Paper No 2012–17

Gupta, V., 'A Brief History of Blockchain' *Harvard Business Review*, 28 February 2017 <https://hbr.org/2017/02/a-brief-history-of-blockchain> Accessed 12th December 2017.

Hauchi, C., 'Dodd-Frank's Swap Clearing Requirements and Systemic Risk' (Winter 2013) 30 (1) *Yale Journal on Regulation*, 279.

Hermansson, H., 'Consistent Risk Management: Three Models Outlined' (2005) 8 (7–8) *Journal of Risk Research*, 562.

Hodgson, D., ' "Know Your Consumer": Marketing, Governmentality and the New Consumer of Financial Services', (2002) 40 (4) *Management Decision*, 318–328.

Hopper, M., and Stainsby, J., 'Principles-Based Regulation – Better Regulation?' (2006) 21 *Journal of International Banking Law and Regulation*, 387–391.

Hu HTC, 'Misunderstood Derivatives: The Causes of Informational Failure and the Promise of Regulatory Incrementalism' (1993) 102 *Yale Law Journal*, 1457, 1464–1465.

Jackson, C., 'Have You Hedged Today? The Inevitable Advent of Consumer Derivatives' (1999) 67 *Fordham Law Review*, 3205.

Johnston, J.S., 'Uncertainty, Chaos and the Torts Process: An Economic Analysis of Legal Form' (1991) 76 (341) *Cornell Law Review*, 97.

Jopson, B., and Rennison, J., 'Trump Administration Calls for Heightened Regulation of Clearing' (6 Friday October 2017) *Financial Times*.

Kennedy, D., 'Form and Substance in Private Law Adjudication' (1976) 89 (1685) *Harvard Law Review*, 1775.

Kent, M., Forbes-Cockell, C., and Melnick, N., 'How EMIR Compares to Title VII' (June 2012) *International Financial Law Review*, 1.

Kuprianov, A., 'The Role of Interest Rate Swaps in Corporate Finance' (Summer 1994) 53 *Federal Reserve Bank Richmond Economic Quarterly*, 58.

Langbein, L., and Kervin, C., 'Implementation, Negotiation and Compliance in Environmental Safety Regulation' (1985) 47 (854) *Journal of Politics*, 880.

Lastra, R., 'Defining Forward Looking, Judgement-Based Supervision' (July 2013) 14 (3–4) *Journal of Banking Regulation*, 221–227.

LCH Clearnet, '$9 Trillion Lehman OTC Interest Rate Swap Default Successfully Resolved' (Press Release, 8 Oct 2008)

Lichtenstein, C., 'The Fed's New Model of Supervision for "Large Complex Banking Organizations": Coordinated Risk-Based Supervision of Financial Multinationals for International Financial Stability' (2006) 8 *American Journal of Law & Medicine*, 283–300.

Majone, G., 'The Rise of the Regulatory State in Europe' (1994) 17 (3) *West European Politics*, 78.

Majone, G., 'From the Positive to the Regulatory State: Causes and Consequences of Changes in the Mode of Governance' (1997) 17 *Journal of Public Policy*, 2.

March, J., and Shapira, Z., 'Managerial Perspectives on Risk and Risk Taking' (1987) 33 (1404) *Management Science*, 1413.

McBarnet, D., 'Law and Capital: The Role of Legal Form and Legal Actors' (1984) 12 *International Journal Sociology of Law*, 233.

McBarnet, D., 'Law, Policy and Legal Avoidance: Can Law Effectively Implement Egalitarian Policies' (Spring 1988) *Journal of Law and Society*, 113.

McBarnet, D., and Whelan, C., 'The Elusive Spirit of the Law: Formalism and the Struggle for Legal Control' (1991) 54 (6) *Modern Law Review*, 848.

McCoy, P.A., Pavlov, A., and Wachter, S.M., 'Systemic Risk Through Securitization: The Result of Deregulation and Regulatory Failure' (2009) 41 *Connecticut Law Review*, 493.

McKenzie, D., 'The Material Production of Virtuality: Innovation, Cultural Geography and Facticity in Derivatives Market' (August 2007) 36 (3) *Economy and Society*, 359.

Myers, R., 'What Every CEO Needs to Know About Weather Risk Management' CME Group, 2008.

Nikil, C., Labelle, N., and Tuer, E., 'Central Counterparties and Systemic Risk' (December 2010) *Bank of Canada Financial System Review*.

O'Malley, P., 'Risk, Power and Crime Prevention' (1992) *Economy and Society*, 252.

O'Malley, P., 'Imagining Insurance: Risk, Thrift and Industrial Life Insurance' (1999) 5 (2) *Connecticut Insurance Law*, 675, 705.

Raz, J., 'Legal Principles and the Limits of Law' (1972) 81 *Yale Law Journal*, 823–854.

Reddy, S., 'Claims to Expert Knowledge and the Subversion of Democracy: The Triumph of Risk Over Certainty' (1996) 25 *Economy and Society*, 222, 254.

Scholz, J., 'Voluntary Compliance and Regulatory Enforcement' (October 1984) 6 *Law and Policy*, 385, 404.

Scott, K., 'US Federal Banking Regulators Issue Risk-Based Capital Guidance For Certain Derivatives' *Financial Services: Regulation Tomorrow*, 22 August 2017 <www.regulationtomorrow.com/us/us-federal-banking-regulators-issue-risk-based-capital-guidance-for-certain-derivatives/> Accessed 12th December 2017.

Shah, A., 'Creative Compliance in Financial Reporting' (1 January 1996) 21 *Accounting, Organizations and Society*, 23.

Siems, T., '10 Myths About Financial Derivatives' (1997) Cato Instituute, *Cato Policy Analysis*, No. 283.

Smialek, J., 'Gary Cohn Calls Clearinghouses a "New Systemic Problem"' Bloomberg, 15 October 2017 <www.bloomberg.com/news/articles/2017-10-15/whitehouse-s-cohn-calls-clearinghouses-a-new-systemic-problem> Accessed 17th October 2017.

Smith, D., and Toft, B., 'Risk and Crisis Management in the Public Sector' (1998) *Issues in Public Sector Risk Management*, 18 (4) *Public Money and Management*, 10.

Smith, L., and Muñiz-Fracticelli, V., 'Strategic Shortcomings of the Dodd-Frank Act' (Winter 2013) (58) *The Antitrust Bulletin*, 4.

Speer, S., 'Regulatory Reform Should Be About Strengthening Legislative Responsibility' *The Regulatory Review*, 23 October 2017 <www.theregreview.org/2017/10/23/speer-strengthening-legislative-responsibility/> Accessed 12th December 2017.

Stafford, P., 'European Banks Face US Capital Hit Unless Rules Converge' *FT.com*, 4 April 2016 <www.ft.com/cms/s/0/bbe6678a-f5c5-11e5-803c-d27c7117d132.html#axzz48oFXlFrR> Accessed 12th December 2017.

Stigler, G.J., 'The Theory of Economic Regulation' (1971) 6 (2) *Bell Journal of Economics*, 114.

Stout, L.A., 'Why the Law Hates Speculators: Regulation and Private Ordering in the Market for OTC Derivatives' (1999) 48 (701) *Duke Law Journal*, 741.

Stout, L.A., 'Derivatives and the Legal Origin of the 2008 Credit Crisis' (2011) 1 *Harvard Business Law Review*, 1.

Terán, N., 'How the World's Largest Default Was Unravelled' *Fin News*, 13 October 2008 <www.fnlondon.com/articles/how-the-largest-default-was-unravelled-20081013> Accessed 5th December 2017.

Tinianow, A., 'Delaware Blockchain Initiative: Transforming the Foundational Infrastructure of Corporate Finance' *Harvard Law School Forum on Corporate Governance and Financial Regulation*, 16 March 2017 <https://corpgov.law.harvard.edu/2017/03/16/delaware-blockchain-initiative-transforming-the-foundational-infrastructure-of-corporate-finance/>

Walker, G., 'Quarterly Review – Regulatory Principles, Efficiency and Financial Stability' *Financial Regulation International*, 1 June 2007 <www.financialregulationintl.com/regulation/quarterly-review-regulatory-principles-efficiency-and-financial-stability-1.htm?origin=internalSearch> Accessed 5th December 2017.

Walker, G., 'Regulatory Review – Northern Rock, Financial Completion and Financial Shock (Part I)' *Financial Regulation International*, 1 February 2008 <www.financialregulationintl.com/regulation/regulatory-review-northern-rock-financial-completion-and-financial-shock-part-i-1.htm?origin=internalSearch> Accessed 5th December 2017.

Walker, G., 'Northern Rock – National Audit Office Report' *Financial Regulation International*, 1 June 2009 <www.financialregulationintl.com/financial-industry/banking/northern-rock-national-audit-office-report-1.htm?origin=internalSearch> Accessed 5th December 2017.

Weinrib, E., 'Legal Formalism: On the Immanent Rationality of Law' (1988) 97 *Yale Law Journal*, 949.

Wilmarth, A., 'The Transformation of the US Financial Services Industry, 1975–2000: Competition, Consolidation, and Increased Risks' (2002) *University of Illinois Law Review*, 215.

Wilmarth, A., 'Reforming Financial Regulation to Address the Too-Big-to-Fail Problem' (2010) 35 *Brooklyn Journal of International Law*, 707.

Wilmarth, A. Jr, 'Dodd-Frank Act: A Flooded and Inadequate Response to the Too Big to Fail Problem' (2011) 89 (3) *Oregon Law Review*, 952.

Yermack, D., 'Corporate Governance and Blockchains' *Harvard Bussiness Review*, 6 January 2016 <https://corpgov.law.harvard.edu/2016/01/06/corporate-gov ernance-and-blockchains/> Accessed 12th December 2017.

Working papers

Baldwin, R., 'Is Better Regulation Smarter Regulation?' (Autumn 2005) *Public Law*, 489.

Black, J., 'The Rise, Fall and Fate of Principles Based Regulation' (2010) LSE Law, Society and Economy Working Papers No. 17.

Borio, C., and Disyatat, P., 'Global Imbalances and the Financial Crisis: Link or No Link?' (May 2011) BIS Working Papers No 346, Monetary and Economic Department.

Boskovic, T., Cerruti, C., and Noel, M., 'Comparing European and US Securities Regulations: MiFID versus Corresponding US Regulations' (2010) World Bank Working Paper No 184.

Briault, C., 'The Rationale for a Single National Financial Services Regulator' (1999) FSA Occasional Paper No. 2.

Committee on Payments and Market Infrastructures, 'Distributed Ledger Technology in Payment, Clearing and Settlement: An Analytical Framework' February 2017, 3 <www.bis.org/cpmi/publ/d157.pdf> Accessed 12th December 2017.

Cusenza, P., and Abernethy, R., 'Dodd-Frank and the Move to Clearing' (September 2010) *Insight*, 22, 23.

Delivorias, A., 'Briefing: Distributed Ledger Technology and Financial Markets, PE 593.565 EN' European Parliamentary Research Service, November 2016 <www.europarl.europa.eu/RegData/etudes/BRIE/2016/593565/EPRS_ BRI(2016)593565_EN.pdf> Accessed 12th December 2017.

Douglas, M., 'Cultural Bias' Occasional Paper 35, London, Royal Anthropological Institute.

Duffie, D., Li, A., and Lubke, T., 'Policy Perspectives on OTC Derivatives Markets Infrastructure' Federal Reserve Bank of New York, 2010, 10.

Georgosouli, A., 'Judgement-Led Regulation: Reflections on Data and Discretion' (3–4 July 2013) 14 *Journal of Banking Regulation*.

Gola, C., and Spadafora, F., 'Financial Sector Surveillance and the IMF' IMF, Working Paper, 1 November 2009.

Hutter, B.M., 'The Attractions of Risk-Based Regulation: Accounting for the Emergence of Risk Ideas in Regulation' (2005) Discussion Paper No. 33 ESCR Centre for Analysis of Risk and Regulation.

IMF, 'Central Counterparties: Addressing their Too Important to Fail Nature' Working Paper, January 2015.

IMF, 'Integrating Stability Assessments under the Financial Sector Assessment Program into Article IV Surveillance: Background Material' 27 August 2010.

IMF, 'The Regulatory Responses to the Global Financial Crisis: Some Uncomfortable Questions' WP/14/46 March 2014.

IOSCO, 'IOSCO Forms Task Force on OTC Derivatives Regulation' (2010) Press Release <IOSCO/MR/11/2010 www.iosco.org/news/pdf/IOSCONEWS191. pdf> Accessed 12th December 2017.

IOSCO, 'Mitigating Systemic Risk: A Role for Securities Regulators' (2011) IOSCO Discussion Paper OR01/11 February.

IOSCO, 'International Standards for Derivatives Market Intermediary Regulation', Final Report Technical Committee (2012) IOSCO, FR03/12 June <www.iosco. org/library/pubdocs/pdf/IOSCOPD381.pdf> Accessed 12th December 2017.

IOSCO, 'Review of Implementation Progress in Regulation of Derivative Market Intermediaries' (2015) IOSCO, FR15/2015 July <www.iosco.org/library/pub docs/pdf/IOSCOPD497.pdf> Accessed 12th December 2017.

ISDA, 'Common Domain Model Version 1.0 Design Definition Document' October 2017.

ISDA, 'Whitepaper: The Future of Derivatives Processing and Market Infrastructure' September 2016.

Karmel, R.S., 'IOSCO's Response to the Financial Crisis' 16 March 2012, *Brooklyn Law School*, Legal Studies Paper No 268 <http://ssrn.com/abstract=2025115> Accessed 12th December 2017.

ISDA and Linklaters, 'Whitepaper: Smart Contracts and Distributed Ledger – A Legal Perspective' 3 August 2017.

Komai, A., and Richardson, G., 'A Brief History of Financial Regulation in the United States from the Beginning Until Today: 1789 to 2009', (2011) NBER Working Paper 17443.

Lynch, T.E., 'Derivatives: A Twenty-First Century Understanding' (2011) Indiana Legal Studies Research Paper No. 187, 14.

McBarnet, D., 'When Compliance Is Not the Solution but the Problem: From Changes in Law to Changes in Attitude' The Australian National University, Australian Taxation Office, Centre for Tax System Integrity Working Paper No. 18 August 2001, 8.

Pinna, A., and Ruttenberg, W., 'Distributed Ledger Technologies in Securities Post-Trading: Revolution Or Evolution? European Central Bank – Occasional Paper Series No 172 April 2016.

Osiński, J., Seal, K., and Hoogduin, L., 'Macroprudential and Microprudential Policies: Toward Cohabitation' IMF, Monetary and Capital Markets Department June 2013.

Willem, B., 'Lessons from the 2007 Financial Crisis' (2007) CEPR Discussion Paper No DP6596, December.

Bank of England reports

Bank of England, 'The Role of Macroprudential Policy' (Discussion Paper November 2009).

Bank of England, Prudential Regulation Authority, 'The PRA's Approach to Banking Supervision' (October 2012).

Bank of England, 'The Bank of England's Approach to the Supervision of Financial Market Infrastructures' (April 2013).

'Bank of England's Supervision of Financial Market Infrastructures Annual Report' (March 2015).

Sidanius, C., and Wetherilt, A., 'Thoughts on Determining Central Clearing Eligibility of OTC Derivatives' Bank of England, Financial Stability Paper No. 14 (March 2012).

Financial Conduct Authority reports

Better Regulation Framework Manual: Practical Guidance for UK Government Officials (July 2013).

BIS, *Compliance and the Compliance Function in Banks* (April 2005).

BIS, *Core Principles for Effective Banking Supervision* BCBS (September 2012).

Draft Financial Services Bill – Draft Financial Services Bill Joint Committee, Contents (19 December 2011) para 188.

Financial Crisis Inquiry Commission, *The Financial Crisis Inquiry Report* (Public Affairs New York, 2011) (FCIR).

Financial Services Authority, *FSA Policy Statement 07/16: FSA Confirmation of Industry Guidance.*

Financial Services Authority, *Internal Audit Report on Northern Rock* (FSA, London, 2008).

Financial Services Authority, *Reasonable Expectations* (FSA, London, 2003).

FSA, *Building the New Regulator: Progress Report 1* (FSA, London, December 2000) (PR1).

FSA, *Building the New Regulator: Progress Report 2* (FSA, London, February 2002) (PR2).

FSA, *The FCA Approach to Regulation* (FSA, June 2011) ch 5 (para 5.6 to 5.9).

FSA, *Financial Services Authority: An Outline* (October 1997).

FSA, *The Firm Risk Assessment Framework* (FSA, London, February 2003) (FRAF).

FSA, *The Future Regulation of Insurance: A Progress Report* (FSA, London, October 2002) (PR3).

FSA, *Principles-Based Regulation – Focusing on the Outcomes that Matter* (April 2007).

FSA, *Turner Review: A Regulatory Review to the Global Banking Crisis* (August 2009).

FSB, *Increasing the Intensity and Effectiveness of SIFI Supervision, Progress Report to the G20 Ministers and Governors* (1 November 2012).

Hampton Review was commissioned in 2004 by the Cabinet Office, Better Regulation Task Force and HM Treasury.

HM Treasury – FCA, *A New Approach to Financial Regulation: The Blueprint for Reform* CM8083 (June 2011) FCA (2011)

HM Treasury, *Reforming Financial Markets* (London, 2009).

House of Commons Treasury Committee Report, *The Run of the Rock* (26 January 2008).

IOSCO Guidelines to Emerging Market Regulators Regarding Requirements for Minimum Entry and Continuous Risk-Based Supervision of Market Intermediaries (December 2009).

OECD, *Regulating Policies in OECD Countries* (OECD 2002).

Sants, *H Draft Financial Services Bill,* (2012) para 190.

US Government Accountability Office, *Financial Crisis: Recent Crisis Reaffirms the Need to Overhaul the US Regulatory System,* GAO-09-1049T (Washington, DC, 2009).

US reports

Board of Governors of the Federal Reserve System, Securities and Exchange Commission, Commodity Futures Trading Commission, *Risk Management Supervision of Designated Clearing Entities* Report to the Congress, Washington, DC, July 2011

<www.federalreserve.gov/publications/other-reports/files/risk-management-supervision-report-201107.pdf> Accessed 12th December 2017.

The City of New York, Office of the Mayor and United States Senate *Sustaining New York's and the US' Global Financial Services Leadership*, 2007 <www.nyc.gov/html/om/pdf/ny_report_final.pdf> Accessed 12th December 2017.

Government Accountability Office, GAO-05–61, *Financial Regulation: Industry Changes Prompt Need to Reconsider US Regulatory Structure* (October 2004).

International Securities Exchange, *Proposal for Regulatory Reform for the US Financial Markets* (March 2009), 4.

Notice of Filing of Proposed Rule Change, 81 Fed Reg 45, 554 (14 July 2016); 'FTC Announces Agenda for March 9 FinTech Forum on Artificial Intelligence and Blockchain Technology' Fed Trade Commission, 27 February 2017 <www.ftc.gov/news-events/press-releases/2017/02/ftc-announces-agenda-march-9-fintech-forum-artificial> Accessed 12th December 2017.

Office of the Comptroller of the Currency, Board of Governors of the Federal Reserve System, Federal Deposit Insurance 'Corporation Regulatory Capital Treatment of Certain Centrally-Cleared Derivative Contracts Under Regulatory Capital Rules' (14 August 2017).

US Department of the Treasury, 'A Financial System That Creates Economic Opportunities Capital Markets' Report to President Donald J Trump, Executive Order 13772 on Core Principles for Regulating the United States Financial System (September 2017).

Conference papers

Bartle, I., 'Risk-Based Regulation and Better Regulation in the UK: Towards What Model of Risk Regulation?' 2nd Biennial Conference of the ECPR Standing Group on Regulatory Governance, Utrecht University, The Netherlands: 'Regulation in the Wake of Neoliberalism, Consequences of Three Decades of Privatization and Market Liberalization' (5–7 June 2008).

Fisher, P., 'Speech: The Financial Regulation Reform Agenda: What Has Been Achieved and How Much is Left to Do?' (30 September 2015).

Gudmundsson, M., 'How Might the Current Financial Crisis Shape Financial Sector Regulation and Structure?' (BIS, Deputy Head of the Monetary and Economic Department, at the Financial Technology Congress 2008, Boston (23 September 2008).

Henderson, S., 'Speaking at Legal Accounting and Control Challenges of Credit Derivatives' IBC (8 December 1997).

Mullins, D., 'Remarks on the Global Derivatives Study Sponsored by the Group of Thirty' (1993) ISDA Summer Conference.

Tucker, P., 'The Debate on Financial System Resilience: Macroprudential Instruments' Speech to Barclays Annual Lecture, London (22 October 2009).

Encyclopedias

Bert, E., 'Financial Regulation' *The Concise Encyclopedia of Economics* (2008) Library of Economics and Liberty.

Black's Law Dictionary (9th ed, West, 2009).

Hansson, S.O., 'Risk' *The Stanford Encyclopedia of Philosophy* (2007).

US legislation

CFTC, 17 CFR Parts 1, 37, 38, 39, and 40. RIN 3038 – AD01, 'Governance Require-ments for Derivatives Clearing Organizations, Designated Contract Markets, and Swap Execution Facilities; Additional Requirements Regarding the Mitigation of Conflicts of Interest' <www.cftc.gov/idc/groups/public/@lrfederalregister/docu ments/file/2010-31898a.pdf> Accessed 1st November 2017.

'Dodd-Frank Wall Street Reform and Consumer Protection Act' Pub L No 111–203, 124 Stat 1376 (2010).

'Exchange Act Release No 34–73639' (19 November 2014), 79 FR 72252 (5 Decem-ber 2014) ('Regulation SCI') adopting release.

'Financial Stability Oversight Council', 12 CFR Chapter XIII and Part 1320 RIN 4030–AA01 Final Rule Authority to Designate Financial Market Utilities as Sys-temically Important <www.gpo.gov/fdsys/pkg/FR-2011-07-27/pdf/2011-18948.pdf#page=11> Accessed 12th December 2017.

'Securities and Exchange Commission' 17 CFR Part 240 [Release No 34–78961 File No S7–03–14] RIN 3235-AL48 Standards for Covered Clearing Agencies <www. sec.gov/rules/final/2016/34-78961.pdf> Accessed 5th November 2017.

Index

Printed in the United States
by Baker & Taylor Publisher Services